HANDBUCH DER ORIENTALISTIK

Herausgegeben von B. Spuler
unter Mitarbeit von
C. van Dijk, H. Franke, J. Gonda, H. Hammitzsch, W. Helck, B. Hrouda,
D. Sinor, J. Stargardt und F. Vos

HANDBUCH DER ORIENTALISTIK

SIEBENTE ABTEILUNG

KUNST UND ARCHÄOLOGIE

Herausgegeben von J. STARGARDT

ERSTER BAND

DER ALTE VORDERE ORIENT

ZWEITER ABSCHNITT

DIE DENKMÄLER

Herausgegeben von B. HROUDA

B — VORDERASIEN

LIEFERUNG 4

ANCIENT JEWISH ART
AND ARCHAEOLOGY
IN THE LAND OF ISRAEL

ANCIENT JEWISH ART
AND ARCHAEOLOGY
IN THE LAND OF ISRAEL

BY

RACHEL HACHLILI

E.J. BRILL
LEIDEN · NEW YORK · KØBENHAVN · KÖLN
1988

Library of Congress Cataloging-in-Publication Data

Hachlili, Rachel.
    Ancient Jewish art and archaeology in the land of
Israel.
    (Handbuch der Orientalistik. 7. Abteilung, Kunst
und Archäologie, ISSN 0169-9474; 1. Bd., Der alte
Vordere Orient, 2. Abschnitt, Die Denkmäler, B,
Vorderasien, Lfg. 4)
    Bibliography: p.
    Includes index.
    1. Palestine—Antiquities. 2. Excavations
(Archaeology)—Palestine. 3. Jewish art and symbolism—
Palestine. 4. Art, Jewish—Palestine. 5. Synagogue
architecture—Palestine. 6. Synagogue art—Palestine.
I. Title. II. Series: Handbuch der Orientalistik.
Siebente Abteilung, Kunst und Archäologie; 1. Bd., 2.
Abschnitt, B, Lfg. 4.
DS111.8.H33   1987   933'.05   87-8039
ISBN 90-04-08115-1

ISSN 0169-9474
ISBN 90 04 08115 1

PRINTED IN THE NETHERLANDS

TO MY FAMILY
GAD
GUY, SIGAL, NIV

CONTENTS

PART ONE

JEWISH ART AND ARCHAEOLOGY IN THE SECOND TEMPLE PERIOD

PART TWO

JEWISH ART AND ARCHAEOLOGY IN LATE ANTIQUITY

Plates

LISTS OF FIGURES

Chapter 1

Chapter II.

Chapter III

Chapter IV.

Chapter V

Chapter IX

Chapter XI

LIST OF PLATES

105 Panel of Jewish Symbols, Naᶜaran.
106 Inscription, Beth Sheʾan B.
107 Room L, Monastery, Beth Sheʾan.
108 Lintel with Inscription, Nabratein.
109 Lintel with Inscription, Kasyon.

ACKNOWLEDGEMENTS

Most of the photographs are courtesy of the Israel Department of Antiquities and Museums, except: Pls. 6a-c, 8 are courtesy of N. Avigad; Pls. 51, 96a-c courtesy of D. Barag; Pls. 2, 3, 9 are courtesy of M. Ben-Dov; Pls. 23, 26, 29, 35, 41, 42c-f, 88, 90, 92, 94, 98 are courtesy of Z. Maoz.; Pls. 7a,b, 10a are courtesy of Masada Excavations. Pls. 5, 10b, 20, 41a,b courtesy of Israel Government Press Office; Pls. 34, 54, 62 courtesy of Israel Museum, Jerusalem.

Photographs by Z. Radovan: Pls. 2, 10, 11, 21, 22, 24, 26,.38, 40, 49, 61, 71, 74, 76, 78-84, 88, 100, 107; N. Avigad: 6a-e, 8; A. Hay: 73; Z. Ilan: 25, 48; Z. Maoz: 29, 35, 42c-f, 90, 92, 94, 98; M. Pan: 66; J. Simon: 109; D. Harris: 62; the author: 39, 93.

The drawings are by Adi Weichselbaum, except for IV.22, IX.38 by D. Bechar; IV.1b, 2, 4, 20, 21A by A. Cleja; IV.5 by M. Eichelberg; XI.9 by N. Kubie.

My sincere thanks are due to the following individuals and institutions who have helped me and allowed me to use their photographs and drawings:—
N. Avigad, D. Bahat, D. Barag, M. Ben-Dov, A. Berman, M. Dothan, Z. Ilan, Z. Maoz, E. and C. Meyers, J. Naveh, E. Netzer, A. Raban, V. Tzaferis, F. Vitto, Z. Yeivin.
Israel Department of Antiquity and Museums; The Israel Museum, Jerusalem; Israel Government Press Office; Masada Excavations.

FOREWORD

For some time now I have felt that a comprehensive study, which would support my thesis for the existence of an ancient Jewish Art, could be accomplished by a compilation of the material excavated in the past few decades, especially the latest results, together with previous materials and studies. I was, therefore, greatly honoured by the invitation of the late Prof. Dr. J.E. van Lohuizen-de Leeuw, editor of the "Kunst und Archäologie" Series, to write this book; I regret immensely that she herself did not live to see its publication. I was particularly pleased about the invitation because I had been researching and collecting material on this specific subject for the past ten years and had now reached the stage when I wished to present the fruits of this labour.

As a result of the many excavations in the last decades a large body of new material has come to light which now allows for a comprehensive treatment of ancient Jewish art and archaeology. Although archaeology is dealt with in detail, the emphasis of this book, especially in Part II, is on Jewish art. This, because it has been a particularly neglected aspect of the field and one on which my own studies have centered.

The discussion takes the form of a general comparison, divided according to topics such as Jewish symbols and other specific subjects, which together create what I hope is a conclusive case for the existence of Jewish art during the Second Temple period and Late Antiquity. An understanding of the artistic heritage left us by our ancestors can help to penetrate the mists of time separating us from those periods.

Jewish art and archaeology of the Diaspora, which forms an important and supplementary aspect of the subject, will be covered in a second volume in this series and will follow in the near future: as the amount of material for this study is vast it can only be dealt with as a book unto itself.

I should like to express my gratitude to the Memorial Foundation for Jewish Culture for providing funds for parts of the research and to the Dorot Foundation for a grant which helped enable this book to be produced.

A number of people also deserve special recognition. My thanks to Prof. M. Rosen-Ayalon for her recommendation. I should like to acknowledge my gratitude to my late teacher, Prof. M. Avi-Yonah, whose assistant I became during the last years of his life, and who constantly encouraged me in my research. His pioneer work in Oriental Art will long remain the basis for all further studies in this field.

I should like to mention my indebtedness to those who have helped me prepare this book: warm thanks are due to my friend Stephanie Rachum for her encouragement, advice and her thorough reading of the manuscript; a special gratitude to Joan Michaeli, my editor, for her thorough and diligent work; to Martha Adato for her conscientious and precise typing of the manuscript; to Malka Hershkovitz for checking parts of the manuscript; to Adi Weichselbaum for his many drawings published in this book; to my friends and colleagues, Z. Maoz and M. Ben-Dov, whose discussions helped me clarify my ideas; and especially to Dr. L.Y. Rahmani, who read the completed manuscript and who gave me many helpful suggestions and criticisms.

I especially want to thank my husband Gad whose help was immeasurable; he also painstakingly prepared the manuscript using word processing facilities. His help has meant that I have been able to finish the manuscript in less time and with fewer complications than usual. Further affectionate thanks to my children for their enormous and unfailing help, patience, understanding and encouragement.

Rachel Hachlili
Haifa University
November 1984

ABBREVIATIONS

AASOR	Annual of the American Schools of Oriental Research.
AJA	American Journal of Archaeology.
Ant	Josephus *Jewish Antiquities.*
ASR	*Ancient Synagogues Revealed.* ed. L.I. Levine. Jerusalem 1981.
B	Babylonian Talmud.
BA	Biblical Archaeologist.
BAR	Biblical Archaeology Review.
BASOR	Bulletin of the American Schools of Oriental Research.
BIES	Bulletin of the Israel Exploration Society (Hebrew).
BJPES	Bulletin of the Jewish Palestine Exploration Society (Hebrew).
EAE	*Encyclopedia of Archaeological Excavations in the Holy Land*, vols. I-IV. 1975-1978.(ed. M. Avi-Yonah).
EI	Eretz Israel.
IEJ	Israel Exploration Journal.
J	Jerusalem (Palestinian) Talmud.
JAOS	Journal of the American Oriental Society.
JBL	Journal of Biblical Literature.
JPOS	Journal of the Palestine Oriental Society.
KW	Kohl, H. and Watzinger, C. *Antike synagogen in Galilaea.*
Liber Annuus	Liber Annuus Studia Biblici Franciscan
M	Mishna.
PEQ	Palestine Exploration Quarterly.
QDAP	Quarterly of the Department of Antiquities in Palestine.
RB	Revue Biblique.
T	Tosefta.
War	Josephus, *Jewish War.*
ZDPV	Zeitschrift des Deutschen Palastina-Vereins.

INTRODUCTION

By the term Jewish art is meant an art that was created specifically for the Jewish community. Its form and content were determined by the desires of both the upper and lower classes, and it was executed in accordance with the spiritual and secular requirements of local congregations. Art was employed to satisfy both functional and recreational needs.

The time spanned by Ancient Jewish Art, discussed in this book, begins in the Second Temple period and continues until the end of the period of Late Antiquity (late second century BCE-seventh century CE).

Jewish art reflects a culture which came into being, not as a consequence of a nation's isolation, but rather as the result of a necessity to absorb and assimilate, and to compete with, the culture of others. Simultaneously with absorbing and assimilating elements from its Hellenistic, Roman pagan and later Christian surroundings, Jewish art, as will be shown, retained and clung to its fundamentally spiritual basis, and to its essential beliefs and customs.

The worship of objects, whether natural or created by man, was very popular in ancient times. With the proliferation of polytheistic beliefs the necessity for organized symbols was realized. In the case of Judaism, however, visual art was not an indispensable attribute of worship. On the contrary, a constant battle raged between the Jewish religion which was expressed in abstract values, and pagan worship, where symbols and tangible objects were used. Although Judaism in principle rejected pagan symbols, they nevertheless penetrated Jewish art as decorative motifs, void of their original meaning.

Jewish art found expression in various aspects of Jewish life: secular, sacred and funerary. It adorned public and private buildings, tombs, sarcophagi and ossuaries, some of which, such as the synagogue interiors and exteriors and the tomb facades in Jerusalem, are vigorously and splendidly decorated. Jewish art of the Second Temple period (second century BCE-first century CE) is aniconic and non-symbolic. Most of the motifs used are taken from the environment. They consist of plant and geometric motifs expressing growth and productivity and are similar to patterns used in Graeco-Roman pagan art. In the struggle against paganism, Judaism at that time offered staunch resistance, especially by insisting on obedience to the ''no graven image'' commandment and by guarding against its violators. Hence the strict adherence to a non-figurative art form. After the destruction of Jerusalem and its Temple (70 CE) and the Bar Kokhba War (132-135 CE), Jewish art, though retaining a degree of continuity with the past, developed completely different, varied and versatile characteristics.

The Jewish art which evolved during the period of the third-seventh centuries was primarily a popular art, founded on a definitive spiritual outlook. Its study enables us to reconstruct a vivid picture of the past in which the spiritual and material nature of Judaism is disclosed.

As we follow the course of the development of Jewish art, several facts will emerge as indisputable. During the Second Temple period the Jews rejected the representation of figurative images in their art and used only aniconic, non-figurative motifs and patterns, which reflected their struggle against both paganism and Christianity. However, from the third century until the seventh century, Jews employed figurative art, images and symbols. They did so with rabbinical tolerance or even approval. The initiative for the growth of a versatile Jewish art, and especially for its figurative and symbolic aspect, lay with the Jewish population itself, with the national as well as the local communities.

The elaborate decoration of synagogal and funerary art reflected the natural wish of society to live in a visually pleasing environment, as well as the desire of man to conquer material and mould it to his needs. Moreover, it provided an outlet for the human frailty of wishing to impress and attract attention and to demonstrate power through symbols and motifs, through magnificence and beauty.

This study will attempt to examine the available data, and to reach a comprehensive interpretation by determining the meaning and significance of the material presented. It will discuss the extensive history and development of Jewish art, its symbolic and iconographic vocabulary and its characteristic features, and assign them to their proper context. It will attempt to examine both the forces of continuity and discontinuity, thereby drawing attention to what is truly distinctive in Jewish art.

The book will be divided into two sections: Part One, Jewish Art and Archaeology of the Second Temple period; and Part Two, Jewish Art and Archaeology of Late Antiquity.

Explanatory Notes

Chronological terms used for dating are BCE (= Before the Common Era) equating to BC, and CE (= Common Era) equating to AD. As most of the dates mentioned are of the Common Era (C.E.) they have not been labelled; only dates before the Common Era (B.C.E.) are so specified.

The discussion of synagogues in the text as well as their appearance in the chart is by geographical location from north to south.

HISTORICAL BACKGROUND

Present knowledge of the history of the Jews in the Land of Israel is based on literary sources which include the Bible, the writings of Josephus, the Mishna and Talmud, and on extensive archaeological excavations.

The kingdom of Judah was conquered in 586 BCE by Nebuchadnezzar, king of Babylon. The First Temple was burnt down, the capital city of Jerusalem destroyed and the people were taken into exile to Babylonia. Fifty years later, Judah became a province or satrapy of the Persian Empire; it was named *Yehud*. The Persian king, Cyrus, issued a proclamation in 538 BCE, allowing the Jews to return to Jerusalem and to rebuild their Temple (Ezra I). The exiled Jews returned to Judah and Jerusalem in several groups, under Zerubabel (ca. 521 BCE), under Ezra the scribe (ca. 458 BCE), and under Nehemiah the governor of Judah (ca. 445 BCE). They returned with a very strong, national religion, maintained by a priestly caste. Zerubabel rebuilt the Temple, Nehemiah reconstructed the walls of Jerusalem, and Ezra and Nehemiah restored the religious and spiritual life, as well as the economic and social life, of the returning Jews. The province of Judah was granted independence as indicated by the coins and inscriptions bearing the name of the province *Yehud*.

Alexander the Great conquered the Persian Empire in 332 BCE, and Judea became a Hellenistic province often subject to controversy, passing between the Syrian Seleucids and the Egyptian Ptolemies. In 200 BCE, Judea, under the rule of Antiochus III of Syria, gained some administrative autonomy. The priests became the upper class, and were concentrated in Jerusalem. The High Priest was the ruler of Judea and the Temple, and was appointed by the Seleucid king.

Among this upper class Hellenism was predominant in both social and spiritual concerns. In 175 BCE, under Antiochus IV, the city of Jerusalem was granted the status of a Greek polis, and a gymnasium was built. In 168 BCE Antiochus IV built the "Akra" fortress which overlooked the Temple *temenos*. The Seleucids finally began to intervene in Jewish religious practices which caused the successful Maccabean Revolt headed by the Hasmonean family. In the second century BCE, the Hasmoneans gained political independence, and were the rulers of Judea, both as High Priests and kings, throughout the century.

In 63 BCE Judea and Jerusalem were conquered by Pompey, and became a Roman vassal state. During the period 37 BCE-70 CE Herod and his dynasty ruled Judea, with sporadic rule by Roman procurators. Herod the Great (who gave his name to the Herodian period) was the son of Antipater, an Edomite (the Edomites were a people conquered by the Hasmonean ruler John Hyrcanus in ca. 125 BCE and forced to convert to Judaism). Herod succeeded the last of the Hasmonean kings and High Priests, Mattathias Antigonus, becoming king in 37 BCE with the support of the Romans. He was able to extend his rule over most of the Land of Israel and even beyond; he built extensively in other countries as well as at home. The Jews greatly disliked Herod, because of his alien origin, and his being an usurper who had replaced the legitimate Hasmonean kings. Educated in and admiring Graeco-Roman culture, Herod began his building projects accordingly: luxurious palaces, as well as towns with institutions such as theatres, hippodromes and gymnasia were constructed (see pp. 11ff.). The Herodian period is remarkable in its extensive building and in its ornamental art.

Herod's family continued to rule Judea and several other provinces. The Jewish kings of this dynasty were Agrippa I (who ruled in 41-44 CE) and Agrippa II (50-ca. 100 CE).

Full scale war against the Romans broke out in 66 CE, but was suppressed in 70 CE, when Jerusalem and the Temple were conquered and destroyed. Masada, however, maintained resistance, finally falling after a long siege in 73 CE. Upon Titus' conquering Jerusalem in 70 CE, the city became a base for a Roman garrison, for the Tenth Legion ''Fretensis.'' During the reign of the Roman emperor Hadrian a second war against the Romans broke out, and was led by Bar Kokhba (132-135 CE). It was cruelly suppressed: Jerusalem was completely razed and the Roman colony of ''Aelia Capitolina'' was built on its ruins. In the period following the destruction of the Jewish state, and of Jerusalem and its Temple in 70 CE, the Jews continued to live in the area of Jerusalem and Judea until the Bar Kokhba war of 132-135 CE. During these six decades, little art either flourished or survived. After the Bar Kokhba War, Jews were expelled from Judea and began to move to the Galilee in large numbers.

In ca. 190 CE, the Roman Antonine dynasty with its Graeco-Roman traditions was replaced by the Severan and Syrian emperors, whose roots were in the Orient. Several of these emperors maintained favourable relations with the Jews, as indicated by the Kasyon inscription, which offers the dedication of a building by the Jewish community to Septimius Severus and his family (Pl. 109; p. 396). This was a period of political peace and economic prosperity. Such an atmosphere was favourable for closer relations between the Jews and their neighbouring cultures, particularly with the Roman Orient's Hellenistic culture. Thus, the end of the second, and the third centuries CE marked an important period in the evolution of Jewish art. A major change occurred, primarily in the introduction of representational, figurative and symbolic elements into the traditionally aniconic Jewish art, manifesting itself in both synagogal and funerary art. During this period the Jewish communities in the Galilee flourished; towns and synagogues were built. These communities were prosperous and independent, being governed by the Sanhedrin, who were the rabbis and the elders of the family of Hillel. Endeavouring to preserve the beliefs and traditions of Judaism they conducted life according to the *halakha*. The climax of this period was marked by the codification of the Mishna.

In 324 CE, Constantine the Great conquered his eastern enemies, and Christianity became the official Imperial faith. The Land of Israel now became an important religious centre for Christianity. Pilgrims began to pay visits, and the country became a site for vast building projects. Churches and monasteries were constructed throughout the country. The Jews in the Land of Israel found it necessary to protect themselves, both politically and religiously, against Christianity. The Christian church did not prohibit Judaism, but it did have an extremely negative attitude towards the Jews, as is indicated by the anti-Jewish laws which contained insulting language and which provided encouragement to Christian zealots who harmed Jews and Jewish institutions. Christianity also claimed propriety of the Land of Israel because of Christian history and the existence of holy places. In the fourth century, the anti-Jewish legislation of the Christian Constantinian emperors was harsh and strictly maintained to the detriment of Jewish religious and economic life. Many other changes also occurred, caused by new administrative divisions of the Land of Israel. Civil and military rule were separated.

In 351 CE a Jewish revolt in Sepphoris was organized against Galus, the Roman governor in the East. It spread to all of the Galilee, and was suppressed by the destruction of many Galilean towns. Some of the major cities, such as Tiberias, Sepphoris and Lod, were immediately resettled.

During the short rule of Julian (360-363 CE) Jewish hopes were raised as he showed intentions of permitting them to rebuild Jerusalem and its Temple. This prompted enthusiastic Jews to resettle in Jerusalem. They built a synagogue near the Temple Mount, and began collecting funds from all over the Jewish world to rebuild the Temple. Meanwhile, Julian was murdered, and with him went Jewish hopes.

At the end of the fourth and the beginning of the fifth centuries, as Christianity expanded, anti-Jewish legislation became even stricter, and Jews suffered from harsh treatment. The Patriarchy was terminated in this period (425 CE) and collecting money for the Sanhedrin was prohibited. The Jerusalem Talmud was completed at this time. The period of two hundred years from the beginning of the fifth century until the beginning of the seventh century was a difficult one for the Jews

in the Land of Israel. Jewish towns and villages diminished in size. Additional
legislation further harmed Jewish life: building new synagogues was prohibited,
although not actually enforced. However, within this period, the latter half of the
fifth century and the beginning of the sixth was a quieter and more relaxed period
for the Jews. Their economy flourished, and agricultural settlements were established in the south of the country. Synagogues were built and reconstructed, as well
as redecorated.

Hard times returned with the reign of Justinian I (527-565 CE) who renewed anti-
Jewish legislation which discriminated against Jews and relegated them to an inferior status. At the beginning of the seventh century, with the Persian victories over
the Byzantine empire in the east, the Jews revived hopes of regaining their
autonomous rule, fired by strong Messianic hopes. The Persians conquered the
Galilee with Jewish assistance, and, in 614 CE, conquered Jerusalem. Jews were allowed to settle in Jerusalem and ruled there for three years. In 617 CE the Persians
returned to Jerusalem and the Jews resisted them unsuccessfully. Heracles, the
Byzantine emperor, expelled them from Jerusalem and the decrees against the Jews
were further strengthened. Many Jews fled the country.

In 640 CE the Land of Israel was conquered by the Arabs. By now the local
Jewish population had greatly dwindled in number.

PART ONE

JEWISH ART AND ARCHAEOLOGY IN THE SECOND TEMPLE PERIOD

Part I consists of a survey of the art and archaeology of the Second Temple period. The remains of the monuments discussed here belong to the Hasmonean and Herodian periods, and are our source for the study of the architecture and art in those periods. This survey will also deal with the Second Temple synagogue problem, as well as the burial customs practiced by Jews.

CHAPTER ONE

ARCHITECTURE

The architecture of the Second Temple period begins with remains of Hasmonean architecture encountered in sites and structures which were later reconstructed or completely renewed by the Herodian architectural projects. The only exceptional structure with figurative art is found in ʿAraq el Emir, northwest of Heshbon in Transjordan. Here are the ruins of a temple or a palace, probably the castle of Tyre mentioned by Josephus in *Ant.* XII.233, and ascribed to the Tobiad dynasty in the third century BCE. This palace has an entrance with a frieze of monumental lions in profile, symmetrically facing the entrance (Avi-Yonah 1961b: 14). The Herodian projects and renovations left a more enduring impression upon the art and architecture of the period than those of the Hasmoneans.

A) HASMONEAN ARCHITECTURE

Hasmonean architecture survives mostly in remains found of fortifications, desert fortresses, in funerary art, water systems and the recently excavated Hasmonean palace at Jericho. Apart from this palace, most of the other Hasmonean remains will be discussed in the context of their later Herodian reconstructions and expansions. The architectural structures which exhibit features which could be related specifically to the Hasmoneans are the palaces.

The characteristic features of the Hasmonean palaces consist of a central court surrounded by rooms. A hall with two columns *in antis* in the southern part of the court led to the triclinium, and probably served as a reception hall.

This basic plan characterizes all the palaces at Masada, the twin palaces at Jericho and was inspired by Hellenistic architecture (especially Priene—Yadin 1965: 47). Netzer (1982b: 25) maintains that the Masada palaces were built by the Hasmoneans at the same time as they built their palaces at Jericho (see p. 45).

The Jericho Hasmonean Palace (Netzer 1975a, 1977, 1983)

The beginning of the development of the Jericho valley was probably in the days of Alexander Janneus, 103-76 BCE. Jericho was a garden city and royal estate, and flourished during the first century BCE. The Hasmoneans were the first to build

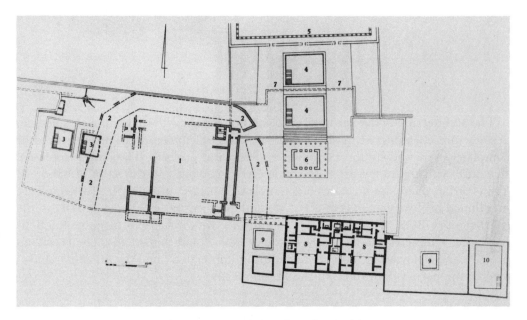

1. The Hasmonean Palace Complex, Jericho.

aqueducts in the western Jordan Valley, one leading from the Wadi Qelt springs, and the second from the Naʿaran springs. Availability of water and land as well as the mild climate enabled the development of agriculture including date palm and balsam cultivation (Pliny *N.H.* 6.14; Strabo, *Geog.* 16.241; Josephus, *War* I.6.6; IV.8.3) which caused economic growth. The above reasons brought about the building of winter palaces, first by the Hasmoneans and later by Herod.

The Hasmonean Palace complex (fig. 1) was built at the outlet of Wadi Qelt on a hill overlooking the Jericho valley. The fortressed central building(1) (50 × 50 m.) was surrounded by a moat(2) on three sides. This moat has been recently excavated. A cistern brought water from the aqueduct to the palace. This building was later covered by an artificial mound constructed by Herod. The palace probably had a central open court. A hall decorated with stucco and fresco was found in the excavations. Remains of a storage hall were also found. The walls remain standing to a height of seven metres, indicating that the palace was probably two storeys high. Two small swimming pools(3) were probably surrounded by a peristyle-shaped building which was decorated with fresco and mosaic floors. The drowning of Aristobolos III, as described by Josephus in *Ant.* XV.53, may have occurred in one of these pools. At the time of the building of the second aqueduct, another pair of

pools four metres apart was constructed to the northwest of the central building
(13 × 18 m.)(4). Their surrounding area was built with a court (60 × 70 m.) (5) serving as a garden, probably surrounded by columns which have not survived. South
of the pools and on the same axis, a splendid building, the "pavilion," was
erected(6). This was a 21 × 17 metre-structure similar to a Doric temple. It probably
was destroyed by an earthquake and only its foundations, columns and architrave
survive. This complex probably served the inhabitants for reception and leisure purposes and had a magnificent view of the valley and Wadi Qelt.

At a later period, the complex was extended to the south. Two "twin" palaces
were found(8) dated to the reign of Queen Alexandra (Shlomzion,76-67 BCE)
(Netzer 1983:103). Each measures 25 × 25 m., has a central open court (9 × 10 m.)
surrounded by rooms, a hall, a bath house and a *miqveh*. The palaces were decorated
with frescoes. Each had an adjacent court with a small swimming pool(9). An additional swimming pool (20 × 12.5 m.) was built onto the eastern palace(10). Other
buildings, houses, installations and *miqveh* complexes were built around the palaces
probably needed in the purification rites of the priests. The Hasmonean palace complex probably still stood at the beginning of Herod's reign.

B) Herodian Architecture

Comprehensive and monumental building projects were undertaken during
Herod's reign, 37-4 BCE. The two sources of data relating to the Herodian construction projects are literary and archaeological. The major literary sources are to
be found in the works of Josephus Flavius, particularly *Antiquities* XV-XVII and *War*
I, II and V. Extensive archaeological excavations undertaken during the last decades
add information which is both complementary and contradictory to the literary
sources. Some of the archaeological finds are not mentioned in Josephus' writings,
whereas some buildings are known to have existed only from the literary sources.
Josephus' detailed descriptions are based on the structures in existence during his
lifetime, and are not mentioned according to their objective importance and splendour. Josephus mentions 33 building projects, twenty of which were within the
borders of Herod's kingdom and thirteen of which were beyond its borders in other
countries. This list of Herodian architectural projects (see map 1) includes mention
of the construction, reconstruction and extension of towns, fortifications, palaces,
and fortresses, as well as of the Temple in Jerusalem (on a raised platform of 36
acres), the largest single structure (the Royal Stoa), the largest palace (the 50-acre
palace at Herodium), and one of the largest harbours ever constructed in antiquity
(at Caesarea). Many of these monumental structures have survived and have been

excavated in the last decades, enabling us to determine the extensiveness and splendour of Herodian architecture. Most of these structures were built during Herod's reign, but renovations and reconstructions were undertaken during the first century CE until the destruction of the Second Temple in 70 CE (see especially the extensive studies done by Netzer, 1975a, 1977, 1981a, 1981b and 1983).

During the first century BCE the Land of Israel contained several towns or Greek poleis, all of which were outside Herod's Jewish kingdom and which accommodated mostly Gentile citizens. The Jews generally resisted living in such a polis because of pagan institutions which included theatres and gymnasia (Broshi 1981: 70-71). In 30 BCE Herod received from Augustus several areas east and west of the Jordan. These areas included foreign towns, such as Gaza and its harbour. Herod built three new towns: ᵓAntipatris, Caesarea with its magnificent harbour and Sebaste (Samaria) with its temple of Augustus. In the newly-established towns Herod built temples, palaces, theatres, stadia, fortifications and harbours. Within the Jewish kingdom Herod carried out several projects. He built extensively in Jerusalem, particularly its Temple, a palace, town fortifications and towers, as well as many public buildings and institutions. In the Judean desert Herod constructed or renovated several splendid palace-fortresses: Masada, Herodium, Alexandrion (Sartaba), Cypros, Machaerus and the winter palaces at Jericho (see map 1).

Two new towns were built by Herod's sons: Tiberias was founded by Herod Antipas in 18 CE and Paneas, which was built by Herod, was extended by his son, Herod Philipos. The Herodian building projects included public structures, private buildings, and villas, as well as other structures such as palace-fortresses which incorporated within them monumental, magnificent sections and utilitarian, functional sections. The palace-fortresses in particular combined luxurious, leisurely living with the need for security.

Netzer (1981b: 61) maintains that Herod's building projects were "an expression of the kings's will and ability to build extensively..." He asserts (1981b: 52-54) that these projects involved innovative and original planning by King Herod as well as a grandiose approach, indicated by the proportions of the huge podium and monumental stones of the Temple Mount and its Royal Stoa, and in the Herodium palace-fortress which was a monumental structure of fifty acres. Levine, (in Netzer 1981b: 63) in contrast to Netzer, contends that "a gifted architect or even a team of experts...determined the sites, designed the program and made the basic planning decisions." He maintains that the king was certainly involved and followed the work done, but did not take an active part.

1. Characteristic Features of Herodian Architecture

Herodian architecture is characterized by the following features (see Netzer's five main principles of planning in the Herodian building complexes: 1981a,105-109; 1981b):

1) High-level planning reflected in the vast areas of the cities, such as Caesarea, Sebaste and Jerusalem.

2) The built-up area extended considerably and the creation of complexes containing buildings, open spaces, pools and gardens. Examples here include the complexes of Masada, Jericho and Greater Herodium.

3) The concept of a commanding architectural focal point for each of these complexes. Topographical locations with either natural or artificial focal points were chosen. This concept is demonstrated by the choice of sites: Masada is built on a high rock in the desert; Caesarea stands by the sea shore; Jericho is a palace-complex constructed on artificial mounds on either side of Wadi Qelt; Herodium is constructed as a palace-fortress surrounded by an artificial mound, and the Temple in Jerusalem is built on a site much higher than its surroundings and elevated by its high retaining walls.

4) A variety of functional purposes creating a combination of structures such as a palace complex which integrated residence, administrative, leisure and entertainment structures within it (the palaces at Jericho, Masada and Herodium). Another example is the hippodrome-theatre at Jericho which combines a race course for chariots and horses with a theatre and a building at its short end.

5) Building techniques:

a) Use of simple and local materials: stone and sun-dried bricks.

b) Plastering of buildings' exteriors and interiors with high-quality plaster. Netzer (1981b: 58) notes that this plastering was considered highly aesthetic; he refutes the generally-held notion that ashlar stone construction characterized Herodian structures (also Ben-Dov 1982: 96-99).

c) An imported Roman method of building was discovered in Jericho, palace III: mud-bricks were placed atop a foundation of rubble stones, were joined together with cement and were covered with *opus quadratum* and *opus reticulatum* (Netzer 1975a: Pl. 8a; 1977: 9).

d) Ashlar stones, used mainly in the Temple retaining walls but also in palace building. This was sometimes imitated in plaster in buildings such as "The Mansion" in the Upper City in Jerusalem (see Avigad 1983: figs. 87, 88). Ashlar stones were a type of ornamental motif in Second Temple period art (see p. 81 and Hachlili 1985: 113, 124).

e) Barrel-vaulting was employed for some instances of roofing (Netzer 1981b: 60).

6) An interesting feature of Herodian architecture is the naming of public and private structures for Herod's relatives and Roman patrons, as mentioned by Josephus. He named Herodium for himself, ꜀Antipatris for his father and Cypros is named after his mother. The three towers in Jerusalem, Phasael, Mariamme and Hippicus, are named for, respectively, brother, wife and friend (*War* V. 161-175). Cities and structures named for Roman patrons include Caesarea, the Augustus Temple at Samaria, the Agrippeum and Caesareum (two triclinia) in the Jerusalem palace (named for, respectively, Marcus Agrippa and Caesar Augustus), and the Antonia fortress at the northwest corner of the Temple Mount in Jerusalem.

7) Some features of Herodian architecture are unique and may have been innovations originated by King Herod himself:

a) The building of the northern palace at Masada on the natural rock steps, and the shaping of this palace's middle terrace like a tholus (Yadin 1966: 59; Netzer 1981b: 53).

b) Multi-storied towers at the Citadel and the Antonia fortress in Jerusalem, and at the Herodium palace-fortress (Netzer 1981a: 80-84, fig. 110).

c) A swimming pool within the Caesarea palace (Levine and Netzer 1978: 73-74).

d) Colonnaded streets at ꜀Antipatris (Kochavi 1981: 83-85), Caesarea (Bull 1982: 39-40), and Antioch in Syria, probably the first in the Roman world (Netzer 1981b: 79).

2. Sources of and influences upon Herodian Architecture
(see Netzer 1981b: 60; Tsafrir in Netzer 1981b: 70-72; Tsafrir 1982: 138-142)

1) Tradition and inheritance from the Hasmoneans.

a) In the case of Masada, other Judean desert fortresses, and the Jericho Winter Palace (figs. 10, 18, 20-22 and Pl. 4.) Herod used building sites which had originally been chosen and established by the Hasmoneans for their palaces and fortresses. The Hasmoneans had founded all these buildings, and had been the first to construct fortresses and palaces in the desert, for political reasons as well as for leisure purposes, as the Jericho Winter Palace (fig. 1, p. 10) and the western palace at Masada (fig. 19a, p. 43). Herod rebuilt and expanded most of these existing buildings.

b) Several architectural aspects of the Hasmonean building projects show the influence on them of the surrounding Hellenistic cultures. These include the incorporation of swimming pools, gardens and pavilions in palaces; water installations; and building techniques which employ local stone and barrel vaulting (in the Jericho Hasmonean palace). The western palace and the other small palaces at Masada and the twin palaces at Jericho were constructed on the lines of Hellenistic prototypes.

c) The ornamentation of the buildings—wall fresco, stucco on walls, columns and ceilings, and mosaic pavements—was influenced by that found in the principal contemporary Hellenistic centres such as Alexandria and Antioch. Such ornamentation techniques were employed in Hasmonean architecture and were later continued in Herodian structures.

2) The influence of Roman architecture upon Herodian buildings:

a) Herod's projects followed imperial Roman models for temples, theatres, hippodromes, palaces, aqueducts and bath houses. Similar projects were built in the Roman Empire for the same religious, cultural, political and economic reasons.

b) Building plans: incorporation of triclinia, peristyle courts and gardens, bath houses and pools. Herod's palaces are somewhat similar to the "domus" type of house found in towns, and to villas (Netzer 1981a: 109-110).

c) Roman building technology was commonly used. Domes, arches and vaults, aqueducts, bridges and staircases were employed in most Herodian projects in the Jerusalem Temple, and the palaces of Herodium, Jericho and Masada. A transient technological phenomenon should be considered here, that of the use of *opus reticulatum* and *opus quadratum* in several Herodian structures. These are found in the Third Winter Palace at Jericho, at a building in Banias, and in a circular building near the present-day Damascus Gate in Jerusalem, and were executed by builders who came from Italy (Netzer 1981b: 60; 1983: 108).

3. Herod's Major Building Projects (map 1)

Herod's extensive architectural projects were conducted primarily in his capital city of Jerusalem (fig. 2), the most prominent and important of which was the Temple, probably the largest temple built in antiquity. Herod also built his chief palace in Jerusalem. His life-style, copied from the style fashionable in imperial Rome, drove him to build many more complexes; the palaces-fortresses at Masada and Herodium were splendid and colossal constructions. The Herodium palace, due to its size, prominent location and detailed planning, was probably meant to be Herod's major summer palace. Masada was his major desert fortress and winter palace. At Jericho Herod built three winter palaces, presumably to serve his family and court for residence, entertainment and leisure.

Herod's most famous building projects, for which excavations provide ample evidence, are:

The Temple Mount in Jerusalem.

The palace-fortress of Masada.

The palace-fortress of Herodium, and Lower Herodium.

The three winter palaces at Jericho, and the Hippodrome.

Caesarea Maritima and its harbour.

Map 1. Herod's building projects.

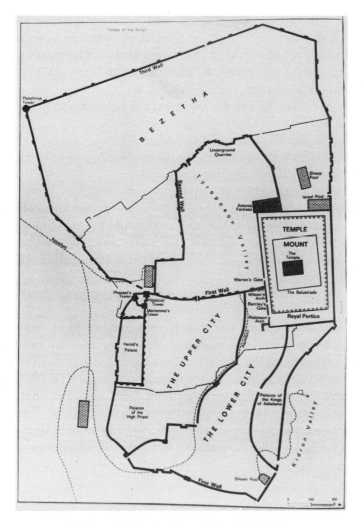

2. Jerusalem in the Second Temple Period.

a) The Temple in Jerusalem
(Jeremias 1969: ; Safrai 1976: 870-907; Schürer *et al* 1979, II: 237-309).

The Temple in Jerusalem has been the spiritual focal point of Jewish national life throughout the ages. It was the centre, furthermore, for the religious, political and artistic innovations of Judaism. During periods of pilgrimage, the gathering of thousands of pilgrims in Jerusalem influenced the economic and social life of the city. National and religious fervour, as well as resentment against Roman rule, could be kindled and manipulated by sages, prophets or others with a message, who found ready and ardent audiences. Pilgrims would also use the public institutions during their stay in Jerusalem.

In order to understand the Temple complex, it is necessary to first survey the worship conducted there.

Daily worship in the Temple consisted of:

1) The whole-offering of two lambs, one in the morning and one in the afternoon, which opened and concluded the day's worship.

2) Between the daily whole-offerings, two further kinds of offerings were sacrificed. One was the obligatory sin- and guilt- and purification-offerings for men and women. The second was free-will offerings, consisting of burnt-, peace-, thanks- and various meal-offerings.

3) An additional offering was sacrificed after the morning whole-offering on feast days, new moons and Sabbaths.

4) Reading of the Torah and prayers were added during the Second Temple period.

All the daily sacrifices and feast sacrifices were accompanied by music and singing, which began and ended with the sounding of two trumpets by the priests.

The worshippers came to the Temple in order to 1) participate in the Temple worship; 2) offer the first fruits, tithes and obligatory offerings; 3) study the Torah; and 4) cleanse themselves after various impurities, such as contamination by contact with the dead. Women also participated in Temple worship. They brought the peace-offering meals and participated in rejoicing, and were obliged to bring offerings after childbirth. Gentiles also made offerings and pilgrimage to the Temple.

The Pilgrimage

Pilgrimage from throughout the Land of Israel and the Diaspora to the Temple in Jerusalem was made on three Feasts: Passover (*Pesach*), Pentecost (*Shavuoth*) and Tabernacles (*Sukkoth*). The obligation of pilgrimage did not necessarily have to be undertaken three times a year; it could be undertaken once a year, once in several years or even once in a lifetime. Most probably, of the thousands who made the pilgrimage on each Feast, most came from nearby Judea. Although scholars have made attempts to calculate the number of pilgrims, they have never succeeded. The obligation of the pilgrims to appear in the Temple to celebrate and rejoice in the Feast actually meant a sacrifice for each obligation (burnt and peace-offerings).

The Temple offices

Temple worship was conducted by the priests who were the politically and socially predominant class. They were assisted by the Levites and the Israelites.

The Priests

The priests constituted a closed circle of privileged families, and were divided into twenty-four courses. Each course served for one week at a time, twice a year, and each had its own organization. Most priests did not live in Jerusalem; they resided in towns (Luria 1973) such as Jericho and Sepphoris, and went up to Jerusalem only for their Temple service, during which time they slept within the Temple precincts.

The ritual was conducted by priests who alternated each week, and whose functions included communal and individual offerings and sacrifices, burning incense, tending to the menorah in the sanctuary, participating in some rites with the Levites and sounding the two trumpets at the start and conclusion to the daily singing. They were the only ones who had access to the altar and to the sanctuary.

The High Priest

The High Priest stood at the head of the Temple hierarchy and had a unique privileged status. He did not serve on a daily basis, although a daily cake-offering which was part of the whole-offering was sacrificed in his name. On the Day of Atonement, the High Priest entered the Holy of Holies in order to burn incense. He also participated in the rites and worship on festivals and on Sabbaths.

The Prefect

The prefect was second-in-command to the High Priest whom he accompanied during the rites. The prefect presided over the daily whole-offering.

The Levites

The Levites were a circle of families divided into twenty-four courses which each served in the Temple one week at a time, twice a year. They were singers and gatekeepers. Their duties included opening and closing gates, guarding the Temple precinct by day and night, supervising the Temple cleanliness and making certain that no unclean worshippers should enter. The Temple guard was conducted by watches stationed in twenty-four locations.

The Israelites

The Israelites consisted of deputations, based on the geographical constitution of twenty-four districts. They were men who stood beside the priests during the rites and sacrifices, and later gathered for daily Torah reading and prayer.

The Temple Treasury

All adult males had to contribute a half-shekel per year to the Temple. Women were not obliged to donate but probably also contributed. The contribution was given on the first day of the month of Adar, so that it could be used in Nisan, the first month of the year. It was collected throughout the Land of Israel and the Diaspora and sent to Jerusalem.

The Temple revenues consisted of fixed contributions derived from the half-shekel donation. However, other contributions were also sent by Jews and Gentiles, and included dedicatory donations for houses, servants or fields. The treasury financed the expenses of the Temple maintainance, as well as the communal needs of Jerusalem.

The Temple Structure (Avi-Yonah 1956; Mazar 1975b; Ben-Dov 1982)

Literary sources describe the history of the Temple and detail its construction: Josephus Flavius' *Antiquities* (XV, 38-425) and *War* (V, 184-227), several references in the *Mishna* (*Middoth* and *Tamid*), and some references in the New Testament (Mark 13:1; Luke 21:5) are the most helpful. Archaeological excavations, particularly the most recent around the Temple Mount, provide proof and reaffirm literary sources for a reconstruction of the Second Temple structure.

The building of the Temple by Herod probably began in the years 20-19 BCE, and officially took nearly ten years to complete, but most likely building continued for many more years until 62-64 CE (*Ant.* XV, 380-402, 420-421; XX, 219; *War* I, 408).

The plan of the Temple consisted of a rectangular *temenos*, surrounded on all four sides by porticos (fig. 2). The inner Temple was erected in the centre, close to the western porticos (fig. 3 and Pl. 1). The construction involved tens of thousands of selected and trained builders, craftsmen and stone masons. One thousand priests were trained to work in the Temple building. Herod originally had organized the work force and materials in order to renovate the earlier Temple. After preparations had been made, the earlier Temple was destroyed and a new one was erected on its site by the Herodian builders (B. *zebahim* 62a; *Ant.* XV, 390-391). Herod's renovations included doubling the size of the Mount by the addition of a platform and retaining walls and building porticos and bridges. The height of the Temple itself was raised by forty cubits. The facade and ornamentation were new.

The Temple Mount itself is a trapezoid-shaped mountain crest.

The Mount is bordered on the east by the Kidron Valley, and on the west by the Tyropoeon Valley (fig. 2). Its highest point is in the north and its total area is

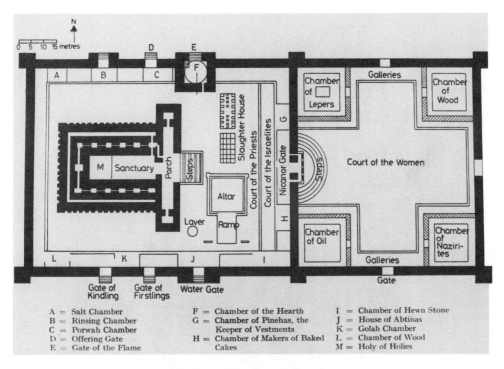

A = Salt Chamber
B = Rinsing Chamber
C = Porwah Chamber
D = Offering Gate
E = Gate of the Flame

F = Chamber of the Hearth
G = Chamber of Pinehas, the
    Keeper of Vestments
H = Chamber of Makers of Baked
    Cakes

I = Chamber of Hewn Stone
J = House of Abtinas
K = Golah Chamber
L = Chamber of Wood
M = Holy of Holies

3a. Plan of the Second Temple.

144,000 sq. m. The dimensions of its retaining walls, which survive to the height of about 30 m. above the paved streets, are: north side: 315 m.; south side: 280 m.; west side: 485 m.; and east side: 460 m. At the corners of the Mount towers were erected 30 m. above the paved streets.

A flat, oblong platform was built around the Temple Mount by quarrying and filling the surrounding valleys, and by adding a vaulted sub-structure (now known as "Solomon's Stables") to the southeastern part of the Mount. The retaining walls of the Temple *temenos* and precinct are formidable. Excavations in the last decades have revealed these well-preserved walls, particularly on the south and on the east. The retaining walls were constructed with huge ashlar stones with the technique of "dry masonry." Several stones are as long as twelve metres and weigh as much as 400 tons (Ben-Dov 1982: 88). The southern part of the western wall is known today as the "Wailing Wall." The upper parts of the western and southern walls were decorated with a row of projecting pilasters (fig. 4), similar to the ones on the Tomb of the Patriarchs in Hebron. Architectural fragments of these pilasters have been

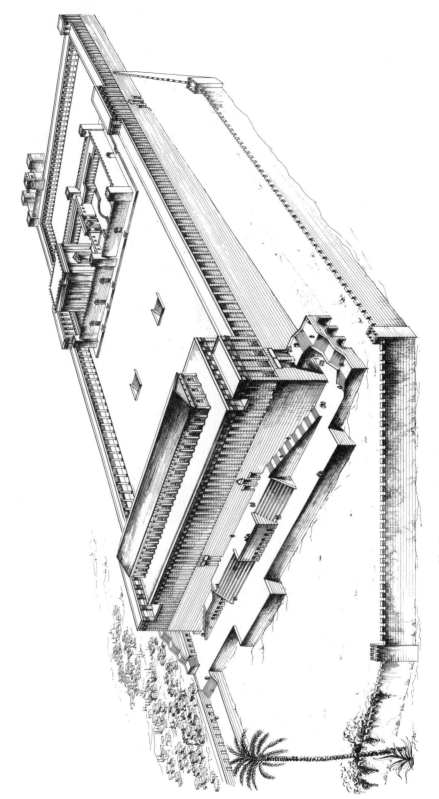

3b. Reconstruction of the Temple on the Temple Mount.

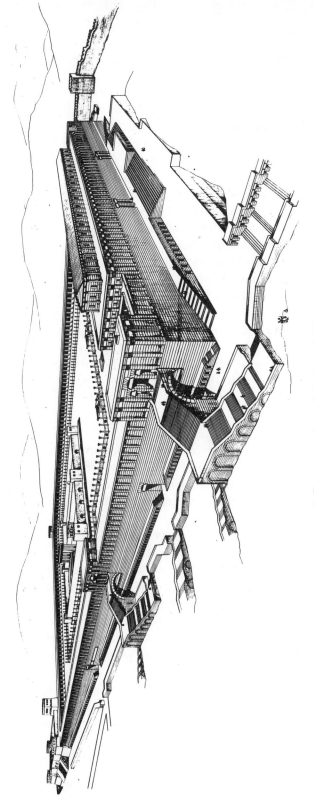

4. Reconstructions of the Temple Mount.

found in the excavations. An important find is the stone inscribed in Hebrew: "To the place of trumpeting." This stone had fallen into the street, and was probably located originally at the southwestern corner of the uppermost wall, marking the spot where the priest blew his trumpet every Friday evening to mark the beginning of Sabbath (*War* IV, 582) (Mazar 1975b: 35, 138; Ben-Dov 1982: 93-96; but see Demsky 1985).

On the Temple Mount several huge stone pavements can be observed today in the area of the Dome of the Rock and Aqsa mosque, and were probably part of a huge paved plaza (Ben-Dov 1982: 100-103).

The Temple Mount possessed both an inner and an outer court (*War*, V, 192-193). The Mishna records (*Middoth* 2:1) only the inner court, and gives the measurement of the Temple Mount as 500 × 500 cubits (ca. 250 × 250 m.). The court was surrounded by porticos of two rows of columns on three sides.

The Royal Stoa, a magnificent basilica-type structure, was built along the entire length of the southern wall (*Ant.* XV, 411-412). Fragments of this structure which were found toppled down during the course of the excavations are ornamented by geometric and floral motifs (Mazar 1975: 25). The Royal Stoa served as an assembly hall before, during and after the Temple services.

The Temple

The reconstruction of the Temple itself has been made by various scholars, based solely on literary sources (fig. 3 and Pl. 1). No archaeological remains of it have been found. The Temple has been reconstructed in miniature by Prof. Avi-Yonah on the grounds of the Holy Land Hotel in Jerusalem (Pl. 1; fig. 5). The description below follows his reconstruction:

The Temple's inner and outer Courts were separated by a screen (*soreg*) bearing an inscription warning Gentiles from entering the inner court (Ben-Dov 1982: fig. on p. 102). Beyond this screen a flight of either twelve or fourteen steps which surrounded the Temple led up to a rampart (*ḥel*) separate from the Temple inner walls. This wall was a fortress with gates and towers (figs. 3, 5). *War*, V, 198-200; *Ant.* XV, 418 and the Mishna (*Middoth* 1, 3) mention seven and ten gates (Avi-Yonah 1956: 408-409). The Temple was divided into three parts (fig. 3): 1) the outer, Women's Court; 2) the inner Court of the priests and the Court of the Israelites; and 3) the Temple Sanctuary.

1) *The Outer, Women's Court* (135 × 135 cubits) (fig. 5). This was so named because women were allowed to enter only as far as this court and no further. It served for communal ritual functions (Safrai 1976: 866). Four corner "chambers," 40 × 40

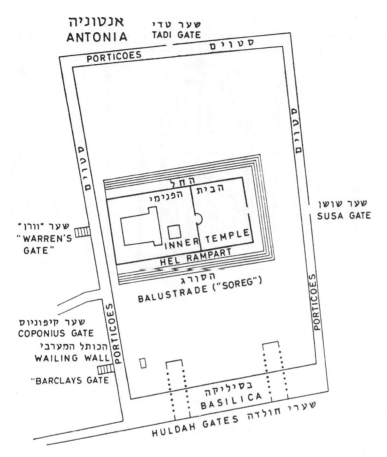

אנטוניה
ANTONIA

שער טדי
TADI GATE

סטוים
PORTICOES

פורק

פורק

הבית הפנימי
החל

INNER TEMPLE

HEL RAMPART

הסורג
BALUSTRADE ("SOREG")

שער שושן
SUSA GATE

שער "וורן"
"WARREN'S
GATE"

PORTICOES

שער קיפוניוס
COPONIUS GATE

הכותל המערבי
WAILING WALL

"BARCLAYS GATE"

PORTICOES

בסיליקה
BASILICA

שערי חולדה
HULDAH GATES

5. Plan of the Temple Mount.

cubits each, were erected in this court: the Wood, Nazirites, Oil and Lepers chambers, each with its own ritual bath serving for purification. The Women's Court was surrounded by porticos and galleries where women assisted in several of the ceremonies.

The Nicanor Gate (figs. 3, 6) was built on the west wall of the court leading into the Israelites' Court. The gate, named after an Alexandrian Jew who donated the bronze doors, was approached by fifteen curved steps on which the Levites would sit while playing instruments and singing.

6. Reconstruction of the Nicanor Gate.

2) *The Second Court* was divided into two parts:

a) The long and narrow Court of Israelites (135 × 11 cubits) ran along the eastern side of the inner Court. In this court men who brought sacrifices could watch the rites performed in the Court of the Priests. On either side of the inner section of the Nicanor Gate was a chamber, one the Chamber of Pinhas, the Keeper of the Vestments, and the other the Chamber of the Makers of the Cakes (*M. Middoth* 1:4).

b) The Court of the Priests (187 × 135 cubits) was surrounded by porticoes, with gates. Colonnades with decorated columns (*M. Tamid* 1:3; *War* V, 200) housed several chambers which all protruded into the court. The Chamber of the Hewn Stone was the seat of the Sanhedrin. The House of the Hearth was used as the centre of the priests on duty in the Temple. The House of Abtinas served for the preparation of incense. Inside this court were two most important structures: the Slaughter House and the Altar, which were erected in front of the sanctuary. The Altar (30 cubits square) was made of stones untooled by iron chisels. This altar was approached by a ramp, and both were whitewashed twice a year. The House of Slaughter was divided into three parts, each of four cubits, containing the marble tables, low pillars and the rings.

3) *The Temple Sanctuary* was 100 cubits in width along the front and 70 cubits in most of its length. It was ''shaped like a lion, broad in front and narrow behind''

7b. The Dura Europos fresco.

7a. Reconstruction of the Temple facade.   7c. The Bar Kokhba Coin.

(*M. Middoth* 4:7). The portal of the Temple was flanked by four engaged columns standing in two pairs (fig. 7a), which have been reconstructed on the basis of the coins of Bar Kokhba (fig. 7c) and the Dura Europos synagogue fresco (fig. 7b). A golden eagle was hung above the portal (*War* I, 650-656; *Ant.* XVII, 149-163). The doorway was covered by a large curtain and twelve steps led up to the sanctuary. The Temple was divided into three parts:

a) The porch, 70 × 11 cubits, had two flanking rooms, each 15 cubits wide.

b) The sanctuary (40 × 20 cubits), access to which was gained through two outer and inner doors, had two walls covered in gold foil. It housed the sacred golden vessels: the menorah, the shewbread table, the altar of incense. The position of these vessels is disputed; they were either placed from north to south (*B. Yoma* 51b-52a), or from west to east (*M. Menachoth* 11:6, cf. *War* V, 216-217).

c) The Holy of Holies (20 × 20 cubits) occupied the western part of the Temple, and its entrance was through two curtains. It was impossible to see into the Holy of Holies. The Second Temple Holy of Holies contained no objects, whereas that of the Solomonic Temple contained the Ark of the Covenant. The High Priest alone was allowed to enter once a year on the Day of Atonement.

The archaeological excavations carried out during the course of a decade (1968-1978) (Pl. 2) have resulted in important data being disclosed concerning the areas of the Temple Mount gates and the areas outside the west, south and east retaining walls. Streets, squares and monumental passageways have been uncovered (Mazar 1975a: 25-30; 1975b: 111-152; Ben-Dov 1982: 105-133).

The Gates of the Temple Mount (figs. 2, 3, 4) (Ben Dov 1982: 135-146; 1983: 134-153)

Josephus describes four gates on the west wall which led into the Temple Mount. By comparison, the Mishna, (*Middoth* I, 3) describes five gates: the two Ḥulda Gates on the south, the Coponius Gate on the west, the Tadi Gate on the north, and the Susa Gate on the east. On the west, as revealed by the archaeological excavations, four gates led into the Temple Mount. Two of these gates, which were situated above the monumental bridge-stairways and whose remains are known today as Robinson's Arch and Wilson's Arch (figs. 8a, 5), probably led to the Royal Stoa and other public buildings on the Mount. Through them ran the western (Tyropoeon) street. The other two gates are known today as Barclay's Gate (figs. 8a, 4), situated between the Robinson and Wilson arches, which can probably be identified with the Coponius Gate through which it is assumed the Gentiles entered the Temple Mount (Ben-Dov 1982: 142; 1983: 141-143, 154), and Warren's Gate, north of Wilson's Arch (figs. 8a, 2) (Ben-Dov 1983: 144).

On the south were the two Ḥulda Gates, separated from each other by a distance of 70 metres, the eastern of which (the Triple Gate) was the main entrance which led into the Temple Mount, and the western of which (the Double Gate) led out of the Temple Mount (figs. 4, 9) (Ben-Dov 1982: 140-141; 1983: 134-140). These gates were decorated with ornamented domes (figs. 9a, II.7 and Pl. 9), and were named for the prophetess Ḥulda, who, according to tradition, is buried nearby (but see Ben-Dov 1982: 136). As these were the main gates to the Temple Mount it is safe to assume that the southern side was the entrance of the Temple Mount. Two other gates are mentioned, but have not been found: the Tadi Gate on the north (*M. Middoth* 1:3), and the Susa Gate on the east, so called due to the depiction of the town of Susa on it. Another gate has been found above the eastern passageway; it was a

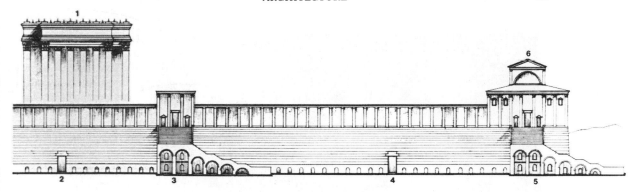

.8a. The Gates at the Western Wall.

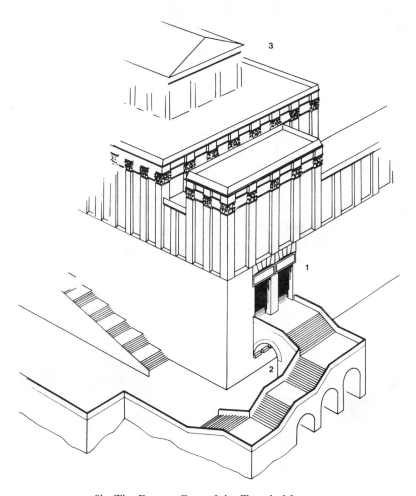

8b. The Eastern Gate of the Temple Mount.

9a-c Huldah Gates, Jerusalem.

double gate that led to the vaults under the *temenos*, probably to the store rooms (fig. 8b; Ben-Dov 1983: 151-152).

Arches and Interchanges

Arches and interchanges protruding from the Temple Mount have been uncovered. Three arches, two on the western wall and one on the eastern wall, were employed as interchanges:

1) Robinson's Arch protruded from the western wall, close to the south-western corner (fig. 4). Its width was 15.20 m. and its length was more than one hundred metres. The diameter of the arch was 13 metres. It rested upon a pier built at a distance of 13 metres from the western wall. A series of smaller piers continued southwards, forming seven progressively smaller arches which together formed a monumental interchange leading from the street up to Robinson's Arch and the entrance above it, and probably to the Royal Stoa on the Temple Mount (figs. 4, 8a) (Mazar 1975a:25-26; Ben-Dov 1982:126-133).

2) Wilson's Arch protruded from the western wall, north of Robinson's Arch (fig. 9). It was also fifteen metres wide and thirteen metres in diameter. Ben-Dov (1982: 123) reconstructs Wilson's Arch and passageway identically to Robinson's Arch. He relies on the following facts: the Upper City buildings found in the excavations reach as far as the eastern pier of Wilson's Arch; thus no series of arches could have been constructed towards the east (see, on the other hand, Mazar 1975: fig. on 26-27). Wilson's Arch seen today *in situ* is a much later arch, probably Islamic in date. The original Herodian arch stones were found fallen onto the Second Temple period street (Ben-Dov 1982: 130; 1983: 147-149).

3) The eastern arch (fig. 8b), similar to the others, was also part of the interchange. It protruded from the eastern wall, close to the southeastern corner. It was smaller than the others, being only seven metres in both width and length. Under it ran the "Eastern Road" along the eastern wall. This eastern interchange, according to Ben-Dov (1982: 116) probably led from the street into the vaults which served as store rooms, under the Temple Mount.

Streets and Squares

Streets and squares were found in the excavations. Three of the four streets found ran along the Temple Mount walls, and two ran under the arches and interchanges.

1) A wide street (10 m.), paved with large stones, was flanked by small buildings which were probably shops. On the west they abutted the western retaining wall. The street ran under Robinson's Arch and Wilson's Arch (figs. 4, 8). It probably carried a large flight of steps leading from the Tyropoeon Valley through an en-

trance to the Royal Stoa. The pillar of Robinson's Arch (as well as Wilson's Arch) was also built with four shops inside it, and inside these the excavators found coins, stone vessels and weights. The area was probably a commercial section (fig. 4) (Ben-Dov 1982: 113-114, photo on p. 108).

2) A second street found during the excavations was the one which wound north of Robinson's Arch towards the Upper City. This street was built on vaults which housed an extensive drainage system and connected the Temple Mount to the Upper City (Ben-Dov 1982: 115)

3) Along the southern retaining wall, another street, paved with slabs, was reached by stairs (fig. 4), some of which were built on vaults along the eastern part of the street. The street runs adjacent to the Hulda Gates. Near the Double Gates a monumental stairway was found (figs. 4, 9 and Pl. 3), about 64 m. in width (Mazar 1975a: 30). A plaza paved with flagstones was found 6.50 m. south of this stairway.

4) A fourth street ran along the eastern Temple Mount wall. It must have been narrower, because the eastern arch is much smaller (Ben-Dov 1982: 115-116).

Herod's Temple in Jerusalem is the largest known temple in antiquity. One of the architectural wonders of the ancient world, and a unique structure, it must have made a magnificent impression on visitors. The Temple was the focal point for the Jewish nation, the centre for worship and the place where political, economic and spiritual affairs of world Jewry could be discussed and determined. It was also the destination for pilgrims during the Feasts, and therefore needed to accommodate thousands of people who gathered there to celebrate. One of the major reasons behind the enormity of the Herodian Temple building project was in order to meet this exigency.

b) Herodian Palaces

King Herod's reign is remarkable, in the architectural sphere, for the many monumental edifices either renovated or newly-built in both towns and fortresses. Herod especially concerned himself with building palaces which could be used for both administrative as well as for recreational purposes. In order to exploit the climatic differences as well as the strategic features between the various areas under his control, he built both fortresses, and winter and summer palaces. The Judean desert and the Jericho Valley, where his winter palaces of Masada, Jericho and Cypros were situated, as now, had ideal, temperate winter climates but were inconveniently hot in summer. Furthermore, the isolated and easily defendable rock upon which Masada is built provided excellent conditions for a fortress-palace. The high altitude and proximity to Jerusalem of Herodium, and the nearby sea at Caesarea, both assured pleasant climates for his summer palaces. Two additional palaces, probably for summer use, are mentioned by Josephus but have not yet been positively identified: ʾAscalon (*Ant.* XII, 321; *War* II, 98); and Sepphoris (*Ant.* XVII, 271; *War* II, 56). (Excavations at these two sites began in the summer of 1985.)

Typical Features of the Plans of Herodian Palaces

These features followed the common plans of the Roman "domus" and "villa" (town and country house respectively). A Herodian palace was usually an elaborate building with several wings:

1) The main wing contained:

a) The triclinium. This was a prominent feature consisting of a large hall with three rows of columns parallel to three walls and a wide entrance open to the landscape or an inner court.

b) A peristyle court, with rows of columns and double columns in its corners.

c) An inner garden.

d) A bath house.

e) Dwelling rooms.

2) The extended palace complex usually also included entertainment facilities:

a) Pools for swimming and sailing boats.

b) Elaborate gardens, such as the sunken garden at Jericho, palace III.

c) Water installations, such as aqueducts and channels, to bring water to the pools and gardens, as well as to the residential wings.

Herod's Palace in Jerusalem

Josephus describes Herod's magnificent palace which was situated close to three towers in the area of the present-day Citadel (*War* V, 176-182). Josephus' description of the Jerusalem palace is substantiated by the Jericho palaces which contain architectural features such as triclinia and gardens which are mentioned as having existed in the Jerusalem palace (p. 36). Archaeological excavations conducted south of the present-day Citadel (David's Tower) have revealed remains of this palace (Bahat and Broshi 1975). From the citadel in the north it was built on a raised platform which extended over 300-350 m. north-south and at least 60 m. west-east. No superstructure of the palace has been found and only supporting walls have survived. The palace in Jerusalem was Herod's chief palace and was probably in use throughout the year.

Jericho—Three Herodian Winter Palaces (fig. 10) (Netzer 1975a, 1977, 1983)

1) *Winter Palace I* (''Gymnasium'') (fig. 10(b))

This palace, which served for residential and ceremonial purposes, is dated to the early years of Herod's reign, following his defeat of Mattathias Antigonus in about 35-30 BCE. At that time, Cleopatra was given the Jericho valley by her lover Mark Anthony; Herod rented from her the date palm and balsam plantations. At this time the Hasmonean palace north of Wadi Qelt was still extant. The Herodian palace, a splendid villa, was built south of Wadi Qelt (fig. 10b). It was, in plan, a rectangular building (46 × 86 m.) with a central peristyle court (35 × 42 m.), a triclinium, a peristyle hall (12.50 × 18.50 m.), a bath house, and a pair of pools which may have served as a ritual bath (*miqveh*).

2) *Winter Palace II* (figs. 10(c); 11)

In 31 BCE an earthquake destroyed the Hasmonean palace complex. After the Battle of Actium Herod succeeded in regaining control of the Jericho valley (*Ant.* XV). He rebuilt and extended the palace complex which included several wings:

a) The south wing (1) was a small building erected over an artificial platform under which the Hasmonean palace was buried (fig. 11.1). It probably served as Herod's private residential villa (Netzer 1977:11; 1983: 106). Of the remains of the Hasmonean complex, the two pools were retained and now combined into one large swimming pool (fig. 11.2) and another smaller pool (fig. 11.9), surrounded by gardens.

b) Gardens were also planted (fig. 11) over the remains of the destroyed Hasmonean ''twin'' palaces.

c) The eastern wing was constructed on two levels. On the upper level a peristyle court (5) was surrounded by rooms on three sides, and had a hall decorated with frescoes (6). The lower level consisted of two swimming pools remaining from the Hasmonean palace (7, 9) inside a peristyle court. Attached to these was a bath house (8). It seems that this wing served for recreational purposes.

3) *Winter Palace III*, an enlarged palace (figs. 10(d); 12; 13).

At the end of each winter, the Wadi Qelt springs overflow, and the wadi becomes a river for a few weeks. Herod built his enlarged palace on both sides of Wadi Qelt. It consisted of a ''northern wing'' (4) on the north bank of the wadi (fig. 12.4), and

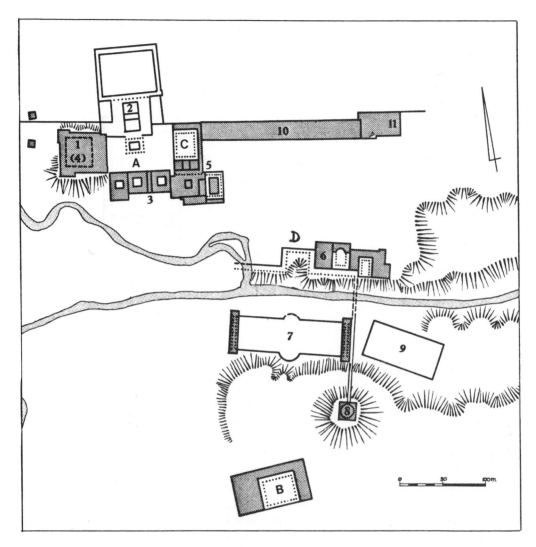

10. The Winter Palaces at Jericho: The Hasmonean Palace.(a) Herod's Winter Palace I.(b) Herod's
Winter Palace II.(c) Herod's Winter Palace III.(d)

a sunken garden (2), a large pool (40 × 92 m.) (3) and an artifical mound with a
building (1) on the south bank of the wadi.

a) The "Northern Wing" (4) is constructed of mud brick and concrete covered
with *opus reticulatum* and *opus quadratum* (Netzer 1975: 93, Pl. 8:A; 1977: 9, fig. 12).

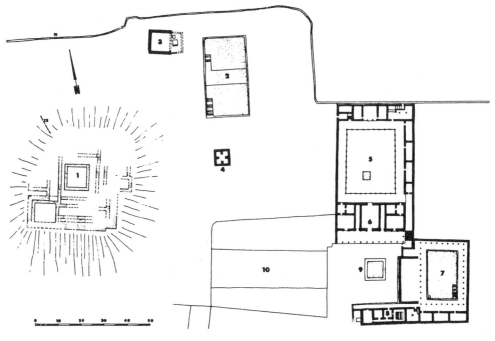

11. Jericho Winter Palace II.

This wing contained two triclinia and one large hall (29 × 19 m.) (B70) with three rows of columns open to the south to Wadi Qelt. The hall was paved in *opus sectile* stone slabs (Netzer 1975a:9, fig. 11). Also included in the northern wing was a five-room bath house (fig. 26c) which included a round frigidarium with four semicircular niches and a caldarium similar to those at Herodium and at Masada (fig. 25a, b). This wing also possessed two peristyle courts, the western of which had a wide semicircular apse. Several other rooms as well as the entrance were also included in the northern wing, which probably served as a leisure area.

b) The Sunken Garden (fig. 12) (2), which measured 140 × 40 m., had an impressive facade containing a semicircular structure in its centre. On both sides of this structure were 24 rows of niches. Two colonnades were located at either end.

c) The Large Pool (fig. 12) (3), west of the sunken garden, was built on an orientation different to that of all the other structures, probably because it is parallel to the natural slope. It served for swimming and water games.

d) The South Mound (fig. 12) (1) had a rectangular exterior and round interior. It probably was the foundation of a round cement-constructed hall, 16 m. in

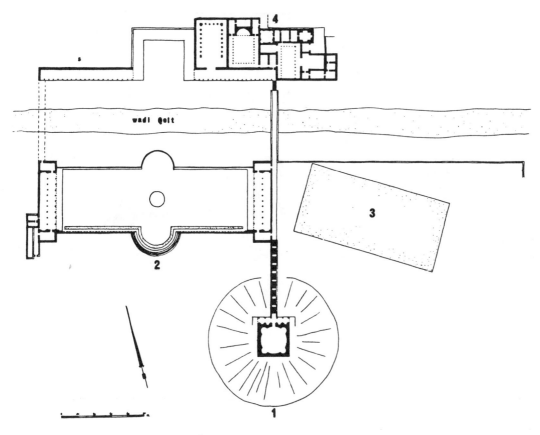

wadi Qelt

12. Jericho Winter Palace III Complex.

diameter, and similar to the frigidarium. It may have been another triclinium. A bridge connected the mound with the garden (figs. 12; 13.). Netzer (1983: 110-112) also postulates the existence of a bridge above the Wadi Qelt (fig. 13).

To sum up, Palace I ("Gymnasium") comprised Herod's first residential structure. Later, in palace complex II he built a smaller structure on an artificial platform which buried the previous Hasmonean palace (fig 1), to serve as his private residential villa. Most of the winter palace II complex (fig. 11) and all of the winter palace III complex (figs. 12; 13) served Herod and his court for recreational purposes.

Greater Herodium (Netzer 1981a)

Herodium is 12 km. south of Jerusalem. Herod built the Herodium palace-fortress, named it after himself, and chose it as the site of his burial. Sources for this

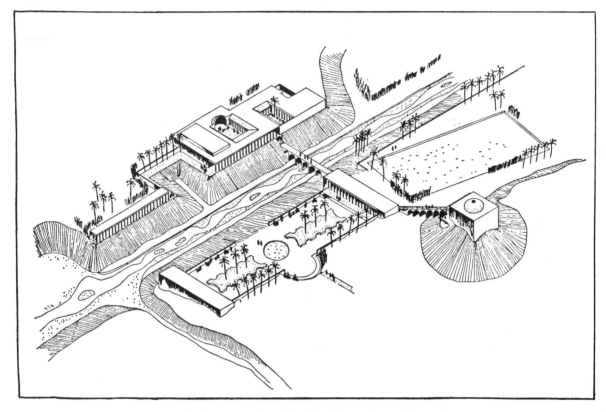

13. Reconstruction of Jericho Winter Palace III.

palace-fortress are the writings of Josephus (*Ant.* XIV, 359-360; XV, 323-325; *War* I, 265, 419-421) and the extensive excavations carried out during the last decade. Greater Herodium (fig. 14, Pl. 5) consists of an upper mountain palace-fortress (1) and a lower area containing a building complex (3-13).

1) *The Mountain Palace-Fortress* (1) (fig. 15)

This palace was built on top of a hill and was the first building constructed at Herodium (Netzer 1981a: 80-84, fig. 110). The structure is built in the shape of a cylinder of 63 m. in diameter, and consists of two concentric circular walls with a corridor (5) 3.5 m. wide between them (Netzer 1981a: 85-101, figs. 120, 130, 131). A massive fill was added to the outside of this cylinder, creating a steep slope. Four towers were built outside the cylinder walls, three of which are semicircular (2-4).

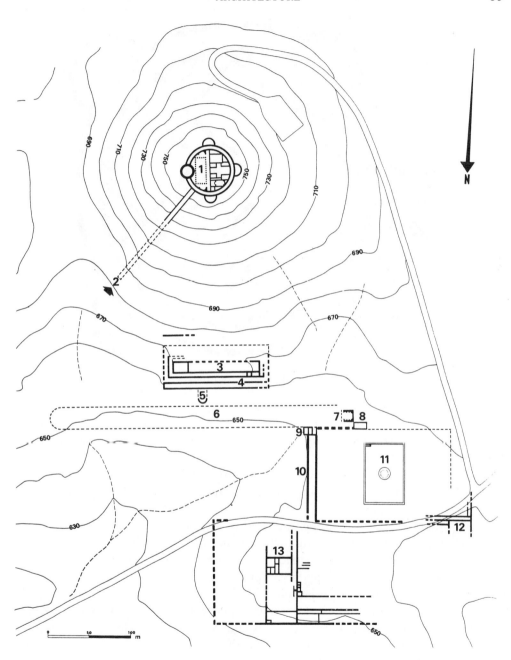

14. Plan of Greater Herodium.

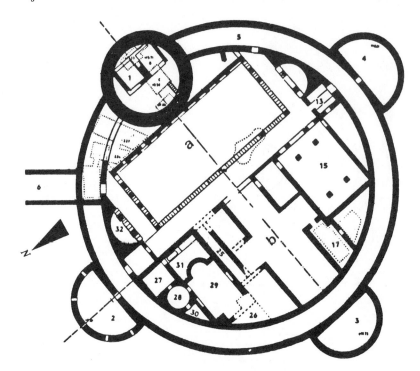

15. Herodian Palace-Fortress.

The fourth, the eastern tower (1), was the tallest, and was probably a multi-storeyed tower, similar to the three towers of Jerusalem. The structure was five-six storeys high and contained rooms.

Netzer (1981a: 100-101) asserts that the prototype for the Herodium palace-fortress was the Antonia fortress in Jerusalem. Herodium is similar in design except that it is circular in plan.

A steep stairway, partly a tunnel quarried in the mountain, was built directly up to the palace. Within the encircling fortress walls and towers Herod built a palace, as a residential villa, which is divided into eastern and western wings:

a) The eastern wing (a) has a peristyle courtyard with semicircular niches at either end, and probably served as a garden.

b) The western wing contained the living quarters consisting of rooms surrounding a central courtyard (b). South of this courtyard is the triclinium (15) (later a synagogue, p. 84). North of the courtyard is the bath house with its caldarium (29) similar to those at Masada and Jericho, and its tepidarium (28) which was a circular room (see also p. 57, fig. 26b).

2) *Lower Herodium* (fig. 14)

Below the mountain palace-fortress and at the foot of the mountain, remains of structures have been uncovered in recent years by Netzer (1981a: 10-51).

a) The pool complex (11) (fig. 14) was the architectural focus of Lower Herodium and must have been an outstanding feature. Surrounded by formal gardens, its centre contained a circular colonnaded pavilion (Netzer 1981a: 28-30, fig. 47). The pool served for swimming, sailing boats, and as a water reservoir.

b) The large central palace (3-5) (fig. 14) was built on an elevated platform, and served as a palace for Herod and his court.

c) The course (6), 350 m. long and 25 m. wide, was almost level. At its western end stand the remains of a monumental building (7) which is connected to the course.

d) The monumental building (7) (fig. 14) is massive, measuring 14.9 × 14 m. and containing a hall with niches, once covered by frescoes. This building may have formed part of a burial complex, with the course serving as a "funeral course" (Netzer 1981a: 33-45).

e) The northern wing (fig. 14.13) consists of several buildings which probably served as dwellings for Herod's family and court, as service wings or as residences for the administrative staff (Netzer 1981a: 45-51).

f) The aqueduct built by Herod brought water from Urtas to the Lower Herodium complex.

Masada (Yadin 1965, 1966)

Eight palaces were found at Masada in the northern and western parts of the rock mountain (fig. 16; Pl. 4). The two main palaces are: 1) the Northern Palace or palace-villa; and 2) the Western Palace or the ceremonial and administrative palace. Several smaller palaces were also uncovered: 3) a group of three small palaces serving the royal family (33, 34, 26 = XI, XII, XIII) (fig. 19); and 4) a further group of palaces which served as residences for high officials and as administrative centres (Palaces VII, IX, XI, XII; fig. 19).

1) *The Northern Palace-villa* (fig. 17)

This palace is a most unusual structure which utilized the rock cliff in a unique manner. The palace, consisting of three terraces, one above the other, is built on the northern edge of the rock. The entrance was on the east side of the upper terrace.

a) The upper terrace (III) consists of rooms along the sides of an open court, living quarters and a semi circular balcony (porch) which probably had two rows of columns.

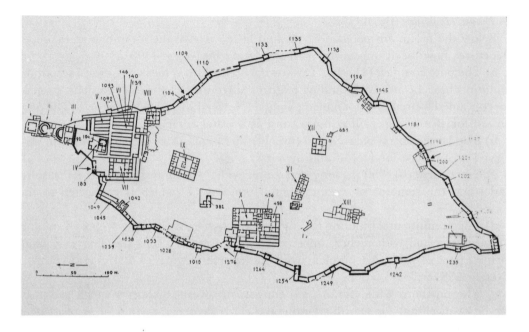

16. Plan of Masada.

b) The middle terrace (II) is about twenty metres beneath the upper terrace and consists of a circular pavilion structure. The foundation of this building has survived and consists of an outer and inner wall. The space between the two walls is filled with stones. This structure was a type of tholus with two rows of columns. South of the circular building was a staircase connecting the upper and middle terraces. A large hall on the east is decorated with a colonnade, a "false facade" and fresco imitating marble. The middle terrace served as a pavilion, a relaxation and leisure area.

c) The lower terrace (I) is about fifteen metres beneath the middle terrace. The building measures 17.6 × 17.6 m. and is constructed on a raised area of supporting walls. The central area is porticoed, (fig. 17) consisting of a double colonnade of half-columns made of sandstone which are plastered with coloured Corinthian capitals. The lower parts of the portico walls are decorated with marble-imitative fresco (fig. II.3). Behind the porticoed area is a "false facade" wall, with half-columns attached to the rock and fresco panels between them (fig. II.3) (Yadin 1965: Pl. 3). On the east is a small bath house, and on the west is a staircase leading from the middle terrace to the lower terrace.

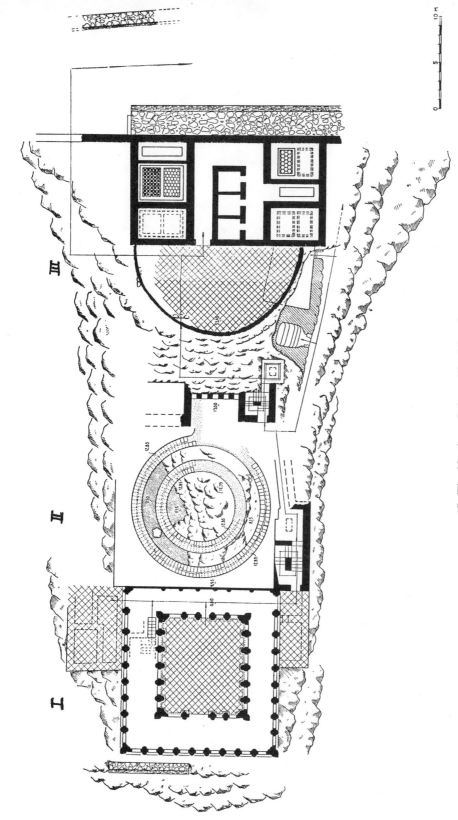

17. The Northern Palace-villa, Masada.

This palace had only a few living rooms on the upper terrace and was intended mostly for leisure.

2) *The Western Palace* (X) (fig. 18.X)

This is the largest among several similarly-planned palaces at Masada. The plans of the two groups 3) and 4) are quite similar and follow the plan of the western palace apartment wing. Built close to the western gate (fig. 16), it is the largest of all the palaces, occupying about four thousand square metres, with a main entrance on the north. The palace contains four parts: a) the southeast section containing the royal apartments; b) the northeast service wing and workshop; c) the southwest storerooms; and d) the northwest administrative wing and residence for palace officials.

a) The royal apartments are built around a central court. A hall is located in the middle of the southern part and two Ionic columns in the north side mark the opening into the court. Three entrances from this hall lead into a throne room. One of the eastern rooms of the royal apartments contains a mosaic floor (Pl. 7a). North of the court is the bath house, ritual bath and other installations. The floors here are also paved with mosaics (Pl. 7b). This wing probably had several storeys, and is similar in plan to the twin Hasmonean palaces at Jericho (fig. 19) (Netzer 1982b: 25).

b) The service wing and workshops are built around a court. The north side contained dwelling rooms whereas the remaining rooms were workshops.

c) The storeroom wing consists of several long storerooms in the southwestern part of the palace. A row of storerooms abuts the south wall of the royal apartment wing. These rooms belong to the second stage of the palace buildings.

d) The administrative wing consists of three blocks of buildings. The northernmost of these served as the residence of the palace officials and is similar to the other palaces of Masada.

3) *Palaces XI, XII and XIII* (figs. 16, 18)

These were erected close to the western palace. They each have a central court, and a hall with two columns leading into another corner hall which was probably a reception room. This room could also be entered through a small corridor or waiting room.

4) *Palaces VII and VIII* (figs. 16, 18)

These are close to the storeroom. They have the same general plan as the other palaces. Building VII has a storeroom attached to it which probably contained valuable commodities.

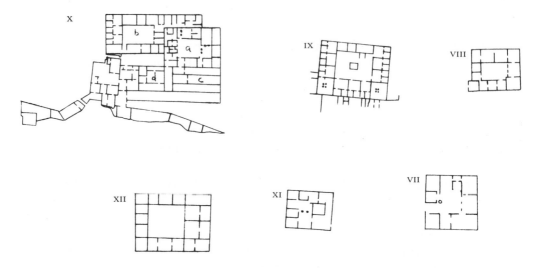

18. The Palaces of Masada.

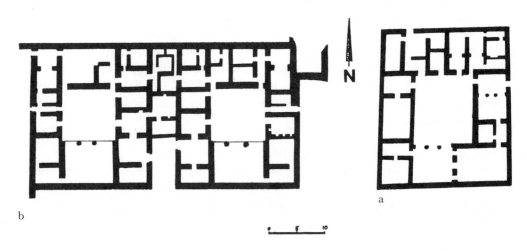

19. Masada, Western Palace, Royal Wing (a), and Twin Palace of Jericho (b).

5) *Building IX*

This has a different plan (figs. 16, 18). Its central court is surrounded by rooms consisting of small units, each of which has two small rooms and a court. Three units lie on three sides of the building. The east side contains two large halls and the main entrance. This building probably served as a barracks for the guard.

The Masada palaces differ in plan from the usual Herodian palaces of Jericho and Herodium. They are characterized by a simple, central court, and by halls each with two columns in antis, leading to a triclinium, usually in the southern part of the court (fig. 18). They are closely related in plan to the twin buildings of the Hasmonean palace at Jericho (fig. 19) (Netzer 1982b: 23, 25). The plan of the Masada palaces follows basic elements of Hellenistic architecture (Yadin 1965: 47, note 37; Netzer 1981a: 110). Netzer (1982b: 25) asserts that these differences in plans prove that the Masada palaces had been already built by the Hasmoneans, and were only expanded and improved by Herod. However, it is also possible that Herod, when building the Masada palaces, utilized a plan which had also been used earlier by the Hasmoneans.

c) Fortresses

Seven fortresses known to have been built in the Judean desert, Masada, Herodium, Cypros, Hyrcania, Alexandrium, Machaerus and Doq, constitute an important component of Herodian architecture. The fortresses were located in the desert, within view of each other. They were isolated and autonomous. Built on mountain tops, they were strongly fortified, and had extensive systems for the entrapment and storage of water. They functioned primarily as military bases for defence, but also as places of refuge for political and spiritual reasons, and as shelters in times of violent confrontation and upheaval. The fortresses also served as administrative centres for important routes, agricultural and royal farm areas and palaces; they also were used for guarding borders. They even served as burial places both for the Hasmoneans and for Herod. Elaborate palaces were constructed on their premises. Masada was the most spacious of all and had several palaces on its summit, which served as leisure resorts. The fortresses sometimes extended into the lower areas of their mountains; Herodium had buildings and installations built below the mount.

The history of the fortresses, known from literary sources as well as from archaeological excavations (Tsafrir 1982), begins in the Hasmonean period. Three fortresses (Alexandrium, Hyrcania and Machaerus) are mentioned by Josephus

(*Ant.* XIII, 417; *War* VII, 166) as being related to the Hasmoneans in about 69 BCE. This is attested to by their names: Alexandrium is probably named after Alexander Jannaeus (103-76 BCE) and Hyrcania after John Hyrcanus I (135-104 BCE). These three fortresses played roles in the skirmishes and struggles between the Hasmonean kings and the Romans. In 57 BCE they were destroyed by the governor Gabinius.

The earliest mention of Masada is from 42 BCE (*Ant.* XIV, 296; *War* I, 236-238); Herod fled to Masada in 40 BCE, and it became his stronghold against the Hasmoneans. The fortresses were also extensively used in the First War against the Romans (66-73 CE), especially Masada, Herodium and Machaerus, which still stood after the fall of Jerusalem (70 CE). The last Hasmonean stronghold was Hyrcania (*War* I, 364). Upon establishing his rule in about 30 BCE, Herod rebuilt and refortified all the existing fortresses as well as building Herodium. Splendid palaces were built within all fortresses. He also used the fortresses as administrative centres, for executions and as burial places.

Masada (Yadin 1965) (fig. 16)

The fortress of Masada is built on the rock cliff about 25 kilometres south of ʿEn-Gedi. The rock is rhomboid in shape, measuring about 600 m. north-south and 300 m. east-west. The fortress itself is encircled by a casemate wall with four gates, thirty towers and seventy rooms. The wall is built of local dolomite stone. The gates' plan consists of a room with an outer and inner entrance, and benches along the walls. The towers are small casemates built according to the topography at unequal distances.

On the northern edge of the cliff stands the palace-villa. Next to it are the public storehouses, bath house and additional palaces. Other palaces were built on the western part of the rock.

Herodium (fig. 14) (Corbo 1963, Netzer 1981a)

Herodium is a symmetrical, circular mountain fortress built on a natural hill south of Jerusalem. Two walls shaped as concentric circles enclose the structure, and a fill is added between them. Four towers are added to the circular wall according to the exact points of the compass. Three of the towers are semicircular. The eastern tower is multi-storeyed and circular. Inside the fortress is built a palace. A further palace and other buildings were uncovered in lower Herodium.

Alexandrium/Sartaba (fig. 20) (Tsafrir & Magen 1984)

Alexandrium was the northernmost of the Judean desert fortresses during the Second Temple period. It had probably been built as a fortress in Hasmonean times,

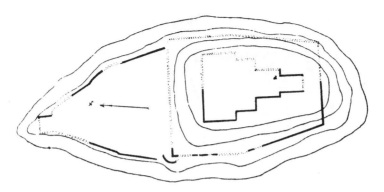

20. Alexandrium, Plan of Remains.

and named after either Alexander Janneus or his wife Salome Alexandra (first half of the first century BCE). The Hasmonean fortress was destroyed by Gabinius in 57 BCE, and was later rebuilt on a more elaborate scale by Herod.

According to Josephus, Herod left his wife Mariamme and her mother in custody at Alexandrium in 30 BCE. In 15 BCE Marcus Agrippa was Herod's guest there. After Herod murdered his two sons, they were buried in the Hasmonean dynasty tomb at Alexandrium (*War* I:27; *Ant.* 16, 394). Several architectural fragments in the Doric order are all that remain of the Hasmonean fortress. Most of the fortress is built on the mountain summit, and was found in ruins, probably due to an earthquake, with stones, columns and capitals collapsed in a pile. However, remains indicate a peristyle structure. A west wall with a stone vault seems to indicate a second storey, probably of a palace with two terraces. Many column drums, stucco and fresco fragments were uncovered in the structure and around it. The centre of the peristyle hall was paved with mosaic.

Cypros (fig. 21) (Netzer 1975b)

Cypros is a desert fortress built on a mountain dominating the Jericho valley. It was first built by the Hasmoneans, and later Herod constructed splendid buildings on the site, which he named for his mother Cypros. Herod built, as was his custom, retaining walls on the slopes, and thus expanded the fortress area.

Remains of a palace have been uncovered on top of the mountain. In the northwest corner of the summit a bath house was found (fig. 25d; see p. 59) and a further building was discovered in the lower area. This also has a large bath house (fig. 25e) which is probably earlier in date than the upper bath house.

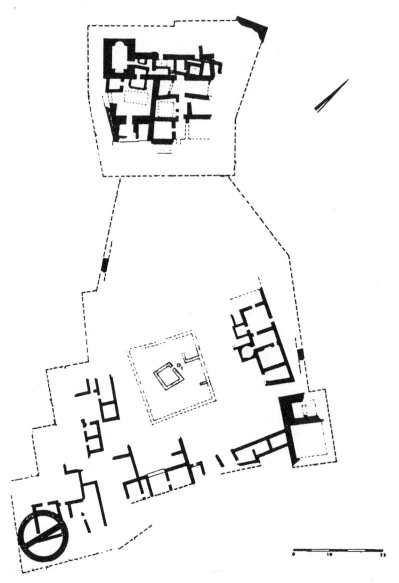

21. Plan of Cypros.

The function of the palace-fortresss at Cypros is not exactly clear. It could have served either as another winter palace for Herod, or as a place of refuge to which Herod could flee from Jericho during periods of unrest. It may also have been a palace for the royal family or other important personages. Cypros was probably burned and abandoned in The Jewish War (66-70 CE).

Hyrcania (Wright 1961: 8)

Hyrcania is a fortress in the northeastern section of the Judean desert whose remains were uncovered during a trial excavation. Fortress walls and towers were found on the summit of the hill. The enclosure contained a court surrounded on three sides by rooms. A water system had been also in use.

Machaerus (Corbo 1979, 1980)

The fortress of Machaerus is situated east of the Dead Sea. Excavations on the site uncovered a fortification wall with several towers (fig. 22,1). The wall encloses a unit similar to other desert fortresses. It consists of three main sections: first, a paved peristyle court in the upper centre of the site (2); second, another paved court in the lower part, and a bath house to the west of this court containing a stepped frigidarium (5) and large caldarium (4); and third, storerooms on the eastern side of the court (3).

Jerusalem

In Jerusalem two important fortresses or citadels were built. One was the Antonia, which commanded the Temple Mount, and the other was the citadel near Herod's palace.

The Antonia Fortress

This fortress was rebuilt by Herod before 31 BCE, and is named for Mark Anthony. It was situated close to the northwest corner of the Temple Mount, and dominated the Temple (fig. 2). Four square towers, one of which was taller than the others, were situated at the corners. The interior of the fortress was designed and furnished as a palace, as described by Josephus (*War* V, 238-245). The precise location of the fortress is subject to debate (Benoit 1975; Bahat 1981b). Netzer (1981a: 100-101) maintains that the Antonia fortress is the prototype for the palace-fortress of Herodium which differs only in its circular plan.

The Jerusalem Citadel

A citadel with three towers was built at the northwest corner of the city wall, north of Herod's palace (fig. 2). The towers were named Hippicus, Phasael and Mariamme, for Herod's friend, brother and wife respectively. Only the base of one of these towers has survived. It is 21 m. in length, 17 m. in width and has a solid

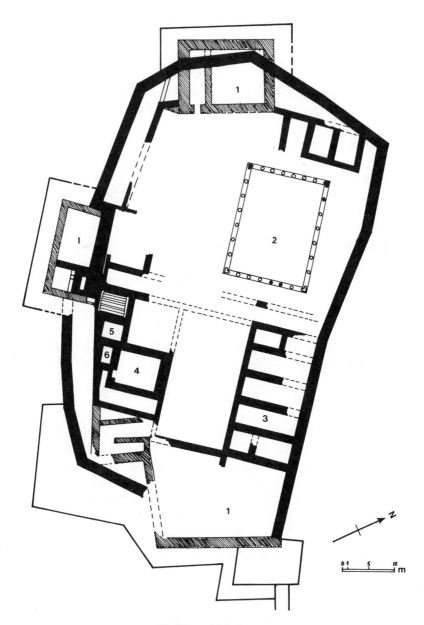

22. Plan of Machaerus.

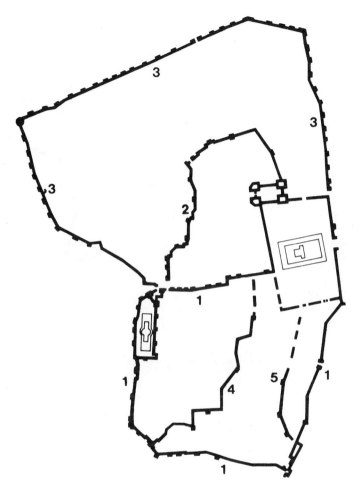

23a. Jerusalem City Walls.

foundation. This was a multi-storeyed tower, identified by scholars either with Hippicus or Phasael (Geva 1982: 71).

d) *The Jerusalem City Walls* (fig. 23a,b)

The Hasmoneans began to refortify the city of Jerusalem and sections of the city wall have been uncovered in excavations (Avigad 1983: 65-74). The fortification of Jerusalem is known from the writings of Josephus and from extensive excavations

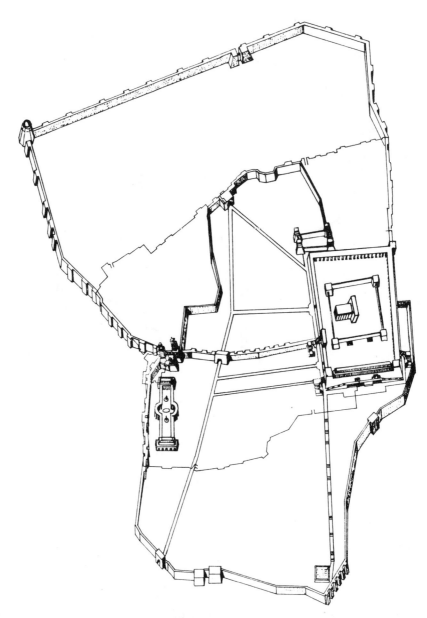

23b. Jerusalem City Walls.

carried out during the last decade. The *First Wall* encompassed the whole western hill, and encircled the Upper and Lower Cities (figs. 2, 23). It linked up with a section of the earlier wall of Israelite Jerusalem near the Siloam pool, and, according to Josephus, had about sixty towers. The northern line of the First Wall ran from the Herodian palace towers in the area of the present-day Citadel, to the Temple Mount. Its eastern line ended at the southeastern corner of the Temple Mount. Ben Dov (1983:43 and plan on p. 47) proposes that the eastern line continued for about thirty metres on the eastern slope of the Kidron Valley.

The reconstruction of the *Second Wall*'s line is subject to controversy. According to Josephus it ran from the "Gennath Gate" in the First Wall to the Antonia Fortress. It had only twelve towers, probably due to its fairly short course. The remains of the Herodian gate foundation under the Damascus Gate are considered to be part of this wall, which is ascribed to Herodian city fortifications.

The *Third Wall* was built by King Agrippa I (41-44 CE), Herod's grandson. Its construction including its ninety towers ended abruptly and was only renewed during the First War against the Romans in 67 CE. It ran north from the Hippicus tower and turned east until the northeast tower of the Temple Mount. Its exact course, like that of the Second Wall, is subject to controversy (Ben Dov 1983:45-47).

e) Caesarea Harbour (Raban and Hohlfelder 1981). fig. 24

Herod's most important undertaking in Caesarea was the harbour named Sebastos, a marvel of engineering and one of the greatest harbours known to have been built in antiquity. Underwater excavations in recent years have yielded important information about the Herodian harbour which was fully described by Josephus (*Ant.* XV, 334-338; *War* I, 413). Herod built two stone breakwaters: a southern curved breakwater about 480 m. in length, and from 40 to 60 m. in width, and a shorter northern breakwater, over two hundred m. long and 50 m. wide. Its inner face held several interior loading platforms. At the head of the northern breakwater huge ashlar stones (some fifteen metres in length) were found in the underwater debris. These stones presumably formed the base of one of the towers built on either side of the entrance to the original Herodian harbour, as described by Josephus. At the head of the southern breakwater, ruins of a massive building, probably a lighthouse, were discovered.

The distance between the two breakwaters was 18 metres and probably marked the entrance into the harbour. The harbour moles were destroyed by earthquake. The total space of the harbour was about 1500 sq.m.(fig. 24).

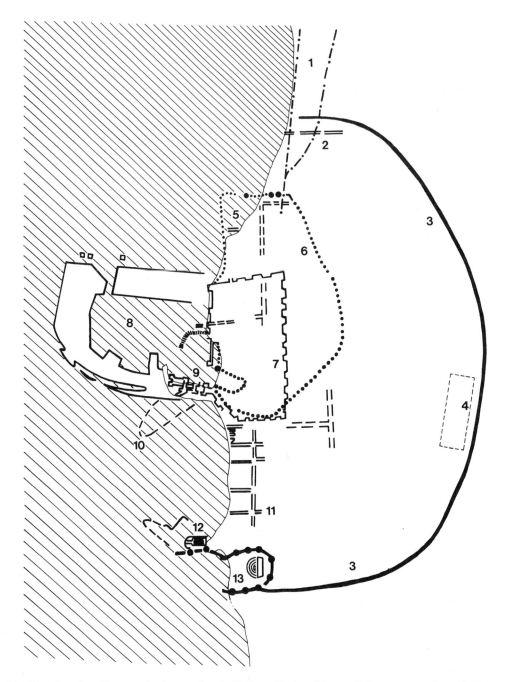

24. Plan of ancient Caesarea harbours after A. Raban, *Guide to Sebastos*: 1) Roman aqueduct; 2) Herodian main sewer; 3) Byzantine city wall; 4) Roman hippodrome; 5) Hellenistic harbour; 6) City walls of Straton's tower; 7) City wall; 8) Herodian harbour; 9) Crusader harbour; 10) Later Roman harbour; 11) Roman streets; 12) Fish Market; 13) Roman theatre.

The land excavations (Bull 1982: 34-36) uncovered about five vaulted complexes of warehouses, which were part of the vast Herodian harbour warehouse and shipping installations built along the harbour front. These vaulted warehouses opened onto streets, and several opened onto the Cardo Maximus.

Huge quantities of fragments of large amphorae typical of Italy, Spain, and other countries were found inside these vaulted structures. They attest to the fact that Casearea was a large, international harbour in antiquity.

4. Other Herodian Structures

Jerusalem Houses

Residential houses of the Herodian period are mostly known from those uncovered during the excavations of the Upper City and the Temple Mount area in Jerusalem. The streets were not laid in a uniform plan and their direction followed the topography of the area.

The houses of the Upper City were built close to each other. Each house was usually structured around a central court. Rooms were decorated with mosaic floors, wall paintings and stucco, and had elaborate water installations (fig. 25) (Avigad 1983: 83-98). Some of the buildings, such as the Mansion (fig. 25b), contained two levels: a ground floor for dwelling, and a basement with water installations. Houses similar to those in the Upper City have been uncovered near the Temple Mount (Ben-Dov 1982: 149-153). In the Armenian Quarter outside the Zion Gate, remains of houses with rooms, courts and water installations have been found. Many of the installations were vaulted over and many of the houses had two storeys. Splendid fresco fragments with birds have been found (Broshi 1975: 57-58, Pl. III).

The Palace of Ḥilkiya (Damati 1982)

In the Hebron area a splendid palace, Herodian in plan and ornament, has been uncovered. The palace is a rectangular building, having a peristyle court (8 × 10 m.) with an open triclinium in its centre. Thick walls surround the whole structure. The palace contains rooms in rows around the court. Some of these rooms have barrel vaults and they are decorated with stucco. The gate to the palace was uncovered in the south. A bath house was found in the northern wing. In the west a tower measuring 13 × 13 m. was constructed.

Many architectural fragments were found during the excavations: Nabatean capitals, column bases and drums, some of which bore masons' marks and Hebrew letters.

The palace was named Ḥilkiya after a Greek inscription on a limestone slab which mentions Ḥilkiya, son of Simon.

25. Jerusalem Houses: a) Residence; b) Palatial Mansion .

Herod's Tomb

The location of Herod's tomb is subject to much debate. A site for his mausoleum, favoured by many scholars, is Herodium. Netzer (1981a: 100-101), however, asserts that Herodium was not Herod's tomb, because first, no remains of any significance which may suggest a mausoleum have been found either at the palace-fortress or in Lower Herodium; second, the palace of Herodium was used for more than seventy years, and would not, simultaneously, have served as a tomb; and finally, the suggestion by scholars that the mausoleum of Augustus in Rome had supplied the prototype for the Herodium palace-fortress is unacceptable for architectural and functional reasons. Netzer suggests that a circular building in Jerusalem (opposite the present-day Damascus Gate) whose foundations are preserved, may have served as Herod's family mausoleum (Netzer & Ben Arieh 1983:171).

Bath Houses

The bath houses of the Herodian palaces and houses are modelled on familiar and common Roman baths (Gichon 1978). The Roman bath generally consists (fig. 26) of a caldarium (hot room)(1), a tepidarium (tepid room)(2), a frigidarium (cold room)(3), and an apodyterium (entrance and disrobing room)(4). Usually the caldarium is connected with the frigidarium. The furnace is usually built in the courtyard.

Masada possessed three bath houses:

1) A large bath house is located next to the storerooms (fig. 26a). Most of it, including the ceiling, was decorated with fresco. The floor of the tepidarium was paved with *opus sectile*, and the courtyard was paved with mosaics. The caldarium heated by a hypocaust, which probably had a domed ceiling, had two niches, one round and one rectangular. One contained a huge tub and the other a basin (Yadin 1966: 75-85).

2) A private bath house was uncovered in the Western palace (Yadin 1966: 127).

3) A further private bath house was discovered on the lower terrace of the Northern palace (Yadin 1966: 47).

Herodium contained two bath houses:

1) In the fortress-palace was a large private bath house (fig. 26b). The caldarium is similar to the one at Masada. The frigidarium or tepidarium was a round room, with a domed ceiling. The walls were covered with fresco and the floor was paved with geometric mosaics.

2) A bath house was found in the northern wing in Lower Herodium (Netzer 1981a: 47-84, figs. 77-78).

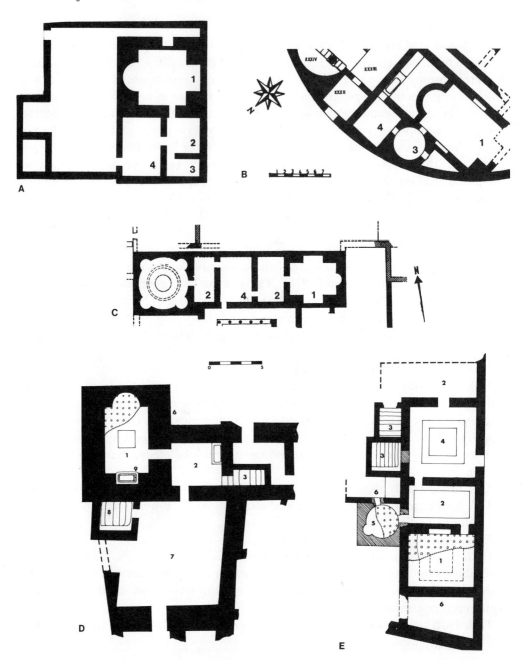

26. Bath Houses: a) Masada; b) Herodium Palace-Fortress; c) Jericho Winter Palace III; d) and e) Cypros;
1) Caldarium; 2) Tepidarium; 3) Frigidarium; 4) Apodyterium.

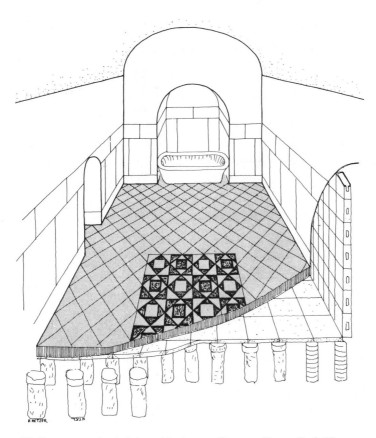

27. Reconstruction of the caldarium at Cypros, Upper Bath House.

Jericho also had two bath houses:

1) A bath house was found in the Herodian palace II. Its rooms were set in a row (fig. 11).

2) A large bath house was uncovered in the northern wing of Herodian palace III (fig. 26c). It was situated close to the triclinium and the peristyle court, thus being part of the reception and leisure wing. The bath house rooms were constructed in a row.

Cypros had two bath houses (Netzer 1975b):

1) The upper one was in the palace-fortress (fig. 26d) and may have served the king and his court. It had a large entrance hall(7). The caldarium(1) had a rectangular niche with an alabaster tub which was found *in situ* (fig. 27) (Netzer 1975b:

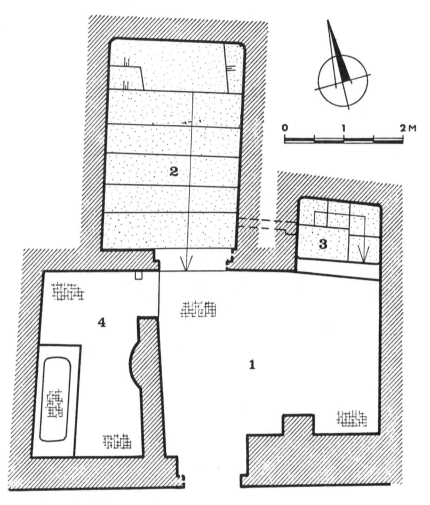

28. Ritual Bath, Jerusalem ; 1) Vestibule; 2) Ritual Bath; 3) "Store" Pool; 4) Bathroom.

57). Fragments of a basin were found in the other, semicircular niche. The floor was paved with *opus sectile* pavement, and under it was situated the hypocaust (fig. 26e). Some of the rooms were covered with fresco.

2) The lower bath house was smaller, and its rooms were built in a row. The caldarium(1) was unusually shaped: a rectangular room with one niche. The tepidarium(2) and apodyterium had mosaic floors.

Palace of Ḥilkiya (Damati 1982: 117) The northern wing of this palace had a bath house in its first level; a caldarium and a hypocaust; a tepidarium with a mosaic floor and a frigidarium containing a pool.

Machaerus (Corbo 1979) had a large bath house in its southwestern corner, flanking a court (fig. 22). Its frigidarium had steps and the tepidarium was paved with a mosaic floor (Corbo 1979: Pl. 44b).

Ritual Baths

A structure unique to Jewish architecture is the ritual bath. Many of the laws of Judaism concern ritual purity and requirements for this purity were particularly strict among the priests; thus it is not surprising that ritual baths (*miqveh, miqvaoth*) have been found in Jerusalem close to the Temple, in the Temple Mount and Upper City excavations. Similar baths have also been found in Jericho, which was also a city of priests. According to Jewish law, the ritual bath must hold about 750 litres of either rain or spring water. It generally consisted of two pools, in one of which the participant had to be immersed, having steps to ascend and descend, and in the other of which called the ''store pool'' the pure water was held. The two pools were connected by a pipe through which the water from both pools could come into contact, thus purifying the water for ritual immersion.

In Jerusalem many ritual baths have been found: about 48 were found in the Temple Mount excavations (Ben Dov 1982: 151-152), and many others were also found in the Upper City (fig. 28) (Avigad 1983: 141-142, figs. 143-149).

The ritual baths of Jericho received their pure water from the aqueducts of the Jericho valley (Netzer 1982a). Some of the Jericho ritual baths were already constructed in the Hasmonean period and were in use during the Herodian period, during which time several new ones were also built. There were many ritual baths in Jericho and their plan was slightly different from those in Jerusalem. The pools and their steps were of different sizes. They were very deep, probably to be able to hold a large amount of water. These baths probably served many of the inhabitants of Jericho, particularly its priestly families (Netzer 1982a: 119).

Several ritual baths were found at Masada having been constructed according to the ritual regulations. Most of them were built and used by the Zealots, the defenders of Masada after the Temple of Jerusalem was destroyed (Yadin 1966: 164-167).

At Qumran several ritual baths were found (see p. 122).

Buildings for Purposes of Culture and Amusement

a) *The Hippodrome at Jericho* (fig. 29) (Netzer 1980b). This building complex unique

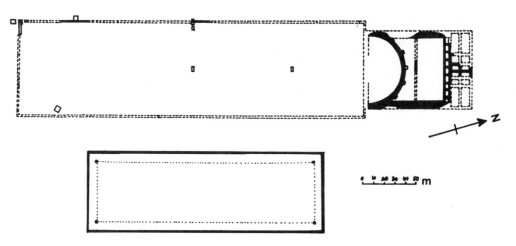

29. Hippodrome at Jericho and Samaria stadium.

in the Graeco-Roman world is a combination of a hippodrome, a course for chariot and horse racing, and a theatre at the rear of which a building is attached. It was uncovered at Tel el-Samarat, 600 m. south of ancient Jericho. The hippodrome course has a rectangular shape and its walls have been excavated, but no remains of the *spina* have been found. The spectators presumably sat in the theatre-like structure at the northern end of the course. This structure has survived nearly intact, but lacks its benches, steps, and passages. It is built on an artificial platform. A large building measuring 70 × 70 m. was found behind the theatre, and is also constructed on a platform. It surrounded a large court.

Netzer (1980b: 105-106) asserts that this hippodrome complex was used for "Olympic" games, which were observed from the theatre-like structure. The building may have served as a royal reception wing, or a gymnasium, or possibly a combination of both.

b) The Hippodrome of Caesarea lies to the east of the harbour (Bull 1982: 32). Its remains include granite *metae*, turning posts for chariot races, and fragments of an obelisk which stood in the centre.

c) The Theatre at Caesarea (Frova *et al.* 1965: 55-244). Built by Herod, the theatre is situated in the southern part of the town. The remains of the theatre indicate that it is a Hellenistic type, particularly in its cavea, seats and its gangway. The orchestra and its floor are decorated with painted plaster in various patterns. The walls are decorated with marble-imitative fresco. The *scenae frons* has a square central exedra flanked by smaller niches, which are all covered with plaster. The pulpitum was also painted. Fragments of stucco which decorated the theatre have also been found.

d) The Stadium of Samaria-Sebaste (Crowfoot *et al.* 1942:41-50, fig. 12-17). This stadium was built probably by Herod. It is 230 m. long and 60 m. wide and is located in the northeastern part of the city. The stadium was surrounded by four porticos with Doric columns and its walls were plastered (fig. 29).

Colonnaded Streets

Colonnaded streets were built by Herod in several towns. Excavations at Samaria have revealed a street of this type containing about 600 columns. The street began at the western gate and continued for some 800 metres. In ʾAntipatris (ʾAphek) an eight-metre wide Cardo runs north-south and has elevated pavements, shops and workshops on either side (Kochavi 1981). In Caesarea the Cardo Maximus which was uncovered in the recent excavations is dated to either the late Roman or Byzantine periods, and probably followed the route of the original Herodian street (Bull 1982: 40).

Aqueducts

a) The Jerusalem aqueducts (fig. 2) (A. Mazar 1975: map on p. 83). Jerusalem in the Second Temple period had a problem of a limited water supply which was solved by the construction of several aqueducts. The sources for the aqueducts lay south of Jerusalem, and were located in three places: Wadi ʿArrub, Biyar and the area of Solomon's Pools. A network of four aqueducts has been found, the oldest part of which is the Lower Aqueduct.

1) The ʿArrub aqueduct runs in a circuitous route from ʿAin Kuweiziba in the south to Solomon's Pools. It consists of a channel partly hewn and partly constructed, partly exposed and partly covered by stone slabs. Solid dams bridge the wadis. This earliest aqueduct was probably constructed in the Second Temple period, possibly by Pontius Pilate, with Temple funds. A second stage was added in the Mameluke period.

2) The Wadi Biyar aqueduct is completely different in construction. It is short and follows a route which is quite straight, mostly through hewn tunnels 3 m. in height. This aqueduct was an exellent hydraulic project.

3) The lower aqueduct is 21 kms. long, and runs from Solomon's Pools to the Temple Mount. It consisted originally of two tunnels (one of which is now blocked). The aqueduct ran to the Temple Mount over Wilson's Arch into a huge cistern system. This aqueduct was possibly built by the Hasmoneans, and was also in use in the Herodian period.

4) The upper aqueduct ran from the uppermost of Solomon's Pools to the Roman Tenth Legion camp in the area of the present-day Citadel. It is either rock-hewn,

or man-made; one section 2.5 m. in length consists of stone pipe segments, some bearing inscriptions of the Tenth Legion commanders.

b) Caesarea. The high-level aqueduct nearly thirteen miles long originated at a spring in the Carmel Mountains. It was partly carried over a series of arches and partly hewn into the rock. The aqueduct actually consists of two adjacent aqueducts, the easternmost probably built by Herod and the western by Hadrian.

A low-level aqueduct following the same route is Byzantine in date (Bull 1982: 29-30).

c) Herodium. An aqueduct was built by Herod to bring water from Urtas for the north wing, the pool complex, the gardens and other structures in Lower Herodium (Netzer 1981a: 53).

d) Samaria. Samaria had three aqueducts: one coming from the southeast, another from the east and a third from the Shechem springs. The third aqueduct is 15 kms. in length and is partly a tunnel and partly a bridge.

CHAPTER TWO

ART

Second Temple period Jewish art is a decorative art characterized by a mixture of native traditions and Hellenistic-Roman features. Hellenistic-Roman culture greatly influenced the upper classes (of all the Near Eastern countries), as is attested to by the predominance of Hellenistic-Roman architecture and by the use of the Greek language and its institutions which affected many aspects of everyday life. Politically the country was first under Hellenistic, and later under Roman, rule. However, resistance to the intrusive culture was strong, because of the force and vitality of the Jewish religion which completely controlled the community's activities. Judaism also conceptually dominated its decorative art so that neither figurative nor symbolic representations were depicted.

The various ornamental devices and the repertoire of motifs used were part of the general stream of Roman art, especially its provincial and eastern tributaries. Decoration in Herodian architecture attests to the influence of Roman art. Hellenistic tradition, moreover, survived into the later Herodian period. A locally developed style is encountered mainly in funerary art, on tomb facades, on ossuaries and on sarcophagi. The style of Jewish art followed the basic Oriental elements: a) The "endless" and "all-over" patterns. b) Symmetrical stylization. c) Deep carving resulting in contrast between parts, intensifying the play of light and shade. d) *Horror vacui*—Ornament filling all available space.

Decoration of buildings, palaces, houses and bath houses of the Second Temple period mainly focussed on the use of wall paintings, stucco-plaster mouldings and ornamental floor pavements. The decorative elements, motifs and designs are characterized by a total lack of animate motifs and symbolic emblems. This stems from the reluctance of all Jews, including the ruling families such as that of Herod and his dynasty, to decorate any building or tomb with religious or iconic symbols. The Biblical prohibition of "no graven image" was carefully kept (Ex. 20:4; Deut. 4:16; 27:15).

A) FLOOR PAVEMENTS

Two types of floor pavements are found in the Second Temple period buildings: 1) mosaic pavements and 2) floors paved in *opus sectile*.

1) Mosaics

Mosaics decorated the floors of Second Temple period buildings, in Herodian palaces as well as in the private homes of the upper class Jerusalemites.

a) Herodian Palaces

Masada—Several mosaic floors were found at Masada. In the northern palace, a simple mosaic of black hexagons covers the upper terrace floor. An identical mosaic is found in the bath house court of the Western Palace (Yadin 1966: 61, 84) which has two other mosaics. In one room a coloured mosaic floor has a geometric border and a central rendition of popular vegetation motifs: pomegranates, vine leaves, grapes, and fig leaves with a frame of stylized olive branches (but see Balty 1981 who call this motif *chainette*: 358, n. 52). The centre is rendered as a circle containing a number of intersecting circles (Pl. 7) (Yadin 1966: 119-127). The second mosaic is located in the bath house corridor and portrays a circle consisting of radial segments within a square. Yadin proposes that the bath house had a mosaic floor which was later replaced by an *opus sectile* pavement (see below).

Herodium—Simple black and white mosaic floors were revealed in the bath house of the palace.

Jericho—A crudely-fashioned and simple mosaic floor with squares and triangles was found in one of the rooms of palace III (Netzer 1974: Pl. I).

Caesarea—A mosaic carpet with a design similar to and probably imitative of *opus sectile* floors such as at Jericho (Levine & Netzer 1978: fig. on p. 74) was found here.

Cypros—A simple geometric mosaic floor was found in the bath house (Netzer 1975b: Pl. A) (fig. I.27).

Alexandrium (Sartaba)—A crudely made and simple mosaic paved the centre of the peristyle hall (Tsafrir & Magen 1984: 31).

Machaerus—The tepidarium had a mosaic floor (Corbo 1979: Pl. 44b.).

b) Private Houses (in the Upper City of Jerusalem)
(Avigad 1983: 144-146, figs. 150-151, 160-165)

Ten ornamented and plain mosaic pavements, several of which paved bath rooms, were found in these houses (Pl. 6). The central motif of these floors is usually a six-petalled rosette(Pl. 6b), but in one case it is a three-petalled rosette (Avigad 1983: figs. 162, 163). One bath complex has a mosaic with a wave border motif enclosing a circle with a multicoloured and multipetalled rosette. In the corners were palmettes and a spindle bottle (Pl. 6c)(Avigad 1983: fig. 161). Only three mosaic floors have survived in living rooms: one has a rosette within a square frame. The corners bear a geometric pattern similar to the "gamma" motif (Avigad 1983: 146, fig. 164). Another mosaic floor which has partly survived bears a central carpet of intertwined meanders framed by wave, guilloche and "crow-step" patterns (Pl. 6a)(Avigad 1983: 144, fig. 165).

2) Floors in Opus Sectile (coloured stone tiles)

Jericho—The triclinium reception hall (B70) has a floor in *opus sectile* with designs of octagons and squares in the central carpet, surrounded by simple designs (fig. 1). A mosaic may have filled the space of the destroyed centre.

Masada—The bath house was paved with an *opus sectile* floor. It probably replaced an earlier mosaic floor (Yadin 1966: 81).

Cypros—Fragments of an *opus sectile* floor were found in the bath house caldarium (Netzer 1975b: 57-58) (fig. I.27).

Jerusalem—A floor with traces of *opus sectile* tiles was found in a room of one of the Upper City houses. It depicts a design of interlocking circles made of black squares and red triangles (fig. 2).

Usually, all that remains of these floors consists of a few tiles found in the debris of the structures. The pavements which were made by this technique have usually disappeared. Only the bedding survived, and it is this bedding which contains the impression of the tiles which formed the design, the patterns of which may be reconstructed from the surviving impressions.

B) Wall Paintings

Many of the palaces, mansions and houses were adorned with coloured wall paintings. A wall painting has also been found in a monumental tomb in Jericho. Most wall paintings are made by the fresco technique: the wall is covered with wet lime plaster consisting of a coating of sand and slaked lime. The painting is executed with colours onto the wet plaster. In this way the painting is absorbed into and dries with the plaster and can neither be rubbed nor peeled off; because of this method wall paintings have survived in good condition through the ages. Another technique used in wall painting is secco, where paint is applied to dry plaster. However, in this case the paint tends to peel off. Most of the wall paintings which have survived were made by the fresco technique.

Masada—Painted walls are found in the Northern Palace. The wall painting of the lower terrace has a marbled pattern (fig. 3) (Yadin 1966: 44-49). Fragments of a frescoed wall were found in the debris of the upper terrace (Yadin 1966: 69). In the bath house, frescoes covered the tepidarium and the apodyterium, and fragments

2. Opus Sectile Pattern in a Jerusalem House.

1. Opus Sectile Floor Patterns from Jericho. Winter
Palace III.

of ceiling fresco were found as well (Yadin 1966: 79-80). Other palaces also had wall
paintings of framed panels (Yadin 1966: 136-137).

Herodium—Frescoed walls decorated the bath house and other rooms of the palace-
fortress (Corbo 1963: 241-247, 260-262, figs. 9, 10, 12, 18, 20). These
multicoloured frescoes depict framed marbled patterns.

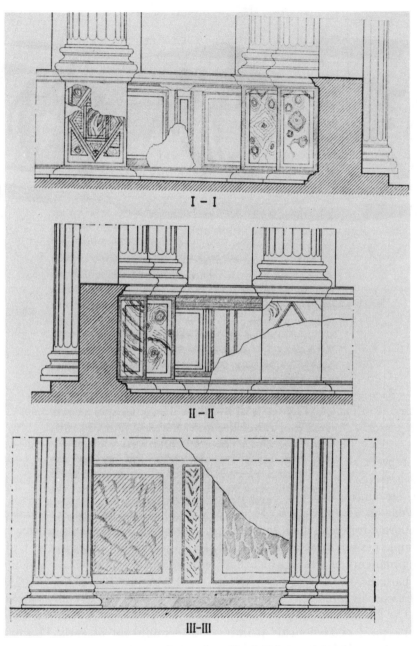

I – I

II – II

III-III

3. Marble-imitative Fresco from North Palace at Masada.

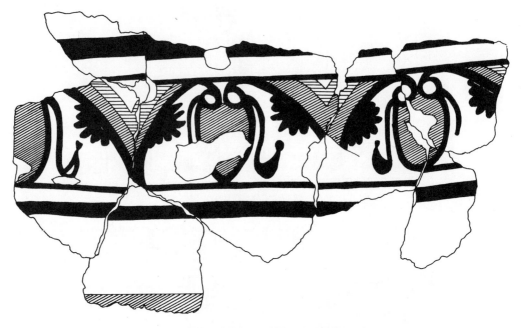

4. Painted Frieze of Floral Motifs.

Jericho—Fragments of coloured imitation-marble patterned fresco were found in the Hasmonean palace. The walls of the third Herodian palace were covered with marbled patterns and various other designs (Netzer 1975a: Pl. 8b).

Cypros—The bath house walls were covered with frescoes in red and yellow. Fresco fragments were also found in a hall (Netzer 1975b: 58, Pl. B).

Alexandrium (Sartaba)—Fresco fragments were found in the debris of the fortress' peristyle structure (Tsafrir & Magen 1984: 30).

Jerusalem—a) The so called ''House of Caiaphas'' on Mount Zion was adorned with elaborate frescoes which include bird portrayals, a unique appearance in Second Temple period art (Broshi 1975: Pl. III). b) Several houses in the Upper City contain fragments of fresco which had once adorned walls. Many had imitation-marble patterns.

The frescoes in Jerusalem include designs of plants (fig. 4) as well as architectural motifs. The garlands, pomegranates, apples and leaves depicted show a high artistic standard typical of Hellenistic painting and reminiscent of early Pompeian wall paintings (Avigad 1983: 149-150, figs. 103-106; 168-174).

Caesarea—In the theatre, the orchestra walls were decorated with fresco of imitation marble patterning.

Jericho, Goliath Family Tomb—Jewish tombs do not usually have wall paintings. However, a unique wall painting decorated the monumental Goliath tomb in Jericho (Hachlili 1985). Depicted on three walls of the upper room of the tomb (figs. IV, 20, 21), the main theme consists of vine branches with leaves and grapes. Birds are rendered perched between the branches. Other motifs appearing in the wall paintings are a wreath and ashlar stones which are depicted on the wall opposite the entrance (fig. IV, 21).

C) Stucco

Stucco mouldings were found in many of the Herodian palaces and buildings. The original styles and the standard of execution point to local workmanship even though generally the ornamentation followed the Roman examples. Stucco usually decorated ceilings and upper parts of walls, as well as covering columns made of local stone in order to make them appear fluted.

Masada—Stucco fragments were found on the lower terrace of the Northern Palace. Bases and column drums covered with stucco imitative of fluting characterizes this terrace (Avi-Yonah *et al.* 1957: Pls. 10:1,3; 12:2; 14:1,2).

Herodium—Stucco with various profiles such as egg-and-dart decoration and tongue mouldings were uncovered at Herodium (Netzer 1981a: 73-74, figs. 101-103).

Jericho—Stucco moulded panels decorating walls which were sometimes also painted were found in the palace at Jericho (Kelso & Barᶜamki 1955: Pls. 19, 20a).

Cypros—Fragments of moulded stucco were found in the palace (Netzer 1975b: 59, 60).

Machaerus—Fragments of stucco were found in the bath house (Corbo 1979: Pl. 48).

In other Herodian palaces stucco fragments were also uncovered: at the Ḥilkiya palace (Damati 1982: 120) and at Alexandrium (Tsafrir & Magen 1984: 30).

Jerusalem—The Mansion in the Upper City had a large reception hall which was ornamented with white stucco imitating ashlar stones. Moulded plaster fragments which probably had fallen from the ceiling were found in the debris of the hall, and many of them bear the egg-and-dart motif (Avigad 1983: 99-103, figs. 87-91). Avigad (1983: 102) maintains that the method of imitating ashlar stones by modelling them in plaster is not derived from any local Jerusalem style, but is rather an earlier stylistic tradition which had survived in the East longer than it did in its original Hellenistic context.

D) STONE CARVING

A new type of ornament, indigenous to Jewish art, appears at this time and is produced by a special technique of stone carving (*Kerbschnitt*). This new technique using compass, ruler and chisel, results in deep carvings and in a variety of characteristic designs such as rosettes, and is found in architectural decoration and on stone objects.

Decorative stonework features in architecture of buildings and tombs. It is characteristic of funerary art: tomb facades were decoratively carved and stone sarcophagi and ossuaries, in particular, exhibit a vast ensemble of local decorative stonework.

Architectural Ornamentation

Fragments of capitals, lintels, friezes and other architectural members were found along the west and south Temple retaining walls in Jerusalem. They probably came from the pilasters of the upper courses of the walls and from the Royal Stoa (Mazar 1975a: 25). Identical Corinthian capitals were found in the north palace at Masada (Yadin 1966: 70-71) and in Cypros (Netzer 1975b: Pl. B). Both are carved out of local stone and painted in gold which has survived only in traces. Parts of stone columns, capitals and bases were found in the Temple Mount (fig. 5) and Upper City excavations: a Corinthian capital made of hard local stone bears lily scrolls, the stonemason's own addition, on one side (Avigad 1983: 150-165, figs. 157, 200); a huge base and a finely-executed Ionic capital from monumental columns (fig. 6) were uncovered, indicating the existence in Jerusalem of monumental architecture and craftsmanship of a high standard. The entrances of the Ḥulda Gates of the Temple Mount were built of stone domes more than five metres in diameter and carved with geometric and floral motifs (fig. 7 and Pl. 9) surmounted on columns and with walls built of ashlar stones.

Stone Objects

Tables

Several stone tables were found during the excavations in the Jewish Quarter in Jerusalem (Avigad 1983: 167-174). Fragments of tables have also been discovered in other excavations. Finds may be divided into two types:

1) A table with a rectangular top and a single, central leg which is carved in the form of a column. The edges of the table top are generally decorated with a carved design (fig. 8) (Avigad 1983: figs. 185-186) having either floral or geometric motifs (see

5. Capital from Temple Mount Excavations.

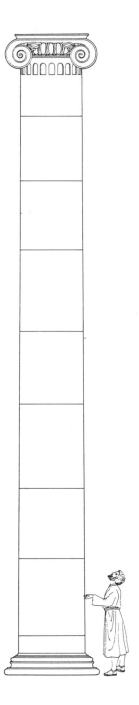

6. Ionic Capital from Upper City Excavations .

7a. Decorated Stone Dome of the Huldah Gates.

7b. Decorated Stone Dome of the Huldah Gates.

7c. Decorated Stone Dome of the Huldah Gates.

8. Stone Table Top.

9. Stone Table Tops.

pp. 79-80). One edge is usually plain, suggesting that the table was meant to stand against the wall. One ornamented table top edge itself portrays such a table with vessels standing on it and with several large jars supported by the table leg (fig. 9) (Rahmani 1974; Avigad 1983:figs. 194-195).

2) A round table which is smaller and lower than table type 1; and which stood on three legs probably ending in animal feet (Avigad 1983: figs. 188-192). Hellenistic and Roman paintings which depict such tables prove that the rectangular table type was used to hold drinking vessels and that the round type was used for meals (Avigad 1983: 191-192).

Vessels

Most of the stone vessels are made of soft limestone and have a distinctive form which is either 1) carved by hand, or 2) made on a lathe. Hand carved stone vessels such as cups with handles, square bowls and vessels with multiple compartments were found in Jerusalem and at other sites. They are considered to be "measuring cups" for dry and liquid measures (Avigad 1983: 174-183, figs. 197, 198, 207-209; Ben Dov 1982: 158-160).

The phenomenon of this particular craft of stonework being so highly cultivated can be explained by the Jewish law that stone vessels do not become contaminated by contact with uncleanliness (*Mishnah Kelim* 10:1; *Parah* 3,2). Because of this law stone vessels were very popular containers (Avigad 1983:183).

D) Stonemasons

Stone carving became, particularly in Jerusalem, a highly skilled craft, as is evidenced by the elaborately decorated examples of funerary art which remain: tomb facades, sarcophagi and ossuaries are carved and incised in an instantly recognizable style which developed from local artistic traditions. Stone vessel carving was also highly developed. Recently quarries have been found in the Jerusalem area which were probably the workshops of the stone craftsmen.

Rahmani (1982: 112) proposes that there were two types of local stone artisans: stonemasons who executed tomb facades, sarcophagi and ossuaries; and stone carvers who prepared stone vessels from the local limestone.

The existence of Jewish stonemasons is indicated by the appearance of stonemasons' marks and Hebrew letters on column drums. At Masada each column is composed of several drums: in order that they would be correctly fitted together, each column was assigned a letter, and each drum a number. Stone cutters' marks with Hebrew letters (Yadin 1965: Pl. 21:A; 1966: 68-69) were found on a number of column drums. The many drums which had to be amalgamated into columns necessitated the use of Palaeo-Hebrew script, Latin letters as well as geometric signs in order to provide enough differing combinations. The use of Hebrew letters at Masada shows that the stonemasons were Jewish. A similar system of marking must have been used in the Ḥilkiya Palace where one such cutter's mark was found (Damati 1982: 120).

Further evidence for the existence of Jewish stonemasons and artists may be gathered from the choice of designs found on ossuaries, artefacts and monuments. The standard ossuary design consisting of a decorated frame enclosing a tripartite design of symmetrically carved rosettes sometimes flanking a central motif, continues into Late Antiquity in Jewish synagogal art, where tripartite designs are popular (p. 359). This continuity of design suggests that the original conception was also associated with Jewish artistic notions. Furthermore, the cluster of grapes consisting of a central bunch flanked by two smaller ones (fig.IV, 8) which Avi-Yonah (1981: 70) maintains is a preferred type in Jewish art, as depicted on monuments such as the Tomb of the Kings and the Grape Tomb (figs. IV, 8,9), follows an Oriental model.

E) Motifs

The repertoire of Second Temple period Jewish art consists of ornamental motifs which can be divided into the following types:
1) Plant—floral and vegetation motifs and patterns.
2) Geometric patterns.
3) Architectural motifs.
4) Varia.
5) Faunal motifs: birds and fish.
6) Temple vessels: Menorah and Table.
7) Motifs on Jewish coins.

1) *Plant motifs* (Avi-Yonah 1981a: 66 ff.) were part of ornamental art and were common designs in ancient art. They were used in architectural ornamentation, and as funerary ornament. Floral and vegetation motifs were considered suitable for aniconic expression, for repetitive patterns and for filling spaces. Plant motifs were either adopted from earlier Oriental designs or were imitations of local flora. Their form and composition are sometimes stylized into abstract or geometric patterns.

Floral motifs include the palmette and the lotus. Palmettes are found on a Jerusalem house mosaic (Pl. 6b) and on a glass pitcher (Avigad 1983: figs. 95, 96, 161) whereas the lotus appears on a Jerusalem house fresco (Avigad 1983: fig. 173).

Leaves are present on a fresco and on a stone table from Jerusalem (figs. 4, 8) (Avigad 1983: 106, 185).Floral motifs such as acanthus leaves, lilies, flowers, branches, wreaths and garlands are found in funerary art: on Jerusalem tomb facades (figs. IV. 8-10; Tomb of the Kings, the Frieze Tomb and the Cave of Jehoshaphat), on ossuaries (Rahmani 1982: 115; Figuras 1983: 45-53) and on sarcophagi (fig. IV.18).

Vegetation motifs include pomegranates, olive leaves, vine branches and leaves and grapes. Pomegranates appear in the frescoes and mosaics of the Jerusalem Upper City houses (Avigad 1983: figs. 108, 166) and in the mosaic of the western palace at Masada (Yadin 1966: 124-125). Olive leaves decorate a stone table (fig. 8) and pottery bowls from Jerusalem (Avigad 1983: figs. 94; 115) and Herodium (Netzer 1981a: Pl. 7). Vine branches, leaves and grapes are popular motifs which decorate several architectural fragments from Jerusalem (Avigad 1983: 184). This motif is even more popular in funerary art and appears in the wall painting in the Goliath family tomb in Jericho (fig. IV.21) (Hachlili 1985), on tomb facades in Jerusalem, on the Tomb of the Grapes (fig. IV.9), on the Nazirite sarcophagus (Pl. 8) and some ossuaries (Pl. 18).

The palm or date tree with stylized leaves occurs on a Masada fresco (Yadin 1966: 47) and also decorates ossuaries (Rahmani 1982: 115; Figueras 1983: 42-43).

Only one record of the appearance of an apple motif has been recorded, on a fresco fragment from a Jerusalem house (Avigad 1983: fig. 167).

2) *Geometric patterns*. The rosette is the most prominent motif in Jewish art and could be said to exemplify it (Avi-Yonah 1981a: 97-111). Executed with the aid of a compass, the rosette developed from a traditional geometric motif. It occurs in almost all aspects of Jewish art, such as in architectural decoration, on stone tables (fig. 8) and a sundial from Jerusalem (Avigad 1983: figs. 116, 185), and in mosaics from Jerusalem and Masada (Pls. 6, 7). In funerary art the rosette fills the spaces in Doric friezes on tomb facades such as the Frieze Tomb (fig. IV.7) and also appears on sarcophagi (fig. IV, 18). It is also the motif which most frequently occurs on ossuaries (Rahmani 1982: 114; Figueras 1983: 36-41) (figs. IV.15-17). Other geometric motifs include meanders, waves, guilloches, lozenges and hexagons. They are depicted in mosaics as borders or in the centre of the pavement design, as at Masada (Pl.7) or in the Upper City of Jerusalem (Pl. 6) (Avigad 1983: figs. 108, 161, 165). These motifs also occur in fresco and stucco (Avigad 1983: figs. 90, 91, 174; Mazar 1975a: 28-29; Ben-Dov 1982: 138). A capital from the synagogue of Gamla is ornamented with a meander design (Maoz 1981a: 36).

Geometric patterns also appear in funerary art, and usually consist of circles and intersecting lines. On ossuaries the zigzag motif frequently appears as a frame (figs.15-17).

3) Architectural patterns are found rendered in fresco and stucco, as well as decorating funerary art. A frequent design shown is the "ashlar stone" pattern. A mansion in the Upper City of Jerusalem has a large reception hall covered in white stucco which imitates ashlar stones (Avigad 1983: 99-102, figs. 87, 88, 90, 101). This technique is common in Hellenistic cities and is also seen later at Pompeii (until the first century BCE). The same motif is depicted in funerary art in the wall painting of the Goliath family tomb at Jericho (figs. IV.20, 21) (Hachlili 1985: 124), and on ossuaries (Rahmani 1982: 114).

Architectural decorative patterns such as walls covered by imitation marble are found in fresco in the Herodian palaces of Masada (Yadin 1966: 46) and in the Jerusalem houses (Avigad 1983: 168-171), which also exhibit friezes of dentils (Avigad 1983: figs. 172, 173). Ossuaries are decorated with metope patterns (Rahmani 1982: 114). In several instances the motif of a *nefesh*, a tomb monument, is rendered on ossuaries and wall decoration (fig. IV.22; Pl. 17a) (Rahmani 1968; Hachlili 1981).

4) Varia. Other motifs are found in the art of the Second Temple period. The cornucopia and pomegranate are common motifs on Herodian coins (Meshorer 1982, II: 27-28), and appear also on a stone table top from Jerusalem (Avigad 1983: fig. 186). The amphora is depicted on ossuaries (Rahmani 1982: 116; Figueras 1983: 73-74). A rare depiction of a spindle bottle is portrayed in the corner of a mosaic pavement in Jerusalem (Pl. 6c)(Avigad 1983: 144, fig. 161).

5) Faunal Motifs rarely occur in the Second Temple period. Birds are rare (Hachlili 1983: 87, fig. 12); in Jerusalem they appear on a palace fresco (Broshi 1975: Pl. III) and incised on the handle of a stone vessel (Ben Dov 1982: 160). In the Jericho Goliath family tomb wall painting several birds appear among the vine branches (fig. IV.21). An eagle is depicted on one Herodian coin type, and is probably associated with the golden eagle Herod had installed over the Temple gate (Meshorer 1982, II: 129). A stucco fragment with an outstanding motif consisting of animals was found in a private building alongside the Temple Mount (Ben Dov 1982: 151). One depiction of a fish appears on a stone table top in Jerusalem (fig. 8) (Avigad 1983: fig. 185:4).

6) Temple Vessels. The most significant designs appearing in this period are the Temple Menorah and Table which were the most important Temple vessels. They appear, for example, on the Arch of Titus in Rome (Pl. 53) and a graffito of the menorah and table is incised on a plaster fragment from Jerusalem (fig. IX.1) (Avigad 1983: 147-149; see also pp. 237-238). Incised menoroth are rendered on a sundial in Jerusalem (fig. IX.2a). Examples of the menorah manifested in funerary art include the graffiti on the wall of the corridor of Jason's tomb (fig. IX.2b) and two incised menoroth on ossuaries (Rahmani 1980: 114-115). This depiction of Temple vessels on the Arch of Titus was meant to reflect Roman victory over Judea, whereas the other incised depictions of the menorah represented spontaneous attempts by people who probably had seen the Temple Menorah and wished to draw it from memory (see also pp. 237-239).

7) Motifs on Jewish Coins. Emblems depicted on coins are carefully chosen and show designs which are meant to express immediate needs and can serve as a short term symbol. Both kings Antigonus and Herod wished to obtain the maximum propaganda effect by their selection of specific emblems for their coinage. Mattathias Antigonus (40-37 BCE), the last Jewish Hasmonean king, minted his coins during a difficult time when, although supported by a people loyal to his Hasmonean heritage, he was being usurped by Herod Antigonus' coins depict the Temple vessels, the Menorah and the Table (Pl. 59a, b) (Meshorer 1982, II: 87-97); in this way he hoped to enhance and establish his status as Jewish king and high priest. Simultaneously with his rule, Herod, who came from a non-Jewish Edomite family, was appointed king of Judea by Rome. In order to substantiate his right to reign he issued coins. Meshorer (1982, II: 18-30) maintains that these consisted of two groups: one group of coins was struck in Samaria in 40-37 BCE, and the other was of undated coins struck in Jerusalem in 37-4 BCE. The coins of the first group were minted to rival those of Antigonus, and deliberately depicted designs imitative of the Roman Republican coins of 44-40 BCE. In this way Herod hoped to prove that his kingship, contrary to that of Antigonus, was legitimate and had Roman support. The second group of coins, struck in Jerusalem after Herod had become the sole king, depicts designs relating to the Jewish Temple and Jewish art. Meshorer further states that all the Herodian kings (Herod, Agrippa I and Agrippa II), who were appointed and backed by Rome, used designs on their coins which imitated Roman issues, although the emblems did not necessarily convey the same connotations.

Motifs depicted on the coins of the Jewish War (66-70 CE), and later on those of the Bar Kokhba War (132-135 CE), are of religious and national significance, and include the chalice and the bundle with the four species of the Feast of Tabernacles (Meshorer 1982, II: 106-122).

Thus, motifs on coins were significant emblems which were used for their national, political or religious meanings.

Motifs in Jewish art derived from traditional elements in local, native art, although they were occasionally taken from Hellenistic-Roman art and from that of neighbouring cultures. A further source of inspiration was the natural environment from where floral and faunal subjects were borrowed and adapted. Ossuaries were decorated with motifs derived from Jerusalem tombs, thus reflecting a funerary context (Rahmani 1982: 112, 115-117; cf. Figueras 1983: 83-110).

What is most conspicuously lacking in the Second Temple period ensemble of motifs is any figurative representation or any motif indicating symbolic significance. It is only later, in the third century, that motifs acquire a symbolic status (for example the menorah, see p. 236ff.). Consequently it can be stated that the Jews of the Second Temple period honoured the Biblical injunctions by refraining from representations of humans and animals in their art. However, whereas official and public art was strictly aniconic, private dwellings did sometimes use ornamentation which portrayed figurative motifs, usually birds.

In conclusion it can be seen that a Jewish art developed in the Second Temple period which exhibits several characteristic features:

1) Stonework, carving and use of relief characterize Jewish Second Temple period art and continue later in Jewish synagogal art. Stonework was one of the most prevalent crafts of Jewish art which flourished in Herodian times. It utilized the locally available stone, and created a new type of ornament. The designs were sketched in by compass and ruler and carved out by chisel in a deeply incised and stylized manner. Stonework features in the architecture of buildings and tombs and in funerary art. Stone craft is also used for objects of daily life, such as ornamented stone tables and domestic vessels.

2) The repertoire of ornamental aniconic motifs reflects a rigid choice of floral, geometric and architectural patterns, some of which were adopted from Hellenistic art.

3) Jewish art style displays many Oriental elements.

These elements characterize all Jewish art, including the simple local art encountered mainly in funerary art, as well as that seen in the palaces and tombs. Differences lie usually in the quality of execution and in the attention paid to decorative detail.

Thus evolved a local Jewish art, strictly aniconic, using neither figures nor symbols. In their struggle against paganism and idolatry the Jews refrained from using animate motifs and representational art. Only with the decline of paganism during the third century did the attitude of Jewish art change, resulting in the use of figurative motifs.

CHAPTER THREE

SECOND TEMPLE PERIOD SYNAGOGUES

Several public structures of the Second Temple period which have been discovered in the last decades are considered to be synagogues: at Masada (Pl. 10a)(Yadin 1965, 1981), Herodium (Pl. 10b) (Foerster 1981), Gamla (Pl. 11)(Gutman 1981; Maoz 1981a) and Migdal (Corbo 1976) (fig. 1; Table 1; Pls. 10-11), and another synagogue, now lost, reported at Chorazin. The rarity of discovery of synagogues of this period is due to several reasons (Maoz 1981: 35): later structures may have either covered or destroyed them; and a lack of distinguishing architectural features, and the lack of symbols, creates difficulties in classification. Nevertheless, the excavated structures are assumed by scholars to be synagogues because of the circumstantial evidence of similarity to each other in architectural plan, and therefore, in function, even though no actual proof has been uncovered. These common architectural features inlcude (fig. 1, Tab.1): a) All structures built as oblong halls. b) Hall divided by rows of columns into a central nave and surrounding aisles. c) Stepped benches erected along all four walls of the hall facing the centre.

The structures also share a similar date for their construction in the first century CE (although Gamla may have been erected already by the end of the first century BCE). Only the structure at Gamla was adorned with architectural ornamentation, such as that found on lintels and capitals. The buildings were probably single storeyed. The Gamla synagogue was an independent, intentionally designed assembly structure, whereas the Masada and Herodium structures having originally been triclinia were converted into synagogues, which then served as reception and ceremonial halls. This change was carried out by altering the arrangement of the columnation (that is, by reusing the columns in different places), and by adding the stepped benches along the walls. The synagogue halls of Masada and Herodium also included additional, small rooms which probably served as repositories (*genizah*) and adjacent ritual baths (*miqveh*). The Masada and Herodium structures have similar dimensions (12 × 15 m. and 10.5 × 15 m. respectively). Gamla is larger (19.60 × 15.10 m.) (see table 1).

A small building was uncovered in Migdal (fig. 1d), situated on the western shore of the Kinnereth (Sea of Galilee), and is dated to the first century. In the First Jewish War against the Romans, Migdal became a Zealot stronghold and the synagogue

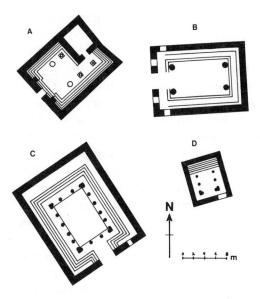

1. Second Temple Period Synagogues: a)
Masada; b) Herodium; c) Gamla; d) Migdal
building (Synagogue?).

Table 1: Second Temple Synagogues

Synagogue	Date in centuries CE unless stated	Measurement W. L.	Entrance Orientation	Columns 2 Rows	4 Rows	Cor- ner	Benches	Floor Plaster	Stone
Masada	1st	12.0 × 15.0	East	+			+	+	
Herodium	1st.	10.5 × 15.0	East	+			+	+	
Gamla	1st BCE-1CE	15.1 × 19.6	S W		+	+	+	+	+
Capernaum	1st	18.5 × 24.2	East	+			+		basalt
Migdal	1st	7.0 × 8.0	N W (?)			+	+		

was destroyed by the Romans in 70 CE (Corbo 1976), becoming a water installation. The Migdal small synagogue was 8.16 × 7.25 m. and contained five rows of
benches along its northern wall and three rows of columns, the southern ones of
which were corner columns. Netzer (1980a: note 13, p. 116) and Maoz (1981a: 39)
assert that the small structure at Migdal is a nympheum.

A synagogue belonging to this period has been uncovered recently at Capernaum,
under the later synagogue, and is possibly the only one of these early synagogues

found buried under a later synagogue. Renewed excavations during the last few years date this early synagogue to the first century (Corbo 1982; also Strange and Shanks 1983). This evidence consists of several basalt walls and a basalt cobbled pavement abutting them. The walls run under the south wall and east and west stylobates of the prayer hall of the later synagogue (II), and were later reused as foundations for the limestone walls of this later building (II)(Corbo 1982:Photos 1,2,5,8,10). Benches are assumed to have lined the aisles, but no entrance has been discovered. The plan of the earlier building appears to conform to the plan of the later prayer hall. The dating of the early synagogue to the first century is based on pottery which was found under and in the basalt cobbled pavement. Thus, the excavations prove that the synagogue of the fourth-fifth centuries at Capernaum was erected above an earlier first century basalt synagogue, which is somewhat similar in plan both to the later Capernaum synagogue and to the other Second Temple period synagogues.

These structures were erected according to an architectural conception which saw the hall as serving as a place of assembly for a congregation which would gather to worship. Such a structure might have had a focal point in the centre of the hall (as suggested by Maoz 1981a: 38-41; Huttenmeister 1982:3).

The Origin of the Architectural Plan

Scholars propose several sources for the origin of this type of synagogue: Avigad (1967: 96-97) suggests that the Hellenistic basilica was the source of inspiration, mainly because of the similar style of columnation of the hall. Foerster (1981: 28-29) compares the synagogue structure to assembly halls, *pronaoi* of the eastern pagan temples, as at Dura (already rejected by Maoz 1981a: 40-41 and Chiat 1981: 50-52). Yadin (1965: 78-79), followed by Maoz (1981a: 41) proposes that the Masada synagogue plan is derived from those of secular Hellenistic halls (the ecclesiaterion, the bouleuterion, and the telesterion).

Yet it seems entirely unnecessary to seek so far afield for the sources of the architectural inspiration. By placing these structures within their historical as well as their actual context it becomes obvious that they were the result of local improvisation. Built at a time of war not conducive to architectural innovation, the structures were built by modification of previously existing buildings; changes made were only those essential to serve their new function. By the reuse at Masada and the supplement at Herodium of columns, and by the addition of benches around the walls, the prior Herodian triclinium was thus altered into an assembly hall required by the new congregation (the Zealots). At Gamla an assembly hall was also created with the addition of benches. Its plan probably followed the triclinium plan common in the Herodian palaces of Jericho and elsewhere.

Maoz (1981a: 40) is correct in his emphasis on the benches as being the most important element of these synagogue structures (also Chiat 1981: 51-52), as they must have been specifically added for the congregants to sit upon during their assembly and worship. This arrangement of benches lining all the walls is the most distinctive feature of the Second Temple period synagogues; it also continues into the later synagogues, where the benches, however, occupy less space. By contrast the focal point in the later synagogues becomes the Torah shrine which is constructed on the Jerusalem-oriented wall (see p. 166f.).

Are These Structures Synagogues?

Synagogues in the Second Temple period are known mainly from literary sources (Safrai 1976: 909-910). Rabbinical literature mentions synagogues in Jerusalem: *B. Ketubot* 105a and *J. Megilla* III, 1, 73d assert that Titus and Vespasian destroyed either 394 or 480 synagogues in Jerusalem and a Jerusalem synagogue is recorded in *T. Sukka* 4, 5. Synagogues in other places are mentioned by Josephus at Tiberias (*Life* 277), Dor (*Ant.* XIX, 300) and Caesarea (*War* II, 285-290). A Capernaum synagogue is recorded in the New Testament (Mark 1:21; Luke 7:1). However, despite the literary sources, very little actual proof has been uncovered until now. One Greek inscription from a synagogue found in Jerusalem and dated to the first century (*ASR* 1981: fig. on p. 11) mentions a synagogue "built for the purpose of reciting the Law and studying the commandments." Yadin (1981: 21) bases his contention that the Masada structure is a synagogue upon finding there a type of *genizah* with scrolls and an ostracon with the inscription "priestly tithe" (cf. Netzer 1981c: 51).

Upon the evidence of the structures themselves, it should be noted that they differ from later synagogues in plan, function and decoration. First, from the architectural point of view no new conceptions in construction have been discerned (also Chiat 1981: 54-56), but the impression is rather one of local extemporization. Second, these structures only existed for a short time in the first century CE, and were never built again, except at Capernaum. Only in the case of the first century building under a later synagogue at Capernaum can one assume that it is a synagogue, due to its location. Third, these assembly halls lack the most important feature of the later synagogue: the Torah shrine. Finally, during the first century the Temple in Jerusalem was still the centre for worship and ritual for the entire Jewish community in Judea and the Diaspora where they could participate in the ceremonies, in the teaching of the Law conducted in the Temple courtyards, and could settle administrative questions in the Temple courts. These local centres of worship probably existed as community assembly halls, where service would be conducted probably only on Sabbaths and feast days (see Chap. VII, pp. 138-139).

The assembly structures of the Zealots at the fortresses of Masada, Herodium and Gamla probably served as local assembly halls during the years of the revolt against Rome, a time during which it was extremely difficult for their congregations to travel to Jerusalem in order to participate in Temple worship. At the same time as these structures were serving as small community centres, worship presumably was also being conducted in them, although no convincing proof of this supposition has been found. With the destruction of the Temple, local structures began to flourish which, of necessity having to replace the national centre, the Temple in Jerusalem, became sites of local worship and community centres. In these halls reading of the Torah was emphasized, and thus the distinctive feature of the later synagogues, the Torah shrine, emerges.

CHAPTER FOUR

FUNERARY CUSTOMS AND ART

A) Burial Customs of the Second Temple Period

Two cemeteries of the Second Temple period in Jerusalem (Avigad 1950-51; Rahmani 1981; Kloner 1980) and Jericho (Hachlili 1980a; Hachlili & Killebrew 1981, 1983a) constitute our data for funerary customs and art. They were located outside the town limits, in accordance with Jewish law (*M. Baba Bathra* 2, 9). The Jerusalem cemetery consisted of tombs surrounding the walls of the city, in three major areas of concentration to the north, south and east (Kloner 1980a: 259-268) and the Jericho cemetery was located outside the town, on the hills flanking the Jordan Valley (Pl. 12).

The Jerusalem necropolis developed as the result of tombs being randomly scattered wherever the rock was soft and could be easily hewn. Roads and paths led to the tombs, and plants and trees landscaped the surroundings. Families purchased burial plots presumably according to their means. Several of the loculi tombs have richly ornamented facades and a group of monumental rock-hewn tombs, the Kidron Valley tombs, probably belonging to prominent Jerusalem families, have a memorial or *nefesh* in the shape of a pyramid or tholus standing above the ground. In spite of the lavish ornamentation, burial was probably similar to that of the simpler, undecorated loculi tombs. Apart from two tombs where sarcophagi were discovered, all were found in a disturbed, robbed state. Several crowded burial quarters exist in the present-day areas of Mount Scopus, Dominus Flevit and French Hill (Kloner 1980a: 268).

A large necropolis at Jericho with approximately fifty tombs, containing either primary burials in wooden coffins or secondary collected bone burials in ossuaries, was excavated, and approximately 75 robbed tombs were surveyed (Hachlili 1979a; 1980).

The tombs found in these two cemeteries may be divided into two types: the first consists of rock-hewn loculi tombs and the second type is a monumental tomb which is rock-hewn and has a memorial or *nefesh* standing next to or above it. Two basic tomb plans exist; one is called the loculi type (*kokhim*) and the other is the arcosolia type. Some tombs are equipped solely with a burial room. Both types of plans are found in the Jerusalem necropolis, but the Jericho cemetery consists of loculi tombs

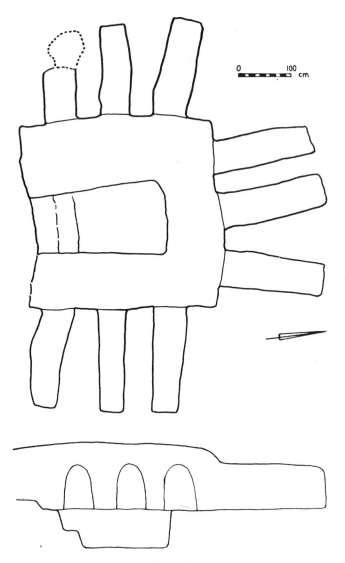

1a. Loculi Tomb Plan.

only which are hewn into the hillsides (Pl. 12), serving as family tombs but with provision for separate burial of each individual.

The form of the loculi tomb (fig. 1) consists of a square burial chamber, often with a pit dug into its floor to enable a man to stand upright. The edge of the pit forms

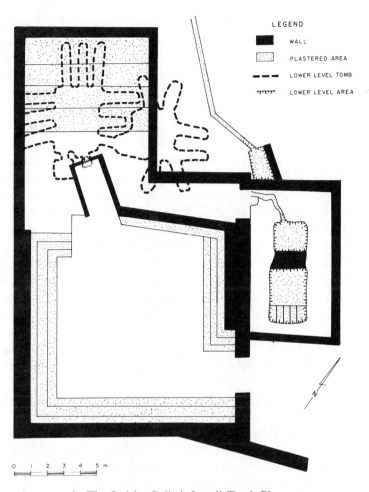

LEGEND

�--	WALL
░░	PLASTERED AREA
- - -	LOWER LEVEL TOMB
┬┬┬	LOWER LEVEL AREA

0 1 2 3 4 5 m

1b. The Jericho Goliath Loculi Tomb Plan.

three or four benches, on each side of the tomb. From one to three arched loculi 1 m. high and 2 m. long (*kokhim*) are hewn into three walls, the entrance wall excepted. The entrance to the tomb is square; in Jerusalem it sometimes has a forecourt and a moulded facade (Avigad 1950-1951: 98, fig. 3) or an ornamental facade (see pp. 104-106). It is closed either by a rectangular blocking stone, sometimes in the shape of a large "stopper," or by mudbricks and small stones. Occasionally, single-loculus tombs were constructed.

The evidence from Jericho proves conclusively that loculi tombs were first designed and used for primary, that is, permanent, burial in coffins. This is indicated by the length of the *kokh* (ca. 2 m.), which is the length of a coffin. The same tomb plan continued to be used in the case of ossuary burials (also Kloner 1980a: 218-228). In previous research scholars have claimed that the *kokh* was "intimately" connected with secondary burial (Meyers 1971: 64-69; Avigad 1976: 259). If this was the case and the loculi tomb had been designed for 70 cm.-long ossuaries there would have been no need to dig a 2 m.-long *kokh*.

Few tombs have a courtyard such as that of the monumental tomb at Jericho (Fig. 1b)(Hachlili 1979; Hachlili and Killebrew 1983a: 112-113). The courtyard was used probably for mourning and for memorial services similar to the "eulogy place" mentioned in Jewish sources (*B. Baba Bathra* 100b; also Safrai 1976: 779). Similar courtyards with benches are known from other contemporary Jerusalem monumental tombs but are usually smaller in size and lack the ritual bath (*miqveh*) found here (Kloner 1980a: 210, 244). Courtyards with benches dating to the third century are also found at Beth She‘arim and probably served a similar purpose (Avigad 1976: 41-45, 81-82, figs. 23-24, 35, 61, Pl. XXX:1).

The origin of the plan for the rock-cut loculi tomb of the Second Temple period in Judea is to be sought in Egypt, particularly in Leontopolis, from as early as Hasmonean times (*Ant.* XIII 63, 67; XIV, 99, 131-133) (Hachlili and Killebrew 1983a: 110-112; for a summary of theories on the origin of the loculi tombs see Kloner 1980a: 228-231).

In some Jerusalem tombs another type of burial is found: the arcosolia which is a bench-like aperture with an arched ceiling hewn into the length of the wall. The arcosolia is a later type of burial, in addition to common loculi tomb, in use at the end of the Second Temple period. In the Beth She‘arim catacombs the arcosolia was usually reserved for more expensive burials. In several cases the deceased was interred in a trough grave hewn in the arcosolium. From the third century on, the trough grave became the prevalent type of burial (Avigad 1976: 259).

1) *Burial Types*

Two distinctly different types of loculi tomb burials, primary and secondary, were discovered during the excavations in the Jericho cemetery. They can be classified typologically, chronologically and stratigraphically into primary burials in wooden coffins (type 1) and secondary burials of collected bones which were either placed in individual ossuaries (type 2a), or piled in heaps (type 2b) (but see Bennet 1965:532-534).

Type 1: *Primary Burial in wooden coffins* is the earliest type of burial in the Jericho cemetery. The coffins were placed in the rock-cut loculi tombs, each loculus holding one wooden coffin (with the exception of one loculus which held two coffins, one containing a woman and the other her child)(fig. 2). The deceased were evidently brought to the cemetery inside their coffins. The coffin itself would be pushed through the entrance of the tomb, although it was necessary to remove the gabled lid in order that the coffin would fit. Once inside the tomb, the lid was securely placed on the coffin which was then deposited in the loculus; only when all loculi were filled, would further coffins be placed on the benches or in the pit.

Coffins took the form of a wooden chest with a post at each corner, and were constructed by means of mortising. Several types of wood were used in the construction of the coffin: the most common types were sycamore, Christ-thorn and cypress. The lid of the chest was usually gabled and consisted of one plank on each side and a pediment at each end (Fig. 3). One well-preserved example, however, has a hinged lid. Iron nails and knobs found with the coffins were probably used only for decoration or structural support. The coffins were decorated with painted red and black geometric patterns and designs.

Contemporary coffins in Israel, different in their construction and decoration were found in tombs near 'En-Gedi, in a Jericho tomb , and in the Qumran cemetery (de Vaux 1973: 46-47) (Hachlili & Killebrew 1983a:115). Earlier examples of similar wooden coffins, dating to the fourth century BCE have survived in Egypt and South Russia (Watzinger 1905).

Manner of Burial: All the bodies were extended, face upwards, in the coffin, usually with the head to one side and hands close to the side of the body (fig. 2). Most coffins contain one individual, but sometimes a mother and small child (infant or foetus) are found together in a coffin. There are several occurrences where one or two bodies have been added to a coffin that already contained an individual, but no more than three bodies have ever been found in any one coffin. It is probable that a later body was placed in the same coffin because the individual was related to the previously interred person (*Semaḥot* 13, 8 in Zlotnick 1966: 84, 164).

Orientation of the bodies in the *kokh* and tomb does not seem to be significant as the heads face various directions (fig. 2). No special marks were found on the coffins which might have indicated in which direction the head should be oriented in the loculus. This is in contrast to the Qumran cemetery, where the orientation of most of the tombs is consistent—generally north-south (de Vaux 1973: 46; Bar Adon 1977: 22).

The discovery of several coins inside skulls may indicate that coins had been placed in the mouth of the deceased (Hachlili and Killebrew 1983b). In Jericho the

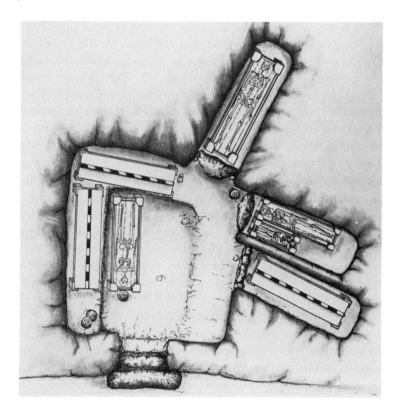

2. Tomb with Coffin Burials, Jericho.

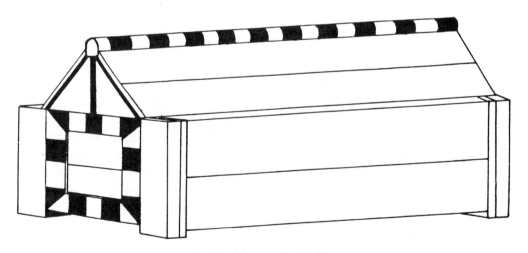

3. A Jericho wooden Coffin.

remains of twig-filled leather mattresses found in some of the coffins attest to the fact that the deceased had been placed upon them. Possibly the deceased was brought up to the tomb on a mattress and then placed inside the coffin. Another possible explanation is that an individual who died in his home was felt to have contaminated his mattress, and, instead of its being burned, the mattress was buried with the deceased in the coffin.

The imprint of woven material found on several bones and a skull suggests that the body was wrapped in a shroud.

It should be noted that the wooden coffins in Jericho were used for primary burials only and never as containers for secondary burials (cf. Avigad *et al.* 1962: 180 where wooden coffins at ʿEn-Gedi were reused as ossuaries).

Grave Goods: In most of the coffin tombs, grave goods consisting of both personal possessions and objects of daily use were found with the deceased, usually placed near either the head or the feet. Found only with women and children, they include wooden objects such as bowls, spatulas and beads, and a glass amphoriskos. Leather sandals were also commonly found, placed at the head of the deceased inside the coffin. Objects of daily use were found on the floor or in the pit of the tomb and storage jars were placed outside the entrance to the tomb.

Type 2: *Secondary Burial in Ossuaries*: This type was at first practiced only in Jerusalem but later spread to other parts of the Land of Israel (Rahmani 1982: 109). From the finds and stratigraphy of the ossuary burials in Jericho (but see Bennet 1965:532-34) it is clear that they post-date coffin burials. *Ossuaries* were hewn from one large block of limestone usually in the shape of a small, rectangular box resting on four low legs, and measuring ca. $60 \times 35 \times 30$ cm. for adults, and less for children. A stone lid— flat, slightly curved or gabled—was placed on top. The ossuaries were often decorated (Pls. 17, 18, pp. 110-115). They do not show any influence on them of wooden coffin design, neither in construction nor in decoration. Only a few pottery ossuaries, but none of wood, have been discovered until now.

Manner of Burial: The ossuaries were placed in the loculi or on the benches. Often two ossuaries would be stacked one above the other or placed next to each other (Hachlili 1978: 45; Kloner 1980a: Pls. 11, 13, 16, 23). In one loculus four ossuaries were found together (fig. 4; in the Goliath tomb at Jericho) (Hachlili 1979: 56-57). The occupants of ossuaries placed in the same loculus were usually related to each other, as can be concluded from the inscriptions found on the ossuaries. Ossuaries are sometimes found on the benches or floor even though the tomb contains empty loculi: this indicates that ossuary burial did not develop due to a necessity of saving space.

4. Four Ossuaries in One Loculus, Jericho.

The bodies were prepared for secondary burial by being first buried in a primary burial to allow the flesh to decay until only the bones remained (but see Hachlili & Killebrew 1983a:119). It has been claimed that the body was placed in the loculus of the family tomb and that after a year the relatives of the deceased would come to gather the bones and put them in the ossuary (Rahmani 1961: 117-118; 1978: 104; Kloner 1980a: 226-227, 248-252). In Jerusalem tombs, bones have been found inside loculi, and sometimes even under ossuaries (Kloner 1980a: 225). However, up to now no such evidence has been found in the Jericho cemetery.

The bones were placed inside the ossuary in a customary order: long bones lengthwise at the bottom with the bones of the arms and hands on one side and those of the legs and feet on the other side. The remaining bones of the body were placed on top of them and the skull was placed on top of all the bones at one end (Pl. 13). Usually the bones of one individual were placed in the ossuary, but there are several occurrences of more than one individual being interred in one ossuary: small children were buried with their mothers, three children were placed together, or two adults were interred together (Hachlili 1979: Table 1; Hachlili & Smith 1979: 67).

It is clear that the relatives were careful to place the deceased in the correct ossuary. At Jericho inscriptions mentioning the name and occasionally the age always correspond to the sex and age of the individual found inside the ossuary (Hachlili & Smith 1979); hence the bodies must have been carefully labelled during the period in which they were left to decompose.

Grave Goods discovered with ossuary burial tombs include unguentaria, bowls, Herodian lamps and cooking pots, and glass vessels and were identical to those used in daily life. No personal objects were found inside the ossuaries. They were usually placed close to the ossuaries or in the pit. In one Jericho loculus, two ossuaries were stacked one above the other together with an inscribed funerary bowl (Pl. 15)(Hachlili 1978: 48-49). It is noteworthy that some of the objects in the tombs were defective at the time of their placement, for example cooking pots were cracked, and pottery was left in fragments. This raises the question whether it was considered economically preferable to place a defective item in the tomb or whether the act was symbolic (Kloner 1980a: 257; Hachlili & Killebrew 1983a: 121, note 16).

Several explanations have been proposed regarding the purpose of these vessels inside the tomb. Storage jars, some found *in situ*, were often placed outside the entrance of coffin tombs in Jericho and may have contained water for purification. Small vessels such as juglets and bottles were apparently used for funerary ointments. Lamps found in the tombs may have been used to illuminate the tomb for visitors or may have been lit and placed at the head of the deceased out of respect.

The practice of placing burial gifts with the dead was widespread throughout the Hellenistic and Semitic-Roman pagan worlds, but the Jews, although following the custom, gave it their own interpretation by ignoring the connotation of an offering to the dead for their use in the afterlife. Possibly Jews placed personal belongings in the tomb of the deceased because the scene aroused the grief of the onlookers.

2) *Inscriptions on Ossuaries*

The Second Temple period onomasticon has been greatly enriched in recent years by incised, scratched or written inscriptions which have been discovered on

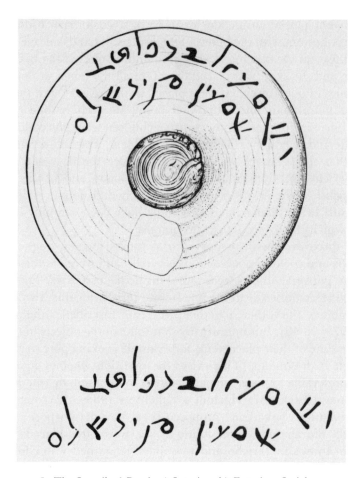

5. The Inscribed Bowl: a) Interior; b) Exterior. Jericho.

ossuaries. No particular place was reserved for the inscriptions and they are found on the front, back, sides and lid. Quite often the inscription is written more than once on the same ossuary and some are bilingual, written in Jewish and Greek script. The inscription usually includes the name of the interred and his family relationships (Pls. 14, 19), but in several cases additional information is also given, such as place of origin and age (Hachlili 1978: 48-49), or status, for example "freedman" (Hachlili 1979: 33). An abecedary, consisting of the first eight letters of the Greek alphabet, appears written in charcoal upon a re-used ossuary lid (Hachlili 1979: 47-48; 1984a). A unique inscribed funerary bowl, found in an ossuary tomb in Jericho

(Hachlili 1978) mentions a three-generation family which originated in Jerusalem, but probably lived, died and was buried in Jericho (fig. 5a, b; Pl. 15). In Jerusalem most of the inscriptions consist of names and family relationships. Sometimes a profession, like that of "Simon the master builder," appears, or an Aramaic inscription appears in archaic Hebrew script (such as the Abba cave inscription (Naveh 1973)). An intriguing aspect of the inscriptions is the identity of their authors. They were probably professional scribes or family members, but the latter seems more likely because of the great variety of hands that are evident in the execution of these inscriptions.

A consideration of the inscriptions leads us to conclude that first, ossuary tombs contained at the most three generations of a particular family; second, the recurrence of names is common in successive generations of a family (Hachlili 1979: 53; 1984b: 188-211) and third, Jewish families were literate and bilingual in Aramaic or Hebrew, and Greek.

The more personal duties associated with the burial of the deceased, such as carrying the coffin and its orderly placement in the tomb, the collecting of bones and laying them in the ossuaries, mourning, and the writing of inscriptions, were probably carried out by relatives and friends of the deceased (see Josephus *Against Apion* II, 205). Contemporary and later sources mention charitable societies, the *Hever ʿir*, who probably dealt with other duties involved in the preparation of the body for burial (see *Semahot* 12, 4-5 in Zlotnick 1966: 80-81; Safrai 1976: 775).

3) Dating

Dates for the burial customs are still the subject of debate. Nevertheless, the Jericho cemetery can provide a chronology for the two different types of burials (Hachlili & Killebrew 1983a: 124-125): primary burials in coffins can be dated to the mid-first century BCE-ca. 10 CE, and secondary burials in ossuaries immediately followed, dating to the period ca. 10 CE-68 CE. These dates are based on coins found in the tombs, the ossuary inscription mentioning queen Agrippina (Hachlili 1979: 60-62) and other ossuary inscriptions, the comparative stratigraphy of the tombs, as well as the pottery. Rahmani (1966:116; 1977:24-25; 1981: 175) dates the practice of secondary burials in ossuaries in Jerusalem to 30/20 BCE-70 CE, continuing sporadically until ca. 135 CE or the third century (also Kloner 1980a: 252-253). In the light of the new discoveries in the Jericho cemetery, which provide absolute chronology for ossuary burials, previous dates given for the beginning of ossuary burials in Jerusalem should now be considered accordingly.

4) Conclusions

Biblical references never mention the word coffin (ʾaron) except in the case of Joseph (Gen. 50:26) who died in Egypt and whose remains were transported to Canaan in a coffin (see also discussion in Hachlili 1979: 55). Iron Age archaeological evidence gives no indication that coffins were used then by the Israelites, even though coffins are known from this period in the Egyptian and Phoenician world. The isolated case of Joseph, therefore, might be explained as simply following the Egyptian burial practices of his time. The Biblical concept of burial was "to be buried with your people," perhaps indicating a form of tribal burial. After the settlement of the Land of Israel by the Israelite tribes, the custom became one of being buried in a family tomb ("to sleep with" or "be gathered unto your fathers' ancestors"). Thus already by that time the concept of family burial was strong.

The excavations in the extended Jerusalem necropolis and the Jericho cemetery reveal that two completely different burial customs, one chronologically following the other, were practiced by Jews of the Second Temple period. The earlier custom (first century BCE) which first appears among Jews at this time is of a primary individual burial in a wooden coffin. In Jerusalem indications of primary burial have been found in many tombs (Kloner 1980a: 225).

Jewish burial practices of the late Second Temple period reveal a corresponding importance placed on both the individual and the family. This is reflected in the plan of the loculi tomb, which provided for individual burial of coffins or ossuaries in separate loculi while at the same time allowing a family to be buried together in the same tomb. The entire population and not just the upper classes (as in the Israelite period) were given individual burials. This practice is probably related to the increasing importance placed on the individual in contemporary Hellenistic society, and to the Jewish belief in individual resurrection of the body. This belief is reflected in sources dating as early as the second century BCE (Rahmani 1961: 117-118, n. 6).

The second type of burial found in Jerusalem and in the Jericho cemetery, chronologically following the coffin burials, is conscious secondary burial of the bones either placed in individual ossuaries or in communal burials in loculi or pits (Hachlili & Killebrew 1983a:123-124), which was also common in burials of the First Temple and Hellenistic periods. This complete change in burial customs occurs during the beginning of the first century CE simultaneously with a change in the political status of Judea, which now became a Roman province. Up to now no theory has been able to account for this drastic change in burial customs; unfortunately, all sources dealing with ossilegium describe only the custom itself without mentioning the reasons for its sudden appearance. Whereas Meyers (1971) attempts to explain ossilegium as a continuation of earlier, local customs, Rahmani (1961:117-118, nn. 6, 7; 1981:175-177) proposes that ossuary burial began as an attempt to expiate sins through the decay of the flesh, which would then allow resurrection of the purified physical individual. Rahmani's suggestion seems to be the most plausible, particularly in view of the historical and social events of the period.

To sum up, what is most extraordinary in the Jewish burial customs of the Second Temple period is the astonishing fact that within a comparatively short space of time burial practices, usually among the most conservative customs in a society, underwent rapid changes. Loculi tombs appear with primary coffin burials, and within a century secondary burials in ossuaries in similar loculi tombs becomes the prevalent custom, a practice which lacks parallels with any other contemporary neighbouring culture. At the same time, these customs were short-lived and show little affinity with either the earlier Israelite customs or the later Jewish rituals of Late Antiquity which contain only traces of these Second Temple period customs. Archaeological investigation has been unable, moreover, to uncover the causes for these ossuary burial innovations. It may be conjectured that the Jews blamed their loss of independence and their state on their sinful behaviour; the custom of secondary burial of the bones, in ossuaries, after decay of the flesh, became a way to expiate sins.

5) Other Burial Customs

Two completely contrasting Jewish tomb forms and burial customs are encountered in the cemeteries of Qumran and ʿEn-el Guweir belonging to the Second Temple period Jewish sect of the Essenes in the Dead Sea area; and in the second-fourth century burials in the Jewish necropolis at Beth Sheʿarim.

The Essene Burial Customs in the Cemeteries of Qumran and ʿEn el-Guweir

One sect of Jews during the first century CE, the Essenes, practiced a completely different primary burial in individual graves as evidenced by their cemeteries at Qumran and ʿEn el-Guweir. The main cemetery of Qumran is located east of the settlement and contains about 1,100 graves (de Vaux 1973: 46). Its organized plan consists of rows of single graves, usually oriented north-south. The graves are marked by oval-shaped heaps of stones placed on the surface. Several graves contained signs of wooden coffins (de Vaux 1973: 46-47). Most of the excavated tombs contained individual burials; male interments only were found in the main cemetery (de Vaux 1973: 46, Pls. XXV-XXVI; 1953: 102, fig. 5, Pls. 4b, 5a, 5b; Bar-Adon 1977:12, 16, figs. 19-20). On the outskirts of this cemetery and in the smaller cemeteries of Qumran, a few females and children were interred (de Vaux 1973:47, 57-58; 1956: 569, 575). The large number of males found in these graves compared to the small number of women and children points to the importance placed on celibacy in this community (Cross 1961: 97-98).

The Essene burial practices have a few elements in common with those of the Jerusalem and Jericho cemeteries. The coffin burials at Qumran, though later in date, are comparable to those found at Jericho. Grave goods were discovered with women and children at Qumran and ʿEn el-Guweir, as well as remains of cloth (indicating that the dead had been wrapped in shrouds), and mattresses (de Vaux 1973:47, Bar-Adon 1977: 22). Broken storage jars were discovered on top of the graves at ʿEn el-Guweir (Bar-Adon 1977:16, figs. 21:1-3, 22-23) and Qumran (de Vaux 1953: 103, figs. 2:5 and Pl. VI), probably a parallel to the custom of placing storage jars outside the tombs at Jericho.

The contrasts in these burial practices indicate differences in religious philosophy towards the dead among the Jews of this time and reflects the severance of the Essenes from Judaism (de Vaux 1973: 126-138; Cross 1961: 51ff.; Yadin 1983: 304-305). Single-person burials at Qumran and ʿEn el-Guweir cemeteries stress the importance of the individual, rather than the family.

The Beth Sheʿarim Necropolis

The Jewish necropolis at Beth Sheʿarim was the central burial ground for Jews from the Land of Israel and the neighbouring areas. The majority of the catacombs date to the third-fourth centuries. Beth Sheʿarim was expanded after the death of Rabbi Judah in the latter part of the third century. The *terminus ante quem* for the catacombs is the date of their destruction in the year 352 CE (Avigad 1976: 260).

Burial Manner

The Beth Sheʿarim burial place consists of catacombs, with a frontal courtyard and portals constructed of stone doors imitating wooden doors with nails (Mazar 1973: Plan 1-5; Pl VI; Avigad; 1976: figs. 3-5; Pls. 25:1; 27:2; 28:1). Several burial halls spaced out along a corridor were hewn in the rock. The graves were mainly loculi or arcosolia types and it is clear that burial customs, that is primary inhumation in arcosolia, coffins and sarcophagi, have little in common with those of the Second Temple period. On the walls were carved, painted or incised decoration, in a popular art style. Decorated marble or clay sarcophagi contained the primary burials of Jews from the Land of Israel or the reinterred remains of Diaspora Jews (Mazar 1973; Avigad 1976). By this time burial had become a commercialized, public enterprise, and was directed apparently by the burial society (*Hevrah Kadisha*) who sold burial places to any purchaser (Avigad 1976: 253, 265).

The Inscriptions

The Aramaic, Hebrew and Greek inscriptions found in these tombs mainly record the names of the tomb owners; sometimes a sentiment is added. Longer inscriptions are written on the walls. Their purpose was to identify the graves of the deceased for visitors (Schwabe and Lifshitz 1974: 219). The inscriptions found at Beth She^carim indicate that the interred were people of importance such as rabbis, public officers, merchants, craftsmen, and scribes.

6) Reinterment

A differentiation must be made between the custom of secondary burial in ossuaries and the custom of Diaspora Jews being reinterred in the Land of Israel. Scholars (Meyers 1971: 72-79) have claimed that ossuaries contained the bones of Diaspora Jews, citing inscriptions mentioning a person's origin outside of the Land of Israel as proof. What the inscriptions actually indicate is that the deceased had belonged to a community of Jews residing in Jerusalem who were of Diaspora origin (Rahmani 1977: 28 and nn. 123-124). Not until the third century CE did Jews begin to practice the custom of reinterment in the Land of Israel (Gafni 1981), and especially abundant evidence for this practice is to be seen in the Beth She^carim cemetery (Schwabe & Lifshitz 1974:219).

B) FUNERARY ART

Funerary art of the Second Temple period is a rich and varied art. It consists of ornamentation of tomb facades, sarcophagi and ossuaries, as well as wall paintings and graffiti.

1) Tomb Decoration

The composite style, an amalgamation of stylistic features influenced by Hellenistic-Roman architecture and by Oriental elements, is characteristic of ornamented tombs in Jerusalem, and its execution is typical generally of Jewish art of the Second Temple period. This composite style is found on:

a) Facade ornamented tombs with either i) a Doric frieze together with Ionic columns, or ii) an ornate gable.

The most common of the tomb entablatures consists of a Doric frieze, sometimes with an addition in the centre and around the entrance as at the Tomb of the Kings, and usually combined with Ionic columns. The gable ornament is filled with plant motifs, consisting of a central focus which spreads to both sides of the triangle. The pediment is completely filled in accordance with the Oriental element of *horror vacui*.

b) Monumental tombs exhibiting a mixture of classical features and Egyptian pyramids and cornices.

The ornamentation of the monumental tombs reveals the existence of a composite style which sometimes combines the classical and Oriental styles, as in the tomb of Zachariah (Pl. 16), or even is a combination of three styles, as in the case of the monument of Absalom, which has a Doric frieze, Ionic capitals and an Egyptian cornice.

a) Tombs with Ornamented Facades (Avigad 1950-1951; 1956; 1975)

i) Three rock hewn tombs portray a combination of features which characterize Jewish funerary art in Jerusalem. Each has a Doric frieze and Ionic columns with an unusual addition: a distyle in antis entrance with Ionic columns.

Umm el ʿAmed (fig. 6) has a Doric metope frieze containing rosettes, above which is a row of dentils which is an Ionic feature. Below it are Doric guttae. The architrave is relatively low in relation to the frieze, which is characteristic of Hellenistic architecture. The rock face of the facade is carved with ashlar stone decoration.

The Frieze tomb (fig. 7) has a Doric metope frieze with rosettes flanking a central wreath. Surmounting it is an elaborately decorated Corinthian cornice, which is characteristic of Roman architecture, usually more elaborately ornamented than Hellenistic architecture.

The Tomb of the Kings (Kon 1947) has a richly decorated facade. The opening is distyle in antis, with Ionic columns. Enclosing this facade is an unfinished decorative band with leaves, fruit and pine cones with a rosette in the centre. Surmounting it is a Doric frieze whose central motif is a triple bunch of grapes flanked by wreaths and acanthus (fig. 8). The impressively elaborate composite style of this tomb's facade is unique.

ii) Several tombs have facades decorated with ornamented gables.

The Tomb of the Sanhedrin has an entrance decorated with a gable and acroteria. The gable is filled with acanthus leaves among which fruit are placed.

6. Umm el-ʿAmed Tomb.

7. Frieze Tomb.   8. Restored Facade of the "Tomb of the Kings".

9. The Grapes Tomb.

10. The Gable of the Tomb of Jehoshaphat.

The Grapes Tomb (fig. 9) has a similar gable and acroteria over the entrance. The pediment is decorated with vine branches. Two bunches of grapes flank the central rosette.

The Tomb of Jehoshaphat, which is adjacent to the Absalom monument, has a flatly carved gabled facade and acroteria. The pediment is decorated with a highly stylized design of branches creating medallions which are filled with fruit. The branches grow out of a central acanthus leaf (fig. 10).

b) Monumental Tombs

Monumental tombs are characterized by a partly rock-hewn and partly built free-standing monument either above or next to the chamber and loculi tomb. The monument usually has a pyramid or tholus surmounting a cube-shaped base. A group of monumental tombs, located in the Kidron Valley (Avigad 1954) from south to north (fig. 11) consist of the Tomb of Zachariah (late first century CE), the Bene Hezir tomb (dated to the Hasmonean period—early first century BCE), and the Absalom tomb (first century CE) with its adjacent Tomb of Jehoshaphat. All the tomb names, except for that of the Bene Hezir, are later folklore appendages.

The Bene Hezir tomb is the earliest of the tombs and probably belongs to the Hasmonean period (early first century BCE). It is a rock-hewn tomb with chambers and loculi and an entrance hall with a decorated facade. Its facade is distyle in antis, with two Doric columns crowned by a Doric frieze (fig. 12). A Hebrew inscription is incised on the architrave and mentions the "priests of Bene Hezir." This monument is not only chronologically earlier than the others, but also its ornamentation differs in that it is not in the composite style characteristic of the other Jewish tomb facades.

The Tomb of Zachariah (Pl. 16) is a free-standing monument with a small rock-hewn chamber. It consists of a cube-shaped building surmounted by a pyramid and is decorated with an Egyptian cornice carried on engaged Ionic columns with pillars in the corners. This monument was intended to be a memorial, a *nefesh*, either of the Bene Hezir tomb or of a nearby unfinished tomb.

The Monument of Absalom and the Cave of Jehoshaphat is a family tomb complex with many rock-hewn chambers (Avigad 1954b: fig. 51). The monument has a lower rock-hewn cube and an upper drum and cone built of ashlar stones. The lower cube is decorated with engaged Ionic columns bearing a Doric frieze and an Egyptian cornice. The drum and conical roof are crowned by a petalled flower (fig. 13). The upper built part is the *nefesh* (Avigad 1954b: figs. 69-70).

The two free-standing monuments of Zachariah and Absalom are magnificent examples of the composite style of Jewish art which consists of a combination of common Ionic and Doric styles together with an Egyptian cornice and pyramid. Similar monumental tombs which combine both a tomb and a *nefesh* memorial have been found in the following tombs of Jerusalem:

The Tomb of the Kings (fig. 8) has been identified as the tomb of Helene, Queen of Adiabene, who settled in Jerusalem after she and her family converted to Judaism. They were buried here in ca. 50 CE. Situated north of the present day Old City, the tomb is large and impressive. It has a rock-hewn court, staircase, an or-

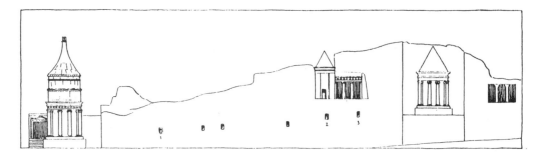

11. The Kidron Valley Monumental Tombs.

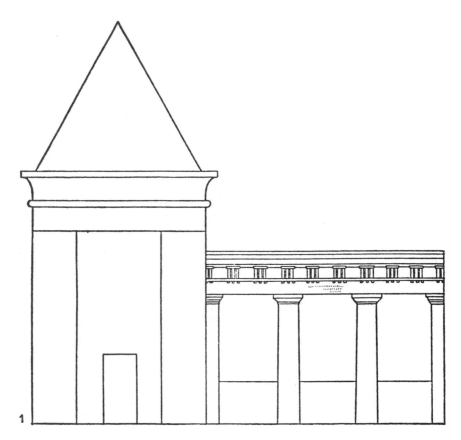

12. Bene Hezir Tomb Facade and its Restored *Nefesh*.

13. Monument of Absalom.

namented facade and chambers with niches and arcosolia. Three small pyramids similar to those in the Kidron Valley probably stood on top of the tomb (described by Josephus in *Ant.* XX, 4, 5).

Jason's Tomb in the western part of modern Jerusalem is named after the person mentioned in the inscription found there. It has three courts and two chambers, one of which has loculi, and a facade (which is mono stylos in antis) with one column only. The tomb is topped by a pyramid. It also bears wall carvings (see p. 238). It is dated to the Hasmonean period, first century BCE (Rahmani 1967).

The Tomb of the Family of Herod (fig. 14) (adjacent to the modern King David hotel, west of the Old City). Remains of what is conjectured to be a monument stand in front of the entrance. The plan is different from that in the other tombs (see p. 57 for Netzer's proposal of Herod's tomb in Jerusalem).

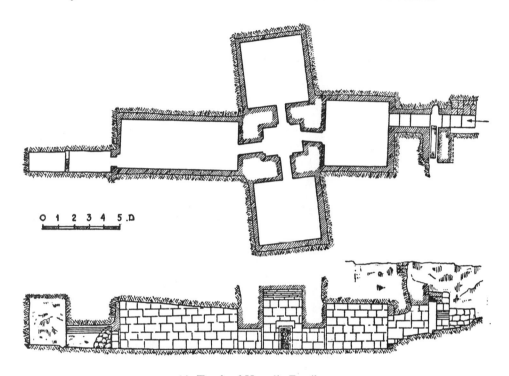

14. Tomb of Herod's Family.

Jewish funerary art as expressed in ornamented tombs reflects a Hellenistic tradition, executed locally.

2) Ossuary Ornamentation

Of all the ossuaries found in Jerusalem, most are undecorated, whereas in Jericho most are decorated. Ornamentation of ossuaries has been recently comprehensively researched by Rahmani (1977) and Figueras (1983).

The repertoire of motifs decorating ossuaries is quite numerous (about 35 motifs were gathered by Rahmani and Figueras), and consists of plant, geometric and architectural motifs. These motifs are similar to those appearing in other arts of the Second Temple period (pp. 79-82). However, the variation on each motif is greater, probably due to the large quantity of ossuaries found (see for instance Figueras 1983: Pls. 9-10 for rosettes and Pl. 30 for amphorae). Other architectural patterns may also be added to the repertoire and include those generally associated with tombs, for example, the column pyramid (Hachlili 1981) and facades. Stone ossuary workshops and artists probably had a repertoire, presumably in the form of a pattern book, to which reference could be repeatedly made.

The ornamentation is carved into the soft stone of the ossuaries with the aid of tools such as a ruler and compass. Few ossuaries are painted. The commonest type of ossuary ornamentation is a scheme consisting of a frame of zigzag lines, incised or chip-carved, within two straight lines. This frame is divided usually into two, and sometimes more, metopes which are filled generally with six-petalled rosettes (figs. 15-17; Pl. 17a, b). This general scheme is based on the metope frieze common in tomb facade decoration. It is a traditional, fully developed Oriental geometric form (Avi-Yonah 1981a: 96-97).

Three general types of ossuary ornamentation can be distinguished (Figueras, 1983: 26, Pl. 4, proposes eight types but, as the distinctions are confused, they cannot be considered separate types):

a) Two symmetrical rosettes enclosed in a frame constitute the standard type of ossuary decoration. The variety of rosette styles is extensive, from simple, incised six-petalled rosettes (fig. 15a; Pl. 17a) to chip-carved (fig. 15a; Pl. 18), and to elaborately designed and executed rosettes (Goodenough 1953: figs. 180, 193, 211; Rahmani 1982: 116; see also Figueras 1983: Pls. 9-10, chart of rosettes). The majority of the decorated ossuaries have depictions of two or more rosettes.

b) Another group of ossuaries portrays the standard rosettes flanking a central motif consisting of various patterns, for instance a tomb facade (fig. 16b), a column (Pl. 17b) or an amphorae (Figueras 1983: Pl. 30).

c) The third group of ossuaries is rendered with a design which covers the entire front of the ossuary, but lacks rosettes; for instance, the ossuary with an ashlar stone motif, with arches, columns and with other designs (fig. 15b). Occasionally several rosettes are incorporated into this general design (Figueras 1983: Pls. 18; 19; 26:134, 144; 28: 380, 566, 576, 580; 29: 172; 30:16; 31:317).

It is very significant that generally, dissimilarly decorated ossuaries are found within the same tomb, from which it appears that the families chose a differently decorated ossuary for each member. For example the Jericho "Goliath" tomb contains twenty-one ossuaries (Hachlili 1979), all of which are different, two being exceptionally elaborate (Pl. 19). In Jerusalem the same phenomenon occurs in a tomb in Givʿat HaMivtar for instance (Kloner 1980c: figs. 11, 12, 23),although a preference for a certain lily plant motif between rosettes may be seen. However, the design and execution of this motif are different in each case.

Research conducted into these elements of decoration has resulted in a controversy as to their meaning and interpretation (see the discussion in Rahmani 1982:

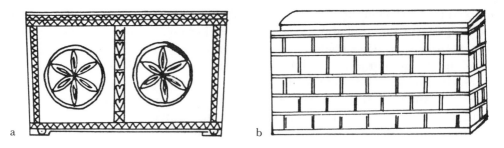

15. Ornamented Ossuaries from a Workshop

a

b

c

d

16. Ornamented Ossuaries from a Workshop

116-118; Figueras 1983: 78-86). Several scholars maintain that the ornaments possess symbolic value and represent hope of an afterlife, in other words, they are symbols with emotional content (Goodenough 1965: 70). Others suggest that ossuaries as well as the custom of ossuary decoration express the beliefs of Judaeo-Christians (already rejected by Rahmani 1982: 116-119). Figueras (1983: 83-110) continuing in the vein developed by Goodenough, asserts that the decorated ossuaries suggest eschatological belief. Rahmani (1982: 117-118) contends that the motifs decorating the ossuaries represent actual contemporary funerary art and architecture in Jerusalem. In fact, no symbols are depicted on the ossuaries, neither are any motifs connected with every-day life or the Temple portrayed. Rahmani's contention seems to be the most acceptable. The repertoire of motifs used to decorate the ossuaries is part of a general ensemble of decorative patterns used in Second Temple period art, several of which are found solely in funerary art.

Ossuary workshops

Evidence for local workshops can be seen in the ornamentation of ossuaries, where similar, sometimes even identical, elements are portrayed.

A group of ossuaries, all found in Jerusalem except for one discovered in Jericho, contains similarities in execution and patterns to such an extent as to suggest that all examples of the group are from one workshop (Rahmani 1967: 190). The front panel of each ossuary is enclosed by two incised frames. The outer of these two frames is depicted by closely-spaced carved lines with squares in all four corners. The inner frame is narrower and is rendered by groups of two widely-spaced, incised lines (fig. 16). The only exception is the Jericho ossuary on which the order of the frames is reversed: the outer frame has widely-spaced lines and the inner has closely-spaced vertical lines. Both frames enclose a tripartite decoration of two six-petalled and chip-carved rosettes flanking a central motif. Noteworthy are the identical rosettes of the Jericho and Jerusalem ossuaries, the ends of which are joined by six leaves with six small circular depressions between the petals. The sole variation in these ossuaries is the design of the central motif which shows diverse structures:

a) One leitmotif consists of two pillars which are depicted on three of the ossuaries (fig. 16a).

b) Another motif appearing on six ossuaries is a door or gate which is sometimes arched, and in one instance is double (fig. 16b). Each gate is flanked by two pillars similar to a).

c) A motif probably representing a tomb facade which appears on two ossuaries from Jerusalem and on an ossuary fragment from a Jericho tomb (fig. 16c) consists

17. Ornamented Ossuaries from a Workshop.

of the facade of a structure flanked by two or three pillars of type a) surmounted by a gabled roof with a rectangular projection. The gable has a frieze decorated either with metopes or with a zigzag pattern (fig. 16c). Motifs of both this type and type b) are flanked by two pillars which in turn are flanked by a pair of rosettes.

d) One unusual ossuary from Jerusalem which belongs to this group displays similar frames to those described above. However, it differs in its central motif, it lacks rosettes and it shows five pillars with arrows filling the spaces between them (fig. 16d). As mentioned above, all the ossuaries, with the exception of one found in Jericho, were discovered in the Jerusalem area. The question thus arises whether the Jericho ossuary was imported from Jerusalem, and if so, whether all the ossuaries found in Jericho were manufactured in Jerusalem workshops and then transported to Jericho. On the other hand, it may be possible that artisans or apprentices came from Jerusalem to work in Jericho. Whatever the answer, the craftsman who made the Jericho ossuary must have worked at the same time and in the same workshop which produced the identical Jerusalem ossuaries.

A second group of ossuaries which, due to similar decorative elements and affinity of execution, seem to have been produced in one workshop, consists of seven examples discovered in Jerusalem (fig. 17) (Goodenough 1953: figs. 205, 206, 207; Figueras 1983: Pls. 33: 420; 34: 422; Rahmani 1982: 117). The facade decorations of these ossuaries consist of the following identical elements:

a) A chip-carved zigzag double frame usually incised on all four sides. Occasionally the bottom line of the frame is single.

b) Within the frame are depicted two chip-carved six-petalled rosettes.

c) In the centre between the rosettes, a stylized depiction of a knife is shown, which Rahmani (1982: 115 and fig. on 117) asserts represents stylized palm trees. An exception to this is one ossuary (Figueras 1983: Pl. 420) which shows a stylized, geometric design.

d) Several ossuaries show triangles chip-carved onto the bottom frame (fig. 17.

e) An interesting element common to all these ossuaries is the two lines incised from the lower part of the two rosettes to the bottom frame, which may have functioned as aids to the mason in carving the triangles. Two of the ossuaries are slightly differently decorated: one (Goodenough 1953: fig. 206) has two twelve-petalled rosettes, and the other (Figueras 1983: Pl. 33: 420) has a different central motif.

3) Sarcophagus Ornamentation

A few sarcophagi have been found in tombs in Jerusalem. Made of hard stone, their ornamentation differs from that of ossuaries in both design and execution, although the motifs are similar, consisting of plants, rosettes, vine branches and bunches of grapes, and acanthus leaves. Two similar sarcophagi from the Tomb of the Nazirite and from Herod's Family Tomb are of high quality, and are beautifully carved with symmetrical ornamentation of a central motif such as a vase or a leaf with grape bunches, and with leaves and flowers filling the space (Pl. 8; fig. 18). This design resembles the tomb facade ornamentation (fig. 9, the Grapes Tomb). Two sarcophagi from "Dominus Flevit," and one from the Tomb of the Kings are also of high quality, and are richly carved with elaborate rosettes in a row (fig. 19), or flanking a bunch of leaves.

Differences are noticeable between sarcophagi and ossuary decoration and ornamentation. The sarcophagi are usually depicted in high relief, are skillfully executed, and their design is richer and more elaborate. They are similar in style and execution to the tomb facades of Jerusalem. However, their style, symmetrical execution, play of light and shade, and *horror vacui* are similar to the style of ossuary ornamentation (Avi-Yonah 1961b: 21). The richly adorned sarcophagi well executed in relief were probably much more expensive so that only wealthy families would have been able to afford them.

4) Wall Paintings

Jewish rock-cut tombs of the Second Temple period are not known to have been decorated. However, a wall painting was discovered in the monumental "Goliath" tomb in the Jericho necropolis (Hachlili 1985). Traces of a wall painting enclosed

18. Sarcophagus from Herod's Family Tomb .

19. Sarcophagus from the "Tomb of the Kings".

by a painted red frame appear on three walls of the tomb (figs. 20, 21). The painting is executed in various shades of red, brown and black. The loculi are outlined by a thick black line flanked by two thinner red ones, forming an arch above every loculus. The vine motif is the subject of paintings on both the north and south walls. Several birds perch on the vines. The worst preserved section of the wall painting faces the entrance on the west wall and shows ashlar stones or brick masonry, probably portraying a structure, and floral designs (fig. 21). Three main non-figurative motifs, vine branches, wreath and masonry, appear in the wall painting. The vine

20. Reconstruction of Jericho Tomb with Wall Painting.

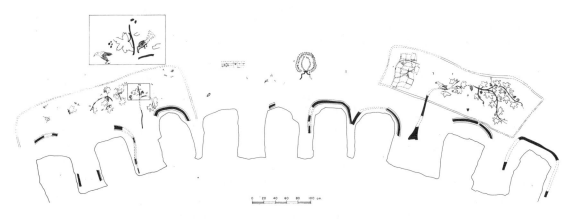

21. Drawing of the Jericho Tomb Wall Painting.

branch motif in contemporary Jewish art of the first century CE is rare but appears in the Grapes Tomb (fig. 9), and on two ossuaries and two sarcophagi from Jerusalem (Pl. 18).

The Jericho tomb painting was most likely accomplished at the same time as the tomb itself was hewn, evidently for the benefit of the tomb's visitors and to indicate the family's prominent position. In no way can it be considered as or compared to tomb graffiti that occasionally appear on tomb walls and seem to have been executed by tomb visitors. This tomb, based both on absolute and relative chronology, can be dated to 10-70 CE, thereby dating the wall painting to the beginning of the first century CE; it probably was inspired by the Graeco-Roman tomb frescoes prevalent at this time.

5) Drawings

A charcoal drawing of a *nefesh*, a column pyramid, was discovered on a tomb wall in the Jericho cemetery (Hachlili 1981). The drawing depicts three columns and part of a fourth (fig. 22). Each column consists of a fluted shaft on a raised rectangular base, with an Ionic capital surmounted by a pyramid. Palm trees fill the spaces in between the columns. A similar three dimensional fragment of a stone *nefesh* grave marker was also found at Jericho (fig. 23). Similar columns are carved on several ossuaries (Pl. 17b) (Hachlili 1981: fig. 3; Pls. V; VI).

Several drawings in charcoal appear on the northern and southern walls of the porch of Jason's tomb. They probably were executed by one artist at the same time (Rahmani 1976: 69-75). Three ships, one warship pursuing two other ships, are drawn in detail on the western wall of the porch (Rahmani 1967: fig. 5). Over the entrance, on the northern wall of the porch, a recumbent stag is drawn (Rahmani 1967: fig. 6). On the eastern wall of the porch graffiti of five menoroth are scratched (fig. IX.2b). Rahmani (1967: 73) maintains that these graffiti are later than the drawing of the ships, about 30 CE. Some other indistinguishable graffiti also are found in the tomb. Rahmani (1967: 96) contends that the porch drawings served as identification for one of the interred, and are meant to indicate the occupation of the deceased. The stag may represent either a symbol of strength or may refer to a family name (Rahmani 1967: 97). Thus, the drawings in Jason's tomb were drawn as a reference to those interred in the tomb and not as a purely decorative embellishment while the tomb was being hewn, as is the case with the Jericho wall painting.

Jewish funerary art consists mostly of decorations of tombs, facades, pediments and friezes in Jerusalem and a tomb wall painting at Jericho, as well as funerary

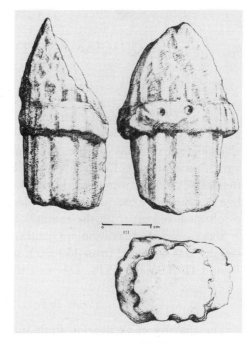

22. Drawing of *Nefesh* on a Tomb Wall, Jericho.   23. A Three-Dimensional Stone *Nefesh*.

receptacles, richly ornamented ossuaries and sarcophagi. Aniconic art is used, with geometric, floral and architectural motifs. The origin of this art is Hellenistic with local execution by stone masons and artists.

CHAPTER FIVE

QUMRAN AND THE DEAD SEA SCROLLS

A) QUMRAN

Khirbet Qumran lies at a height of 50 m. overlooking the coastal plain of the Dead Sea (Pl. 20). The community who wrote the Dead Sea scrolls are known from archaeological remains at the community centre at Qumran, from the nearby agricultural area at ꜤEn Feshka and ꜤEn el-Guwher and from the Dead Sea scrolls themselves, which were found and excavated in nearby caves. Those who came to live at Qumran chose this remote place for religious reasons, as a spiritual as well as physical retreat from the mainstream of Judaism and Jewish life.

Six seasons of excavation at Qumran and the surrounding area have revealed that the site was occupied from 150 BCE until 68 CE in three main phases: periods Ia, Ib and II (de Vaux 1973; Davies 1982).

Period Ia (ca. 150-103 BCE) (fig.1)

The sparsity of excavation finds indicates that the earliest community of period Ia was small. The inhabitants probably built upon the ruins of a building, an Israelite structure, which had been abandoned three hundred years before. The building consists of two wings, a western and an eastern (fig. 1). It also has several circular and rectangular cisterns (1-3), a decantation basin (4) which serves the cisterns, two channels (5-6) which provide for the collection of water, several small rooms (7-9) of unknown purpose, and two potters' kilns (10-11) on the east. Period Ia is the least well preserved phase at Qumran. Its pottery is very similar to that of Ib. Several silver coins which are dated to 130 BCE have been found, but it is uncertain whether they belong to Ia as silver coins are known to have remained in circulation longer than did those of bronze.

Period Ib (ca. 103-31 BCE) (fig. 2)

In period Ib the existing building was expanded, probably because the community increased to about three or four times its original number. In this period it became an autonomous settlement. The building now had three main parts: the main or eastern block, the western block and the potters' workshop.

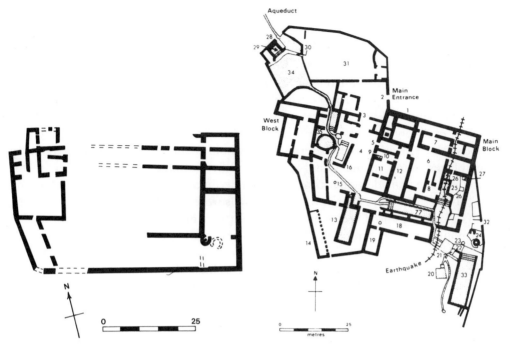

1. Qumran, Plan of Period 1a.   2. Qumran, Plan of Period 1b.

1) The main (eastern) block consists of a tower (1) overlooking the main entrance (2), and store rooms on the ground floor. Its courtyard (6) is surrounded by kitchens (7) and small rooms (8). The most interesting rooms in this block are (11) and (12). (11) has benches running along its walls, and probably served as some kind of an assembly room. (12) is the "scriptorium," the upper room where the Dead Sea scrolls were written. Several finds were discovered including mudbrick fragments covered with plaster (later reassembled into tables) and one pottery and one bronze inkwell (Davies 1982: 44-46; but see Golb (1980:3,5,11) rejecting the concept of the Scriptorium).

2) The western block was developed around existing cisterns and has an elaborate water system. It contains a large cistern (13), a central corridor (15) with a circular platform with a groove for millstones and a baking oven (16). Two rooms are located in the southern part: a refectory (18) and its adjoining room (19), a pantry, where thousands of crockery fragments were found. The refectory is the largest room at

Qumran and has on its west a circular paved area for the priest who presided over the meals and ceremonies.

3) The potters' workshop contains several features: a shallow, plastered basin (20) where clay was washed with water from the channel, a pit (21) where the washed clay was left to mature, a trough (22) in which the final mixing was carried out, a stone-lined pit (23) in which the wheel stood, and two kilns (24) for firing the pottery. This sole workshop apparently provided all of the pottery used at Qumran, which is probably the reason for a lack of variety and development in the types of periods I-II. However, the pottery on the whole is similar to other contemporary assemblages found in the Land of Israel. Other installations at Qumran in this period include two additional cisterns with a decantation basin (25), a small bathing area (26), a store room (27) in which iron tools were found, an entrance (28) on the north, a bath (29) used before entering the settlement proper, an aqueduct (30), an outer courtyard (31), and what is probably the southwest corner entrance (32).

4) The cisterns. Because of its desert site, water was a matter of great importance at Qumran and for this reason the cisterns dominate the entire complex. They are linked by water channels which provide all areas with water, probably rainwater, which is carried by an aqueduct some 750 metres into the northwest corner of Qumran.

Dating of period Ib is provided both by pottery and by coins. The pottery consists mainly of late Hellenistic types dating from the beginning of the second century BCE until the middle of the first century BCE. The coins, including those of silver mentioned above, probably belonging to period Ia, are dated to the early part of the first century BCE, ca. 100 BCE. Period Ib occupation ended in fire and earthquake around 31 BCE, at which time the site was abandoned. The reasons for the desertion, the site to which the community moved and the date of its return are all open to conjecture. What is clear is that the same community resettled the site in period II. The gap in occupation at Qumran is contemporaneous with the reign of Herod, 31-4 BCE.

Period II (ca. 4 BCE—68 CE (Davies 1982: Plan 4))

Period II buildings are identical to those of Ib in function, organization and size. Beginning and end of occupation of this period is dated by coins which show that life at the Qumran community ceased in the third year of the War against the Romans (68 CE).

'En Feshka

South of Qumran on the Dead Sea coast (Davies 1982: 64-69), the site was excavated in 1958 and contains a few remains: a rectangular building (25 × 20 m.) consisting of a courtyard surrounded by rooms, a lean-to structure on the south, and an enclosure on the north (Davies 1982: Plan 6, Pl. 21). From evidence provided by coins and pottery it seems that the building was inhabited during periods I-II of Qumran, with three stages of occupation. It was also partly inhabited during the second Jewish War of 132-135 CE. 'En Feshka was probably part of the Qumran complex: the structure's connections with agricultural activity in the area suggest that 'En Feshka was the Qumran "farm," or its agricultural and industrial annexe with stores, workshops and enclosures. The springs of Feshka would have provided water for flocks and herds. The date palms which grew in abundance were used for limited industrial work: mats were made from reeds and the palm trees were used for timber. There is some evidence for a tannery.

The Qumran community was self-sufficient, its primary activity being the production of manuscripts by scribes in the scriptorium. The buildings show that vessels were also manufactured in the potters' workshop, and the finds from 'En Feshka indicate farming and industry.

B) THE QUMRAN LIBRARY

The Dead Sea Scrolls
(Cross 1961: 4-53; 163-194; Vermes 1978: 9-86; Dimant 1984)

The Hebrew writings on leather and papyrus found in eleven caves at Qumran belong to a library of religious manuscripts of Biblical and post-Biblical Jewish literature. The scrolls and the fragments of texts were deposited in the eleven Qumran caves during the First War of the Jews against Rome in 68 BCE. (But see Golb 1980, suggesting in his well argued hypothesis that the manuscripts are remnants of Jerusalem libraries hidden away in the Judean desert prior to 70 CE.)

Biblical Literature: The Qumran library yielded about 200 manuscripts of the Hebrew Bible, dating from the third century BCE until the second century CE. The manuscripts include every book of the Bible except for Esther. About seventy are of the Pentateuch, with Deuteronomy predominant. Four are complete scrolls. These and a large number of Biblical commentaries, along with Aramaic and Greek translations of parts of the Bible, indicate that the Essenes were greatly interested in Bible study.

Several of the texts diverge from one another (Vermes 1978: 200-205). These variations in the Biblical manuscripts testify to a plurality of textual traditions, explained by scholars by a theory of geographically local texts (Cross) or by a theory that textual traditions of distinct socio-religious groups were current in the period preceding Qumran (Talmon). This plurality was later compounded into a unified text as the result of religious authority; the Bible was canonized in ca. 100 CE by the rabbis at Jamnia (Vermes 1978: 206-209).

Post- and non-Biblical manuscripts: These comprise four classes according to Vermes (1978: 45-86): 1) rules (5 manuscripts); 2) poetic, liturgical and wisdom texts (12 manuscripts); 3) Biblical interpretations (23 writings); and 4) three miscellaneous compositions including the Copper Scroll, Horoscopes and a Messianic Horoscope. (A register of the entire library including the Biblical, Apocryphal, Pseudepigraphical and Sectarian writings is found in Fitzmyer (1975: 11-52) and Vermes (1978: 27-28).)

The Qumran scripts: On the basis of palaeography, these belong to three periods (Cross 1961):

1) A small group of Biblical manuscripts in archaic style is dated to 250-150 BCE. These were probably master scrolls brought to Qumran by the sect when it was first founded.

2) Several Biblical and non-Biblical manuscripts exhibit a style which reflects the Hasmonean period, ca. 150-30 BCE. Sectarian scrolls, which were composed and copied at Qumran, appear in the mid-Hasmonean period, 100 BCE.

3) A large group of manuscripts are dated to the Herodian period, ca. 30 BCE-70 CE.

The majority of scrolls are written on leather in the formal "Herodian" script. The skins were sewn together and bound onto a piece of wood, with the title inscribed on their surface. The scrolls were then placed in jars, in some cases first being wrapped in linen. The scrolls' dates cover at least the period from the second and first centuries BCE to the first century CE. The majority of the manuscripts were composed or copied during the lifetime of the Qumran community, from about 150/140 BCE to 68 CE. A few Biblical manuscripts are older: some are dated to the third century BCE (the Samuel text from Qumran cave 4 is dated to ca. 225 BCE). Thus, a *terminus a quo* of 150-140 BCE for the establishment of the sect in Qumran may be posited and a *terminus ad quem* of 68 CE, when it was destroyed by Rome, during the First War. (Among the texts from Masada, one sectarian fragment, known also from Qumran, was found as were other fragments of Ben Sirach and several papyri (Yadin 1966: 168-179).)

The actual establishment of the Qumran sect was in ca. 150-140 BCE; however, it had probably existed for some years previously. The community's origins were probably in the pre-Maccabean and Maccabean periods; they were an unorganized group which originated in the "Ages of Wrath" at the beginning of the second century BCE, and which was guided by a "Teacher of Righteousness" (Vermes 1978: 142-150).

C) COMMUNITY CUSTOMS AND ORGANIZATION
(Vermes 1978: 87-115; Schürer, Vermes and Millar. 1979,II: 575-577).

The community at Qumran claimed to be the true Israel, and to represent the genuine religion. It was divided into priests, Levites and laity, and maintained a symbolic grouping of twelve tribes as well as smaller units. Governed by priests, the "Sons of Zadok," and a general assembly, it had a council of the community presided over by the priest-president. They decided upon matters of doctrine, legal affairs and property, debated the Law and selected newcomers. The community affairs were managed by a guardian *mebaqqer*. A priest had to be present at any gathering of ten or more men for debate, study or prayer. The precedence of the priests was absolute, in contrast to the priests in mainstream Judaism. The highest rank was that of the Guardian or Master (*maskil*), who instructed and taught the community, as well as presided over assemblies and community councils.

The customs of the Qumran community (Vermes 1978: 94-96; Schürer, Vermes and Millar, 1979, II: 581) were those of a life of worship with prayers daily at dawn and at dusk. Festivals of the community were celebrated on different days to those of the regular Jewish festivals and all Biblical feasts were observed. The community members followed strict laws of purity and cleanliness. The most important institutions of the community were the council and the common, sacred meal which was presumably a substitute for the sacrificial meals of the Temple. Only the faultless were allowed to sit at the common table. The sectaries probably immersed themselves in a ritual bath before the meals, which would be first blessed by the priest.

Induction into the sect was conducted in two stages: first, a person entered the covenant by swearing loyalty to the Mosaic laws in accordance with the particular interpretation of the priesthood of the sect, and second, the newcomer undertook a course of training before entering the congregation. The sect was probably celibate, although some bones of woman and children have been found in the cemeteries (de Vaux 1973:47,57-58).

Two branches of this sectarian religious movement, having both similarities and differences, are known (Vermes 1978: 97-109):

1) The desert sectaries in Qumran comprised a voluntary religious community group with common ownership of property living together in seclusion and celibacy, and forming a monastic society. These features are described in the Community Rule and are verified by the archaeological finds at Qumran. The Qumran sect rejected worship in the Jerusalem Temple, but Torah study was an integral part of its life. The Guardian was directly responsible to the council. Only at Qumran did the sect keep a common table and the laws of "purity." Offending sectaries in the Qumran community were excluded from communal life. New members joining Qumran underwent two years of training and studies in the doctrine of the "two spirits."

2) The town sect described in the Damascus Covenant, Messianic Rule and sometimes in the War Rule, had a life style which differed from that of the Qumran community. Members lived as families in close contact with the surrounding Jews and Gentiles, had privately owned property and conducted regular lives. Town sectaries handed their wages over to a charitable fund which distributed help to the needy; they also participated in Temple worship. The Guardian in town was independent of the council. Judges were appointed; offenders were either condemned to death or handed over for corrective custody.

Both branches of the sect had similar religious principles and followed the Zadokite priesthood and Mosaic law according to their own interpretation. Forms of organization and government were similar: both were governed by priests and by the principal *mebaqqer*. Induction into both branches was through entry into the Covenant. Both branches conducted their lives according to their own liturgical calendar which completely differed from the general formal Jewish calendar (Vermes 1978: 176-178; Davies 1982: 83-85). The two branches of town and desert were united in organization and theology, and through regular contact between them. Vermes (1978: 107) proposes that a joint annual Feast of the Covenant took place at Qumran. Furthermore, Vermes maintains that the Qumran Guardian was the highest official for both town and desert camps. The annual festival at Qumran was probably celebrated with the participation of the town sectaries. This assumption is based on archaeological finds, consisting of bone deposits, at Qumran, which represent the remains of meals of large groups, probably connected with the festival. The bones of women and children found in the outer cemetery of Qumran may also point to the participation of the town sectaries in the annual festival. Thus, Qumran was the spiritual and organizational centre of both the desert and town branches of the sect.

D) The Identification of the Qumran sect with the Essenes
(Vermes 1978: 116-186; Schürer, Vermes and Millar 1979, II: 580-585; Yadin
1983:398-399; but see Golb 1980).

The identification of the Qumran community has been the subject of much debate; the most popular opinion identifies the Qumran sect with the Essenes, described by Josephus and others, based on the following assumptions:

1) Many similarities are noted between the Essene sect and the Qumran sect. These similarities include customs, rites, and theology, such as the Calendar, the refusal to participate in the Temple cult, and their own interpretation of the Law.

2) The sect's settlement at Qumran appears to coincide with the location of that of the Essenes, mentioned by Pliny (*NH* V: 17) as being between Jericho and ʿEn-Gedi.

3) The period during which the Essene sect is assumed to have existed is approximately the same as the occupation at Qumran, from the mid-second century BCE to the First War against Rome in 68 CE.

CHAPTER SIX

THE BAR KOKHBA PERIOD (132-135 BCE)

The cause of the Bar Kokhba War (132-135 CE) has been much debated by scholars. It appears that two facts, mentioned by Dio and the Historia Augusta, probably caused the revolt (Schürer, Vermes & Millar 1973, I: 535-542). The first was the founding by Hadrian of a pagan city, Aelia Capitolina, on the ruins of Jerusalem, and his intention to erect a temple to Jupiter Capitolinus on the site of the destroyed Temple. The second was the ban against circumcision, which, although not primarily directed against the Jews, deeply offended them. These two causes, particularly the first, meant the end to any hopes of a reconstruction of the city of Jerusalem or the rebuilding of the Temple, and probably created enough of a reaction among the Jewish populace which would lead to a general revolt.

The discoveries in the Judean desert (Murabbaʿat, Naḥal Ḥever and Naḥal Ze'elim, as well as other excavations) have extended our knowledge about this war. According to the documents of the Judean desert, the leader of the war was Shimeon Bar Koziba, renamed Bar Kokhba—Son of the Star—by Rabbi Akiba, probably in connection with Messianic connotations. His enemies called him Bar Koziba—son of the Lie, or Deceiver (Schürer, Vermes & Millar 1973, I: 543-544). On coins he is termed "Shimeon, prince of Israel" (Meshorer 1982, II: 136).

The war spread quickly throughout the Land of Israel and beyond its borders. Several strongholds at Bethar, Herodium, ʿArabia, ʿEn-Gedi and Gofna were held by the Jews with an administrative centre probably at ʿEn-Gedi. The revolt was suppressed by Tineius Rufus, the governor of Judea, but only with the help of large numbers of reinforcement troops. Later, Julius Severus, a general of Hadrian, directed the hunt to track down rebels who were still hiding in caves and subterranean hideouts.

Ironically, the war probably never reached Jerusalem (Schürer, Vermes & Millar 1973, I: 550). Bar Kokhba's last stronghold was Bethar where a lengthy and major battle was fought, which resulted in the fall of the stronghold in 135 CE.

By the end of the war most of Judea had been destroyed, and in Jerusalem stood the Roman city of Aelia Capitolina with its temple of Jupiter. No Jews were allowed to enter the city and those remaining in Judea scattered, resettling in other areas, particularly in the Galilee.

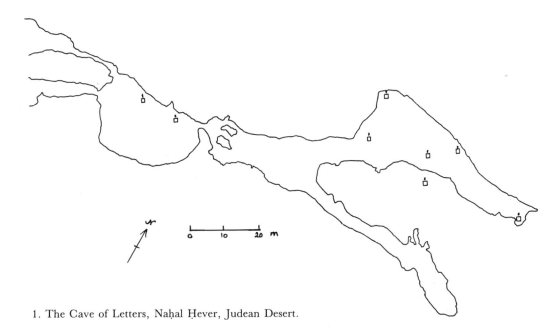

1. The Cave of Letters, Naḥal Ḥever, Judean Desert.

Information on the Bar Kokhba War is obtained from: 1) documents; excavations of 2) caves and 3) subterranean hideouts; and 4) coins.

1) The Bar Kokhba documents (Benoit, Milik & de Vaux 1961; Yadin 1971; Vermes 1978: 14-19 and bibl. p. 26; Schürer, Vermes & Millar 1973, I: 546-547) were found in the Judean desert caves of Murabbaᶜat and Naḥal Ḥever. They are written in four languages, Hebrew, Aramaic, Greek and Nabatean in a formal and cursive script. The documents include legal contracts, deeds and secular manuscripts. The Murabbaᶜat and Naḥal Ḥever caves yielded a most important group of letters connected with Shimeon ben Kosiba (= Bar Kokhba). Other manuscripts from this site include old documents, legal texts and Latin papyri, dated to the second century CE. A most important group of manuscripts was found in the Naḥal Ḥever Cave of Letters by Israeli archaeological expeditions to the Judean desert (fig. 1). Aramaic, Hebrew and Greek documents from the Bar Kokhba period were found in the Cave of Letters (Yadin 1971). They consist of the Simeon Bar Kokhba letters, several parchment fragments of Biblical manuscripts, and an interesting archive of 35 legal documents in Aramaic, Nabatean and Greek, which belonged to Babata, a Jewish woman, and her family. The texts are dated from 93 to 132 CE. This ar-

chive contains Babata's property deeds and tax returns as well as her marriage con-
tract. The Bar Kokhba papyri manuscripts have important historical value as they
are the only source which deals with several aspects of the Second Jewish War. The
letters were written by Shimeon ben (bar) Koziba, later named Bar Kokhba, to his
commanders in their Judean desert strongholds. These strongholds included ʿEn-
Gedi, Herodium and Tekoʿa. The letters also provide a picture of the revolutionary
government at about 132 CE. The land was divided into districts commanded by
military governors and the civil communities were governed by officials who
cooperated with each other. The texts also attest to the fact that all the Jewish
religious customs were strictly kept.

2) Caves in the Judean desert were used as places of refuge from the Roman
enemy; and excavations in the caves reveal evidence of the times both preceding and
during the Second War. Apart from documents, artefacts such as pottery and glass
vessels, bronze objects and pieces of cloth and leather were found in the caves
(Avigad *et al.* 1961; 1962; Yadin 1963). The main occupation in these caves seems
to have been during the Second Jewish War against the Romans, the Bar Kokhba
War (132-135 CE). This is confirmed both by archaeological finds such as coins, and
also by the contents of the manuscripts.

3) Subterranean hiding places (Kloner 1983a) were used by the fighters when the Bar
Kokhba revolt spread. In the Judean foothills about 150 cave-complexes have been
discovered at seventy sites. These were series of caves hewn into the limestone and
connected by tunnel-like passages. Each complex had its own individual water
source. Similar hiding places have also been discovered in the Hebron mountains
and at Herodium. Several characteristic features indicate that the cave-complexes
were places of hiding and refuge:
   a) The entrances are small, low and intentionally concealed, and could be closed
and defended from the inside.
   b) Tunnel-like passages, referred to as "burrows," are a characteristic feature of
such complexes. These burrows, hewn low and narrow so that passage was possible
only by crawling on all fours, connected the various rooms of the complexes. Some
passages served for storage purposes, as water reservoirs, for ventilation or as means
of escape. They could be completely or partly sealed off.
   Some subterranean complexes had several levels joined by vertical shafts which
could be blocked for defensive purposes. In many of the rooms and burrows, lamp
niches are hewn at various levels into the walls. Two types of cave-complexes have
been classified: 1) Small groups for families; and 2) large public complexes. Each

of the small caves had an entrance, burrow and several small rooms, several of them hewn beneath the living quarters. A cave could hold from 20 to 40 people, probably several families. The public complexes were much larger including halls and long passages.

Dating of the Complexes

The complexes post-date the Hellenistic and early Roman periods. This is based on the fact that some of the caves cut into older installations dated to the third-first centuries BCE. Bar Kokhba coins have been found in several excavations and many of the coins reaching the present-day market probably come from these complexes. Pottery discovered in the subterranean hiding places is dated to the first and second centuries CE, in the period following the destruction of the Second Temple. Dating, literary sources and the fact that the Judean foothills were under the control of Bar Kokhba, indicate advance planning and construction of the subterranean hiding places. This is also attested to by a similarity in plan, method and technique, and by the defence installations found in the complexes. This dating of the construction of the complexes to a time earlier than 132 CE indicates that they served as temporary hiding places (and not as permanent dwellings) where weapons and provisions could be stored in preparation for the revolt.

4) Bar Kokhba Coins (Meshorer 1982, II: 132-150) were not minted in Jerusalem; Jerusalem was never conquered by Bar Kokhba and no coins of the period have been found there (Schürer, Vermes & Millar 1973: 500; Meshorer 1982, II: 134). Instead existing Greek and Roman coins were overstruck with Jewish symbols and political, religious and national inscriptions. Meshorer (1982, II: 159) suggests that the Bar Kokhba coinage was minted in several places: in ʿEn-Gedi, the administrative centre, or in any of the other Jewish cities. It is also possible that the mint master followed Bar Kokhba, minting coins wherever and whenever necessary. Designs depicted on the coins were meant as propaganda and were connected with the Temple and other Jewish emblems. They include the Temple facade (fig. I, 7c), the bunch of the four species, (lulav (palm branch), ethrog (citron), willow and myrtle), several Temple vessels such as the amphora and jug, and musical instruments such as the two trumpets and the harp (*nevel*). Also depicted are clusters of grapes and leaf, palm tree and branch. These designs evoked a hope for the restoration of the Temple in Jerusalem and the redemption of Israel. The Temple facade was not an illustration of the actual facade but rather was a symbolic design of the concept of the Temple (suggested by Meshorer (1982, II: 140)). The four species on the coins probably symbolized the hope of rebuilding the Jerusalem Temple at the same time as defying Roman laws forbidding their use (Meshorer 1982, II: 141).

Art of the Bar Kokhba period

Art, obviously, did not flourish during this period. Finds connected with the concealment in the Judean desert caves, however, include clothing, glass, vessels taken from a Roman camp and other artefacts (Avigad *et al.* 1961; 1962; Yadin 1963). A group of lamps from the Hebron area attest also to the art of the period (Sussman 1982). They are dated from the time after the Temple destruction until the Bar Kokhba revolt. The designs depicted on these lamps represent fruit and floral patterns, the four species, vessels, baskets and various other artefacts. Sussman observes connections between the lamp design and ornamentation, and ossuary decoration. This may very well have been the case as they were part of a popular art repertoire, and may have been produced by the same artists. These designs are similar to coin emblems so that a common source of inspiration seems credible.

PART TWO

JEWISH ART AND ARCHAEOLOGY IN LATE ANTIQUITY

Part II is devoted to an analysis of the art and archaeology of a structure which represents a new concept in Jewish life: the synagogue. Its development in Late Antiquity is followed, beginning in the late second century and continuing until the seventh century. Till recently, its environment has been much less investigated than the synagogue itself.

The architecture and art of the synagogue is comprehensively defined. Specific symbolic and iconographic themes are delineated; taken together with distinctive features which are revealed, they show the presence of an ancient Jewish art.

Table 2 shows only those synagogues excavated or surveyed of which remains of the structure have survived. It is unfortunate that of all those synagogues excavated in the last decades very few have been published in more than a preliminary report.

CHAPTER SEVEN

THE SYNAGOGUE

A) The Location of the Synagogue

Beth Ha-Knesseth in Hebrew and *syn-agogue* in Greek both mean "House of Assembly." The synagogue institution was a revolutionary concept in terms of worship and faith: first, as a place of worship, not only for the privileged few, that is the priests, but rather for a large, participating community; second, as a place which contained inside it a central place of worship in a prominent position; and third, as an assembly house used for communal as well as for religious occasions.

Synagogue buildings were generally erected on a high place in a city or village, in the centre of town or near a water source. Local topographic conditions, however, were also taken into consideration in their construction. Both the spiritual and social concepts of these places of worship dictated the external design as well as the interior plan (figs. 1, 2).

A central hall, occasionally with structures attached to it, composed the main building. The most prominent interior synagogue feature was the Torah shrine (p. 166ff.); worship was always facing Jerusalem.

Archaeological remains of synagogues provide information about various areas of Jewish life which are otherwise sparsely documented: these areas include the importance of symbolic, decorative and representational art for local Jewish life.

The great concentration of synagogue remains in the Galilee can be dated from the end of the second century to the third and fourth centuries, which testifies to the area having been the centre of Jewish life at that time. Simultaneously, however, synagogues began to be built in Judea and elsewhere.

B) The Origin and History of the Synagogue

The origin of the synagogue is still disputed (see Gutmann 1975; 1981). As early as the mid-third century BCE, inscriptions mention Egyptian synagogues; Jews in the first century CE believed the synagogue to be a very ancient institution dating back to the time of Moses; Talmudic tradition mentions the fact that there were synagogues during the Babylonian exile.

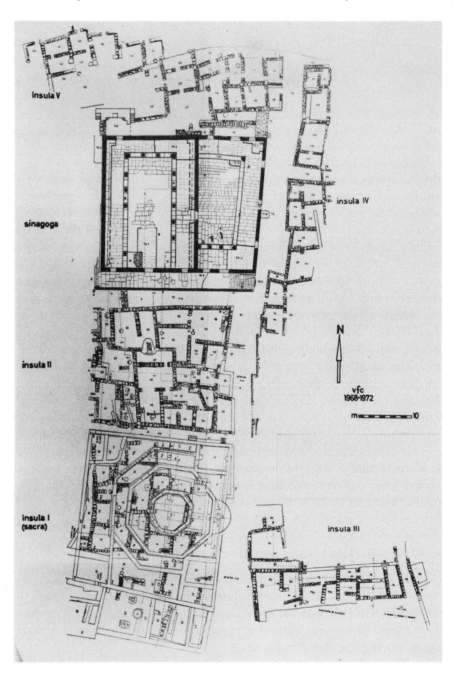

1. Capernaum, Plan of Buildings and Synagogue.

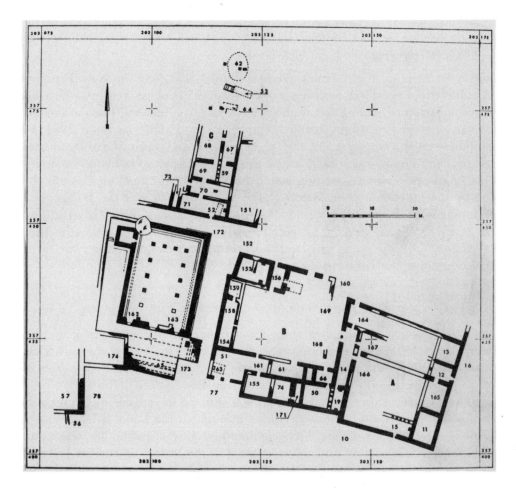

2. Chorazin, Buildings and Synagogue.

Some scholars assume that the synagogue was established by Diaspora Jews (Avi-Yonah 1961a: 155-156). However, synagogues existed both in the Diaspora and the Land of Israel during the late Second Temple period. The Theodotus inscription from Mount Ophel records a synagogue in Jerusalem. This first century Greek inscription (Frey 1952: no. 1404) records the dedication of a synagogue for the use of pilgrims from abroad:

Theodotus the son of Vettenus, priest and archisynagogus, son of the archisynagogus and grandson of an archisynagogus built the synagogue for the reading of the Torah and the study of the Commandments, and the hostel, chambers and water installation to provide for the needs of itinerants from abroad, and whose father, with the elders and Simonides founded the synagogue.

Literary sources, such as Josephus (*Against Apion* 2, 175) and the New Testament (*Acts* 15:21), also attest to the existence of synagogues in the first century which were centres of Scripture reading and studies. Archaeological finds indicate the existence of synagogue-type structures in the first century (see pp. 84-88). Gutmann (1981: 3-4) maintains that the emergence of the synagogue was the result of the Hasmonean revolution in second century BCE Judea, when the synagogue, an institution unique to the Pharisees, became a meeting place where prayers and ceremonies were practiced by the individual Jews. Safrai (1976: 912-913, 918) sees the synagogue as developing from the public Torah reading assemblies at the time of Ezra (fifth century BCE). Originally devoted to special rituals on feast days and Sabbaths (in the first century CE), the synagogue later developed into a daily meeting place for the local community for Torah reading and prayer.

C) The Function of the Synagogue compared to the Jerusalem Temple

1) The Temple was the only centre for national activity which took the form principally of an animal sacrifice ritual. By contrast, the synagogue was a centre solely for the local community. Worship in the Second Temple synagogues was probably conducted only on feast-days and Sabbaths. (Safrai 1976: 918).

2) The Temple, according to tradition, was situated in Jerusalem. On the other hand, synagogues could be built anywhere throughout the Land of Israel and the Diaspora. Thus the synagogue, by becoming the centre of public life, was a most revolutionary development and a new concept in the history of ancient Judaism.

3) A small group of priests practiced in the Temple, and entry into the Holy of Holies was allowed only to the High Priest himself. The ordinary worshippers who came to the Temple were relegated to the outer courtyards of the Temple precincts. In the synagogue, by comparison, all the participants were involved in and conducted the ceremonies. Worshippers took turns in reciting prayers and reading the Scriptures.

4) Scripture reading was not an essential part of the Temple service and was introduced only during the Second Temple period. Furthermore, Scripture reading was not a substitute for Temple sacrifices or liturgy: it simply supplemented Temple worship (Safrai 1976: 912). Prayer and study in the local synagogue replaced sacrifice in the national Temple as the means of serving God. Synagogue services took place at regular times, on the Sabbath, feast days and special occasions (as did

offerings in the Temple). Later, the plan of the synagogue building, with its Torah shrine housing the Ark of the Scrolls in a prominent position, attests to the fact that the congregation came to pray and read Scripture; Jewish synagogal and funerary art which bear representations symbolizing the Temple testify to a continuation of Temple customs.

D) THE SYNAGOGUE AND THE COMMUNITY

1) The Variety of Synagogal Activities

a) Reading the Torah, the Scriptures, was the primary purpose for the synagogue's congregation who participated both in reading and in attending to other readers.

b) Study: Local sages conducted the reading, study and interpretation of the Scriptures in the synagogues. Often, scholars would be employed by the synagogue fathers.

c) Prayer: In the Second Temple period, prayer took the form of blessing the congregation. Regular prayer services were held on the Sabbaths and the feast days. Daily prayers involving a large number of worshippers were established only after the destruction of the Second Temple (Safrai 1976: 922-927).

d) The assembly hall and town hall for the local Jewish congregation, served as a centre for community fund-raising, charitable collections, congregational affairs, and as a type of court of public interests (Safrai 1976: 942).

e) Institutions adjoined the synagogue, and included schools and, in annexes, hostels, guest houses and residences for synagogue officials. Sometimes ritual baths (*miqvaoth*) were also built on.

f) The synagogue or an adjoining room would serve on occasions of the New Moon or the Sabbath (Saturday) evening as a dining room (Safrai 1976: 943).

2) Administration of the synagogue (Safrai 1976: 933 ff; Schürer, Vermes and Millar 1979,II: 427-439).

The synagogue generally belonged to a local community and was governed by three representatives: 1) the archisynagogus (*Rosh Ha-Knesset*), the president, 2) the receiver of alms, who was a civic official, and 3) the minister (*Hazzan*). The archisynagogus managed religious and financial affairs and the *hazzan* was the executive officer in charge of the practical details of running the synagogue. He was the master of ceremonies, and a paid employee (Safrai 1976: 935-937).

Construction of a synagogue would be decided upon by the heads of the community and would be financed by private and public donations. This is known by the numerous dedicatory synagogal inscriptions found in excavations. The donors who paid for the erection, repair and rebuilding of synagogues were usually Jews. Inscriptions generally mention the name of the donor and his donation, which was usually in the form of money. Most of the inscriptions are in Aramaic; thus, Avi-Yonah deduces (1961b: 32) that the donors did not belong to the Hellenized classes.

CHAPTER EIGHT

SYNAGOGUE ARCHITECTURE AND DECORATION

The synagogue building functioned as an assembly hall for the local congregation as well as a spiritual, religious and social centre. Its use as a community assembly centre determined its architectural plan which took the form of a large hall divided by supporting columns, and with benches around it.

The many different architectural styles uncovered verify that no universal or uniform synagogue plan existed. Opinions vary considerably as to the evolution of synagogue architecture. Several attempts have been made to categorize and explain the different types and the divergence in style of the synagogues scattered throughout many regions. Avi-Yonah (1961a: 1973:32-33) divides synagogue plans into three chronological types: 1) the earliest Galilean and Golan type dating from the second century onwards, and with an ornamental facade and a portable wooden construction serving as the Torah shrine; 2) the transitional type from the fourth and fifth centuries, sometimes called ''broad-house.'' In this type three new principles appear: a) a fixed shrine in the Jerusalem-oriented wall, b) entrances in the opposite wall, c) changes in the style of ornament from relief to mosaic. And 3) the later type of the fifth to eighth centuries with a basilical plan and mosaic pavements. Meyers (1980: 97-108) attempts a different classification of synagogue development according to its plan: 1) the earliest, the basilica, the so-called ''Galilean'' type; 2) the transitional type (the broadhouse); and 3) the latest, apsidal synagogue. Another method employed for classification of synagogue architectural development has been the creation of regional divisions (as suggested by Meyers *et al.* 1976: 99; Kloner 1981: 15-18) (see map 2).

Excavations of synagogues in the last decade have challenged the above assumptions concerning typology and chronology (see pp. 396-400) to such an extent that such assumptions can no longer serve as guides for the clarification of synagogue architectural development. Although the regional theory remains useful, and this study points out characteristics shared by synagogues in the same region irrespective of chronological distinction, an attempt will be made in this work to establish essential characteristics typical to the architecture of the majority of synagogues, regardless of geographical location. Divergencies among the types of synagogue buildings will be shown to be due to the social standing of the donors, the financial means of the

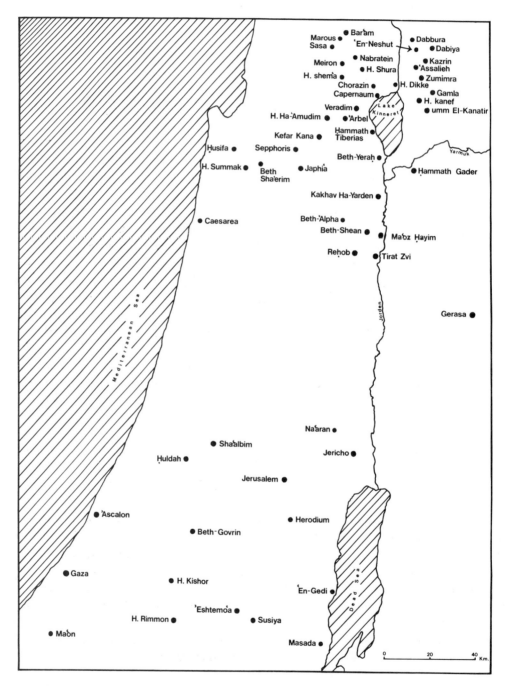

Map 2. Ancient synagogue sites in the Land of Israel.

congregation and to the local construction traditions and practices of the craftsmen and masons involved in the construction.

A) CHARACTERISTIC FEATURES OF SYNAGOGUE ARCHITECTURE

Generally the internal plan of the synagogue building consists of two rows of stone columns which divide the main hall lengthwise into a central nave and two side aisles. The majority of synagogue plans are oblong and all have longitudinal axes. Apart from these general characteristics, synagogues in the Land of Israel exhibit several other common features, the most prominent of which are the facade and its portals, the Torah shrine, and the gallery.

1) The Facade

An analysis of the synagogue facade can best be undertaken by a separation of its various components: both triple and single portal, the Syrian gable surmounting the facade, and the central arched window.

a) The Triple Portal

One of the most characteristic features of the ancient synagogue is the facade with its triple entrance built in one of the short sides of the structure. This entrance consists of a high central doorway with a lower one on each side (see table 2a), and is common in the Galilean synagogues, the Barᶜam synagogue facade being a well-preserved example (Pl 21) and see also Meiron, Pl 22). Remains of entryway thresholds and doorposts have been preserved in most of the other synagogues (figs. 1-4).

The main differences between the (triple) facades of the various synagogues are:

1) Orientation. Characteristic of the Galilean synagogues is the location of both the facade and the Torah shrine on the same Jerusalem-oriented southern wall (see p. 167ff.). In other well-preserved synagogues, particularly those of the fifth and sixth centuries, the facade is usually in the wall facing the Torah shrine. Exceptions are the synagogues of Susiya, ᵓEshtemoᶜa and ᶜEn-Gedi which all have triple facades on the eastern or western side wall not facing the niches (fig. 3).

2) Ornamentation. The facades of the Galilean and Golan synagogues are richly ornamented, by comparison with the plain facades of all other synagogues.

The orientation of the facade is secondary in importance to that of the Torah shrine, which is always built on the Jerusalem-oriented wall (see pp. 196-199).

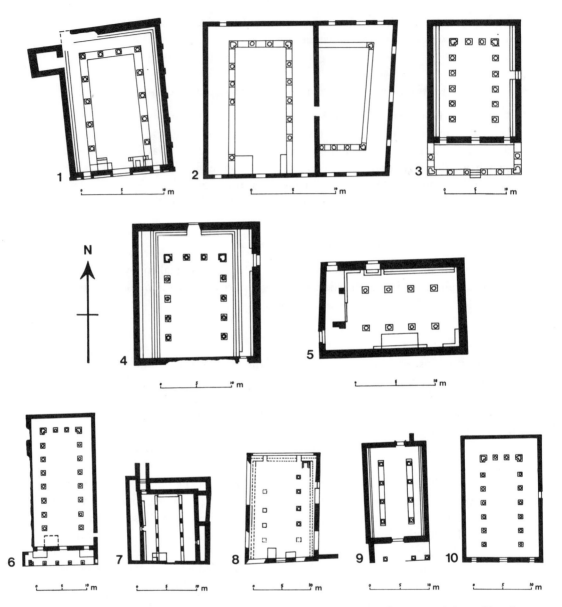

1. Plans of Galilean Synagogues: 1) Chorazin; 2) Capernaum; 3) Bar‘am; 4) Arbel; 5) Shem‘a; 6) Meiron; 7) Hush Ḥalav; 8) Marous; 9) Nabratein; 10) ‘Ammudim.

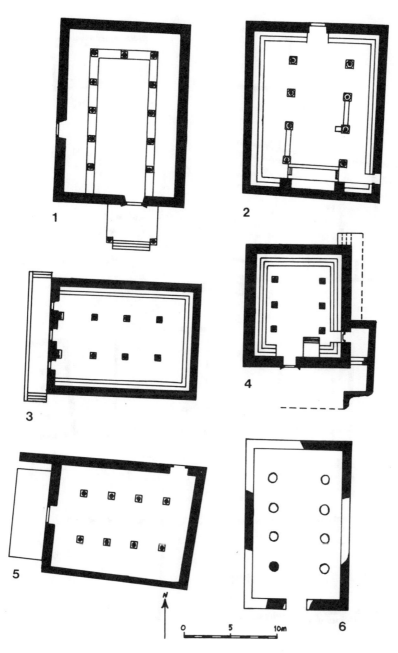

2. Plans of Golan Synagogues: 1) Umm el-Kanatir; 2) Kazrin; 3) Dikke;
4) ʿEn Neshut; 5) Kanef; 6) ʿAssalieh.

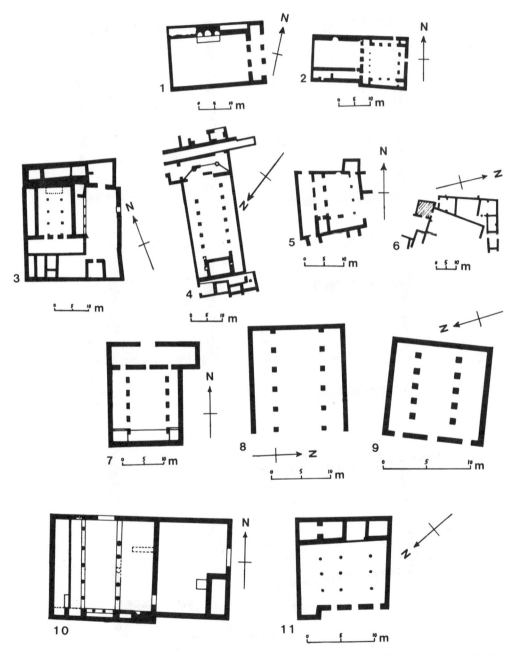

3. Plans of Synagogues with Niches: 1) ʾEshtemoᶜa; 2) Susiya; 3) Rimmon; 4) Beth Sheᶜarim; 5) ᶜEn-Gedi; 6) Beth Sheʾan B; 7) Reḥov; 8) Japhiᶜa; 9) Ḥuseifa; 10) Ḥammath Tiberias A; 11) Ḥammath Tiberias B.

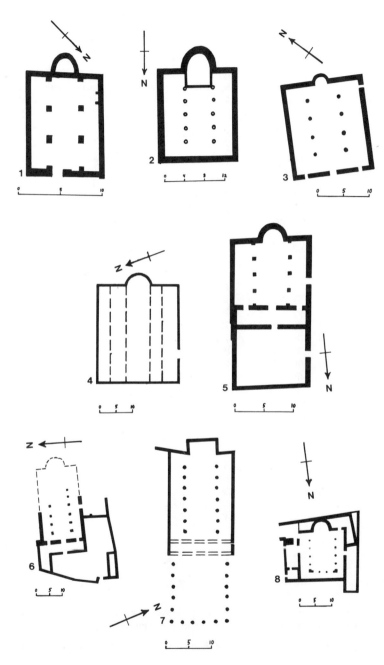

4. Plans of Synagogues with Apses: 1) Jericho; 2) Maᶜoz Ḥayim; 3) Maᶜon; 4) Gaza; 5) Beth ʾAlpha; 6) Naᶜaran; 7) Gerasa; 8) Ḥammath Gader.

Table 2: Ia: The Synagogues in the Land of Israel

Name of Synagogue		Date in centuries (CE)	Dimensions in Metres	Orientation towards Jerusalem		Court-yard	Exterior Facade Narthex Portico	Entrances triple single
				F	T			S
1. ʾArbel		3rd - 4th	18.2 x 18.6		+			+ E
2. ʿAmudim		3rd - 4th	14.1 x 22.5	+	+ (?)			+
3. Barʿam		3rd	15.2 x 20.0	+			+	+
4. Capernaum	I	1st	18.5 x 24.2					
	II	4th - 5th	18.6 x 20.4	+	+	+	+	+
5. Chorazin	I	3rd - 4th	16.7 x 22.8	+	+			+
	II	4th - 5th	16.7 x 22.8	+	+		+	+
6. Gush Ḥalav	I	250-362	10.6 x 13.7	+	+		+	
	II	362-551	10.6 x 13.7					+
7. Meiron		280-360	13.6 x 27.4	+	+		+	+
8. Nabratein	I	135-250	11.2 x 9.4	+	+			+
	IIa	250-306	11.2 x 13.8	+	+			+
	IIb	306-350/363	11.2 x 13.8				+	+
	III	564-700	11.2 x 16.8	+			+	+
9. Marous	I	4th - 6th	17.0 x 18.7	+	+		+	+
	II	5th - 6th	17.0 x 18.7	+	+		+	+
	III	6th - 9th	17.8 x 19.3	+	+			
10. Shemʿa	I	284-306	18.0 x 9.0		+			+ N
	II	306-419	18.0 x 9.0		+			+ N
11. Shura		5th - 7th	14.5 x 17.0	+				+ ?
12. ʿAssalieh		5th - 6th	16.0 x 18.0	+				+
13. Dabiya		5th	13.2 x 15.1	+				+
14. Dikke		5th	10.4 x 13.8				+	+ W
15. Dir ʿAziz		5th	10.7 x 17.9					+ W
16. ʿEn Neshut		5th - 6th	11.3 x 12.5	+	+			+
17. Kanef		5th	13.3 x 15.0					
18. Kazrin	I	4th - 5th	15.3 x 15.2		+			+ N
	II	6th	15.0 x 17.2		+			+
	III	7th - 8th	15.0 x 17.2		+			+
19. Umm el-Kanatir		Late 5th-6th	13.3 x 18.8	+			+	+
20. Zumimra		5th - 6th	14.4 x 18.9					
21. Ḥammath Gader	I	3rd						
	II	4th	13.0 x 13.9		+		+	+ E
	III	5th - 6th	13.0 x 13.9		+		+	+ E
22. Hammath-Tiberias A		4th - 5th	12.0 x 12.0		+	+		+

Synagogues: 1-11 are Galilean synagogues; 12-20 are Golan synagogues; 21-42 are synagogues listed geographically from north to south; 43 is situated in Transjordan

Abbreviations: *Orientation*: F = Facade; T = Torah shrine; *N, S, E, W* mean that entrances face these directions

Table 2: Ib: The Synagogues in the Land of Israel

Name of Synagogue		Date in centuries (CE)	Dimensions in Metres	Orientation towards Jerusalem		Court-yard	Exterior Facade Narthex Portico	Entrances	
				F	T			triple	single
23. Ḥammath Tiberias B									
	I (II B)	3rd	13.0 x 15.0	+			+		+
	II (II A)	4th	13.0 x 15.0		+		+	+	
	III(I a,b)	6th - 8th	24.0 x 31.0		+		+	+	
24. Beth Yeraḥ		4th - 5th	22.0 x 37.0		+				
25. Ḥuseifa		4th - 5th	? x 10.1					+	
26. Japhiᶜa		4th - 5th	15.0 x 19.0						
27. Summaqa		3rd -4th	14.0 x 19.3					+	
28. Beth Sheᶜarim	I	3rd	15.0 x 35.0	+				+	
	II	4th	15.0 x 35.0		+	+			
29. Beth ʾAlpha		6th	10.8 x 12.4		+	+		+	
30. Beth Sheʾan A		5th - 7th	17.0 x 14.2		+	+		+	
31. Beth Sheʾan B		6th	7.0 x 7.0		+				+
32. Maᶜoz Ḥayim	I(a)	3rd - 4th	12.5 x 14.0		+				+
	II(b)	5th	12.0 x 14.5		+	+			
	III(c)	6th - 7th	12.0 x 14.5		+	+			
33. Reḥov	I	early 4th	17.0 x 19.0		+			+	
	II	late 4th-5th	17.0 x 19.0		+			+	
	III	6th - 7th	17.0 x 19.0		+		+	+	
34. Caesarea	I	3rd	?						
	II	5th	?				+		+
35. ʾEshtemoᶜa		4th - 6th	20.0 x 10.0		+		+	+	
36. Susiya	I	end 4th-5th	15.0 x 19.0		+	+	+	+	
	II	6th - 8th	15.0 x 19.0		+	+	+	+	
37. Rimmon	I	mid 3rd	?		+				
	II	4th - 6th	?						
	III	6th - 7th	9.5 x 13.5		+	+	+	+	
38. Maᶜon		6th	15.0 x 17.0		+	+		+	
39. Gaza		early 6th-7th	26.0 x 30.0		+		+		
40. Jericho		late 6th - 7th	10.0 x 13.0		+				+
41. Naᶜaran		6th	15.0 x 22.0		+			+	
42. ᶜEn-Gedi	I	3rd	10.0 x 15.5	+				+	
	II	4th - 5th	10.0 x 15.5		+				
	III	6th	10.0 x 15.5		+	+	+	+	
43. Gerasa		5th - 6th	14.0 x 28.0					+	

Table 2: IIa: The Synagogues in the Land of Israel

		Exterior						Interior — Torah Shrine				
Name of Synagogue		Carved Pilasters	Arched Window	Syrian Gable	Side Entrance	Windows	Outside Stairs	Aedicula	Niche	Apse	Bema	Fragments
1. ʾArbel					+				+			
2. ʿAmudim			+		+			+ ?				
3. Barʿam			+	+	+	+						
4. Capernaum	I			+	+	+	+	+ 2				
	II	+	+									
5. Chorazin	I	+	+	+	+	+		+ 2				+
	II				+							
6. Gush Ḥalav	I				+		+	+				
	II				+		+	+				
7. Meiron					+							
8. Nabratein	I				+			+ 2				+
	IIa				+			+ 2				
	IIb				+			+ 2				
	III				+							
9. Marous	I–III		+		+			+ 2				+
10. Shemʿa	I				+			+				
	II							+				+
11. Shura					+	+	+	+				
12. ʿAssalieh		+			+	+						
13. Dabiya			+		+							+
14. Dikke					+	+						
15. Dir ʿAziz					+							
16. ʿEn Neshut					+	+	+ (?)	+				+
17. Kanef					+							+
18. Kazrin	I		+		+	+	+	+				+
	II		+		+	+	+	+				+
	III				+	+	+					+
19. Umm el-Kanatir			+									+
20. Zumimra		+	+ ?									
21. Hammath Gader	I										+	
	II				+					+		
22. Hammath-Tiberias A	III				+				+			

Table 2: IIb: The Synagogues in the Land of Israel

Name of Synagogue	Exterior						Interior — Torah Shrine				
	Carved Pilasters	Arched Window	Syrian Gable	Side Entrance	Windows	Outside Stairs	Aedicula	Niche	Apse	Bema	Fragments
23. Hammath Tiberias B											
I (II b)				+				+			
II (II b)				+				+			
III(I a,b)				+					+		
24. Beth Yeraḥ											
25. Huseifa											
26. Japhiʿa											+
27. Summaqa											
28. Beth Sheʿarim I				+					+		
II									+	+	
29. Beth ʾAlpha								+			
30. Beth Sheʾan A									+		
31. Beth Sheʾan B									+	+	
32. Maʿoz Hayim I(a)							+				
II(b)								+			
III(c)							+				
33. Reḥov I				+			+				
II				+			+				+
III											+
34. Caesarea I										+	
II										+	
35. ʾEshtemoʿa I							+	+3		+	
36. Susiya I				+				+			
II										+	
37. Ḥ. Rimmon I								+			
II											
III							+				
38. Maʿon				+					+	+	
39. Gaza									+		
40. Jericho									+		
41. Naʿaran											
42. ʿEn-Gedi I											
II								+		+	
III							+				
43. Gerasa									+	+	

Table 2: IIIa: The Synagogues in the Land of Israel

Name of Synagogue		Columns — Rows 2	Columns — Rows 3	Order Dor	Order Ion	Order Cor	Corner Columns	Pedestal	Benches 2	Benches 3	Gallery	Gallery Dor	Gallery Ion	Gallery Cor
1. Arbel			+			+	+			+	+		+	
2. ʿAmudim			+			+		+	+	+	+			
3. Barʿam		+	+		+		+	+	+					
4. Capernaum	I	+				+	+	+	+					
	II	+	+				+	+	+		+			+
5. Chorazin	I	+			+			+	+		+			
	II	+	+					+		+				
6. Gush Halav	I	+			+		+	+	+					
	II	+			+		+	+		+				
7. Meiron		+	+		+		+	+		+	+			
8. Nabratein	I	+		+	+		+	+	+	+	+			
	IIa	+						+	+					
	IIb	+						+	+					
	III	+						+	+					
9. Marous	I–III	+	+		+			+	+	+	+		+(?)	
10. Shemʿa	I	+		+	+			+	+	+				
	II	+		+	+			+	+	+				
11. Shura		+			+			+	+	+				
12. ʿAssalieh		+			+					+	+	+		
13. Dabiya		+		+						+	+			
14. Dikke		+			+				+					+
15. Dir ʿAziz		+			+									
16. ʿEn Neshut		+						+		+	+			+
17. Kanef		+						+		+	+	+		
18. Kazrin	I	+					+	+		+				
	II	+			+		+	+		+	+			
	III	+			+		+				+			
19. Umm el-Kanatir			+								+			
20. Zumimra		+										+		
21. Hammath Gader	I		+								+			
	II		+						+	+	+			
	III		+						+	+	+			
22. Hammath-Tiberias A		+												

colums orders: Dor = Doric; Ion = Ionic; Cor = Corinthian

Table 2: IIIb: The Synagogues in the Land of Israel

Name of Synagogue	Columns Rows 2	Columns Rows 3	Columns Order Dor	Columns Order Ion	Columns Order Cor	Corner Columns	Pedestal	Benches Lining Walls 2	Benches Lining Walls 3	Gallery	Gallery Column Order Dor	Gallery Column Order Ion	Gallery Column Order Cor
23. Hammath Tiberias B													
I (II B)		+											
II (II A)		+											
III(I a,b)		+											
24. Beth Yerah	+												
25. Huseifa	+												
26. Japhiʿa	+							+					
27. Summaqa	+									+			
28. Beth Sheʿarim I	+												
II													
29. Beth Alpha	+									+			
30. Beth Sheʾan A	+			+			+	+		+			
31. Beth Sheʾan B										+			
32. Maʿoz Ḥayim I(a)	+			+									
II(b)	+								+				
III(c)	+												
33. Reḥov I	+					+							
II	+												
III	+												
34. Caesarea I	+							+					
II													
35. ʾEshtemoʿa	+												
36. Susiya I	+												
II													
37. H. Rimmon I	+					+							
II													
III													
38. Maʿon	+									+			
39. Gaza		+ 4											
40. Jericho	+												
41. Naʿaran	+												
42. ʿEn-Gedi I								+		+			
II	+												
III													
43. Gerasa	+												

Table 2: IVa: The Synagogues in the Land of Israel

Name of Synagogue		Archit. Frag.	Ornamentation Floor Pavements				Walls		
			Mosaic	Stone Slabs	Plaster	Fresco	Lime-stone	Basalt	Stone, Concrete
1. ʾArbel		+		+			+		
2. ʿAmudim		+	+	+			+		
3. Barʿam		+		+			+		
4. Capernaum	I			+				+	
	II	+		+			+		
5. Chorazin	I								
	II	+		+				+	
6. Gush Ḥalav	I	+		+			+		
	II	+		+			+		
7. Meiron		+		+			+		
8. Nabratein	I				+		+		
	IIa	+		+			+		
	IIb	+		+			+		
	III	+		+			+		
9. Marous	I-III	+	+	+			+		
10. Shemʿa	I	+	+			+	+		
	II		+						
11. Shura		+		+				+	
12. ʿAssalieh		+						+	
13. Dabiya				+				+	
14. Dikke		+		+				+	
15. Dir ʿAziz								+	
16. ʿEn Neshut		+			+	+		+	
17. Kanef		+						+	
18. Kazrin	I				+			+	
	II	+	+					+	
	III	+			+			+	
19. Umm el-Kanatir		+		+				+	
20. Zumimra		+						+	
21. Ḥammath Gader	I		+						+
	II			+					
	III		+						+
22. Ḥammath-Tiberias A			+	+					+

Table 2: IVb: The Synagogues in the Land of Israel

| Name of Synagogue | Archit. Frag. | Ornamentation Floor Pavements | | | | Walls | | |
		Mosaic	Stone, Slabs	Plaster	Fresco	Lime-stone	Basalt	Stone Concrete
23. Ḥammath Tiberias B								
I (II b)		+						+
II (II b)		+						+
III(I a,b)		+						+
24. Beth Yeraḥ		+						+
25. Ḥuseifa		+			+			+
26. Japhiᶜa		+						+
27. Summaqa			+			+		
28. Beth Sheᶜarim I			+		+			+
II			+		+			+
29. Beth ʾAlpha		+						+
30. Beth Sheʾan A		+						+
31. Beth Sheʾan B		+						+
32. Maᶜoz Ḥayim I(a)			+					
II(b)	+			+				
III(c)		+						+
33. Reḥov I	+	+						+
II		+			+			+
III		+			+			+
34. Caesarea I		+						+
II		+						+
35. ʾEshtemoᶜa		+						+
36. Susiya I		+						+
II		+						+
37. Ḥ. Rimmon I	+			+	+			+
II								
III			+					+
38. Maᶜon		+	+					+
39. Gaza	+	+						+
40. Jericho		+						+
41. Naᶜaran		+						+
42. ᶜEn-Gedi I		+						+
II		+						+
III		+						+
43. Gerasa	+	+						+

Whenever the Torah shrine is built on a different wall than usual, the entrance is aligned on the opposite or side wall. Thus, the location of the Torah shrine determines the orientation of the facade. An example of this is the synagogue at ʾArbel (fig. 1) which probably originally had its entrance on the Jerusalem-oriented wall, like most other Galilean synagogues. Later, changes occurred, and a niche for the Ark was built on this wall, necessitating changes in the location of the entrance.

Although the facade consists of three doorways, this triple entrance does not always lead directly into the nave and aisles. The ʾEshtemoʿa and Susiya synagogues contain no aisles (figs. 3,5,6). At Ḥammath-Gader (fig. 7) the doorways do not correspond to the aisles. It seems, therefore, that the triple-entranced facade had not only a structural function, but also intrinsic significance. Goodenough (1953:183, 265; 1965:41, 84) suggests it is a symbolic front, directed towards Jerusalem, "toward the *shekina* in all three of its symbolic manifestations." Another, more probable, explanation is that the use of the triple entryway represents a recollection of the Nicanor Gate which was the main entrance to the Second Temple of Jerusalem (fig. I,6).

The triple portal is usually compared to examples of Syrian architecture, particularly to the pagan temples (see KW 1916:147-173; Goodenough 1953:183). Similarity between these buildings and synagogues is more one of a general impression than an actual fact. Few of the Syrian pagan temples have triple portals: for example, the temple of Suweda in the Hauran and the Tychaion is-Sanamen (Butler 1903: Pl. 118; 1907,V: fig. 292; Hachlili 1971: Pls. 12:1, 17:1,pp. 168-171) have wider and higher central doorways with two smaller side entrances. Note also that above each side entrance is a niche. Other temples have only one main entrance, sometimes with niches flanking it, as, for example, the temples of Atil, Habran, and Braka (Butler 1903: figs. 121, 123; 1907, VII: Pl. 29). The difference in size between the central and side entryways in the facades of most synagogues is less exaggerated than of those in the pagan temples. A further reason for a general impression of similarity between the triple portal facade of the synagogue (especially the Galilean and Golan examples) and that of the Syrian pagan temple is the close resemblance of the rich ornamentation. Nevertheless, it seems that the real reason for the preference for the triple entrance of the synagogue hall, and its establishment as a characteristic feature was, as mentioned above, the connection with, and reminder of the triple Nicanor Gate, the main entrance into the Second Temple of Jerusalem (see pp. 25-26).

Several of the synagogue facades, such as the Galilean examples of Gush-Ḥalav (see Meyers *et al.* 1979:44), Nabratein and Marous (fig. 1) have only one entrance on the Jerusalem-oriented wall. Ḥurvat Shemʿa has a main portal set into the north

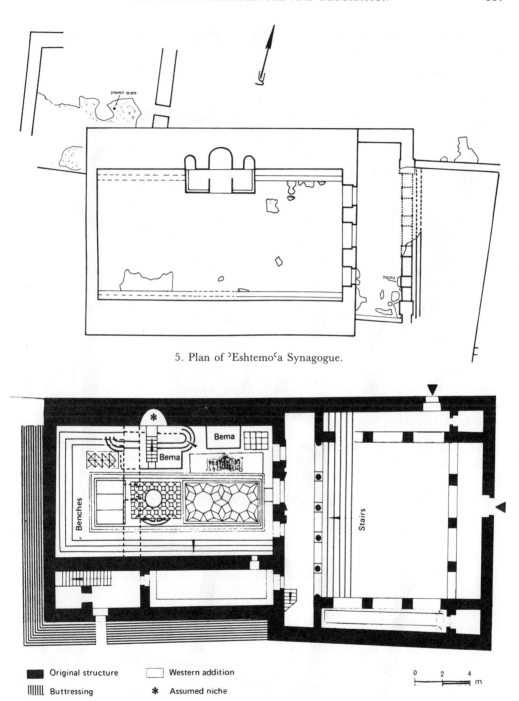

5. Plan of ʾEshtemoʿa Synagogue.

6. Plan of Susiya Synagogue.

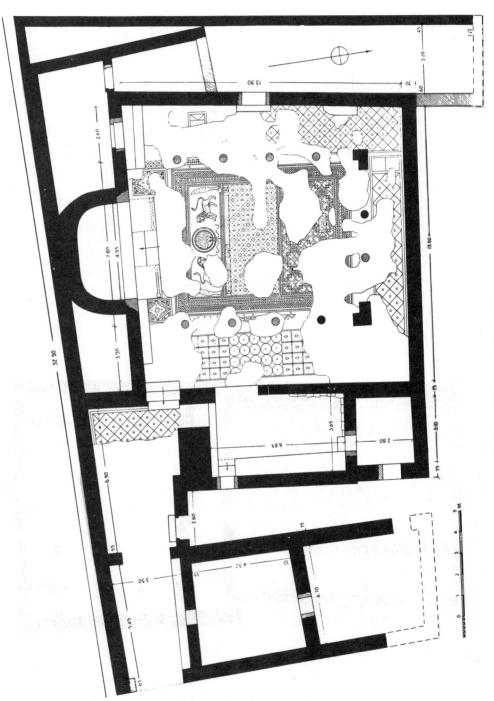

7. Plan of Hammath Gader Synagogue.

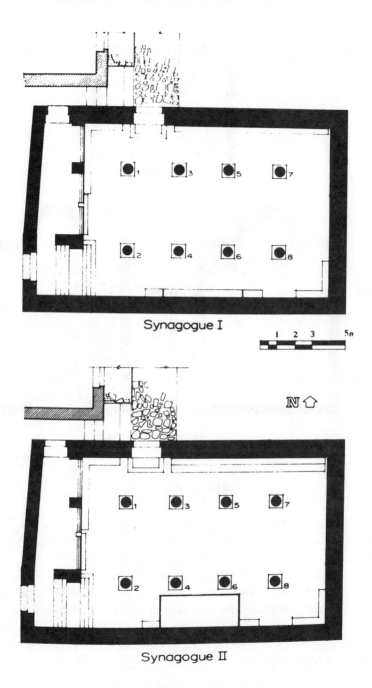

Synagogue I

Synagogue II

8. Plan of H. Shemᶜa Synagogue.

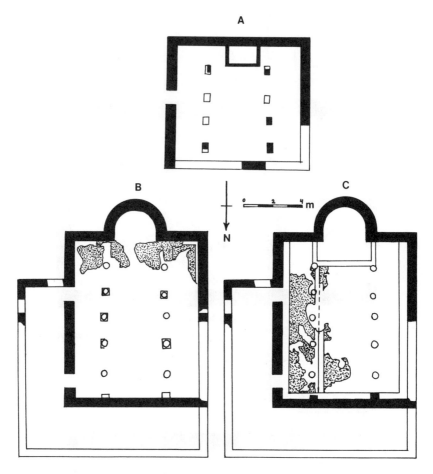

9. Ma'oz Ḥayim Plan, 3 Phases.

wall (fig. 8). Most of the Golan synagogues have only one entrance (fig. 2, table 2): the Dikke synagogue with its triple portal entrance is an exception (fig. 13). Four synagogues (Umm el-Kanatir, ʿEn Neshut, Dabiya and ʿAssalieh, (fig. 2) have their facades on the Jerusalem-oriented wall. Some of these entrances were possibly flanked by windows or niches, in a manner similar to the Syrian pagan temples discussed above. This feature thus preserves the triple rhythm of the facade. Two other synagogues have one main portal: these are the Jericho synagogue and the Ma'oz Ḥayim synagogue, which has one entrance in phase one and probably two entrances in phases two and three (fig. 9).

b) The "Syrian" gable

This type of gable surmounting the facade consists of a pediment with its base curved into an arch, and is an Oriental variation of the classical pediment (see Avi-Yonah 1944: 146-147; also Brown 1942: 389, 391, 399; Hachlili 1971: 88-94). Enough architectural fragments have survived from several Galilean and Golan synagogues to enable the reconstruction of a Syrian gable. Kohl and Watzinger reconstruct several gables on the evidence of sculptured fragment remains: the Barᶜam synagogue is reconstructed with a Syrian gable on the portico, the arch surmounting the two central columns (KW 1916: figs. 186, 191). Another Syrian gable based on ornate sculptured fragments (KW 1916: figs. 89, 107) is reconstructed on the upper part of the facade at Chorazin (KW 1916: fig. 191). This reconstruction has been verified by recent excavations and restoration work (as yet unpublished). At Capernaum, Kohl and Watzinger (1916: Pl. I) postulate that there was a Syrian gable on the facade on the evidence of fragments such as a corner of the gable (KW 1916: fig. 35). In two Golan synagogues, Kohl and Watzinger also reconstruct Syrian gables: Dikke (fig. 13) and Umm el-Kanatir (fig. 14) (KW 1916: fig. 251, 272). Moreover, they suggest that the Syrian gable was constructed along the complete width of the synagogue's facade and they compare it to the basilica at Shabba, el Musmiye, and the Tichayon of is-Sanamen (KW 1916: figs. 285-287).

Some scholars prefer reconstructing a gable along the facade's width for other synagogues, for instance at Beth Sheᶜarim (Yeivin 1942: fig. c, p. 13), Beth ʾAlpha (Sukenik 1932: fig. 19) and Susiya (Gutman *et al.* 1980: 124).

It seems more probable, however, that the gable was built on part of the facade only, that is, a "narrow" gable (see fig. 10). (See Yeivin (1942: fig. a, p. 75) who reconstructs a narrow gable for the Beth Sheᶜarim synagogue, like the gables on most of the Syrian Christian churches (Baccache 1979: figs. 14, 48, 100, 184, 201, 217, 255, 285, 300, 323, 338, 376, 402; 1980: 255-260, 450, 463).) Syrian gables are also found in Nabatean and Roman structures in Syria dating from the first century BCE until the third century CE. Examples include the facade of the temple of Dushara at Si (Butler 1907: figs. 332, 335), the west facade of the temple of Bel, the city gate of Baalbek, the eastern facade of the Heliopolis temple (Wiegand 1921: Pls. 4, 27), the facade of the adyton in the Bacchus temple of Baalbek and the round temple of Baalbek (Wiegand 1921: Pls. 14 and 62).

Taking into account the surviving sculptural fragments, it seems possible to theorise that a few of the Galilean and Golan synagogues did have narrow Syrian gables over their facades (fig. 10).

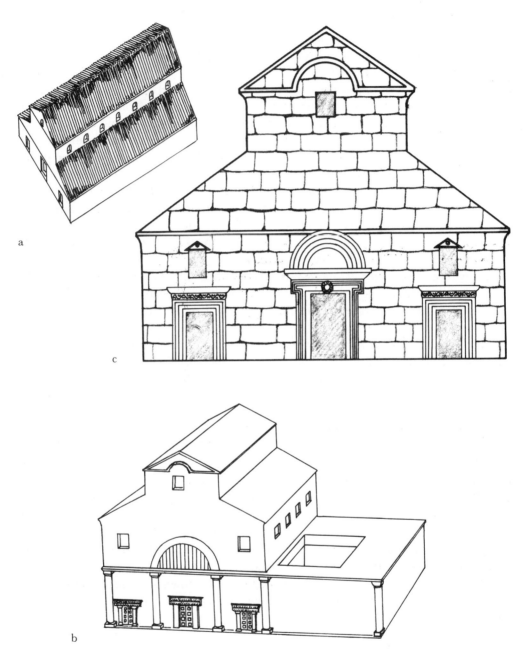

10. Reconstruction of Synagogue Buildings with "Syrian" Gable: a) General reconstruction; b) Capernaum — new reconstruction; c) Barʿam — new reconstruction.

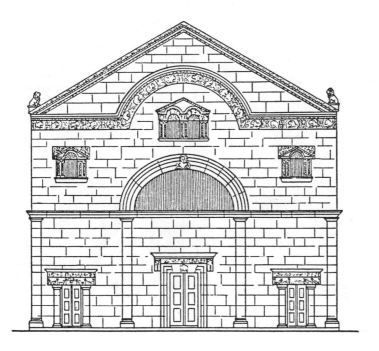

11. Reconstruction of Capernaum synagogue.

12. Reconstruction of H. ʿAmmudim. Synagogue Facade.

13. Reconstruction of Dikke Synagogue.

14. Reconstruction of Umm el-Kanatir Synagogue.

c) Arched Windows

At least ten of the Golan and Galilean synagogues have a large, semi-circular window above a central portal lintel, surmounted by a richly ornamented and sculptured arch, and probably with a metal grille filling the space. This arched window provided an important source of light for the synagogue interior. Many of the Galilean synagogues retain fragments of this arch, and at Barᶜam it is still in place (Pl 21). Fragments of this arch were found at Capernaum (KW 1916: Pl. I and abb.25), Chorazin (KW 1916: figs. 84, 104), and KW propose an arched window for H. ᶜAmmudim (fig. 12) and Gush Ḥalav (KW 1916: figs 205). Golan synagogues with fragments of this arch include Kazrin (fig. 15); here a fragment of a decorated arch was found and holes for a grille are preserved in the upper part of the lintel, Umm el-Kanatir (fig. 14) and Dikke (fig. 13). ᶜAssalieh probably also had such an arched window on the facade. This is an innovative feature of synagogue architecture which seldom appears in other buildings (cf. for instance, the facade of the fifth century Syrian church of Qalat Kalota (Baccache 1979: fig. 217).

 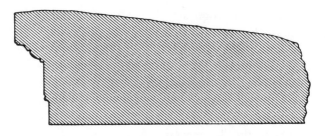

15. Architectural Fragment, Kazrin Synagogue.

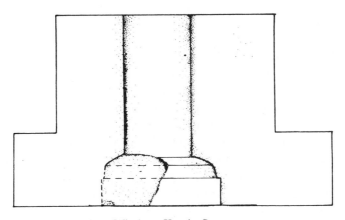

16. A Window, Kazrin Synagogue.

d) Windows

Stone fragments in several of the Galilean and Golan synagogues indicate the presence of windows.

In situ windows are found in the facade of the synagogue at Barᶜam (Pl. 21). Based on this, Kohl and Watzinger reconstruct elaborately decorated windows in the facades of synagogues such as Capernaum (fig. 11), Dikke (fig. 13), and Umm el-Kanatir (fig. 14), using as evidence fragments which may have belonged to windows (see KW 1916: 228-229, 233-234, figs. 8, 22). Other fragments of stone slabs with bases, columns and capitals, which created the frames of the windows, are found in Kazrin (fig. 16), Kanef (Maoz 1980: 13), Dikke (KW 1916: fig. 232; Maoz 1980: 11), Umm el-Kanatir (Maoz 1980: 21), Chorazin , Nabratein (KW 1916: fig. 200), and Shura (Foerster 1983a). These were windows of the side walls of the upper gallery or the clerestorey. The capitals at Chorazin were Corinthian and at Kazrin were decorated with a spiral row (fig. 16). Each window was probably structured of from four to six stone slabs, each carved with part of the base, column or capital.

2) The Torah shrine: the Focal Point

From ancient times until the present day the Torah (the Scriptures) has been a major factor in the life of the Jews. Consequently, it became a symbol of survival and preservation for the Jews throughout the ages, and is a major constituent of the Jewish spirit. Reading the Torah was always the most important duty in the synagogue. It is clear, therefore, that the repository for the Ark of the Scrolls, that is, the Torah shrine, would become the most prominent feature of the synagogue. In fact, the major architectural feature of ancient synagogues was the Torah shrine, an architectural structure which contained the Ark of the Scrolls, and which was always located on the Jerusalem-oriented wall. Until recently, it was thought by most scholars that the early Galilean synagogues had no fixed structure for the Ark of the Scrolls. The accepted explanation was that in early synagogues the Torah scrolls were placed in a receptacle, a portable chest, probably on wheels, which was brought into the room when needed; only later, probably during the fourth century, a change occurred, and as seen in the Beth-She'arim synagogue, the Ark was placed in a permanent structure in a niche or apse (Sukenik 1934: 52-53; Goodenough 1953, I: 210; Avi-Yonah 1961a: 172; Avigad 1967: 100). One very important fact has emerged, however, after recent excavations in Israel: nearly every excavated synagogue yields either fragments, or traces of a site, or the actual site itself for the Torah shrine, which may be classified into the following architectural categories:

a) *A raised platform* as a base for the *aedicula*, made of stone or wood.

b) A *niche*, probably to hold a wooden Ark of the Scrolls.

c) An *apse* to hold the Ark of the Scrolls and sometimes the menoroth.

Each of these categories had its own structural form, but all served as repositories for the Ark. (Some exceptions do exist: synagogues without any traces of a permanent place for the Torah shrine include Umm el-Kanatir, Dikke, Kanef, 'Assalieh,

Ḥuseifa, Yaphiᶜa, Naᶜaran. But most of these are either unexcavated or destroyed to such an extent that it is impossible to locate the site of the Torah shrine.)

d) *Bema*. In some synagogues, a bema was added in front of the Torah shrine.

As confusion exists regarding the meaning of the term *bema*, which up to now has been used whenever a stone base has been found in a synagogue no matter its site or size, it would be helpful to clarify and define this term, as well as others which will be used in the text:

Torah shrine: this general expression denotes the architectural stone structure which was the *housing* for the Ark of the Scrolls built on the Jerusalem-oriented wall. The enclosing structure is either an aedicula, niche or apse.

Aedicula: this is a stone structure added to the synagogue interior on the Jerusalem-oriented wall, housing the Ark, and consisting of a stone base and stone ornamented facade.

Ark of the Scrolls: the actual ark or chest (usually wooden) which contained the Torah scrolls stood in a repository, either the aedicula, niche or apse (see also Meyers *et al.* 1981: n. 3 on 243).

Bema: this is a raised stone platform built in front of a niche or apse, which *did not* house the Ark, and was probably employed in the reading of the Torah.

Types of Torah shrines

a) Aedicula

An aedicula existed in many synagogues. This is confirmed by two types of existing fragments discovered during excavations: first, a few stones of a stone base or platform have survived in some synagogues, whereas in others, several (two to five) courses of stone have been found. This base has been incorrectly called a *bema*. On top of such a base stood a structure usually consisting of a facade, columns, and lintel, which together created the aedicula. This structure was always built as an interior addition to the already existing Jerusalem-oriented wall: aediculae bases added to the walls and standing very close to the previously constructed columns, have been excavated, for instance, at Capernaum, Ḥ. Shemᶜa, and Gush Ḥalav (figs 1,8). Second, stone fragments found in several synagogues either of small columns of unusual size or shape, or decorated lintels, have been designated as aediculae.

The form of the aedicula, reconstructed from remains found in some synagogues, consists of a base which is a platform of stones, topped by a structure consisting of single or double columns (Chorazin, Kazrin, figs. 17a,19 and Umm el-Kanatir, Pl. 23), supporting a decorated lintel (Nabratein, fig. 18, Pl. 24). Access was usually from the front or, in some cases, from the sides (Kazrin, Reḥov, figs. 2: 2, 3: 7) and

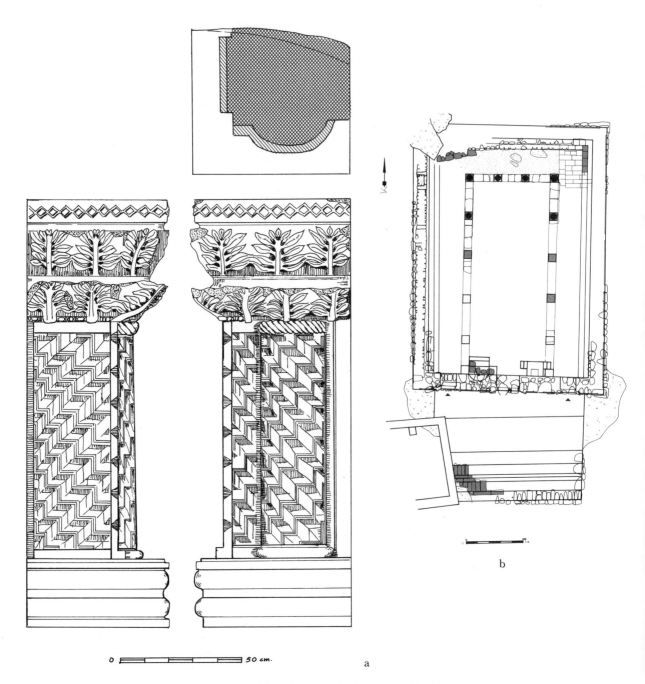

17. Chorazin: a) aedicula column; b) plan.

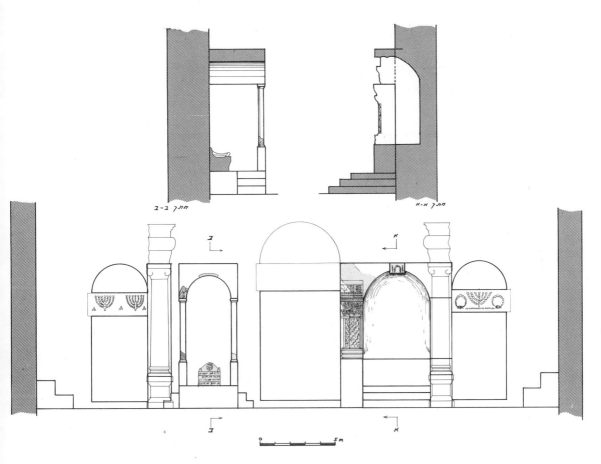

17c. Reconstruction of inner facade.

was usually gained by steps (figs. 29, 30). Reconstructions of aediculae have been attempted in plans of Meiron (fig. 22), Gush Ḥalav (fig. 21), and in the Diaspora synagogue of Sardis (in modern Turkey) (fig. 25).

Aediculae have been found in several locations within the synagogues: i) either constructed on the inside of the facade wall, the Jerusalem-oriented wall, between the main and side entrances; or ii) flanking the interior main entrance on the Jerusalem-oriented facade wall (two aediculae); or iii) built on the inside of the Jerusalem-oriented wall opposite or adjacent to the main entrance wall.

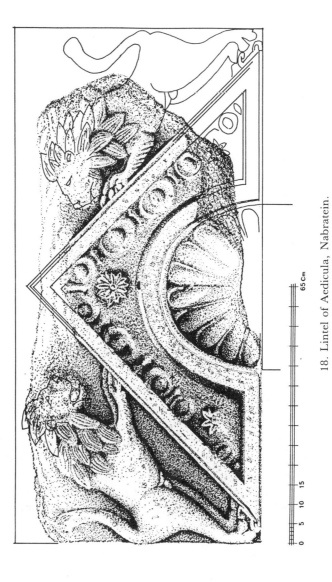

18. Lintel of Aedicula, Nabratein.

19. Kazrin Aedicula Column.

65 cm

0 5 10 15

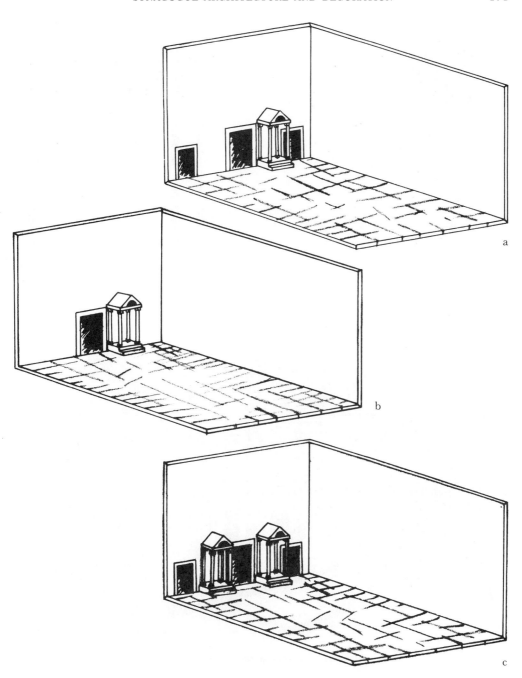

20. Aedicula Reconstructions: a) one aedicula between the main entrance and one of the side entrances; b) an aedicula flanking the single entrance; c) two aedicula flanking the main entrance.

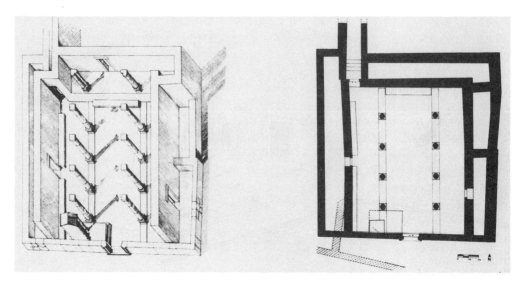

21. Gush Ḥalav, Plan and Reconstruction.

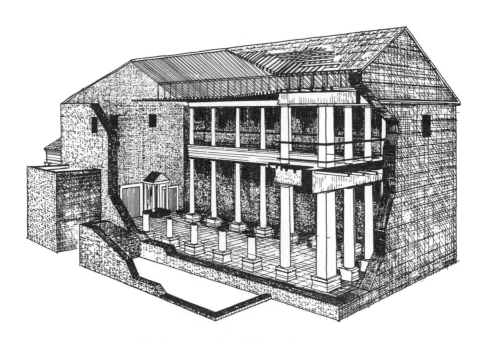

22. Reconstruction of Meiron Synagogue.

i) One aedicula, situated between the main and side entrances, on the interior of the Jerusalem-oriented south facade, survives in one Golan and several Galilean synagogues: (fig. 20a, b)

Gush Ḥalav I (fig. 21)—A large rectangular stone structure, dated to the Late Roman period (stratum VI), extends two metres beyond the Jerusalem-oriented wall, west of the main entrance. A depression, ca. 0.50 m. × 0.75 m., was scooped out of the structure.

Gush Ḥalav II (fig. 21)—A smaller structure than at Gush Ḥalav I (1.46 m. × 1.17 m. × 0.30 m.) was added during stratum VIIa, mid-fourth-fifth centuries, onto the earlier base. Small architectural fragments found among debris were probably parts of an aedicula (Meyers *et al.* 1979: fig. 7; 1981: 76, Photo on 77).

Meiron (fig. 22) (Meyers *et al.* 1981: 12, fig.2.5)—The excavators conjecture an aedicula on the west side of the main entrance.

H. ʿAmmudim (Levine 1981a: 79)—Several stones forming a square were found inside the entrance, in the centre of the south section between the main and eastern entrances and may have been a base for an aedicula (KW 1916: 74 and Pl. 10).

ʿEn Neshut (Maoz 1981b: 108)—West of the main entrance on the south wall remains of one stone and stamps of other stones suggest an aedicula (fig. 2, 4). A stone found near ʿEn Samsam (Pl. 6) is suggested by Maoz (1981b:112) to have come from ʿEn Neshut, and to have been used there as a base for the aedicula. Another fragment of a relief of a lioness may also belong to the aedicula (Maoz 1981b: 110). Maoz (1980: 24) suggests that the aedicula's position was the reason for the entrance not being in the exact centre of the southern facade, an explanation he also proposes for the Golan synagogues of Beth-Lavi and Zumimra.

ii) Two aediculae flanking the central entrance and built on the interior of the Jerusalem-oriented southern wall (fig. 20c) are found at two of the Galilean synagogues and at Sardis in Asia Minor.

Nabratein—In recent excavations at the synagogue at Nabratein several phases were discovered (Meyers *et al.* 1981: 36-39; 1982: 40-43): Synagogue I dates to the second-mid-third centuries CE and Synagogue II is of the late Roman period. Synagogue I has two stone platforms flanking the main entrance, the western slightly larger. Both protrude 3.0 m. from the inner south wall (fig. 23a). Synagogue II (fig. 23b) had two phases: IIa (250-306 CE), when the platform levels were raised, and to whose aediculae belong a carved stone arcuated lintel (fig. 18); and IIb (306-363 CE), when the platforms were rebuilt and the damaged stone lintel was removed from its place and incorporated into one of the renovated platforms. (It should be noted that in Synagogue III of the late Byzantine phase (sixth century) no aediculae were found (Meyers *et al.* 1981: 39; 1982: 43).)

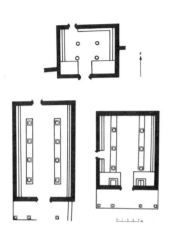

23. Plans of Nabratein
Synagogue, 3 phases.

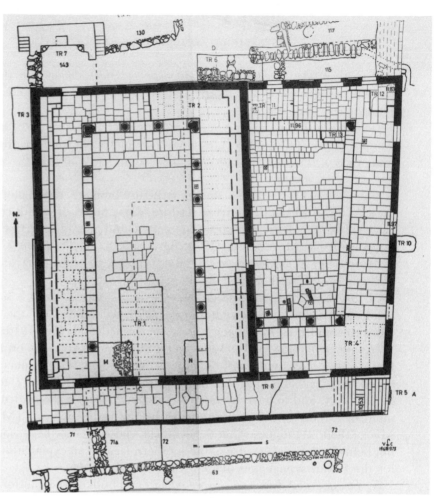

24a. Plan of Capernaum Synagogue.

24b. Capernaum Synagogue, reconstruction of synagogue interior.

Capernaum II (fourth-fifth centuries—fig. 24)—"Platforms" M and N flanking the inner side of the main entrance on the Jerusalem-oriented facade would seem to be the bases of two aediculae. They are constructed of a layer of strong lime mortar laid over gravel which rests upon a 0.25 cm. thickness of basalt flagstones (Corbo 1975: 118-121, fig. 18, photos 52, 55). (Possibly some fragments at Capernaum such as those illustrated by KW may have been parts of such aediculae—see KW 1916: figs. 21, 22, 70, 71.)

Chorazin—In the renewed excavations of the Chorazin synagogue several base stones were found attached to the south wall between the central and side entrances. Some architectural fragments were also revealed, among them an elaborately decorated pillar (fig. 17a-c). Several stones of the base on the west, inner side of the Jerusalem-oriented south wall were also recovered. Yeivin (1985:272-273, figs. 1,2,8) suggests it was a niche.

Small architectural fragments found in the synagogue during the course of the previous excavations point to the existence of an aedicula on the south wall (Sukenik 1934: 24; KW 1916:55-57, abb. 103).

Marous—On the internal southern facade of the synagogue, one aedicula flanks the west side of the single central portal, abutting the southern Jerusalem-oriented wall (fig. 1,8). The west aedicula is in a better state of preservation than is usual: from three to four courses of stone were found, to a height of approximately 1.30 m. The northwest and southwest corners of the aedicula have two antae with bases carved out of the stone, facing the prayer hall (see Pl. 25). Ilan and Damati (1984-5:64) propose the existence of a second aedicula on the eastern side of the entryway, of which only the foundation of its base is preserved. Several architectural fragments, including a gable fragment, a small capital, a column and some carved stones which probably belonged to these aediculae, were found inside the cave, in front of the synagogue portal (Ilan and Damati 1984-5:65).

Sardis—A typical example of double aediculae was discovered in the Diaspora at Sardis in Asia Minor (fig. 25a). Flanking the central doorway on the eastern end of the synagogue hall, two platforms for aediculae (shrines NS and SS) were found, in synagogue stage 4 (fig. 25; Seager 1972: 426, 434; 1975: 89, fig. 13; also Seager and Kraabel 1983:170).

Depictions of double aediculae on a lintel from Kochav HaYarden (fig. 26) and on carvings from Beth She'arim (fig. 27) support the archaeological evidence that in fact there were synagogues which had two aediculae flanking the main entrance. The existence of an aedicula in other unexcavated Galilean synagogues such as Bar'am is theoretically possible if one takes into account the fact that the southern-most columns have been erected far enough away from the entrance so as to allow

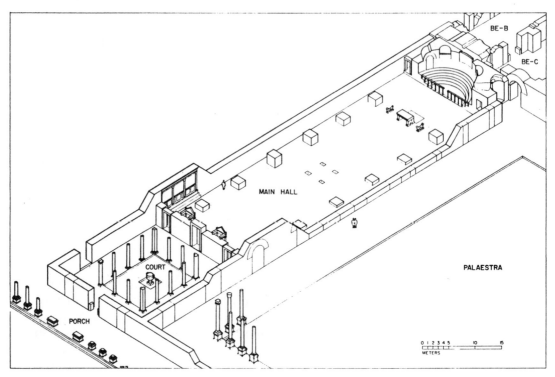

a

b

25. Sardis Synagogue Reconstruction: a) interior looking west; b) interior looking east.

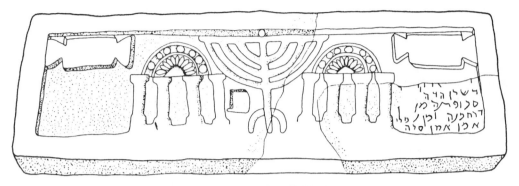

26. Lintel of Kokhav HaYarden.

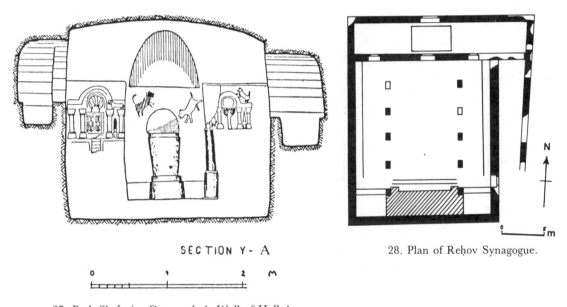

SECTION Y - A

28. Plan of Reḥov Synagogue.

27. Beth Sheᶜarim Catacomb 4, Wall of Hall A.

room for an aedicula abutting onto the inner southern facade (fig. 20). Remains drawn by Kohl and Watzinger (1916: Pl XII) seem to support this conjecture, as do the remains of Umm el-Kanatir. As the Dikke plan (KW 1916: Pl. XVI) shows that the central section of the south wall is completely destroyed we can only surmise that an aedicula was situated there, although it would not have been on the facade wall, which is the western wall in this Golan synagogue.

iii) *Aediculae on the Jerusalem-oriented wall facing or adjacent to the entrance*: the bases of these aediculae were usually small, apart from two large ones found at Kazrin and Reḥov.

Shemᶜa, Synagogues I, II (fig. 8)—In both phases of the synagogue, a fragment of a stone base on the south, Jerusalem-oriented wall was found (Meyers *et al.* 1976: 72-73). To this must be added fragments of columns and capitals adorned with acanthus leaves which belonged, Meyers suggests (Meyers *et al.* 1976: 49, figs. 3.9,3.11), to the stone aediculae of phase I, although for phase II he proposes a wooden aedicula on the stone base (Meyers 1981: 74).

Kazrin (Golan)—An elevated (three level) stone base (5.50 × 2.50 m.) was excavated on the southern Jerusalem-oriented wall (Maoz 1980: 16; 1981b: 105). The aedicula probably stood on top of the elevation and entrance to it was gained from both sides of the base, as can be seen from surviving thresholds. A double stone column (fig. 19), probably belonging to the aedicula, was found in secondary use in the western aisle (Maoz, Killebrew, Hachlili 1987).

Ḥammath Gader, phase II (probably fourth century)—A stone base plastered and painted was found under the apse of phase III on the Jerusalem-oriented wall, facing the entrance (Foerster 1983b: 11-12).

Reḥov II, III—In phase II (end of fourth-fifth centuries) a large stone base (9.0 m × 3.0 m.) was constructed onto the south, Jerusalem-oriented wall (fig. 28). The base was flanked by stairs on both sides, so that the approach to the aedicula was from either side, as at Kazrin (fig 2,2). Several small, limestone columns, bases and capitals, and a fragment of a limestone sculptured block ornamented with a lion were found in secondary use incorporated into the base of phase II (fig. X,13). They probably belonged to a phase I aedicula (fourth century) (Vitto 1981a: 165, Pl. 24:1). In phase III (sixth-seventh centuries) the base was enlarged, the side stairs were blocked and two wing stairs were built in front. A low wall was also added parallel to the facade, probably to hold the chancel-screen found there (Vitto 1980: 215-216; 1981: 93).

It is significant that both the aediculae of Kazrin and Reḥov are larger than usual and both synagogue entrances are situated on the opposite wall.

Maᶜoz Ḥayim I (A) (end third-fourth centuries)—A stone platform protruded into the main hall in the centre of the southern Jerusalem-oriented wall (fig. 9). It was probably enclosed by a marble screen (Tzaferis 1982:217-218, figs. 2-3).

H. Rimmon III (sixth-seventh centuries)—On the north, Jerusalem-oriented wall several stones of a rectangular base (5.0 m. × 1.70 m.) survive (Kloner 1980b: 227; 1983b: 69).

Excavations at two Judean sites suggest the likelihood of the presence of an aedicula in both synagogues. If this is correct, then it must have replaced the niche as Ark repository:

Ḥ. Susiya (Gutman et al. 1981: 125)—the secondary eastern base may have been an aedicula in a later stage.

ʿEn-Gedi III (Barag *et al.* 1981: 117)—An aedicula base may have existed in (later) synagogue III in front of the square niche.

b) Niche

The niche is a stone structure built inside the Jerusalem-oriented wall during the fourth century, to serve as a repository for the Ark of the Scrolls. Niches were constructed in two forms (also Maoz 1972: 18-25):

i) A semicircular structure constructed as an addition to the internal wall, protruding from the wall into the main hall and approached by steps. Most niches have only their lower part surviving. Its facade consisted of columns (or pillars) surmounted by a semicircular arch decorated with a conch. The niche was sometimes decorated like the Dura-Europos niche (Pl. 27) or had a relief facade with flanking pillars and a conch decorating the arch. These facades probably closely resembled the aediculae facades described above.

ii) The second form of niche is rectangular and was built as the result of blocking an entrance, thus dictating the rectangular form.

From the size of the niches it seems reasonable to infer that an Ark was placed inside the niche, as depicted on the Susiya mosaic (Pl. 104).

i) Semicircular niches

Naveh—A niche was found on the wall of a building identified as a synagogue, about 2.20 m. above the floor, flanked by two carved pillars and with a conch decorating it (Mayer and Reifenberg 1936: 8, fig. 8, Pl. 3).

ʾArbel (fig. 1,4)—On the Jerusalem-oriented southern wall, a niche was originally built (Avigad 1967: 98-100, fig. 5). It is the sole Galilean synagogue of the common Galilean-type plan which has a niche.

ʾEshtemoʿa—On the north, Jerusalem-oriented wall, three semicircular niches were built, approximately 2.0 m. above the floor, and approached by steps. The central niche is larger than the two flanking side niches. A later niche was added to the front of the former ones, possibly replacing them (Yeivin 1981: 121; also Maoz 1972: 27).

Susiya—A small niche is assumed to have existed on the centre of the north Jerusalem-oriented wall, similar to the ʾEshtemoʿa niche (Gutman *et al.* 1981: 124).

The most famous niche of this type is in the Diaspora synagogue of Dura-Europos, dating to the mid-third century (Pl. 27).

[On Mount Zion, Jerusalem, the building now called "David's Tomb" might have been a synagogue structure with a niche on its north wall, possibly dated to the fourth century (Pinkerfeld 1960: 41, 43, fig. 1.]

ii) The rectangular niches (fig. 3), which were created mostly as a result of blocking an entrance seem to indicate that an earlier stage had employed a different Torah shrine (aediculae?), but no proof has been uncovered (fig. 3).

Hammath Tiberias A—Four small columns enclose an area on the Jerusalem-oriented southern wall. This probably created a rectangular niche (Slousch 1921).

Hammath Tiberias B—A small rectangular and raised room apparently served as a type of niche or as a repository for the Ark (Dothan 1981: 65; 1983: 30-32; Avi-Yonah, 1973:41, calls it a square apse). A depression was found in the floor at the western part of the room and probably was used for the *genizah* (see p. 192-193).

Beth She'an B—small synagogue—The southern Jerusalem-oriented wall was a relatively thick wall, and a niche is assumed to have been built in its centre (Bahat 1981a: 82).

Beth She'arim II—The central door was walled up in the synagogue building and a niche was added inside (Mazar 1973:18; Avi-Yonah 1961a: 174).

'En-Gedi II—This synagogue's northern Jerusalem-oriented wall had an entrance which was later blocked by a wall which created a rectangular niche 1.50 m. × 0.40 m. (Barag *et al.* 1981: 118-119).

Ḥ. Rimmon I—A rectangular niche was found on the northern Jerusalem-oriented wall, plastered with red bands (Kloner 1983b: 67).

c) The apse

With the innovation of the apse as repository for the Ark in the late fifth century, the Torah shrine became an integral element in the synagogue building and was constructed at the same time as the building itself. It was usually a semicircular structure extending outside the main hall, along the width of the nave, approached by steps and sometimes having a decorated mosaic floor. Its facade probably consisted of columns and an arcuated lintel decorated with a conch (see figs. IX 22, 23). Some scholars suggest that the apse's structure evolved from that of the niche (Sukenik 1935: 165; Galling 1956: 176; see also Meyers *et al.* 1981: 241, who suggest that "the sacred niche was transmitted to Christianity in the form of the apse"). However, the necessity for a larger, permanent place for the Ark and other ceremonial objects seems to be the most logical reason for the development of the apse. It was much larger than the niche or aediculae, and, therefore, could house the Ark and probably the menoroth which were also needed in the ceremony.

The dominant feature of most of the synagogues built during the sixth century in the Beth She^oan Valley and in the southern part of the Land of Israel is the apse (fig. 4). Up to now, no Galilean or Golan synagogues containing apses have been discovered. The two synagogues of Ḥammath-Gader and Ma^coz Ḥayim had their aediculae replaced by newly-built apses in the fifth century (fig. 9).

Ḥammath-Gader III, (fig. 7) (Sukenik 1935: 122, fig. 10)—On the south wall remains were found of an apse (4.50 m. × 2.10 m.) with steps leading up to it. It had originally been partitioned off by a screen (Sukenik 1935: Pl. VIIIa). The floor was lower than the highest step, and was paved with plain mosaics.

Beth She^oan A (fig. XI,2) (Zori 1967: 149-152)—The apse in the southern wall of the synagogue probably had two levels. It was built 0.50 cm. above the floor level of the hall. Set into the floor was a large fragment of plaster which may point to furniture such as a wooden Ark (see p. 273) having stood there.

Ma^coz Ḥayim II, III (B,C) (fig. 9) (Tzaferis 1982: 218, 220, 222, figs. 5, 6, 7, Pls. 30A, 31A)—The apse was added during the later two phases (fifth century), and replaced the earlier aedicula. An apse which protruded about 3 m. was built on the southern Jerusalem-oriented wall. It probably had a higher floor level than that of the main hall, and may have been enclosed by a chancel screen (found in fragmentary condition). During phase III (C) a bema was located in front of the apse and a sunken area was added in the rear part.

Beth-Alpha (fig. 4,5) (Sukenik 1932: 13)—The apse was built in the middle of the southern wall of the synagogue. Three narrow steps led to the floor of the apse which was 0.75 cm. above the floor of the hall. Two rounded cavities were found on the surface of the lower level of the platform, and probably held the columns which bore the curtain (*parochet*).

Jericho (fig. 4,1) (Baramki 1936: 75)—At the southwest end of the nave two steps led to the semi-oval apse, the walls of which were not bonded into those of the synagogue.

Na^caran (fig. 4,6)—The southern part of the structure was destroyed, but it probably included an apse (Sukenik 1932: 53; Vincent 1961).

Ma^con (fig. 4,3) (Levi 1960: 6-7)—The semicircular apse stood on the Jerusalem-oriented wall on the axis of the building, and was constructed of limestone ashlar (width 3.20 m., depth 1.8 m.). A small cavity in the pavement of the apse probably indicates the site where the Ark stood.

Gaza (fig. 4,4) (Ovadiah 1981: 128)—An apse, some 3.0 m. in diameter is conjectured to have existed at the southwestern end of the building.

Gerasa (figs. 4,7; IX, 33a)—A square protruding apse was found on the eastern Jerusalem-oriented wall. Sukenik (1932:53) maintains that the form is not that of an apse, but rather a small square chamber projecting from the western wall.

Ḥammath Tiberias B—Level I, the latest synagogue (Dothan 1981: 68). Three steps led up from the southern end of the nave to an apse built within the external wall of the building.

d) Bema

The bema is a raised stone podium or platform added to the wall found only in front of the niche or apse. Several theories have been advanced as to its function in the synagogue building. First, the simplest solution suggests that some of these additional podia served as footholds for ascending to the niche or apse; second, that it may have been used as a support for holding other ritual objects, particularly the menoroth. This could be the explanation for the bema in the synagogues of Susiya and ʿEn-Gedi where the niche itself is too small to have held more than the Ark (see also Barag 1977 III: 779 for Maʿon); and third, the bema could have served as a platform for prayer, for reading the Torah and for reciting the lessons of the week (see Sukenik 1934: 57) for example, at the synagogues of Beth ʾAlpha, Maʿoz-Ḥayim III, and Ḥammath Gader.

In fact the problem of where the Torah was read in the synagogue has perplexed many scholars. Some suggest the stone bases found in the Galilean synagogues, such as at H. Shemʿa (Meyers *et al.* 1976: 72, note 44), were used for Torah reading, but these are, in actual fact, bases for aediculae. Meyers contends that one of the two aediculae at Nabratein served for reading (Meyers & Meyers 1981:242; Meyers *et al.* 1981a: 36-37). Other scholars suggest that the reading of the Torah was performed on a raised podium, probably made of wood and placed in the centre of the synagogue (Avi-Yonah 1961a: 172). A depression for a stand was found in Nabratein synagogue I (mid-second century) (Meyers & Meyers 1981: 36; see also the Dura-Europos synagogue, Kraeling 1979: 256). At the Sardis synagogue four slabs of marble were set into the floor in the centre of the hall, creating a small structure, probably a bema (Seager 1972: 426 and note 8).

Two kinds of bema were found in the synagogues: those which stood in front of a niche, and those which stood in front of an apse.

i) Bema in front of a niche

ʾEshtemoʿa—A protruding rectangular structure is built in front of the three niches on the northern, Jerusalem-oriented wall (fig. 5). It has a semicircular niche in its centre. Yeivin (1981: 121) proposes that this is a bema. Others assume that it is a later-period niche which had replaced the previous one.

Susiya (Gutman *et al.* 1981: 125- 126)—Two bema were found on the northern Jerusalem-oriented wall (fig. 6). The main bema stands slightly to the west, and is said to have undergone various changes: it had two steps approaching the niche, and posts and chancel screens were built around the bema which may have served to hold the menoroth. The secondary bema further to the east has a mosaic pavement in front of it.

ᶜEn-Gedi (Barag *et al.* 1981:117-118)—In front of the semicircular niche (on the northern Jerusalem-oriented wall) is a rectangular area which enclosed a mosaic panel, forming a bema measuring 2.0 m. × 4.0 m. At the four corners of the bema are small sockets which held the posts of a wooden chancel screen.

Traces survive on the ᶜEn-Gedi and Susiya secondary *bemoth* which suggest they possibly had canopies erected over them. It is also possible that these *bemoth* served as platforms for reading the Torah.

ii) Bema in front of an apse (also Maoz 1972: 29)

Beth ʾAlpha (Sukenik 1932: 13, Pl. V1, 2; fig. 47).—A small bema is built in front of the apse (1.55 m. long, 0.90 m. wide, 0.45 m. high) and has a step leading up to it.

Maᶜoz Ḥayim III (Tzaferis 1982: 222-223)—A bema (2.0 × 6.0 m.) was built in front of the apse, in the third phase . It protruded into the nave and was paved with stone slabs, laid on an earlier mosaic. A screen surrounded the area of the bema.

Hammath Gader (Sukenik 1935: 32, but see Foerster 1983b: 11-12)—A bema was found in front of the apse in its centre. It is of the same length as the apse (4.55 m. long and 1.20 m. wide). Two steps lead up to its centre, and posts and a chancel screen were found which probably stood on either side of the steps.

Gerasa (Sukenik 1935: 166)—Traces of a panel projecting into the nave indicate that a bema may have stood in front of the apse.

Maᶜon (Levi 1960: 7; Barag 1977, III:779). A platform, that is, a bema, is built (0.75 m. × 0.60 m.) in front of the apse. A sunken area, the width of the nave, existed in front of the bema. Four post-holes are visible in the mosaic floor, and may have held the posts for a veil (C—F in plan).

The Form of the Torah shrine

The form of the Torah shrine can be reconstructed by reference to artistic renditions on stone and mosaics, and by architectural fragments belonging usually to aediculae, found in excavations of synagogues.

a) Artistic renditions of the Torah shrine (fig. 29 and fig. IX,24)

i) Several stone and clay reliefs depict the facade of the Torah shrine: a frieze fragment from Chorazin (Pl 28), a relief fragment from Chorazin (fig. 29), a lintel fragment from Kokhav HaYarden (fig. 26), a lintel from ʿAssalieh (Pl 29a), the relief on the Shell sarcophagus (fig. 30), a depiction on a clay lamp, the depiction on the black ceramic fragment from Nabratein (fig. 29) and its comparable design on a clay lamp.

ii) Other stone reliefs as well as mosaic pavements render the Torah shrine facade with an Ark inside it (see also p. 273ff.) (fig. 30). The drawings and incision (Pl. 31) on the Beth Sheaʿrim catacomb walls, a stone relief from Pekiin (Pl. 32), a stone tomb door from Kfar Yasif (Pl. 33), stone plaques (Pl. 34), a lamp and a stone screen from Susiya, all depict the Torah shrine. The shrine is also depicted on mosaic pavements in the synagogues of Ḥammath Tiberias, Susiya and Beth Sheʾan (fig. 30 and Pls.101-103).

All these renditions portray a uniform Torah shrine facade consisting of usually two, but sometimes four, columns which carry an arcuated lintel (straight or gabled) decorated with the conch motif (figs. IX,22,23). The Ark depicted inside these facades takes various forms (see pp. 273-278).

b) Architectural Fragments of Aediculae

Architectural fragments presumed to be from aediculae are also helpful as an aid in reconstructing the Torah shrine's design. The best preserved examples consist of columns, lintels, reliefs and mosaic pavements.

i) Small basalt columns: a richly decorated column from Chorazin (fig. 17a), a double column from Kazrin (fig. 19), a small double column capital of basalt with an eagle relief from Umm el-Kanatir (Pl. 23 and fig. IX,24c), and a relief from Zumimra which depicts a column and a lion, may have belonged to aediculae (Maoz 1981b: 104). The Dikke fragments of the base and capital of a double column, usually identified as window fragments (KW 1916:123, fig. 246-7), may have been aediculae fragments. Fragments of columns and capitals were also found at H. Shemʿa (p. 178). In the Caesarea synagogue the sole remains are several small stone columns which may have belonged to a stone structure (perhaps an aediculae) (Avi-Yonah 1975, I: 279). Some stone fragments were found at Marous (Ilan and Damati 1984-85:65).

ii) Lintels thought to have belonged to aediculae have been excavated at various sites, such as the outstanding Nabratein lintel (Pl. 24; Meyers *et al.* 1981, 1982), the limestone fragment from Reḥov which depicts a striding lion (fig. X,13), and several fragments of basalt reliefs found in the Golan (now displayed in the Kazrin museum). These fragments, however, have been usually ascribed to windows.

29. Torah shrine depictions.

30. Torah shrine depictions.

iii) Reliefs portraying lions or eagles may have been elements in aediculae ornamentation, as seen in mosaic pavements, such as at Beth ʾAlpha (see p. 361. Pl. 102). Similar reliefs have been found in several synagogue ruins in the Golan (Zumimra Pl. 35). Three-dimensional sculptures of lions may also have been used for the ornamentation of aediculae, for example, the lions found at Chorazin, Barʿam, and Capernaum (fig. X,11 and see p. 328).

Whereas synagogues containing actual aediculae and niches portray in their artistic renditions an Ark standing within an aedicula or niche, the synagogues with apses such as at Beth ʾAlpha, Jericho and Naʿaran portray on their mosaic pavements the Ark independent of any enclosure. This Ark probably stood by itself inside the apse.

Additional elements associated with the Torah shrine to be discussed below are the chancel screen, the veil and the *genizah*. A chair of Moses was also part of the interior decoration of some synagogues.

Chancel Screens

Screens have been found in several synagogues. They were used to separate the Torah shrine (the repository for the Ark) from the public prayer hall of the synagogue. The chancel screen was also a characteristic feature of the church of the same period. It served to cordon off the main hall from the bema where only the clergy were allowed to enter.

The screen was formed from several components: posts surmounted by capitals with a vertical groove on either side; a marble slab was inserted into the grooves of the posts (fig. 31). The chancel screen was decorated, sometimes on both sides, and occasionally inscriptions were added, probably because of the prominent position of the screen, (Sukenik 1935: 67). Complete chancel screens as well as fragments have been found in synagogue excavations. Most come from synagogues in the south, the Beth Sheʾan area, and from around Lake Kinneret. No screens, on the other hand, have been found in the Galilean and Golan synagogues.

In several synagogues screen slabs and posts have been found in the area of the apse or aedicula: in the Beth Sheʾan synagogue the negative of a screen was found (Zori 1967: 154, 157, Pls. 27:5, 31:4, 32:1); in Reḥov III a marble screen and two posts were discovered (fig. 32) (Vitto 1980: 215-216); in the Maʿoz Ḥayim III synagogue fragments of a screen were found (Tzaferis 1982: 223, Pl. 36C, D); in Ḥammath Tiberias several fragments of screens and posts were found (Sukenik 1935: 60, Pls. XIII, XIV). A screen (Pl. 36) found during excavations in the town

31. Screens.

of Tiberias may have come from a synagogue. In the apse area of the synagogue of Ḥammath Gader fragments of a screen were found (fig. 32) (Sukenik 1935: 32, 58-60, Pl. XVIIB).

Many marble fragments of posts and chancel screens coming from installations around the *bema* were found in the Susiya synagogue, either plain or decorated (most are not yet published). Many contain incised Hebrew and Aramaic inscriptions (Yeivin 1974). At ᶜEn-Gedi small sockets were found at the four corners of the bema and are considered by the excavators to have held the posts of a wooden chancel screen. At Beth Sheᶜarim, Avi-Yonah suggests (1961a: 173-4) that a reading platform was surrounded by a chancel screen. At the Gaza synagogue fragments of four decorated chancel screens were found (Pl. 99a, b). Several of the screens found are the only indication surviving of a synagogue's presence, as for instance in the case of the screens from ʾAshdod (fig. 32) and ʾAscalon (Pl. 37 a, b).

Screen Ornamentation

The chancel screen slabs are decorated in carved, stylized ornamentation, using openwork and drill technique (Susiya and Gaza, Pl. X,12), but sometimes they are merely incised (Gaza, fig. 32). Most of the screens are decorated with a frame which encloses carvings of various motifs:

1) The menorah is the most popular motif. Alone or flanked by ritual objects, it is shown enclosed by a stylized wreath with flowing ribbons which sprout into leaves. This design is found at Ḥammath Gader, ʾAshdod, Gadara, on a screen of unknown provenance similar to the one at Gadara, and at Reḥov (fig. 32). A menorah flanked by ritual objects is depicted on screens from Gaza (fig. 32), ʾAscalon (Pl. 37). A menorah flanked by birds is depicted on screens from Tiberias (Pl. 36; see also pp. 335-337). A screen from the Susiya synagogue is carved and has two lamps suspended from it (fig. IX,18).

2) A screen found at the synagogue of Susiya portrays a Torah shrine with the Ark inside (fig. IX, 23).

3) Screens decorated with leaves forming medallions filled with grape bunches, leaves and pomegranates are found at Ḥammath Tiberias (done in relief), Gaza (worked in drill technique, Pl. 99), and Susiya (Yeivin 1974: Pls. 49A, B, G, I; 43A, C).

4) Geometric designs are found at Gaza (Pl. 99) and Susiya (Yeivin 1974: Pl. 44E).

5) Figurative motifs: stylized birds flank the menorah (Tiberias Pl. 36) and heraldic lions and eagles appear on a screen from Susiya (Gutman *et al.* 1981:125).

6) Floral designs appear on the screen from ʾAscalon (Pl. 37), and on the reverse of the Ḥammath Gader and Reḥov screens (fig. 32; for Reḥov, Bahat 1973: Pl. 48B).

Many screens bear votive inscriptions incised on the slabs and posts (Sukenik 1935: 67), which usually commemorate the donors (Yeivin 1974:201).

Similar screens have been found in Christian churches, and depict crosses in place of the menorah. These screens may have served as prototypes for the synagogue screens. Moreover, the screens may have come from the same workshop, or have been modelled on the same general patterns, as can be attested to by the similarity of the synagogue screens from ʾAshdod and Ḥammath Gader (fig. 32) on the one

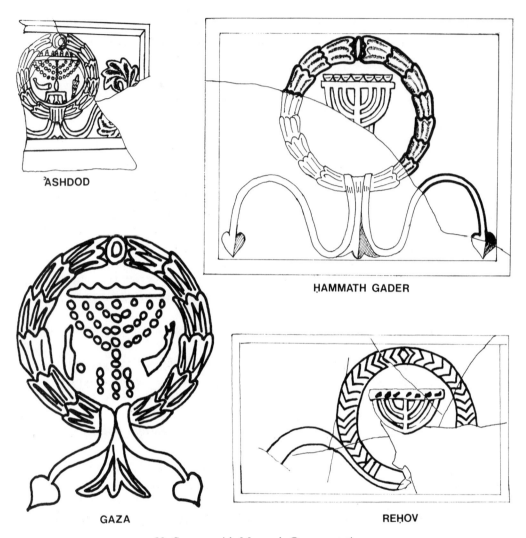

ʾASHDOD

ḤAMMATH GADER

GAZA

REḤOV

32. Screens with Menorah Ornamentation.

hand and the church screens from Beth Sheʾan (Avi-Yonah 1981a: Pl. 16:4, 5) on the other. The screens in synagogues are dated to the sixth century which is the same date as the similar church screens. When found in excavations, their provenance is usually the area of the Torah shrine. It seems the screen's purpose was to enhance the importance and prominence of the Torah shrine. Furthermore, the screen was

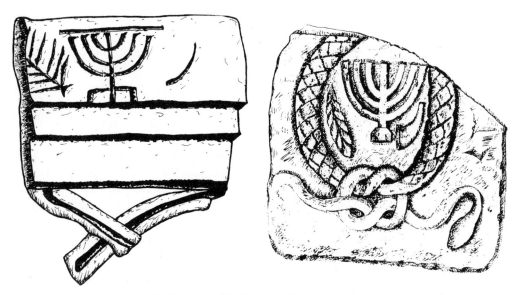

32. Screens with Menorah Ornamentation.

an appropriate place for donors' commemorations, and became a more convenient site for inscriptions than the previously-utilized mosaic floor. The absence of chancel screens in Galilean and Golan synagogues should be noted: these same synagogues also lack apses.

Thus, the chancel screen (although possibly imitating a church prototype where it acted as a barrier between the congregation and the clergy) in the sixth century synagogue served a different function as a token partition between the Torah shrine and the synagogue hall.

The Veil (Curtain), Parochet

The veil, or curtain (*parochet*) hung down in front of, and screened the facade of the Ark or the Torah shrine. The existence of the veil is known by 1) remains found in synagogue excavations and 2) by artistic depictions on synagogue mosaic pavements.

1) At Beth ᵓAlpha, two round holes have been cut into the lower level of the platform steps, probably for columns which held a curtain (Sukenik 1932: 13; 1934: 56-57). At Beth Sheᵓan fragments of an iron chain and rings were discovered close to the apse, Pl 103; (Zori 1967: 163, Pls. 32:6, 33:5, 34:8, 10, 11), presumably belong-

ing to the veil which is also depicted on the mosaic floor. At ʿEn-Gedi, traces of posts and metal ornaments, possibly from the *parochet*, were found in front of the niche. The Maʿon synagogue yielded four post holes, visible in the mosaic floor as veil posts (Levi 1960: 7, C-F in plan), and bronze veil rings (Rahmani 1960: 16). At Susiya, in a corner adjacent to the eastern bema, a stone column is preserved. Gutman *et al.* (1981:125-6) propose that this is part of a canopy which hung above the bema. Similar post holes, presumably for veils, were also found in the Diaspora synagogues of Dura Europos (Kraeling 1956: 257-259) and Sardis (Seager 1975: 109, note 40).

2) Depictions of veils are found on mosaic pavements of synagogues: at Ḥammath Tiberias (fig. IX,8a; Pl. 101) the veil is bound and hangs in front of the Ark. In the Beth Sheʾan A mosaic (Pl. 103) three veils are portrayed: one is suspended between two columns and blocks from view what seems to be the Ark, the second veil is depicted on both sides of the inner shrine, and the third is pictured above the gable. The Beth ʾAlpha panel of Jewish symbols (Pl. 102) is bordered on both sides with a hanging veil.

From the above account it can be seen that the veil appears in three different contexts: first, covering the Ark only, or blocking it from view as at Ḥammath Tiberias and in the Beth Sheʾan A mosaics (Pl. 101, 103); second, screening the Torah shrine (aedicula, niche or apse), as depicted in the Beth Sheʾan mosaic, and third, framing a complete complex consisting of apse and menoroth, as seems to be depicted in the Beth ʾAlpha mosaic (Pl. 102).

Thus, the veil was a Torah shrine fixture, which hid the Ark from view or screened the front of the Torah shrine from the prayer hall, and was probably drawn aside only when the Ark was in use (but see Goodenough (1954,IV:135, 139) who associates the curtain with the tabernacle curtain and the Holy of Holies "that the real presence, or *shekinah* though hidden from all common gaze, was there").

The Genizah

In several synagogues an unusual feature has been observed in the Torah shrine area. A depression (cavity) has been found in the base, and seems to indicate the position of a *genizah* behind the Ark for the community chest and for fragments of scrolls. In the Galilean synagogue of Gush Ḥalav I, a rectangular depression (0.50 m. × 0.75 m.) was found in the early base, close to the southern wall (Meyers *et al.* 1979: 42), similar to one found at Nabratein (Meyers *et al.* 1981a: 242). At Kazrin, the southern rear part of the Torah shrine may have served as a *genizah*. At Ḥammath Tiberias, a sunken pit was found in the western part of the room (Dothan 1983:31). The synagogue of Beth ʾAlpha had a cavity in the platform which contained coins, and thus served as a *genizah* (Sukenik 1935:75). Lately, at the Maʿoz Ḥayim synagogue, a sunken area has been discovered at the back of the apse floor (Tzaferis 1982: 222). At Maʿon, a small pit was discovered in the mosaic pavement, and presumably served as a community chest (Levi 1960:7).

The *genizah* in most of these synagogues usually yielded coins, and probably served, therefore, as the community's hiding place for its treasure and for discarded scrolls.

The Chair of Moses

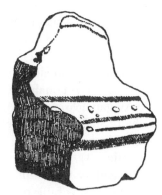

33. Seat of Moses from Ḥammath Tiberias.

34. Seat of Moses from Chorazin.

Another interior feature appearing among the furnishings of the synagogue was the "Chair of Moses," a stone seat mentioned in ancient literature (Sukenik 1934: 57-61; Avi-Yonah 1961a: 167). Two types were found in synagogue excavations:

1) A very beautiful basalt stone seat carved from a single stone was found at Chorazin (fig. 34). It is decorated with an Aramaic inscription on the front, with a carved rosette on the back, and has sculptured hand-rests. The Ḥammath Tiberias A seat is carved out of limestone (fig. 33). It is partly damaged and was found *in situ* next to the southern Jerusalem-oriented wall. Another marble seat was found in Delos, Greece (Sukenik 1934: 61, fig. 19).

2) At the ʿEn-Gedi synagogue, two steps created a seat which abutted the wall east of the niche (Barag *et al.* 1981: 117). It was identified as the "Seat of Moses." A similarly built seat was found in the Diaspora synagogue of Dura Europos (Kraeling 1979: 17).

Opinions differ as to the use of the seat: most scholars consider it the seat of the elders (Sukenik 1934: 58-59; Kraeling 1956:17; Avi-Yonah 1961a:167) whereas others believe that it served as a kind of stand for the scrolls during worship and stood in an aedicula or niche (Yeivin 1985:274-275 and fig. 8).

3) The Gallery

Second-storey galleries are an innovation of synagogue architecture; evidence of their existence is drawn from several facts: in many synagogues the columns along the three sides of the prayer hall are known to have supported a gallery which would have left the centre of the main hall unobstructed. Such an arrangement of columns occurs in the Galilean synagogues of ʾArbel, Barʿam, Gush Ḥalav (cf. Meyers 1979:41), Ḥ. ʿAmmudim, Chorazin, Capernaum, and Meiron, and at Umm el-Kanatir in the Golan (figs. 1,2). The ⌐⌐-shape form of the gallery was dictated by the rows of columns on all sides of the hall, except for the wall containing the entrances (fig. 1; see Avi-Yonah 1961:163-164; Sukenik 1934: 47, 48; Goodenough 1953,I: 182; Avigad 1967: 30). Another type of gallery was built on the two long sides of the hall. Such galleries are encountered at Kanef and ʿEn Neshut in the Golan (fig. 2) (Maoz 1981b: 103, 108), and probably at other synagogues such as Beth ʾAlpha (fig. 4) (Sukenik 1934: 16-19; Avigad 1975,I:188). In several synagogues the gallery was built possibly on part of the main hall only: a second storey, for example, was built on the west wall at Ḥ. Shemʿa (fig. 8). A railing or screen probably separated the gallery from the main room of the synagogue (Meyers et al. 1976: 56-58, fig. 3.10). At Susiya a second storey rested upon the southern wing (fig. 6) (Gutman et al. 1981: 124).

Further evidence which points to the existence of a gallery is indicated by the remains of smaller columns and capitals which probably formed its colonnade and which have been found at most Galilee and Golan synagogues: Barʿam, Ḥ. Shemʿa, Nabratein, Capernaum, Dikke, Umm el-Kanatir, ʿEn Neshut, ʿAssalieh and probably at Kazrin and ʾArbel (table 2 and figs.1,2).

Additional corroboration of the presence of a gallery is seen in staircases found at excavations which lead to an upper floor, and are usually situated outside the main hall. At Capernaum remains of such stairs were found at the northwest, rear corner, fig. 24a (KW 1916: Pl.II) and a similar staircase was found at the northern, rear corner of the synagogue at Chorazin (see also Sukenik 1934: 72,). At Barʿam the restored plan indicates a staircase (fig. 1, KW 1916: Pl. XII; but see Seager 1975: note 36). A staircase is also found at Gush Ḥalav, located at the same northwestern end (fig. 21). At Ḥ. Shemʿa the stairs lead to an upper floor (fig. 8, and

Meyers *et al.* 1976:56-58). Kanef and ʿEn Neshut also possessed staircases, probably leading to a second floor (Maoz 1981:103, 108). At Susiya the steps at the southern end of the narthex led to a second storey (Gutman *et al.* 1981: 124). Ḥammath Tiberias synagogue level IIA had a staircase on the north leading to a second storey or perhaps a roof (Dothan 1981:65). Interesting evidence is found in an Aramaic inscription on an architrave fragment from Dabbura (Golan) which reads:

ʾElʿazar the son of (Ra)bbah made the columns above the arches and beams...

It appears that the inscription refers to columns of an upper storey or a gallery (Naveh 1978: 26-27). At the Maʿon synagogue the aisles and the southern part of the nave are paved with limestone slabs, indicating, in Barag's opinion (1977, III:779) that an additional storey was built above this part of the hall. At Ḥammath Tiberias, Dothan (1981:65) asserts that the eastern aisle of the synagogue of level IIb (fig. XI,1) may have been intended for female worshippers, with a temporary partition being placed between the columns.

The Function of the Gallery

The most prevalent view among scholars regarding the gallery is that it served as the women's section, which implies that segregation existed between men and women in the synagogue (Sukenik 1934: 48; Avi-Yonah 1961: 164; Goodenough I,1953: 182). Safrai (1963; 1976: 939) objects to this view, stating that he finds no indication of segregation in Talmudic literature, and maintains that women probably gathered along the walls or sat on the back benches; furthermore, he states that as there is no reason to allocate them to the balcony, the gallery must have served other purposes.

In the Galilean synagogues the all-round gallery enabled the onlookers to observe the central hall and, what was more important, the southern, Jerusalem-oriented wall with its aediculae, for instance Capernaum, Meiron (figs. 24, 22). The same situation also exists in the Golan synagogue of ʿEn Neshut. At Ḥ. Shemʿa, the west side of the upper storey enabled observation of the aedicula on the southern wall (fig. 35). At Susiya, the upper storey is located opposite the Torah shrine (fig. 6).

One fact is certain: it was possible to have an unhindered view of the main hall, as well as of the Torah shrine, from the upper gallery floor.

It seems therefore, that the gallery played an integral role in the synagogue performance centered around the Torah shrine and *bema*. The gallery enabled the worshippers to follow and observe the ceremony conducted below, which implies that it was built with this purpose in mind. It had, therefore, a twofold function: first as a separate area, and second as a means of observing and following every rite,

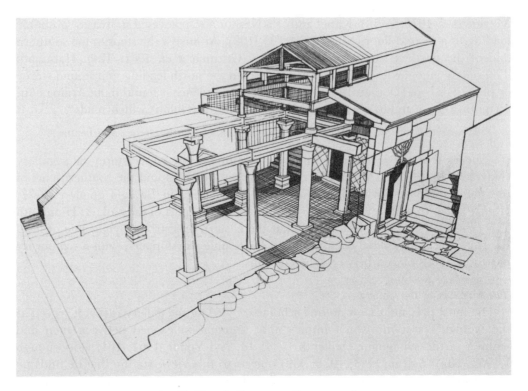

35. H. Shemʿa Synagogue Reconstruction

ceremony and form of worship without being observed. The question still remains as to who would need such a segregated observation post; the most logical answer seems to be the one already given by many scholars: that the gallery served as the women's section.

Conclusions

The major architectural feature of the synagogue was the Torah shrine. From its inception following the destruction of the Jerusalem Temple, the Torah shrine became a permanent fixture in the synagogue building. The Nabratein synagogue I, which already included an aediculae by the mid-second century, corroborates this hypothesis. Always built on the Jerusalem-oriented wall, the Torah shrine took the form or structure either of aedicula, niche or apse.

The preponderance of aediculae found in excavated Galilean and Golan synagogues indicates that the aedicula was the characteristic structure for containing the Ark in these regions. In the Beth She'an area, two synagogues possess aediculae: Ma'oz Hayim I (in its earliest phase only) and the synagogue of Rehov during all of its phases. The Judean synagogue of Hurvat Rimmon (phase III) possibly had an aedicula. The sizes of the aediculae bases range from 1.46 m. × 1.17 m. (Gush Halav), to 5.50 m. × 2.50 m. (Kazrin II) and to 8.50 m. × 3.00 m. (Rehov).

As has been shown above, aediculae were constructed on two sizes of bases; it seems reasonable to infer, therefore, that where the base is small (Gush Halav II, Meiron, 'En-Neshut and Sardis) the aedicula was erected on the whole platform; and where the base is large (Nabratein, Kazrin, Rehov) the aedicula was built only on part of the platform. In the case of synagogues which possessed two flanking aediculae, it seems that they had separate functions. One aedicula served to house the Ark of the Scrolls, and the second aedicula may possibly have held the menorah (Hachlili 1976: 43;1980b: 59). Incised wall decorations in the Beth She'arim tomb (fig. 27) show an aedicula with an Ark inside it flanking the entrance on one side, whereas on the other side, an aedicula has a menorah inside. (Cf. Meyers *et al.* 1981a: 238, 242, who suggest that the second platform at Nabratein was employed as a raised prayer platform for delivery of the priestly benediction. Seager (1972: 434) proposes that the two shrines at Sardis were built for the purpose of maintaining symmetry.)

Scholars have explained the creation of the niche as a result of changing custom, due to the shrine now being given a permanent place inside the synagogue (Avigad 1967: 100; Avi-Yonah 1961a: 173-174). A permanent place for the Ark, however, had already been established in the early synagogues, as has been shown above, by the construction of aediculae. Although synagogues with niches have been found scattered throughout the Land of Israel, there may have been local as well as traditional influences at work, because two of the niched synagogues are located at Tiberias and three are in Judea (Susiya, 'Eshtemo'a and Rimmon), within close proximity to each other.

Not only is the apse a dominant architectural feature in the synagogue, it is also a characteristic feature of churches in the Land of Israel and Syria. However, the apses of synagogues and churches bear no resemblance to each other, both in terms of style and content:

1) Synagogue structures always contain one apse. A typical church has one apse situated between two side chambers, or three apses, but seldom a single apse.

2) The synagogue apse functions as the container for the Ark and, possibly, the menoroth. By contrast, the apse in the church serves as a *synthronon*—the benches

for the seating of the priests behind the altar, and as a *bema*. This area was devoted to the priests and their assistants.

3) The orientation of the apse as the Torah shrine in the synagogue is towards Jerusalem, that is, it is built on the Jerusalem-oriented wall of the synagogue. Church buildings always construct their apses on the eastern wall.

The concept of the church's apse is considered by Butler (1923: 14) to have been copied directly from temple architecture in Syria. Meyers *et al.* (1981: note 4 on 243) contend that synagogue apses influenced those of the churches.

It seems reasonable to assume that the large bases found in front of apses and niches functioned as reading and prayer platforms, although the possibility still remains that they occasionally served simply to provide access to the Torah shrine. However, whenever a synagogue had two aediculae, the second most likely housed the menorah, rather than serving as a prayer platform.

All three types of repositories were constructed of stone, were elevated on bases and approached by steps. The Torah shrine was the receptacle for the Ark of the Scrolls which took several forms, and was probably made of wood (see p. 273ff.).

Typological differences in the Torah shrines should be attributed, either to local preferences, popular vogues or historical development. Chronologically, the aedicula is the earliest type of Torah shrine, already in existence by the second century, and the most popular type in Galilean and Golan synagogues. Several aediculae dating to the fourth century are known also from Ḥammath Gader II and Reḥov. At Reḥov the aedicula was in use throughout synagogues II and III (fourth-seventh centuries). The Maᶜoz Ḥayim synagogue I aedicula is dated to the third-fourth centuries and was replaced by an apse in the fifth century. The southern synagogue of Ḥ. Rimmon included an aedicula throughout the sixth century. Other synagogues, such as Susiya and ᶜEn-Gedi, possess aediculae in their later phases. In the Galilean and Golan synagogues the aediculae usually continued in use during the third and until the sixth century, probably due to the conservatism of the congregation and local traditions. These synagogues underwent no changes in structure, design, or ornamentation during three centuries of use and consequently there was also no change in the Torah shrine.

The round niche developed during the fourth century and was preferred in some locations such as in the Judean synagogues. However, when the niche was created by blocking previously built entrances, its shape is rectangular. Construction of new synagogues in the sixth century shows a significant change in synagogue architecture by the addition of the apse as Torah shrine enclosure. Several renovated synagogues had their aedicula or niche replaced by an apse already in the fifth century (Ḥammath-Gader and Maᶜoz Ḥayim). In the sixth century the apse was an integrally planned structure. The aedicula, on the other hand, even though built to be used as a permanent structure, was an appendage built onto the original internal wall only after the synagogue building had been constructed.

The bema placed in the front of the niche or apse probably served as a convenient area for reading the Torah, as it would have been in close proximity to the place where the scrolls were stored. Noteworthy is the fact that neither apse nor *bema* has been found in any of the Golan or Galilee synagogues.

The most striking feature of synagogue architecture is the fundamental uniformity of design among synagogue structures. Differences occur, however, when certain structural features have to be adapted to liturgical requirements, for example, to the changes in form of the Torah shrine (aedicula, niche and apse) or to the development of the monumental facade in Galilean and Golan synagogues. Synagogue plans were uniform and from the beginning took the form of a hall divided by columns into nave and aisles. These main characteristic features were usually adopted, but the builders of each synagogue felt free to improvise other structural features, which resulted in a variety of synagogue designs difficult to classify; an exception to this diversity is the northern groups of Galilean and Golan synagogues which retain considerable uniformity of structure.

Generally, the Jews tended to use a spacious hall to serve the congregation for reading the Torah and for prayer, but added the specific features of Torah shrine, benches, and gallery to suit their particular needs. Synagogue plans differ according to fashion and local building practices, the congregation's needs and financial resources, as well as according to the social standing of the donors. Nevertheless, an originality of design can be distinguished in the characteristic triple facade of the building, and in the ornamentation infused with Jewish motifs and symbols.

B) Synagogue Art

The most impressive synagogue ornamentation is seen in the Galilean and Golan synagogues which are extensively adorned with ornate exterior facades, and other architectural decoration within the prayer hall itself. A few other synagogues display remains of similar ornamentation such as ʾEshtemoʿa (Pl. 21, Goodenough 1953,III:figs. 609-616) and Ḥ. Rimmon (Kloner 1983b: 67). Further artistic embellishments include pavements decorated with mosaics which became the major adornment of the synagogue hall during the fourth-sixth centuries: many mosaics depicting figurative images came into vogue during the fourth century. Some synagogues had stone slab floors while others used plaster to floor the halls. Frescos covering the walls were a further method of synagogue decoration.

1: Architectural Ornamentation

The facades of the northern group of synagogues are richly ornamented suggesting that the synagogue was meant to impress and attract attention. The synagogue of Capernaum, for example, which is built and decorated in white limestone, must have been conspicuously impressive among the black basalt buildings surrounding it. The interior is usually kept plain, except at Capernaum and Chorazin where a rich frieze decorates the hall (Avi-Yonah, 1961a: 167, suggests decoration of the upper gallery). Architectural ornamentation consists of relief work on lintels, gables and arches, architraves, friezes, capitals and pedestals. Most synagogue sculpture consists of reliefs carved in either limestone or hard basalt stone, found predominantly in synagogues in the Galilee and Golan. The only known sculpture in the round is that of the lions which probably flanked the Torah shrine (also Avi-Yonah 1961a: 170, see p. 324).

Styles of synagogue architectural decoration were the result of reciprocal influences of east and west which were also important in the development of sculpture styles in all the arts of the area, Jewish, Nabatean, Roman-Syrian and Parthian.

As mentioned above, the northern group of the Galilean and Golan synagogues exhibit considerable uniformity in their stone construction, architectural plan, and, primarily, in their richly ornamented portals and facades which differ from synagogues in other parts of the Land of Israel. It will be necessary, therefore, to describe and discuss these monumental facades in detail, according to entrance frames, lintels, capitals, and architraves.

a) Ornate facade entrance-frames

The entrance-frames can be divided into three different types, differentiated by the ornamentation on their lintels and doorjambs.

Type A (fig. 36): these portals have a moulded stone lintel usually decorated on the face, the upper part forming a torus-like decorated frieze. The lintel was supported by two doorposts which were undecorated, moulded monoliths. The synagogues of Capernaum, Chorazin and Bar°am had consols flanking the central lintel (Pl. 38); the Tybe synagogue in the Golan also had such a feature. To this type belong lintel types I, II, V, and VI (discussed below).

Type B (fig. 37): this type is characteristic of the facade's side entrances. The entrances have a moulded stone lintel which is decorated on its face and sometimes had a torus-like frieze; it is supported by two doorposts carved as pilasters and crowned with Doric or Corinthian capitals (see Capernaum, fig. 51a,b and Ḥ. °Ammudim, fig. 12 and H. Summaqa (fig. 39) (Dar 1984: phot. pp. 73,75)). Lintel types III, and IV belong to this type.

36. Ornate Entrance Frame Type A.

37. Ornate Entrance Frame Type B.

38. Ornate Entrance Frame Type C, ʿAssalieh.

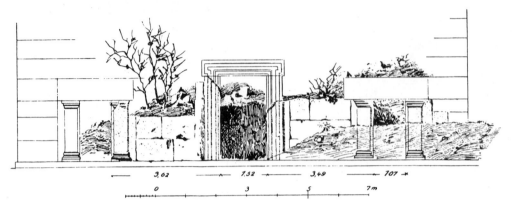

39. H. Summaqa facade.

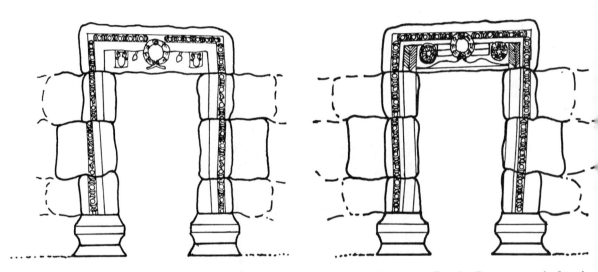

40. Kazrin Synagogue Facade.   42. Tybe Synagogue Facade, Reconstructed after the
Kazrin Facade.

Type C (fig. 38): this entrance type is characteristic and peculiar to the Golan synagogues. Its main feature is the richly carved single entrance whose structure consists of a moulded lintel and doorposts constructed of several ashlar basalt stones on Attic bases. These are usually decorated with a continuous carved frame (see Kazrin, fig. 40; ʿAssalieh, fig. 38 and Ḥ. Kanef, fig. 41. In the first two synagogues the lintel has a broad carved band consisting of a heraldic design). A similar lintel

תה דכד לטב יוסהבר חלקן ברחם

41. Kanef Synagogue Facade.

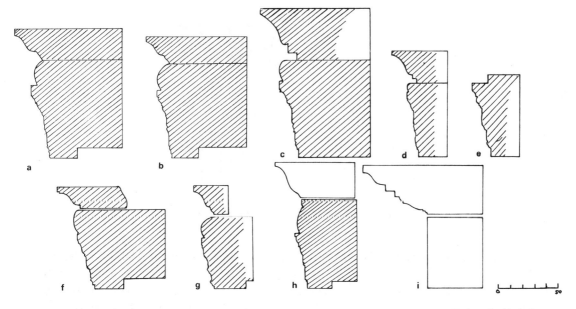

43. Lintels, Type I Mouldings: a-b) Barᶜam; c-e) Meiron; f) Nabratein; g) Gush Ḥalav; h) ᵓArbel; i) Chorazin.

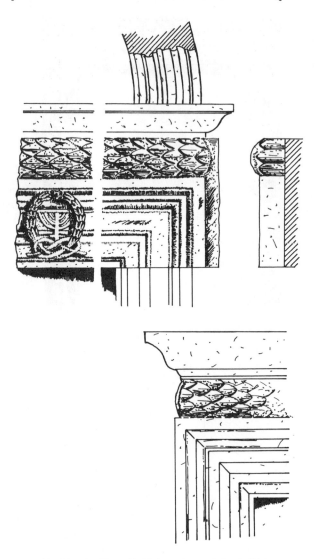

44. Lintels, Type I: Nabratein and Gush Ḥalav .

was found at Tybe (fig. 42) and similar doorposts come from Dabbura (Maoz 1981b: 109), Zumimra (Maoz 1981b: 104), Dabiya (Maoz 1980: 19) and Savitan (Maoz 1980: 33). Lintel type VIII belongs to this type of entrance frame. The only Galilean synagogue with this entrance-frame type is Chorazin (Pl. 39); however the lintel here bears no ornamentation .

A marked difference exists between entrance-frame types A and B on the one hand, and type C on the other: first, the doorposts of types A and B are each made of a monolith, whereas the doorjambs of type C are composed of several stones with Attic bases. Second, the decoration of the portal is concentrated on the lintel in types A and B, whereas type C has a frame-like ornament carved on the lintel and doorposts, with an added design on the lintel face itself.

Entrance-frames of Galilean and Golan synagogues are frequently compared to the portals of contemporary Syrian pagan temples and churches. Most of the Syrian pagan temples have richly ornamented portal frames with a floral ornament on the lintel and doorposts. Mingled classical and Oriental designs are carved on the mouldings. Portal frames with all-over carved ornamentation are already found in the first and second centuries in the Syrian Hauran, and in Nabatean temples (see Butler 1916: ill. 330-332; 328; 339-41; 1919: ill. 371, 376-7). In Roman temples, such as the Tychaion is-Sanamen and others (Butler 1915: ill. 288, 292, 317, Pls. XIX, XXVII) similar portal frames are encountered, for instance, at the Palmyran temples of Baal Shamin and Bel (see Wiegand 1932: Pls. 49, 67, 72, 79), and at the Baalbek temples of Dionysius and Bacchus (Wiegand 1921, I, Pls. 28, 29, 85; 1923, II, Pls. 8, 25, 67, 68). Christian churches continue the tradition of this carved ornamentation, but are less elaborately decorated (see Butler 1903: 133, 136, 144, 146, 191-2, 196, 203, 239, 332, 360, 407). Fourth century north Syrian churches are ornamented with similar floral and geometric all-over patterns which usually extend to the doorposts (Baccache 1980: Pls. 166-167, 177-178, 208, 233, 242, 280-283; some have a cross in the centre of the lintel decoration—see Baccache 1979: fig. 342).

Syrian-Roman portal frames carry an all-over pattern design which is usually continued on the doorjambs, and is most similar to the Golan synagogue entrance frames. Usually, however, no figurative elements are depicted on the lintel (cf. the soffit of the lintel at the Baalbek temple, Wiegand 1921: fig. 38, Pls. 67-8). General appearance of the ornate portals is similar; however, synagogue ornamentation deviates from the common Syrian-Hauranian architectural style in its rich and varied patterns and designs. The thematic variety of design and the style of carving of synagogue architectural decoration indicate an independent development, although influenced by neighbouring art.

In conclusion, it can be said that carved ornamentation in north and south Syria flourished from the first century BCE at least until the seventh century CE and included decoration of temple gates, houses and churches. Developed by local artists, and thus difficult to classify and date (see Butler 1903: 37 ff., 316 ff.), the style takes into consideration the hard basalt stone in which it is worked and exhibits peculiarities which are the trademarks of individual artists. These peculiarities and distinctions are even further foregrounded when figurative elements and Jewish symbols in synagogue ornamentation are interpreted by local artists (see lintel types below).

b) Ornamented Lintels

The three types of ornate entrance frames are associated with several different types of lintels. Most Galilean lintels are moulded in two parts which consist of a wide lower part which itself is divided into three fasciae alternating with irregular caveti, and a narrower upper part decorated with a convex frieze. Lintel decoration is divided into nine different types:

Type I: the lintels are moulded, with three fasciae and without decoration on the main section. Sole ornamentation consists of a frieze on the torus-like upper part. This type of decoration is found on the lintels of Nabratein, Gush Ḥalav, ᵓArbel (figs 43,44), and the side entrances of Barᶜam (Pls. 21,40) and Dikke (fig. 9, KW 1916: 220), which all have identical designs of laurel leaf or scales decorating the convex frieze (the Gush Ḥalav lintel has a decorated soffit depicting an eagle flanked by garlands - fig. X,20a). The Nabratein lintel is also decorated in the centre with a carving of a menorah inside a wreath (Pl. 108, fig. 44). The lintels of Meiron and ᵓArbel have no decoration at all (Pl. 22 and fig. 44).

Lintels of type I fall into two groups distinguished by their moulding style and by their size. The Meiron and Barᶜam central portal lintels are similar in moulding and size: both are 0.80 cm. high and their convex friezes are 0.20 cm. high (fig. 43). The Gush Ḥalav, Nabratein and ᵓArbel synagogues are similar to each other in mouldings (identical to the Barᶜam side portal lintels except that the convex frieze is lower). This could indicate either a change in requirement due to the smaller single entrance at Gush Ḥalav and Nabratein, or a change in moulding style.

The Ḥ. Shemᶜa lintel (fig. 50) which may belong to this group should be noted. The lintel is not moulded, and portrays a menorah as its only decoration. The H. Summaqa central portal lintel probably belongs to this group (fig. 44a; also Dar 1984:74).

Type II: this type includes lintels moulded in two parts. The main front is decorated with a central heraldic design, usually a wreath flanked by Nikae or eagles which hold the wreath and the torus-like upper part is decorated with a convex frieze of floral or geometric motifs. The lintel is surrounded by a cyma-moulded geison. This type is encountered on the Barᶜam central entrance lintel (fig. 36, Pl. 40a), the smaller Barᶜam synagogue lintel (Pl. 40b and fig. 45a) and a lintel said to come from

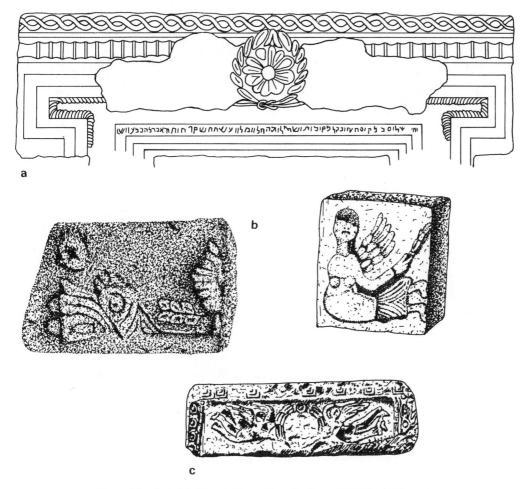

45a-c. Lintels (with Nikae), Type II: a) Bar‘am, b) Dikke, c) Ramah.

Ramah (fig. 45c), all of which portray a wreath flanked by victories. A similar lintel fragment was found at the Dikke synagogue (Golan) (fig. 45b). Similar lintels, such as the Safed lintel, are carved with wreaths flanked by eagles (fig. 46a). Two similar lintels were found at Dabbura in the Golan (fig. 46b,c) but lack the decorated upper frieze.

A fragment of a lintel from Capernaum (fig. 52g) has its upper part decorated with a winding vine frieze; its lower part is broken. To this type belong also two dif-

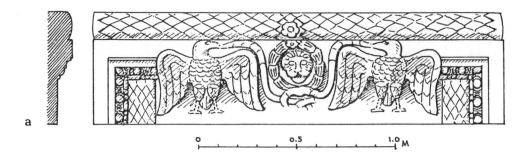

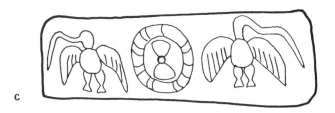

46a-d. Lintels (with Eagles), Type II: a) Safed, b-c) Dab-
burah, d) Japhiᶜa.

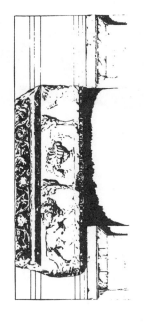

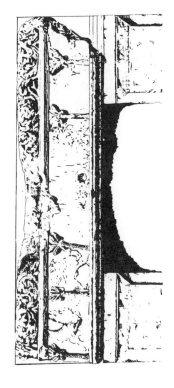

48. Lintels, Type IV.

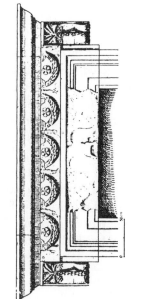

47. Lintels, Type III.

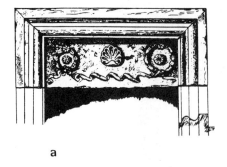 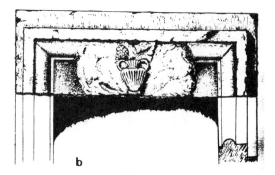

49a-c. Lintels, Type V: a-b) Capernaum, c) Kazrin side entrance.

ferent lintels from ʾEshtemoʿa each with a similar floral frieze on the upper part. On one lintel is depicted the symbol of the menorah and on the other medallions filled with geometric and floral patterns (Goodenough 1953, III:figs. 615,616).

Type III: moulded lintels decorated with a carved central design form type III. The upper part of the lintel is formed of geometric and floral designs in a torus-like decorated frieze. These lintels rest on two fasciae moulded doorposts (Capernaum, fig. 47).

Type IV: this lintel type is decorated with an antithetic design completely covering the lower wider part and is surmounted by a narrow decorated floral frieze (fig. 48).

Type V: the lintel's moulding is found only on its undecorated upper frame fasciae, the lower wider part is decorated by a tripartite design which consists of a central motif flanked by two different motifs (see also Avi-Yonah 1981a:100-103). Examples

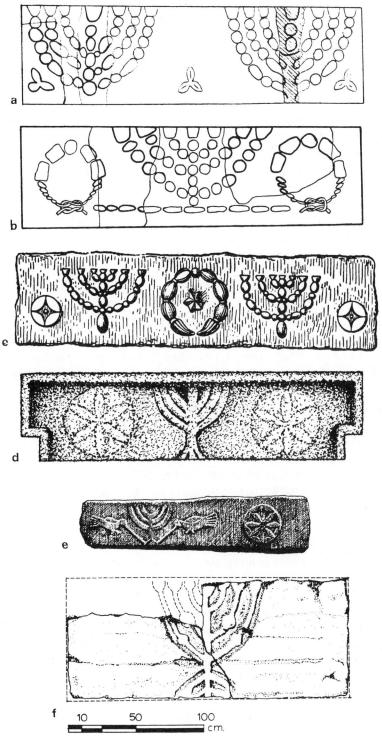

50. Lintels, Type V (with Menorah): a-b) Chorazin, c) Naveh, d)
Japhiᶜa, e) Sarona, f) Shemᶜa.

are the Capernaum lintels of the side court walls (fig. 49a,b), the Kazrin side door lintel (fig. 49c), the ʾEshtemoʿa lintel (Goodenough 1953, III: fig. 613), and the H. ʿAmmudim central entrance lintel (fig. 12) portraying an amphora flanked by two lions with their feet on a bull's head. Two lintels from Chorazin depicting a menorah flanked by wreaths (fig. 50b), and two menoroth flanking a floral motif decorate the internal side portals of the Chorazin facade (fig. 50b, 11b) (reconstructed by Yeivin 1985:fig. 2), and are similar to the Naveh lintel (fig. 50c) as well as to the Japhiʿa lintel (fig. 50d) where a menorah is flanked by two rosettes. To this type also belong some menorah lintels from other sites, such as ʾEshtemoʿa (Goodenough 1953:III,fig. 613) and Sarona (fig. 50e), and the interesting lintel from Kohav Hayarden where the menorah is flanked by two aediculae (fig. 26).

Type VI: these lintels are divided into three metopes by guilloche frame and lines decorated with a central object, such as a wreath or a lion, flanked by floral, geometric or animal designs. To this type belong the lintels of Capernaum (fig. 51a-c), and the lintels of the two side entrances at H. ʿAmmudim which each depict what seems to be a lion in the centre flanked by rosettes (KW 1916: figs 139-141). On the Japhiʿa lintel (fig. 51d) a wreath is flanked by two eagles. To this type also belong the Safsaf lintel (fig. 51e) with a scroll frame within which is a wreath flanked by two bull's heads; a lintel fragment from Faḥma (Goodenough III 1953; fig. 558); and a lintel from Capernaum with a frame of a wavy vine flanking a vase (fig. 52e). A similar fragmentary lintel was found at Kasyun. Kohl and Watzinger (1916: 160-161) compare lintels to wood and stone coffins as well as to wooden screens that, in their opinion, were built around the synagogue gallery. Avi-Yonah (1981a: 101) notes the tripartite arrangement of the lintels in comparison to decoration on ossuaries. (Foerster (1972: 103-105) suggests that this lintel type is specific to synagogues; he dates them to the second century because of the Kasyun inscription (see p. 396).

Type VII: these lintels are decorated with antithetic designs: a central wreath or vase, with vine branches issuing from it, sometimes terminating in amphorae, as appear on the lintel from Naveh (figs. 52a,b). A similar lintel from Naveh has its vine terminated by two menoroth (fig. 52c). A fragment of a lintel, from Bathra in the Golan, is carved with the same design (fig. 52d). A central vase is carved on lintels from Nabratein (fig. 52f) (its upper part has a decorated frieze similar to type I), and on the lintel from ʾAhmedieh (Golan) (fig. 52h). Fragments of probably similar lintels were found at Capernaum, Chorazin (fig. 52g, 52j) and on a side entrance at Ḥurvat Kanef (Golan) (fig. 52i,depicting birds pecking at grapes).

Type VIII: these lintels are characteristic of some of the Golan synagogues. They contain carved ornamental heraldic designs on their flat surface. At Kazrin, the

51. Lintels, Type VI: a-c) Capernaum, d) Japhiᶜa, e) Safsaf.

main entrance lintel is carved with a wreath in the centre flanked by pomegranates and amphorae (fig. 53a). At ᶜAssalieh the lintel is carved with a Torah shrine flanked by a menorah on either side (fig. 53b). At Tybe the lintel bears a wreath flanked by two elaborately carved rosettes in medallions which terminate in two branches (fig. 53c). All these lintels are decorated on their upper parts by convex friezes with an egg-and-dart design which, at Kazrin, ᶜAssalieh and Tybe, (figs. 39-40, 42) is con-

52. Lintels, Type VII: a-c) Naveh; d) Bathra; e) Daliah; f) Nabratein;
g) Capernaum; h) ʾAhmedieh; i) Kanef; j) Chorazin.

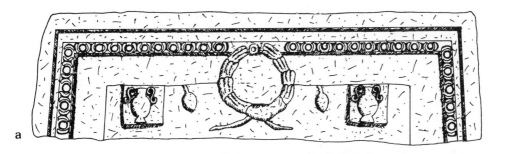

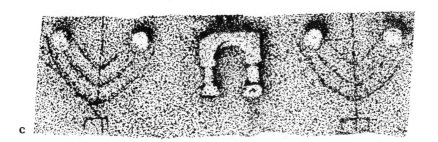

53. Lintels, Type VIII: a) Kazrin, b) Tybe, c) ⁽Assalieh.

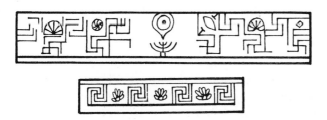

54. Lintels, Type IX: Naveh.

tinued on the doorposts. At Ḥ. Kanef the lintel is carved with a frieze of vine branches and elaborate designs of acanthus leaves and palmettes (fig. 41).
Type IX: these lintels all from Naveh (fig. 54) are decorated with an inhabited
meander frieze.

The most common lintel types in the Galilean synagogues (and elsewhere) are
types I, II and V, which are all similar in their mouldings and type of design. Type
VIII is specific to some of the Golan synagogues.

All lintel type ornamentation exhibits the elements characterstic to Jewish art of
the period, that is, antithetic (heraldic) designs, floral and geometric subjects, and
animate or inanimate themes including Jewish symbols such as the menorah. Most
of the lintels exhibit a preference for carving using the optic treatment, one of the
principles of Oriental art. Lintel decoration is carved on several planes. For instance, on the Kazrin synagogue main entrance lintel, the wreath is depicted in
highest relief, and the two flanking amphorae are placed in a square carved out of
the lintel in shallow relief, whereas the pomegranates are depicted on the lowest
plane (fig. 53a, Pl. 39b). On the ʿAssalieh lintel the aedicula and the two dots on two
of the menoroth branches are in high relief, whereas the flanking menoroth are incised in shallow relief (fig. 53b). A similar two-plane relief is encountered on the
Japhiʿa lintel (fig. 50d). The Tybe lintel is carved in at least two different planes (fig.
53c).

Classifying synagogues according to their different types of lintels may also help
to solve the problem of their dating (see pp. 396ff.). Traditions in northern Israel and
Syria were very strong, yet even so a development can be traced from the earlier
moulded lintel types I and II which have either convex frieze decoration on the upper part (I), or a heraldic design on the front (II) (fig. 43). All these lintels bear the
same profile moulding and belong to the Galilee synagogues of the third century.
Development of the other lintel types seems to have evolved from the earlier type
I into the many rich and elaborate carved designs (types II-VII). Capernaum has
various types of lintel designs which are unique to this synagogue (types III and IV),
but are also related to other synagogue lintels (types I and II).

c) Capitals

Synagogue capitals are elaborately decorated. Three main orders are prevalent in
synagogue architecture: first, the Corinthian capitals, usually massive, and the most
common (Pl 42a,b)(see Avi-Yonah 1961a: 165-166; Fischer 1984); second, Ionic
capitals including simple Ionic, elaborately ornamented diagonal Ionic (Pl 42c,d),

and the "Golan" Ionic (Pl. 42e); and third, Doric-Roman capitals. These different orders are used to support different architraves.

The most significant feature of capitals in synagogue architecture is the fact that decorative motifs are incorporated, usually of Jewish symbols and emblems. A menorah and flanking ceremonial objects appear on Corinthian capitals at Capernaum (fig. Pl. 42a). Similar capitals with menoroth are also encountered on capitals at Ḥammath Tiberias, Caesarea (Pl. 42b), Beth Guvrin and Gerasa. Other emblems, such as a wreath and a lulav occur on Capernaum capitals (see Orfali 1922: figs. 19-21). These same motifs as well as others decorate three sides of the highly ornate Ionic capitals from the Golan synagogue of ʿEn Neshut: a menorah flanked by lulavim (Pl. 42c), a menorah and an altar, and flanking birds (Pl. 42d). Similar, less ornamented diagonal Ionic capitals are also found at Dikke and Chorazin, and are decorated with branches on their volutes. Several Golan synagogues, such as Kazrin and ʿAssalieh, contain Ionic capitals exhibiting a high echinus decorated with a large egg. The side volutes are carved with a geometric design and with a line of astragal around the base (Pl. 42e). Simple Ionic capitals are found at H. ʿAmmudim and Gush Ḥalav (KW 1916: figs. 149-154, 215). Simple Doric-Roman capitals are found in synagogues in the Galilee (Barʿam, Capernaum, and Meiron) and in the Golan (Dikke). Unusual capitals are found in several synagogues: the basket capitals at Umm el-Kanatir (Maoz 1981:106), composite capitals at Capernaum, and convex "Wulst" capitals at Chorazin (KW 1916: fig. l02).

Another exclusive feature of synagogue architecture is the double corner column, the so-called heart-shaped column, found at the rear corner of the row of columnation and the transverse row. These columns are found in many of the Galilee synagogues (ʾArbel, Barʿam, Ḥ. ʿAmmudim, Capernaum, Gush Ḥalav and Meiron—fig. 1), and appear to be a continuation of similar corner columns in buildings of the Second Temple period. A further feature peculiar to synagogue architecture is the unusual colonettes which flank the windows found in Galilee and Golan synagogues. The colonettes are fluted and are surmounted by small Corinthian capitals (see ʾArbel, Capernaum and Dikke: KW 1916: figs. 8, 133, 232, 262).

Remains of capitals found in synagogues prove that the Jews also used common Roman and Byzantine decorated capitals. However, the added motifs and the special decoration of some of the Ionic and Corinthian capitals indicate that local Jewish craftsmen were working in an original style that can be observed in all aspects of architectural synagogue decoration.

A few examples of decorated pedestals are also specific to synagogue art. These are found at Nabratein (Goodenough 1953 III:516-517), ʿEn Neshut (Maoz

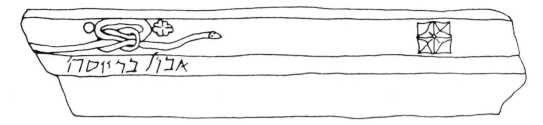

55. ʿEn Neshut Synagogue Architrave.

1981b:108), ʾAscalon and Peḥora (Ilan 1980: 118). The ʾAscalon and Peḥora examples are decorated with a menorah. (Pl. 42f)

d) Ornamented Architraves

The interior of the prayer hall of the synagogue was usually divided into nave and
aisles by two or more rows of columns, which carry moulded architraves. They are
sometimes decorated with formal patterns or special designs (see ʿEn Neshut, fig.
55) and are only found in the Golan and Galilee synagogues. The architraves are
surmounted in one of several arrangements: at Capernaum, Kohl and Watzinger
(1916: Pls. IV, V) reconstruct the architrave as having been placed directly on the
Corinthian capitals; at Dikke, Doric columns carried the architrave; at ʿEn Neshut
an architrave of long basalt stones (fig. 55) was built above the diagonal Ionic
capitals (with their additional side wings). Similar architraves occur also at Chorazin
and Umm el-Kanatir (Maoz 1980: 23). At Kazrin, the many corbel stones which
were found probably supported arches (arcades) (Maoz 1980: 38). Similarly, the
synagogue of Jericho had two rows of capitals which carried arches (Baramki and
Avi-Yonah 1936: 73).

e) A comparison between the architectural ornamentation of the synagogues at Capernaum and Chorazin

The majority of surviving synagogue sculpture comes from Capernaum and
Chorazin, two splendidly decorated and most important synagogues. A comparison
between the style and design of their ornamentation can give a clear indication of,
as well as insight into, the origins and elements of Jewish art in the Galilee during
this period; furthermore it can demonstrate the vast differences in architectural

styles existing simultaneously. Capernaum is the more magnificently decorated, due to the use of white limestone, compared to the black basalt of the Chorazin sculpture. In Capernaum the style of carving is a combination of Hellenistic and Oriental elements, and is executed usually in frontal relief on shallow planes; sometimes the connection between architectural elements and their decoration seems arbitrary.

The frieze is an excellent example of the contrasting styles in the two synagogues. At Capernaum, the frieze is a completely interwoven carving of scrolls of stylistic acanthus leaves creating circles. Emblems of various floral and geometric patterns are portrayed inside the circles (Pls. 43, 44). By comparison, the Chorazin frieze is sharply-defined and deeply carved, the forms developing out of each other, and leaving no empty spaces (*horror vacui*). The frieze is intertwined into the entablature and is an integral part of the stone block. A most common frieze pattern found at Chorazin is the round frame of acanthus leaves which turn in a circular movement (Pls. 45,46) and are carved more naturally than those at Capernaum. Inside these frames a variety of motifs are carved: rosettes, conches, wreaths, round objects, but also images from Greek mythology such as a Medusa head represented frontally as a mask (Pl. 46). Some parts of this frieze are carved on a protruding block (Pl. 45), for example, the carved aedicula which is stylized in deep and skilful relief (Pl. 28). At Capernaum there is a most noticeable difference between the style and execution of the lintels and the frieze: whereas the former are usually ornamented with a tripartite or antithetic arrangement (figs. 49a-c;51a-c), the latter has a fully interwoven carving (Pls. 43, 44). Also remarkable is a wheeled Ark (fig. 56). It is depicted in a three dimensional perspective style, reminiscent of the Hellenistic manner. Noteworthy, too, are the Jewish symbols which appear to be completely unrelated to the design of the Corinthian capitals (Pl. 42a, see also p. 217). The best example, however, of this style of carving at Capernaum is that of the two consuls, one on each side of the lintel of the central facade portal, which have been carved without any stylistic affinity uniting them: the palm trees on front of the consuls are deeply carved with details, whereas the side volutes are depicted in shallower relief (Pl. 38).

By contrast, the Chorazin basalt sculptural decoration, more Oriental in character, is monumental, powerful and impressive because of its execution in basalt, and is furthermore a completely integrated constituent of the architecture. The frieze too, carved with various motifs, is integrated artistically into the entablature. A skilful harmony exists between the hard, black stone and the Chorazin sculptures, both in style and perspective. The artist must have been highly skilled in the technique of basalt relief and the result is sculpture of the highest quality, for instance, the

56. Relief with Ark, Capernaum.

57. Mosaic Floor, Marous.

three-dimensional sculpture of the lion (fig. X,10 and p. 324). An exception to this high standard is the frieze of the vintagers treading grapes, depicted surrounded by interwoven vine branches (Pl. 47a,b), and executed in a more naive manner. All in all, the Chorazin reliefs display a sense of order and of correct proportion in spatial organization.

f) Golan sculpture

Although it is as yet too soon to talk of a distinctive artistic style when considering the Golan synagogues, yet certain features emerge which seem to suggest affinities between them. Golan sculpture is executed in the indigenous, hard, basalt stone, and the style is original and elaborate (also Maoz 1981b: 112); ornamental details enhance architraves, capitals and pedestals (Pls. 23, 26, 29, 35, 90, 98; figs. 53, X:9, 12, 20b). Original Golan variations of the Ionic and diagonal Ionic capitals with their high echinus are found at ʿEn Neshut where they are decorated with Jewish symbols (Pl. 42d); and at Kazrin and ʿAssalieh the common Ionic capital shows an ornate modification. Much figuratively carved stone masonry is found in the Golan, and most can probably be attributed to local synagogues, for instance the carved basalt eagles (Pls. 23, 26, 94) and lions (Pls. 26, 35, 90, 92). Golan sculpture is executed in divergent styles: some show highly stylized reliefs, like the ʿEn Samsam stone (Pls. 26, 88) and the ʿEn Neshut lioness (Pl. 90); others show a skilful competency in the carving such as the relief on the Umm el-Kanatir double aedicula capital which is carved on all sides (Pl. 23); still other sculpture shows simple, shallow carving, for instance, the ʿEn Neshut lintel fragment, the H. Kanef and Dabbura lintels (figs. 46b-c, 52i) and the relief of a man from Dabbura (Maoz 1981b: 112). The lintels of the synagogues at Kazrin and ʿAssalieh (fig. 53c; Pl. 41a) have carvings projecting at various degrees from the plane surface as well as incised decorations. The carved stone menoroth at Dabiya (Maoz 1981b: 106) also show incised decoration.

To sum up, Golan sculpture exhibits a rich and elaborate variety of styles showing affinities to the Galilean synagogue sculpture. Although little of the Golan carvings can compare in excellence of workmanship to the magnificent sculpture of Chorazin or Capernaum (Pls. 43-47), some of the frieze ornamentation at Dikke resembles the ornamentation at Chorazin in artistic quality, even though it is a simpler variation.

2. Floor Pavements

Decorated floors are an integral and important feature of synagogue architecture. They were paved with either a) stone slabs, b) mosaic pavements, or c) plaster, usually on a bed of small stones. Differences in the floor design are due to periodical changes in the synagogal architecture. In some instances an early mosaic pavement, as at Kazrin, would be replaced by a plaster floor; at Marous the mosaic floor was replaced by a flagstone pavement; at Maʿoz Ḥayim the opposite occurred and the stone slab floor of Synagogue I was replaced by mosaic pavements in Synagogues II and III; at H. Rimmon the plastered floor of synagogue I was replaced in Synagogue II by a decorated stone slab pavement (see Table 2).

a) Stone slab floors: most of the Galilean synagogue floors are composed of stone slabs, with the exception of ʿAmmudim, Marous I and Shemʿa which have mosaic pavements, and Nabratein I which has a plastered floor. In the Golan, Dabiye, Dikke and Umm el-Kanatir have basalt slab floors. Beth Shearim and Maʿoz Ḥayim I have flagstone floors. Some synagogues possess unusual stone floors: at Hammath

Gader II the floor is composed of *opus sectile* on a foundation of basalt blocks (Foerster 1983). At Maᶜon the nave is paved with mosaic, whereas its surrounding area is paved with stone slabs which survive in the eastern section (see Levi 1960: 9, Dunayevski 1960: 22). A unique floor decoration was discovered in the last phase of the synagogue of Ḥ. Rimmon (III). The prayer hall is paved with limestone slabs, resembling tiles, on a foundation of packed stones. In the centre, five such "tiles" are decorated with carved rosettes, arranged in a square with one rosette in the middle. North of these decorated tiles, a seven-branched menorah is incised into a slab. (Kloner 1983b: 69).

b) Mosaic pavements ("In the days of R. Abun [4th century] they began to depict designs on mosaics and he did not hinder them" (*J: Abodah Zarah* 42b)): mosaic floors were the principal ornament of many synagogues, mainly in those lacking architectural embellishment. These mosaic pavements depict figured representations and are very richly ornamented with patterns and colours. However, mosaic floors of earlier periods have been found in recent excavations, indicating that mosaic floors adorned synagogues as early as the third century, and this in areas previously thought to be lacking this type of ornamentation, that is, in the Golan and the Galilee. Up to now scholars have assumed that the change in mosaic pavement decoration took place in the third-fourth centuries (KW 1916: 145; Goodenough 1953,I: 239), together with other changes in principles of synagogue construction, such as those connected with the Torah shrine and the entrances (Avi-Yonah 1961a: 173). This new material, consequently, will have to be taken into consideration in any future conceptual revisions concerning this subject.

i) Mosaics in Galilean and Golan synagogues: at Ḥ. ᶜAmmudim (Levine 1981a:80) remains of a mosaic floor with an Aramaic inscription (Levine 1981: photo on 80) and its foundation were found at the northwest corner of the nave (Levine 1981a: Area D plan on p. 79). The excavator concludes that the mosaic floor is the original floor of the building. Thus, this would be one of the earliest synagogues possessing a mosaic floor, dating to around the end of the third century. A mosaic floor was also found recently at Ḥ. Marous, and is probably the original floor of a synagogue (Ilan and Damati 1985). The design of the mosaic is especially interesting and shows a figure surrounded by weapons, with an inscription "Yodan son of Shimon Mani." It probably represents David with the weapon he had taken from Goliath (fig. 57, Pl. 48, see p. 299). This mosaic is dated to the fifth century. At Kazrin, remains of a mosaic pavement in several colours were found to belong to the second phase of the synagogue (fifth century). They were used partly as a fill for the later plaster floor.

ii) Synagogues with Earlier Mosaics:

Ḥ. Tiberias—level IIb—A geometric design fragment of a floor was found in the nave (Dothan 1982: 22,24; Pl. 6:1,7:1-4), and was dated to the third century.

ʿEn-Gedi—A mosaic floor with a swastika as its central pattern was found underneath the later bird-decorated floor (Pl. 96a) and is dated probably to the third century (Barag *et al.* 1981: 118-119).

Susiya—Remains of early mosaic floors of white tesserae were found in the hall under a panelled and figurative polychrome pavement (Gutman *et al.* 1981: 126).

Maʿon (Levi 1960: 9)—Remains of a band of white tesserae were found 0.5 cm. below the later, and upper mosaic floor.

Beth ʾAlpha—Two fragments of an older mosaic laid under the well-known mosaic were found. One shows a design of a snake's head and the other, probably, of a shofar (Sukenik 1951: 26, Pl. XI).

ʾEshtemoʿa (Yeivin 1981: 121-122)—Mosaic pavements with floral and geometric patterns, and an Aramaic inscription, covered the hall and narthex floors.

From the above data it can be concluded that mosaics were used to cover floors as early as the third century, and consisted of geometric designs (ʿEn-Gedi, Ḥ. Tiberias) sometimes with an inscription (Ḥ. ʿAmmudim). Thus, contrary to accepted scholarly opinion, the mosaic floor immediately upon inception became part of synagogue ornamentation; it was also used to decorate some of the Galilean and Golan synagogues. Figurative, richly ornamented floors developed during the fourth century (H. Tiberias) and reached their apogee in the Byzantine period (the sixth century).

c) Plaster floors: few synagogues were paved with plaster. Only one Galilean synagogue, Nabratein I, has a plaster floor. Noteworthy, in the Golan, is the Kazrin early pavement consisting of a plaster floor inscribed with a stone slab pattern. The latest floor level is covered with smooth plaster on a foundation of stone and mosaic fragments which are remains from level II. The ʿEn Neshut synagogue is also paved with plaster (Maoz 1981b: 105, 108). The early Rimmon synagogue has a compressed plaster floor laid on a foundation of small stones (Kloner 1980b: 227; 1983b: 67).

Local tradition and fashions were also strong in the matter of floor paving. The Galilean and some Golan synagogues preferred the stone slab floors, whereas mosaic floors prevailed in most of the other synagogues from the fourth century onwards. Plastered floors were the rarest form of pavement (see table 2).

3. Frescoes

The synagogue most famous for its frescoes is the Diaspora synagogue at Dura Europos, on the Euphrates in Syria (Kraeling 1979; Gutman 1973; Goodenough 1964, vols. IX-XI). Synagogue walls in the Land of Israel were also decorated with frescoes.

Recent excavations of the Reḥov synagogue reveal many fragments of painted plaster which presumably decorated the internal walls. These plaster fragments were covered with polychrome paintings (mainly in red) of geometric and floral designs. A very interesting painting portrays a tree-like menorah and several aediculae, with columns and other details (unpublished). This synagogue also has plastered and painted columns on which were written several Aramaic inscriptions (containing dedications, Halachic laws and other texts of worship) surrounded by wreaths of vine branches (Vitto 1980: 215; 1981a:92-93; 1981b: 166 and Pl. 24:3; 1983: Pl. I). A Hebrew inscription found in the synagogue of Susiya (on the portico mosaic floor of the courtyard) gives a list of donors who, among other things, "plastered its walls with lime..." (Gutman *et al.* 1981: 128). This indicates that plastering of the walls was probably a common practice which was financially supported by donors from among the Jewish congregation.

In several synagogues remains of plaster were found, at Huseifa (Makhouly 1934: 118), Maʿoz Ḥayim (Tzaferis 1982: 219), Ḥ. Tiberias (Dothan 1982:22) and Beth ʾAlpha (Sukenik 1932: 12, 14). At Ḥ. Rimmon coloured plaster probably covered the walls of the early synagogue (Kloner 1983b: 67). The Galilean and Golan basalt-constructed walls were covered in similar white plaster: at Chorazin the bedrock at the northwest corner was incorporated into the building and was covered with plaster decorated with red pottery sherds and imprinted with a herringbone pattern, characteristic of the Byzantine period. The same decorative plaster is found at ʿAssalieh (Maoz 1980: 17, 18). Other synagogues in the Galilee and Golan using this white plaster include Ḥ. Shemʿa's Fresco Room (Meyers *et al.* 1976: 76 ff.), ʿEn Neshut, where one piece of plaster bears an inscription (Maoz 1981b: 108), and Kazrin.

Even though very few frescoed walls have survived, it seems that they were part of the interior decoration of synagogues, and should be taken into consideration as one of the various ornamental features of synagogal art. Frescoes may have as precedent the frescoed walls of Second Temple period structures, as well as mosaic floors of the same period (pp. 67-71). This manner of ornamentation developed into a very fine and rich art, as can be seen in the extraordinary paintings of Dura Europos; the Reḥov synagogue in the Land of Israel indicates how fresco ornamentation also included inscriptions of various worship and donor texts, as well as Jewish symbols.

C) SYNAGOGUE INSCRIPTIONS
(Naveh 1978; Lifshitz 1967)

Synagogues reveal about fifty Greek inscriptions, mostly dedicatory texts, and about 110 Aramaic and Hebrew inscriptions, the majority of which are Aramaic. Inscriptions are found either carved on synagogue stone architectural fragments, such as lintels, column bases and chancel screens, or worked into mosaic pavements. Few are painted on plaster (Reḥov—Vitto 1981a: 93). Most of the inscriptions can be classified in four groups:

1) Dedicatory inscriptions in commemoration of the officials and donors of the synagogue, some of which also mention the artists or builders of the synagogue. Dedicatory inscriptions are found on architectural fragments as well as on mosaic floors (Pl. 49; figs. 34,36). The dedicatory inscription usually begins "may ... be remembered for good," followed by the donor's name and the sum of his donation, and ends with a blessing formula, generally the words *Amen* and *Selah.* Common also are the words *Shalom* (= peace) and "Peace on Israel" (see the Jericho and Ḥuseifa synagogue inscriptions, Pl. 50).

2) Literary texts. Such texts sometimes appear in mosaic inscriptions, the most notable of which are the ʿEn-Gedi inscription (Pl. 51) and the halachic inscription at Reḥov (Pl. 52). Because of their uniqueness, these two, seventh century inscriptions are very important; they are also the longest inscriptions found to date.

a) The ʿEn-Gedi inscription (Nave 1978:31-31; Levin 1981b: 140-145) is divided into four parts (Pl. 51). The first two parts are in Hebrew, the latter two in Aramaic. The inscription begins with an ancestral list of mankind (mentioned in I Chron. 1: 1-4), followed by the names of the twelve zodiac signs, the twelve months, the three patriarchs and the three friends of Daniel. The third part gives a list of donors, and a statement concerning community information and secrets not to be revealed, and the fourth part lists the names of the same donors as mentioned in the third part.

b) The Reḥov Hebrew inscription (Pl. 52) (Sussmann 1981, 147) is an important halachic inscription dealing with agricultural concerns, tithes and seventh-year produce in eight regions of the Land of Israel.

3) Three fragments of marble stones found in ʾAscalon, Caesarea and Kissufim contain lists of the twenty-four priestly courses. This list as reconstructed by Avi-Yonah (1964: 46-49, fig. 1) consists of twenty-four lines, each line including the number of the course, its name and appellation, and the village or town it inhabited after the destruction of the Second Temple. Corresponding to I Chron. 24: 7-19, these lists of the twenty-four priestly courses inscribed on stone tablets are dated to the third-fourth centuries and presumably were fixed to the synagogue wall. By this

method the Jewish communities guarded the memory and tradition of the courses'
service in the Temple, in the hope that as soon as the Temple would be rebuilt the
priests would come up to Jerusalem from their various seats and serve again in the
Temple. This list identifying the order of the courses was probably composed after
the destruction of the Second Temple and the Bar Kokhba War (135 CE) (Avi-
Yonah 1964: 51-52). Each priestly course, while mourning the Temple's destruction, also remembered its appointed dates of service which were preserved in the inscriptions fixed in the synagogues. Lists were incorporated into liturgical poems
during the sixth century (Avi-Yonah 1964:53-54).

The significance of the list of priestly courses lies in its being used as an accurate
device to count off the weeks of the year: each priestly course served twice a year
(two weeks) in the Temple, so that this list serves as a kind of calendar with affinities
to the zodiac signs (Avi-Yonah 1964: 55). Both the inscribed list and the zodiac
panel are essential features in synagogal decoration, and emphasize the importance
of the Jewish calendar as a ritual element in synagogue and community life (see also
p. 301ff.).

4) Explanatory inscriptions of names and text were inserted in mosaic pavements,
next to the portrayals of Biblical scenes and the zodiac panels at Beth ʾAlpha, Ḥammath Tiberias, Naʿaran, Gaza and Japhiʿa (figs IX 35,40 and Pls. 64, 67, 71, 73,
74). A few inscriptions include dates of the synagogue buildings' erection or dedication, such as the inscription at Beth ʾAlpha, Gaza and Nabratein (fig. XI.14).

Position of Inscriptions in Synagogue Design

Inscriptions play an important and organic part in floor composition in the
synagogue, and are usually depicted within a wreath or in a tabula ansata. Inscriptions on mosaic floors can be divided into several arrangements:

1) Many of the inscriptions occupy the centre of an antithetic design, and appear
in a prominent position. An inscription flanked by lions occurs in the centre of a
panel at Ḥammath Gader and Tiberias, flanked by a lion and a bull at Beth ʾAlpha,
and flanked by menoroth in Ḥuseifa (fig. XI.14 a-c). These three panels are found
close to the entrance. In the Beth Sheʾan B (small) synagogue three inscriptions are
flanked by antithetic birds (Pl. 85, fig. XI.14.e). At Gaza the "inhabited scrolls"
pavement has an inscription flanked by peacocks in the centre medallion of row two
(fig. XI.14d, Pl. 86). These inscriptions have parallels in church mosaic pavements.

2) Inscriptions occupy the front section of the entrances to the synagogues of Beth
Sheʾan A, Jericho, Naʿaran, Reḥov and Susiya (figs XI.2,11,13,14).

3) At Ḥammath Gader, inscriptions are depicted on the middle panel's upper border and two inscriptions are framed as part of the geometric carpet in the third panel (fig. XI.12).

4) The middle panel of the House of Leontis at Beth Sheʾan has an inscription framed by a wreath and surrounded by birds (Pl. 69).

5) At Maʿon the inscription is depicted above the "inhabited scrolls" carpet, in front of the apse.

6) A unique inscription at ʿEn-Gedi fills the west aisle (Pl 51) and the longest inscription at Reḥov occupies the synagogue narthex (Pl. 52, fig. 28).

The inscriptions, although sometimes occupying a central position in the synagogue pavement, do not always follow the general orientation of the synagogue hall. See for instance, the front panel in the Ḥammath Tiberias mosaic (figs. X,7a; XI,1) and the Gerasa synagogue narthex pavement (fig. IX, 33a).

D) CONCLUSIONS

Origin and Development of Synagogue Architecture

The origins of the synagogue, especially of the Galilean type, have been researched by many scholars who have suggested various derivations. Broadly speaking, these explanations can be divided into those which suggest that the prototype is to be found in secular Hellenistic basilicae and Roman triclinia (KW 1916: 176-178), and those which suggest that the Second Temple period synagogue is the model for the later synagogue. The former view is supported by Netzer (1980a: 113) who pinpoints the prototype to the Herodian triclinium in the Jericho palaces, because of the similarity of plan and architectural conception. Both the synagogue and the triclinium served as assembly halls, he argues, and in both the exterior is the architectural focal orientation. These seem very unlikely reasons, first because the function of each assembly hall is completely different: the Herodian triclinium is secular in purpose whereas the synagogue is used for religious rituals; second, although the orientation of the triclinium is indeed outside, the focal point in Galilean synagogues, that is, the Torah shrine, is *inside*, on the interior of the facade wall. The latter view of the origins is advocated by Avigad (1981: 42-44) who maintains that the Masada synagogue's plan is the prototype for the Galilean synagogues and is itself a development of the Hellenistic basilica. Foerster (1981a: 47-48) prefers a source for the prototype in Nabatean temple courts. Both these latter suggestions (rejected by Maoz 1981a: 40-41; and see Tsafrir 1981:39-40) are overly concerned with architectural affinities of columnation or arrangement of benches, however, while at the same time ignoring the most significant feature of the synagogue which is completely lacking in the prototypes: the Torah shrine, an internal feature and the focal point of the building, intentionally built on the Jerusalem-oriented wall. This is an innovation which originated after the destruction of the Temple. Moreover, marked differences do exist between the Second Temple structures, on the one hand, and the later synagogues, on the other. During the Second Temple period, the main ritual practices were conducted in the Jerusalem Temple, and the synagogue structure was merely an assembly hall which included stone benches and columns. Such synagogue structures possibly had a central focal point but this has not been decisively demonstrated (see pp. 87-88). By comparison, the later structures operated as a combination of congregational assembly hall and, more importantly, as a place for reading the Scripture. They contained a predetermined, permanently-built focal point, the Torah shrine, which was established on the Jerusalem-oriented wall. Such buildings also had to serve as centres for the ritual practices now concentrated exclusively in the synagogue, which explains the emphasis placed on the Torah shrine, which symbolized the sanctity of the place and acted as a reminder of the Temple. A further fundamental difference between the Second Temple period assembly hall and the later synagogue lies in the positioning of the benches. In the earlier structure they were constructed prominently along all four walls whereas in the later structure they were oriented according to the location of the Torah shrine (see table 2 for list of synagogues which contained such benches).

At the same time, some architectural elements are common both to Second Temple period structures, both religious and secular, and to the later synagogues (as Avigad suggests, 1981: 42-44), such as the columnation of the hall, the benches, the corner double columns of the Herodian triclinia and of the Gamla synagogue, and some motifs of ornamentation (see p. 84).

The early basalt synagogue of Capernaum, uncovered in recent excavations, is dated to the first century and exhibits the same plan found in the later (fourth-fifth centuries) limestone synagogue (pp. 85-86). An important example of the development of synagogue architecture is manifested in the Nabratein synagogue (Meyers *et al.* 1982: 40-42): synagogue I, dated to the second century is a small broadhouse, with benches built along the east, west and north walls. Twin stone bases of aediculae flank the entrance on the south wall (fig. 23a). Synagogue II, dated to the mid-third century, is an enlargement of the earlier: the north wall was moved outwards to the north, thus creating a longitudinal hall; two stylobates divided the hall into nave and two aisles; the bases of the two aediculae were raised; the benches were extended to the north; and a portico was added to the south facade (fig. 23b). Thus, in the mid-third century a building with longitudinal axis and division into nave and aisles was established, and characterized synagogue building plans from then on. Nabratein I also establishes the fact that already by the second century a permanent Torah shrine in the form of an aedicula was being built on the Jerusalem-oriented wall beside the central entrance. This is characteristic of the Galilean synagogues from this time on.

Galilean and Golan synagogues

The Galilean and Golan architectural style is considered to have originated in southern Syria. However, careful analysis and consideration induces us to conclude that the style of the synagogue's facade and portals as well as technical architectural details were influenced by the Hauranic-Roman style only very generally. The Roman-Syrian temples were entirely different both in plan and content. Their triple portals differ from the facades of the Galilee synagogues: the central entrance of the former is usually much higher than the side doors and the ornamentation and moulding profiles of the lintels and doorjambs are entirely different. Pagan temples, considered the god's abode, were small structures serving only a few priests who participated in the rites, and usually contained an idol of the god in the adyton (Hachlili 1971: 29-57). The synagogue, on the other hand, consisted of a large building which had to serve all of the participating congregation within its walls. Jewish art, as it is manifested in synagogue sculpture of the Galilee and Golan, reveals its connection with the prevailing Hellenistic art. Characteristic Oriental elements as well as Syrian-Hauran influences are certainly recognizable in the Jewish art, but it displays some novelty and inventiveness in design which grants it consequence. This can be clearly seen in the architectural features which developed in synagogue construction. For example, the general facade features, especially the triple portal (or single portal) on the southern, Jerusalem-oriented wall, the ornamented lintels, the carved arch above the central portal, are all characteristics specific to Galilean and Golan synagogues.

The earliest synagogues whose ornamented facades bear type A portals are dated to the third century and are distinguished by lintel type I, an arch above the central entrance, and a Syrian gable (Barᶜam, Meiron, Gush Ḥalav I and Nabratein II—fig. 36; at ʾArbel a lintel similar to these may have belonged to the original southern entrance). Later synagogues are generally very similar with portal type A facades, but also have portal type B, and lintel types I-V, with an arch above the central entryway (Capernaum and ᶜAmmudim, fig. 37). The Golan synagogues have impressive facades but are distinguished by a single portal, type C, and by lintel type VIII (figs. 38,53). The exception is Dikke, which has lintel type I.

Many architectural features differentiate the Galilean and Golan synagogues from the remainder of the synagogues in the Land of Israel. Consequently, it would be useful to consider them separately as a group, and also to compare them with the other synagogues.

Galilean and Golan synagogues share some common architectural features (also Maoz 1981b: 113):

1) All the synagogues of this group have stone structures. Most of the Galilean synagogues are built of limestone, except for the Chorazin and Shura synagogues, which, like the Golan synagogues, are built of basalt.

2) Ornamented facades appear on both Galilean and Golan synagogues.

3) The outer walls are built of ashlar stones divided by flat pilasters supporting a cornice (Capernaum and Chorazin).

4) The most important common feature in this group is the location of the Torah shrine, which is always built adjacent to and on the inside of the main entrance (pp. 173-177 figs. 1, 2, 20). Its location is always associated with the orientation of the facade, and in the Galilee and several Golan synagogues, is on the southern Jerusalem-oriented wall. As orientation towards Jerusalem was obligatory for the Torah shrine, and as the facade of the Galilean synagogues was Jerusalem-oriented, it follows that the Torah shrine has to be built on the same wall. There are exceptions to this rule however: the synagogue of ʾArbel in the Galilee probably underwent a later change in the structure: the niche for the Ark was rebuilt on the Jerusalem-oriented wall and the entrance was then moved to the wall opposite it; in Kazrin in the Golan the Torah shrine in the fifth-sixth century synagogue was also built on the southern Jerusalem-oriented wall, even though the entrance facade was constructed on the opposite north wall.

Differences between the Golan and Galilee synagogues lie in some structural details (see also Maoz 1981b: 113):

1) An ornamented monumental facade with a triple portal is more common in the Galilee (figs 36,37) whereas a single portal facade is more common in the Golan (fig. 38; pp. 202-203).

2) In most of the Galilee synagogues the prayer hall has a transverse row of columns, which adds another widthwise aisle (fig. 1). This row of columns usually has corner, heart-shaped columns (fig. 1, Capernaum, Barʿam, ʿAmmudim, Meiron, ʾArbel), a feature absent from the Golan synagogues.

3) The columns in most of the Galilee synagogues were built on stylobates and stood on pedestals. In the Golan, pedestals were only found in excavations at ʿEn Neshut. Another pedestal, probably from ʿEn Neshut, was found in the Golan (from Peḥora, Pl. 42f).

An important difference between the various synagogues' decoration is noted in the emphasis on the exterior in the northern synagogue group, that is, on the facade with its rich ornamentation which must have emphasized the synagogue building and must have made it stand out conspicuously from its surroundings. The other synagogues are sparingly decorated on the exterior; the emphasis is on the interior where the hall is decorated with mosaic pavements (discussed in chapter IX). Avi-Yonah (1961a:180) maintains that this sparse exterior decoration reflects the impoverished state of the Jewish community during the Byzantine period. It seems more likely, however, that the reason for this remarkable contrast in ornamentation is that the elaborately decorated facade with triple or single portals was common only to the northern (Galilean and Golan) synagogues due to local traditions; similarly decorated facades are traditional in Syrian architecture throughout the Roman and Byzantine periods. A very important feature of Syrian architecture followed by synagogue architecture is the conservatism of the carving traditions.

Synagogue buildings in other areas of the Land of Israel usually have a frontal axial courtyard (Beth ʾAlpha, Beth Sheʾan, Maʿoz Ḥayim, Reḥov, Susia, Naʿaran, Gerasa, Ḥammath Gader, figs. 4,6,7,28) (from sometime in the fifth century onward the synagogue also has a narthex) which made a decorated facade unnecessary. These facades were not viewed from outside, whereas the Galilean and Golan synagogues did not use frontal courtyards although some, such as Capernaum (fig. 24), have side courtyards.

Orientation

The orientation of the synagogue has been much debated but generally it has been accepted that the direction of the synagogue was facing Jerusalem. Scholars maintain that in the Galilean synagogues, the facade faced towards Jerusalem, whereas in later synagogues the Torah shrine faced Jerusalem (Sukenik 1934: 50-52, 86; Goodenough 1953, I: 205-208, 216-218, 254-259). Some exceptions to this rule are found including Beth Sheʾan A, Ḥuseifa and Japhiʿa. (Avi-Yonah 1973: 42). Seager (1981: 41) proposes that more than one tradition existed with regard to orientation of synagogue structures. It seems most likely, however, that synagogue orientation was determined by the position of the Torah shrine structure which was always constructed on the Jerusalem-oriented wall. The congregation inside the hall prayed facing the Torah shrine, and, therefore, facing Jerusalem (Hachlili 1976: 52). The *T. Meg.* IV, 2 states:

> "How did the elders sit with their faces toward the people and their back toward the *qodeš* and when the chest is set down, it has to stand with its front toward the people and its back toward the *qodeš*..."

This explanation signifies that the Ark of the scrolls stood with its back to the *qodeš*: in other words, the *qodeš* was the Torah shrine. Prayers were, therefore, conducted facing the Torah shrine, toward Jerusalem, and although the location of the Torah shrine always determined the direction in which the congregation prayed in the synagogue, this location did not necessarily coincide with the orientation of the building itself. In fact, there are several synagogue buildings in which the Torah shrine is built on the Jerusalem-oriented wall, although the synagogue orientation is in a different direction, for example, at Ḥ. Shemᶜa,(fig. 8). In other synagogues, such as at Caesarea, Ḥuseifa and Japhiᶜa, not enough of the building has survived to determine the location of the Torah shrine, which could, however, have been on the southern Jerusalem-oriented wall. Furthermore, the local topographical and environmental conditions were also factors in determining the orientation of these buildings. Beth Sheᵓan A, which some scholars consider to be a Samaritan synagogue, has its apse oriented to the west (perhaps towards Mount Gerizim); Avi-Yonah (1981h: 280) states that the entrances point to the northeast.

In conclusion, it appears that the construction of most of the synagogues in the Land of Israel (as well as in the Diaspora) took into consideration local topography; their orientation, however, is always determined by the Jerusalem-oriented Torah shrine structure. Consequently, the differences in synagogue building orientation depend on local traditions or vogues regarding the location of the Torah shrine. For example, Galilean synagogues (fig. 1) have facade and Torah shrine both on the same Jerusalem-oriented wall, whereas the Judean broadhouse synagogues of ᵓEshtemoᶜa and Susiya have their niches on the northern Jerusalem-oriented wall and entrances on the east, side wall (figs. 5,6); most of the sixth century apsidal synagogue buildings are oriented with their apses on the Jerusalem-oriented wall. The Beth ᵓAlpha synagogue, for instance, has its apse on the southern Jerusalem-oriented wall and its entrances on the opposite wall (fig. XI,3), whereas the southern synagogues of Maᶜon and Gaza have their apses on the northern Jerusalem-oriented wall and their entrances on the opposite wall. The Jericho apse (fig. 4) is built on the western Jerusalem-oriented wall and has entrances facing it.

The synagogues of the Land of Israel were not built according to a stereotyped plan, nor were they designed according to an authoritative law. Synagogue building plans can be classified in two distinct categories:

1) Those where the longitudinal stone structure is columnated, has benches, and is characterized by a richly decorated stone facade (distinctive of the Galilean and Golan synagogues);

2) Those where the broadhouse or "basilical" type of building is characterized by an axial court and narthex in front of the prayer hall, which obviates the need for

a decorated facade. These buildings are usually constructed of concrete, and consist of most synagogues in the Land of Israel.

Furthermore, several features encountered in most of the excavated and surveyed synagogues direct attention to an originality and individuality in their plans. These features include the Torah shrine, the triple portal, the gallery, as well as various methods of ornamentation of the facade, interior and floors. The highly ornamented facade exterior, characteristic of the Galilean and Golan synagogues, is a further original synagogue structural feature. Differences in plans among contemporary synagogues are usually due to regional and local traditions and local priorities as well as fashion. Any changes in synagogue designs probably came about as a result of changes in theological concepts. Whereas Galilean synagogues indicate a preference for entrances and Torah shrines both on the same, Jerusalem-oriented wall, in other localities the Torah shrine is on the Jerusalem-oriented wall with the entrance on another. An important stage in the evolution of the Torah shrine location is the development of the apse during the later fifth-sixth centuries.

Scholarly opinion differs concerning the origin of the synagogue building plan and its sources of inspiration, such as the Hellenistic basilica, pagan triclinium or other public structures. It appears most likely that synagogue structures were a synthesis and accumulation of a variety of plans and architectural features which were themselves influenced by traditional customs as well as by contemporary vogues, together with the Jewish congregation's social and religious needs. The rich ornamentation of the facade, walls, floors and other areas of the synagogue was influenced by contemporary architectural styles in secular and religious buildings in the Land of Israel and Syria. A combination and synthesis of all these elements resulted in a house of worship functionally planned and lavishly decorated by the Jewish congregation for itself. Utilizing previously-constituted tenets within their own tradition, the Jews also adapted various elements of architecture and art from their neighbours. In this way, they succeeded in creating aesthetic and monumental structures which harmonized with the spirit of Judaism in the Land of Israel.

CHAPTER NINE

ICONOGRAPHY AND SYMBOLISM

A) Jewish Symbols

Specific Jewish symbols, such as the menorah, the Ark and the ritual objects, are to be found in both synagogal and funerary art. These symbols express profound and significant values distinctly associated with Judaism, and thus were used frequently throughout Late Antiquity by Jews in the Land of Israel and in the Diaspora where they held a prominent place in the vocabulary of Jewish art. These chosen Jewish religious symbols derived from the Temple rites and ceremonies, which is why only a few symbols were actually used and why the repertoire is so limited.

Many other symbols and images were taken from the contemporary Hellenistic-Roman world; forms were borrowed but were divested of their original meaning. Even if the form of the pagan motif was appropriated it would be wrong to assume that its symbolic value was also transferred. On the contrary, a symbol has a certain value which is applicable only within its context and which loses significance when transplanted into another cultural context.

Avi-Yonah rightly warns (1973: 126) ''...against assuming that transitory symbolical values, good for their own period and environment, can be transferred to another without losing their meaning. Symbols stand for certain values, and certain times, and are not good for all eternity.''

Erwin R. Goodenough's monumental and extensive work assembled into thirteen volumes (1953-1968) deals with the subject of Jewish symbolism in the Hellenistic-Roman world, including relevant archaeological and literary evidence. Goodenough's thesis is as follows: due to the influence of the Pharisees during the Second Temple period, Jews did not depict figurative art. After the destruction of the Temple, and because of a weak religious leadership, Jews accepted symbolism and ornamentation from the Hellenistic-Roman world. As both Jewish and pagan symbols are portrayed together, they must all equally have symbolic meaning. The vocabulary of Jewish symbols is limited, the borrowed motifs being chosen from a much larger repertoire, so that this deliberate, selective appropriation merits consideration. Furthermore, he attributes symbolic meaning to all motifs, whether architectural, floral, geometric or animal. The Jews even began to use pagan art in the full knowledge of its symbolic connotations. Yet with their use in Jewish synagogal and funerary art, these symbols gradually lost their original content and were given new values associated with a mystic, eschatological belief in immortality and hope for resurrection. The Jews who followed this new mysticism excluded themselves from normative Judaism and were a movement of Hellenized Jews who practiced a mystic anti-rabbinical Judaism. Moreover, normative and official Judaism never permitted the use of any image or representational art in any period. Goodenough's conclusions however have not been accepted, in fact his thesis has met with outright rejection (Nock 1955, 1957, 1960; Avi-Yonah 1973; Kraeling 1979: 340-346; Urbach 1959; M. Smith 1967; Neusner 1975a,b; Avigad 1976: 283-286).

In the Second Temple period, the Jews refrained from using figurative art or symbolic motifs and themes. The motifs used were mostly geometric, floral and architectural although occasionally significant emblems were used, such as the menorah. The aniconic Jewish art was a result of Judaism's defence against the Hellenistic assault on their religion and culture at a time when the Hellenistic rulers were attempting to force Jews into idolatry. Jews kept the Biblical prohibition of "no graven image" (Ex. 20:4; Deut. 5:8), as well as many stricter laws. Furthermore, the Hellenistic culture was only able to influence the material values such as the ornamental motifs and the language, but could not turn the Jews into Hellenized thinkers and philosophers. The real threat to Judaism's survival from this time on was from Christianity, which developed out of Judaism and had religious and cultural affinities with it. This challenge to Judaism's independence was even stronger from the fourth century on, when Christianity became the official religion of the Roman Empire. At this time especially the Jews needed to assert their own identity and turned therefore to symbolism. They chose specific symbols which the Jewish communities as well as individuals felt could express their national faith, and could represent religious ideas with which they could identify.

An interesting example of the way an image sign developed into a symbol may be seen in the case of the menorah. The menorah was probably a professional sign of the priests during the Second Temple period, a sign of their duty and office, also signifying the sacred Temple vessel, along with the Table. Only after the destruction of the Temple did the menorah image change from a specific official and limited emblem into a symbol of general but profound connotation, thus becoming the principal Jewish symbol.

The essential Jewish symbols are those phenomenal, unique Jewish objects such as the menorah, the Ark, the ritual utensils and the conch (discussed in this chapter). Goodenough's (1958, IV: 44) contention that "the choice between a menorah and a bird eating grapes was a matter of indifference...so much had the two come to symbolize the same essential religious attitude...'' is utterly unacceptable. The motifs and emblems in Jewish art borrowed from the pagan world were used either lacking their original meaning, for their decorative effect only, or were given a different significance in Jewish art. Other motifs and designs had symbolic meaning, previously absent, attributed to them: the zodiac served as a calendar (p. 309), and lions signified the guarding of the Jewish symbols, the menorah and the Ark (p. 328). Jews carefully selected motifs and iconography of a symbolic character and depicted them in their synagogal and funerary art. By contrast the Christians seldom introduced sacred symbols on their church pavements as to do so was forbidden in 427 CE by an imperial decree (*Theodosian* Code I, tit. VIII). Thus, crosses and other symbols were used for church floors only in a few cases in unimportant places (Avi-Yonah 1960a: 16).

1. The Menorah

The menorah is by far the most dominant and widespread motif in Jewish art and in addition has become one of the symbols of the Jewish People. Its symbolic potency is so strong that the founders of the new Jewish state chose the menorah, as it is represented on the Arch of Titus in Rome (Pl. 53), as the national symbol.

The menorah, or seven-branched candelabrum, as represented in ancient Jewish art consists of a vertical central shaft which supports six branches, three of which are attached to each side of the shaft. The branches are usually depicted curving upwards in a semicircle, although in a few cases they are angled, sometimes attached horizontally to the shaft and then angled vertically upwards. The branches all usually reach the same height, and are joined by a horizontal bar which is laid across them. The menorah usually has a tripod base at the foot of the shaft, but sometimes a solid base with conical profile is shown. An interesting suggestion is that the menorah may in earliest times have reflected the shape of a plant or a tree (Goodenough 1954, IV:73-4; M. Smith 1958:497-512; C. Meyers 1976). Whether this is the case or not, the symbolism has become too stylized for ancient associations to have survived. Other important questions relate to the places where ancient portrayals of the menorah are depicted and to the materials used.

The History of the Menorah

A candelabrum was one of the cult vessels used in temples of ancient times. Candelabra appear in ritual illustrations, their function connected with light or fire. Some of these candelabra are similar to the conjectured menorah of the First Temple

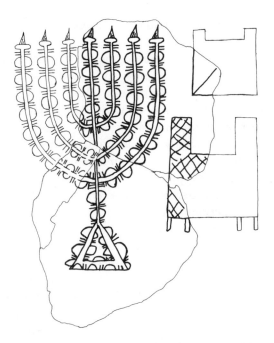

1. Menorah Incised on Stucco from the Jewish
Quarter Excavations, Jerusalem.

(Hachlili & Merhav 1985:257,fig. 1). In the Temple the menorah was lit by the priests as an important element in the ceremony, during the daily ritual, regularly both in the evening and the morning, in order to fix the time and order of the other functions of the Temple (Ex. 25:37; 30:8); the menorah was also lit to mark important events, such as the celebration of the dedication of the Tabernacle (Num. 8:1-4). After Judas Maccabaeus renovated the Temple in c. 168 BCE following his victory, he lit the lamps of the menorah (I Macc. 4:49).

On the three yearly feasts of Passover, Pentecost and Tabernacles, the custom was observed of taking the holy vessels (the Menorah and Table) out to the Temple court. This was done so that the people who came for the celebrations of the feast could approach them and gaze on them (Safrai 1965:179-180; 1976:891); another custom was "drawing back the curtain (*Parochet*) at the entrance to the sanctuary gates". These customs were not particularly connected to the pilgrimage itself but were intended more to show the people the splendour of the sanctuary and its vessels. This could explain the incised menorah and table on the wall of a private house in Jerusalem (fig. 1): someone had seen the vessels and could incise them from memory (Avigad 1983: 147-149).

The menorah is not artistically represented before the second half of the first century BCE (Rahmani 1980). The first known and dated depiction is on a coin of the last Hasmonean king, Mattathius Antigonus (40-37 BCE) (Pl. 59) (Meshorer 1982,I:93-94). As a result of the struggle in 37 BCE between Herod and Antigonus, the future of the Jewish kingdom was determined. Antigonus as king and High Priest was supported by the priestly families and others opposed to Herod. Antigonus stressed his priestly heritage and legitimate lineage by depicting sacred Temple vessels on the coins he minted; this was by way of contrast with the contemporary coins Herod minted which depicted Roman ceremonial objects (Meshorer 1982, I: 84, 94; II: 19-22). The depictions of the menorah and the table on the coins of Antigonus were meant therefore to stress his being a Jewish king and High Priest. By using them to emphasize his legitimacy, however, he rather demonstrated the opposite, that is, the precariousness of his political position at that time.

Several incised depictions of menoroth of the Herodian period have recently been discovered, one of them in the Jewish Quarter in Jerusalem (fig. 1); another on a small stone sun-dial from the Temple Mount excavations (fig. 2a), while several more are lightly incised on a wall in Jason's Tomb (fig. 2b). The most famous of the early depictions is that of the Temple Menorah, which appears on the Arch of Titus,, (Pl. 53, fig. 3) depicted in a panel which shows the Temple treasures being carried out of Jerusalem as booty by Titus' troops in 70 CE, after the destruction of Jerusalem. These early menoroth have branches which curve upwards, and solid conical bases. The Jewish Quarter menorah is the first to have decorated branches as well as to be equipped with light fittings which appear to be lit. All of these are probably depictions of the menorah which stood in the Second Temple (for a detailed discussion see Hachlili §Merhav 1985). All later representations of the menorah seem to be based on this one, the only change to occur being in the base of the menorah, which is later shown as a tripod.

The menorah is found depicted on reliefs, on capitals, lintels, synagogue screens, tomb stones and on synagogue mosaic floors. There are several portrayals of pairs of menoroth flanking the Ark in synagogue mosaics. Only two working menoroth, as distinct from depictions, are known: a stone relief from Ḥammath-Tiberias (Pl. 54) and a bronze menorah from ʿEn-Gedi (Pl. 57). This is probably because the value of the materials which would have been used to manufacture ceremonial articles, such as gold, silver or bronze, would have rendered them liable to plunder. Furthermore, it is unlikely that wood would have survived from antiquity. Lamps found in the Land of Israel and the Diaspora show menoroth depictions with many

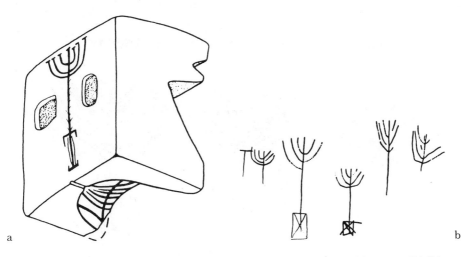

2. a) Small Sun Dial, Temple Mount Excavations, Jerusalem; b) Incisions on a Wall in Jason's Tomb, Jerusalem.

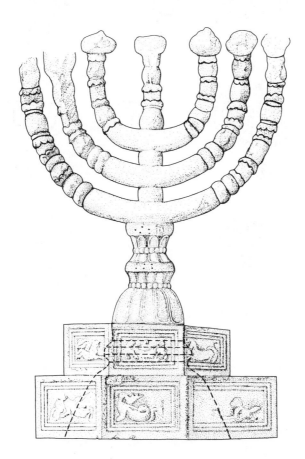

3. The Temple Menorah on the Arch of Titus, Rome.

4. a) Menoroth on Lamps; b) Menorah on Sarcophagus from Rome.

interesting forms (see fig. 4). Some indicate that the menorah was created from several sections (fig. 4; and Sussman 1982:121).

The Form of the Menorah (fig. 5a, b)

The menorah usually appears as a seven-branched candelabrum with a light on top of each branch and the seventh light placed on the centre shaft. From surviving depictions three main components of the menorah can be identified: the base, the branches which are reproduced in many variations, and the light fittings on the top of the branches.

a) The base (fig. 5). The Biblical text does not describe the base of the menorah. Art works which have survived from antiquity provide us with a number of styles. The base of the Second Temple period menorah has a conical shape (figs. 1,3). The menorah on the Ḥammath Tiberias mosaic has a base consisting of a concave plate borne by three animal legs (fig.8a; Pl. 101) as do the ivory plaque from Beth Sheʾan (Pl. 58) and the Dura Europos fresco (fig. 11). A realistic portrayal of three animal legs is to be seen in the Maʿon mosaic floor (fig.14b, Pl. 87), while even more stylized animal feet are to be seen in the Jericho, Gerasa, Beth Sheʾan A and B synagogues (fig. 5,6). The most common form of base consists of a simple tripod, with which the very stylized menoroth discussed above are provided (fig. 5,7). The menoroth of the Beth ʾAlpha mosaic are particularly interesting due to the unusual way in which the artist decided to portray the tripod bases (fig. 8b, Pl. 102).

b) The branches. A description in Exodus 25:33-36 decrees the shape of the menorah which was to be used in the Tabernacle. Each branch must consist of three cups made like almonds, which were each to be surmounted by a capital and a flower. Many depictions of menoroth, dating from the period of the Second Temple and later, appear to conform to this Biblical description (see fig. 5a). One particularly ornate menorah, which probably owes its survival to its being made of stone, was found at Ḥammath-Tiberias (Pl. 54a, b). It has seven branches, each of which is constructed of a sequence of alternating pomegranates and cups. The menoroth which are portrayed in the synagogue mosaic floor at Hammath-Tiberias are strikingly similar to this stone example found nearby (fig.8a, Pl. 101). A similar example is carved on a lintel found at ʾEshtemoʿa and a more stylized example of a tree branch is worked into the mosaic floor of a small prayer room at the Beth Sheʾan synagogue B (fig. 6; Pl. 85). The menoroth shown flanking the Ark in the Ḥuseifa (Pl. 56), Beth ʾAlpha (Pl. 102), and Naʿaran synagogue mosaic floors (fig. 8c), are also equipped with branches in stylized forms of capitals and flowers (fig. 5). A variant is to be found on the magnificent gilded gold glasses which originally came

	BASE	BRANCHES	GLASS	LAMP
HAMMATH TIBERIAS				
BETH SHE'AN A				
BETH 'ALPHA				

5a. Chart with Forms of Menoroth.

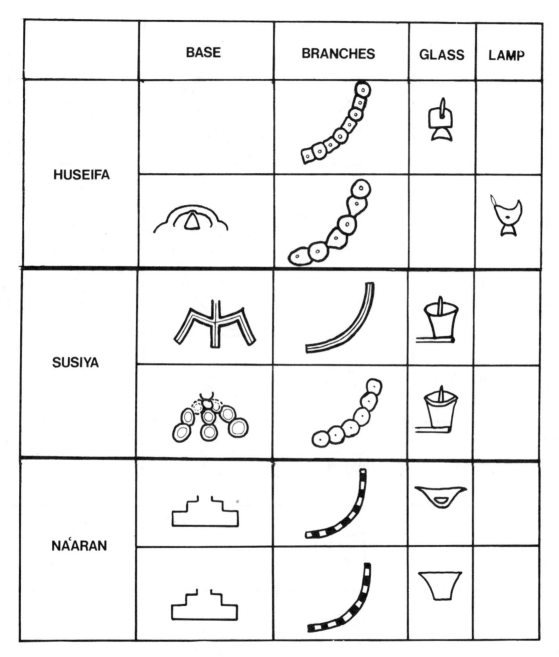

	BASE	BRANCHES	GLASS	LAMP
HUSEIFA				
SUSIYA				
NAʿARAN				

5a. Chart with Forms of Menoroth.

NAME	BASE	BRANCHES	GLASS
MA'ON			
BETH SHE'AN B'			
MA'OZ HAYIM			
JERICHO			
GERASA			
HULDA			
'EN GEDI			

5a. Chart with Forms of Menoroth.

	BASE	BRANCHES	GLASS
JAPHIAᶜ			
H. SHEMAᶜ			
HAMMAT TIBERIAS			
BETH SHEᶜAN			

5a. Chart with Forms of Menoroth.

NAME	BASE	BRANCHES	GLASS
BETH SHEʿARIM			
ʾESHTEMOʿA			
ʾASHKELON			
ʾASHDOD			

5b. Chart with Forms of Menoroth.

6. Menorah from Beth Sheʾan B Mosaic Floor.

7. Menoroth Flanking the Ark, Beth Sheʿarim drawings.

a

b

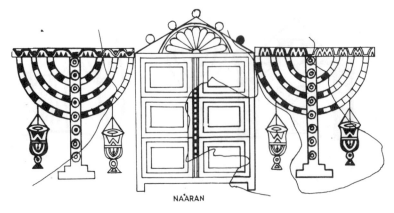

NA'ARAN

c

8. Menoroth Flanking the Ark: a) Ḥammath Tiberias; b) Beth ᵓAlpha; c) Naᶜaran.

9. Gilded Gold Glasses.

from the Jewish catacombs in Rome, two of which are now on display in the Israel Museum (fig. 9a, b). A similar, and equally stylized, menorah was found in the Jewish Quarter in Jerusalem (fig. 1), while a yet more stylized bronze menorah, the branches of which are formed by connected globular balls, was discovered during the excavation of the synagogue at ᶜEn-Gedi (Pl. 57) and is similar to the menorah depicted on the mosaic floor of the Maᶜon synagogue (fig. 14b and Pl. 87). Schematic and highly stylized seven-branched menoroth commonly appear in relief sculpture (fig. 5b), for example, on capitals at Capernaum (Pl. 42a) and ᵓAscalon, on a lintel from Kochav HaYarden (fig. VIII.26), and screens from ᵓAscalon (Pl.37) and Susiya (fig. 18). Similarly stylized menoroth appear on tombstones from Yasif, Tamara and ᶜIblin (Pl. 33), and are seen on the synagogue mosaic floors at Jericho and ᶜEn-Gedi (Pls. 50, 96), and engraved on a limestone slab at Ḥ. Rimmon (Kloner 1983b:70).

The ensemble of menoroth depicted in the Beth Sheᶜarim cemetery shows most of the variants of the shape of the branches: curved upwards, square form and triangular (fig. 10).

c) The light fittings. Light fittings on top of the branches were occasionally made of bronze or pottery lamps (fig. 5), and at other times took the form of glass containers (fig. 5). They were housed on the end of the branches and on the horizontal bar which lay above and linked the branches of the menorah. The appearance of

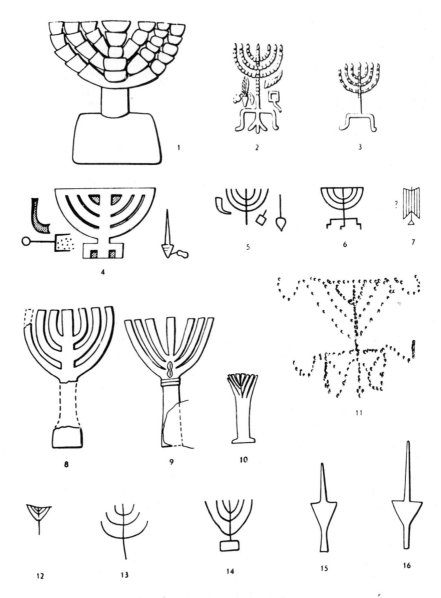

10. Menoroth from Beth She^{c}arim.

these bars on portrayals of realistic lamps on mosaic floors, such as Ḥammath-Tiberias (Pl. 101), Susiya, Beth Sheʾan A and Maʿon (Pls. 104, 103, 87; note the wicks and oil in the glass vessel) suggests that they served a functional purpose, probably to hold the glass containers which served as lamps. Light was provided by an arrangement of oil and wicks. Pottery or bronze lamps are portrayed in the Ḥuseifa mosaic (Pl. 56a, b), in the gilded glass from Rome, (fig. 9a, b) and in the Dura Europos fresco (fig. 11; Pl. 27). The menorah to the left of the Ark in the Beth ʾAlpha mosaic is also equipped with lamps (Pl. 102, fig. 8b). Depictions of the glass containers on mosaic floors are elaborately realistic, allowing one to see the wick inside them and leaving no doubt that they are of glass (fig. 5). Such containers are to be seen on the menoroth in the mosaics at Ḥammath Tiberias, Beth Sheʾan A, Beth ʾAlpha (the right hand menorah), and at Ḥuseifa (fig. 5, Pls. 56, 101-103). Glass containers would most probably have been placed in the seven depressions along the top of the stone menorah from Ḥammath Tiberias (Pl. 54).

Second Temple examples of menoroth (figs. 1-3, 12) have an additional object depicted close to them: a table. On the reverse side of the Antigonus coin a table is depicted (Pl. 59b) (Meshorer 1982,I :94) and is a very schematic depiction of the golden Table located near the Menorah in the Temple. Incisions on a stone from the Jewish Quarter in Jerusalem depict the menorah with the table next to it (fig. 1). The relief panel of the triumphal Arch of Titus shows the menorah, the table and the trumpets (Pl. 53). Similar depictions of candelabra and tables in ritual functions appear in early ancient Near Eastern representations (see for instance Pritchard 1950: fig. 626,628).

Thus, the Menorah as well as the Table are the most important Temple vessels, representing the sanctity of the Temple. In all the above-mentioned depictions they signify the Temple and its spiritual connotations, but do not have the symbolic values which became attached to them only sometime later in the mid second century CE.

During the period between the destruction of the Temple and the Bar Kokhba Revolt, few examples of menoroth are found. When menoroth do appear, they are found mostly in funerary art. By depicting menoroth with more or less than seven branches, or with a different form to the semicircular shape of the Temple menoroth the Jews seem to have avoided the prohibition of direct representations (Sussman 1983: nos.1-6: lamps depicting menoroth dating to the second century CE). The rendering of menoroth on second century ossuaries (Rahmani 1980) can be similarly explained. The reason for the various forms of the menorah might be explained by three passages in the Talmud, where the rabbis prohibit the making of a house in

11. Menorah from the Dura Europos
Fresco.

12. Menorah on the Coin of Mattathias
Antigonus.

13. Five-Branched Menorah, Capernaum.

the image of the Temple; the making of a seven branched menorah in the image of the Temple menorah, or a table in the Temple Table's image (*B. Menahot* 28 b; *Aboda Zara* 43 a; *Rosh Hashana* 24 a,b).

Only from the third century onwards does the seven branched menorah appear as a symbol intimating a complete disregard for this prohibition. Some examples of three-, five- and nine-branched menoroth have been found from this period. See for instance fig. 13, from Capernaum and the examples from the Golan (Pl. 42d,f; Ilan 1980:118-119).

In later periods, from the end of the second century onwards, the menorah is used in the synagogue ritual as a reminder of its function in the Temple (also Goodenough 1954:74-76). This is also attested to by the depiction of the menorah on mosaic floors where it represents the synagogue menorah. There is some proof that a single menorah may have served in some synagogues before the fourth century. This is attested to by the two aediculae, one of which possibly housed a menorah, in both the synagogues of Capernaum and Nabratein (see pp. 173, 175). It is possible that from the fourth century on, two menoroth functioned simultaneously in the synagogue ritual, as attested to by the Hammath Tiberias synagogue mosaic (Pls. 101).

Thus, sometime between the third and fourth centuries, a change in the synagogue ritual must have occurred which required the use of two usually unidentical menoroth which flanked the Ark, as depicted in the Hammath Tiberias, Susiya and Beth 'Alpha synagogue mosaic floors (fig. 8, Pls. 101, 102, 104). This change in the mosaic floor depictions, when a pair of menoroth began to be shown, includes other innovations such as zodiac representations and additional ritual utensils. The expansion of Christianity, and its inherent challenge to the established Jewish religion, may have been the cause of the increasing ceremonial content in synagogue ritual and art.

To sum up, the chronological development of the form of the menorah is as follows: in the first century BCE to the first century CE the menorah of the Second Temple has semi-circular branches and a conical base (see Hachlili and Merhav 1985:259-264). The second century CE menorah depicted on ossuaries and lamps usually has a different number of branches, either more or less than seven. The mid-third century menorah shows the first combination of a conical base with three small round legs suggesting a tripod base (as depicted in the Dura Europos synagogue (fig. 11)). The ornate form of the fourth century Hammath Tiberias menoroth (fig. 8a and Pl. 54) is rendered by pomegranates as "knob and flower" decorated branches, glass containers as lamps, and shows the tripod base common from now on. Chronologically, the horizontal bar connecting the branches begins to appear towards the end of the third century.

The menorah's significance and symbolism

Scholars differ as to the significance of the menorah. Goodenough (1954, IV:71-98) and M. Smith (1957-58:512) maintain that the menorah with the seven lights represents the seven planets. The menorah, whether in the Temple, the synagogue, or on a tomb, portrays for man a great light from God. "The menorah is an image of god ..." "a symbol of god and his rule ..." (Goodenough 1954, IV: 82). "The menorah was significant for Jewish piety in a great variety of senses but essentially as a mystic symbol of light and life—god present and manifest in the world—through which the Jew hopes for immortality" (Goodenough 1954, IV: 92).

Whatever its origins, the fact remains that the menorah came to be the symbol of the Jewish people. Moreover, it is not completely clear whether its origins lie in the Land of Israel or in the Diaspora. It seems probable, however, that it was in places such as Rome, Babylon, and in North Africa during the second century that the menorah came to symbolize the Jewish revolt against the Romans and the Jewish need for self-identity (Avigad 1976:268). From the Diaspora, it returned to Israel, from whence it had probably originally come, and where it had been used as a symbol from the second century onwards (also Rahmani 1980:116-117).

The menorah became particularly prevalent as a symbol specific to the Jews during the fourth century and afterwards and was used as a way of distinguishing them from those who used the Christian cross. The menorah has been found on synagogues, public buildings, and on homes throughout the Land of Israel, leaving no doubt as to which are Jewish structures. In the case of the Maᶜon synagogue mosaic (fig. 41 and Pl. 87), for example, the prominently displayed menorah differentiates the synagogue from the nearby Shellal church mosaic (fig. 43), to which it is similar.

Two most important issues concerning the menorah relate to 1) the reason for and the significance of the seven lights it sustained; and 2) the explanation for the depiction of two menoroth flanking an Ark.

1) The seven lights probably represented the seven days of the week (but see Goodenough 1954, IV: 87): every day of the week a lamp was lighted and only on the Sabbath, the seventh day, did the menorah have all its seven lamps lit. The menorah in the Temple and, later, in the synagogue, was used in a daily ritual which culminated in the Sabbath—a seven day, seven lights ritual. Thus, the menorah was used as a kind of weekly calendar, a time table for the daily and weekly ritual.

2) A simple answer is to be found in the tendency for symmetrical composition in Jewish art, as influenced by Oriental art (see p. 376ff.). Depictions of two menoroth, however, may reflect the actual function of the menorah in the early synagogue.

Such portrayals are, in fact, very often guides to the use of actual objects, and illustrate the internal arrangement of the synagogue, with the Ark in a central position, flanked by menoroth (figs. 7,8), which may also have been placed together with the Ark in the niche or apse of the synagogue (see p. 198). For instance, the three built niches of the ʾEshtemoʿa synagogue probably held an Ark and two menoroth (fig. VIII,5). The two menoroth could have signified the two weeks which the 24 priestly courses had to serve in the Temple (twice a year, one week at a time). Marble slab fragments with inscriptions of the 24 priestly courses were found in ʾAscalon, Kissufim and the Caesarea synagogue (see pp. 225-226).

The menorah was an integral part of the Temple ritual and was the most important of the Temple vessels. Its later representation served the purpose of reminding the Jews of their previous glory as well as their pride in the Temple, and expressed the longing and hope for the renewal of the Temple services and worship. Furthermore, its unique and impressive design made it an excellent choice for a symbol to signify the meaning of Judaism: instantly recognizable, the menorah symbol would be immediately associated with the Jews. So the purposes that the menorah served were many: as a link with ancient rites and worship, as a symbol of the Jewish faith, and as a visual emblem always recognizable. By this process a national symbol was created which satisfied the Jews' need for self-identity, while living among Christians and pagans.

Conclusions

In the course of the above discussion, we have followed the development of the menorah as artefact and as symbol beginning with the very earliest illustration of the Second Temple candelabrum, which was executed during the first century BCE. The menorah and the table, which already appear in the Second Temple period on the coins of Mattathias Antigonus, on stucco in the Jewish Quarter and on the Arch of Titus, were the most important Temple implements. They signify the Temple and its most important ceremonial vessels.

The menorah became a prominent symbol only after the destruction of the Temple. Once the Temple was destroyed, a need for a concrete visual image became strongly felt. It is only at this stage that we begin to see the depictions of the implements associated with the Temple taking on a symbolic significance in funerary and synagogal art. At the same time the actual menorah (such as the Ḥammath Tiberias stone menorah (Pl. 54) takes on a symbolic function in the synagogue, as can be seen by the place of the menorah in synagogal art, on mosaic floors for instance, where it is shown flanking the Ark. In these cases the menorah seems to represent an important feature of the synagogue. During the third to sixth centuries the menorah plays a dual function in Jewish art; first and more commonly, as a symbol of the Jewish people, and second, as an actual illustration of the place and function of the menorah in the Jewish synagogue.

2. The Ritual Objects

The menorah is frequently flanked by ritual utensils usually consisting of the shofar, lulav, ethrog and incense shovel, either severally or together (fig. 14). In some instances another object, the hanging lamp, is shown adjacent to the menorah. This group of ritual emblems is commonly depicted in synagogue and funerary art. Their appearance in synagogal art is more frequent than in funerary art.

a) The Shofar—a Ram's Horn

The form of the shofar is usually that of a horn, open and wide at one end with a knob-like protruberance at the other end (figs. 15, 16). The shofar played a ceremonial and ritual function in the Temple together with a pair of trumpets, and was especially associated with *Rosh HaShanah* (New Year) and *Yom Kippur* (Day of Atonement) (see Goodenough 1954, IV: 168, 193-194; Leon 1960: 200). The most realistic depiction is on the Ḥammath Tiberias mosaic pavement (fig. 14a, Pl. 101), where the shofar is depicted with lines which represent some type of decoration; a very similar shofar is depicted on the Maᶜon and Beth Sheᵓan mosaics (figs. 15, Pls. 87, 103). The Ḥulda (fig. 15 and Pl. 60) and Gerasa (fig. 17) shofaroth are also quite realistic portrayals. Other shofaroth are depicted in filled outline only in Ḥuseifa and Tirath Zvi (Pls. 55, 56). The Beth ᵓAlpha shofaroth are depicted in a stylized fashion (fig. 15, Pl. 102).

Shofaroth first appear in the second-third centuries in funerary and synagogal art. It is the emblem most frequently flanking the menorah, and is commonly depicted paired with the incense shovel on mosaic pavements (for instance, Beth Sheᵓan, fig. 14c) or with the lulav on synagogue screens and architectural fragments (fig. 16). (Whenever the shofar appears to be rendered on its own, for example at Maᶜoz Ḥayim (Pl. 95) or Tirath Zvi (Pl. 55), this is probably due to the fact that the mosaic was damaged and parts of it were lost, particularly those parts including other emblems.).

b) The Lulav—a Palm Branch

The form of the lulav is sometimes a simple branch, although it frequently appears as a bundle of branches, such as palm, myrtle, and willow (fig. 15) (see for instance, the depiction on the mosaic pavements of Ḥammath Tiberias (Pl. 101).

a   ḤAMMATH TIBERIAS

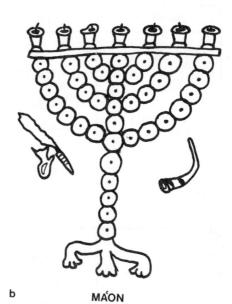

b   MAʿON

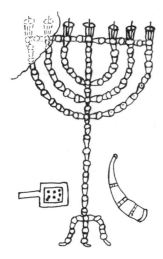

c   BETH SHEʾAN

d   JERICHO

14. Menoroth with Ritual Objects from: a) Ḥammath Tiberias; b) Maʿon; c) Beth Sheʾan; d) Jericho.

NAME	SHOFAR	INCENSE SHOVEL	LULAV, ETHROG
HAMMATH TIBERIAS			
HUSEIFA			
BETH SHE'AN A'			

15. Ritual Objects on Mosaics: Shofar; Incense Shovel; Lulav and Ethrog.

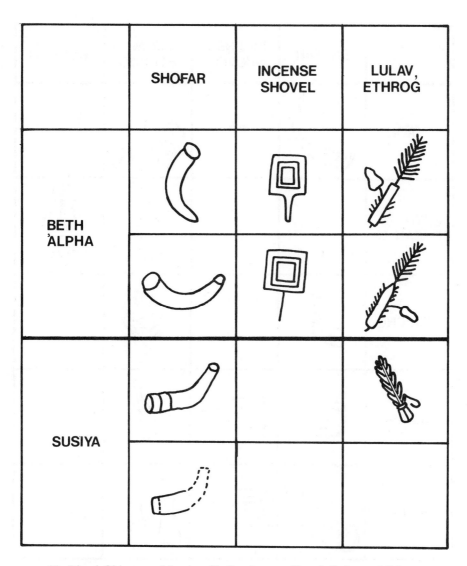

	SHOFAR	INCENSE SHOVEL	LULAV, ETHROG
BETH ʾALPHA			
SUSIYA			

15. Ritual Objects on Mosaics: Shofar; Incense Shovel; Lulav and Ethrog.

	SHOFAR	INCENSE SHOVEL	LULAV, ETHROG	KELILAH
MAʿON				
BETH SHEʾAN B'				
JERICHO				
GERASA				
HULDA				

15. Ritual Objects on Mosaics: Shofar; Incense Shovel; Lulav and Ethrog; *Kelilah*.

NAME	SHOFAR	INCENSE SHOVEL	LULAV, ETHROG
ʾASHKELON			
ʾASHDOD			
BETH SHEʿARIM			
BETH SHEʾAN A			

16. Ritual Objects on Stone: Shofar; Incense Shovel; Lulav and Ethrog.

17. Gerasa, Menorah and Ritual Objects.

c) The Ethrog—a Citrus Fruit

The ethrog is frequently depicted as a circular or ovoid object connected with or tied to the lulav with which it was part of the bundle used in the Feast of Tabernacles (Sukkoth) celebration, the most important of the three annual festivals during which Jews made pilgrimage to the Temple in Jerusalem (see p. 18). The first appearance of the lulav is as an emblem on the Jewish War coins (69 CE, Meshorer 1982, II: 117-120), although palm branches are depicted on some coins of Herod the Great. They reappear on the Bar Kokhba War coins (early second century CE), and also decorate contemporary lamps (Sussman 1982: 21). The lulav is also depicted on many Jewish objects and on synagogue mosaic floors, and is usually paired with the ethrog (figs. 14a, b, 15, 16). On several screens and mosaics the lulav is paired with the shofar, both of which flank the menorah (figs. 14d, 16). In two instances in Beth She'arim the lulav is a solitary emblem (figs. 10, 15, 16) (Avigad 1976: 272-273, fig. 130: 15, 16). On the mosaic floor of the Tiberias synagogue a pair of lulav and ethrog are twice depicted flanking an inscription (Pl. 61).

d) The Incense Shovel

The shovel is a type of rectangular fire pan with a handle. Four bronze incense shovels were found in the Bar Kokhba caves and are dated to the first-second centuries (Yadin 1963: 48-53). Such incense shovels were part of the accessory utensils of the menorah, and were used to clean the lamps of the Menorah in the Temple (Ex. 25: 38). Commonly paired with the shofar (figs. 14c, 15, 16) it is the rarest of all the ritual objects and appears mostly on synagogue mosaic pavements as well as on some synagogue architectural fragments (see Table 3). It should be noted that

Table 3 a

Distribution of the Menorah and Ritual Objects in Synagogue and Funerary Art

DISTRIBUTION CHART (a)

SYNAGOGAL ART

	Total (a + b)	Sub Total	Mosaic Pave.	Screens	Capitals	Columns	Lintels	Archit. Frag.
Total Menoroth	218	95	28	11	11	5	24	16
(1) Menorah alone	139	51	8	4	8	3	18	10
(2) Menorah with Ritual Objects	77	44	20	7	3	2	6	6

Distribution of Ritual Objects Flanking the Menorah in (2)

Shofar	69	36	17	6	2	2	3	6
Lulav	52	26	12	6	–	2	1	5
Ethrog	42	19	11	1	–	1	1	5
Incense Shovel	25	15	11	1	1	–	2	–
Ark	9	5	5	–	–	–	–	–
Suspended Lamp	5	4	2	1	–	–	1	–
Lions	2	2	2	–	–	–	–	–
Scrolls	3	1	–	–	–	–	–	1

the incense shovel is only used in depictions in the Land of Israel and is replaced in the Diaspora depictions by an amphora (fig. 9a, b).

Scholars differ as to the meaning of this emblem. (Sukenik (1933: 225 and fig. on 223) wrongly suggests that it was a lectern), whereas Goodenough proposes that the shovel has eschatological implications. Braslavi (1967: 115-117) contends that the incense shovel was used by the High Priest on the Day of Atonement, and that the Jewish artists used the shovel as part of the symbolic repertoire of the three feasts in the month of *Tishri*: *Rosh HaShanah* (New Year), *Yom Kippur* (Day of Atonement) and *Sukkoth* (Tabernacles). Narkiss (1935) and Avi-Yonah (1964: 30) maintain that it is a snuff shovel used in the synagogue.

Tabel 3 b

Distribution of The Menorah and Ritual Objects in Synagogue and Funerary Art

DISTRIBUTION CHART (b)

FUNERARY ART

	Total (a + b)	Sub Total	Tomb-stones	Tomb Doors	Beth She'arim Cemetry	Lamps	Glass Bottles	Seals	Amulets, Medalions	Bronze Lamps
Total Menoroth	218	123	10	3	41	15	35	10	14	5
(1) Menorah alone	139	89	9	2	34	4	24	6	7	3
(2) Menorah with Ritual Objects	77	44	1	1	7	11	11	4	7	2

Distribution of Ritual Objects Flanking the Menorah in (2)

Shofar	69	34	1	-	3	7	10	4	7	2
Lulav	52	26	1	-	3	2	8	4	7	1
Ethrog	42	23	-	-	3	2	6	4	7	1
Incense Shovel	25	10	-	-	3	7	-	-	-	-
Ark	9	4	-	-	4	-	-	-	-	-
Suspended Lamp	5	1	-	1	-	-	-	-	-	-
Lions	2	-	-	-	-	-	-	-	-	-
Scrolls	3	2	-	-	-	2	-	-	-	-

The four ritual objects flank the menorah in many different combinations and arrangements (fig. 14); rarely is the menorah flanked by a symbol other than these (fig. 8c).

The majority of the depictions of these motifs appears on synagogue objects and ornamentation, and less on funerary art. The situation in the Diaspora is the reverse, where these motifs appear more frequently in funerary art. This may have prompted Goodenough (1954, IV: 147) to observe that the lulav and ethrog were primarily funerary emblems and appear only secondarily in synagogal art (see Tables 3, 4).

A complete assemblage of the four ritual objects flanking the menorah is often portrayed on mosaic pavements (fig. 15a-c). Other artefacts have only two or some-

Table 4

Distribution of The Menorah and Ritual Objects in Synagogue and Funerary Art in the Land of Israel and the Diaspora

COMPARISON CHART

	Land of Israel			Diaspora		
	Total	Synagogue Art	Funerary Art	Total	Synagogue Art	Funerary Art
Total Menoroth	216	95	121	273	25	248
(1) Menorah alone	139	51	88	132	15	117
(2) Menorah with Ritual Objects	77	44	33	141	10	131

Distribution of Ritual Objects Flanking the Menorah in (2)

Shofar	69	35	34	42	8	34
Lulav	52	26	26	83	12	71
Ethrog	42	19	23	48	10	38
Incense Shovel	25	15	10	–	–	2
Flask	–	–	–	35	–	35
Ark	9	5	4	19	–	19
Suspended Lamp	5	4	1	–	–	–
Lions	2	2	–	2	–	2
Scrolls	1	1	–	11	2	7
Ritual Objects alone	6	2	4	25	–	25

times three of the emblems depicted on them (fig. 16). Groups of three of the emblems (figs. 15, 16) flanking the menorah are mostly depicted on small objects— glass bottles, seals, lamps and medallions. These groups also occur on some architectural fragments but only once on a synagogue pavement (Maᶜon, fig. 14b). Most commonly depicted is a pair either of a) the shofar and incense shovel flanking the menorah one on each side (fig. 14c) or b) a pair of shofar and lulav flanking the menorah one on each side (fig. 14d). Most of these pairs are depicted on capitals, lintels and screens (see fig. 16), as well as on lamps and seals (Pl. 62, table 3a). Pair a) is depicted twice on the synagogue pavement of Beth She'an A (fig. 14c and Pl. 103) and pair b) is depicted once on the Jericho synagogue pavement (fig. 14d and

Pl. 50). Note that the pairing of lulav and ethrog is common on some lamps (Pl. 62) and at the Dura Europos synagogue (Pl. 27). On the majority of architectural fragments the menorah is independently rendered (table 3).

Table 3 shows the frequency of the representations of the four ritual objects; a solitary menorah is represented 130 times on about 230 artefacts, and in about 75 instances the menorah is depicted as flanked by the ritual utensils:

> 70 depictions of the shofar flanking the menorah
> 52 depictions of the lulav flanking the menorah
> 42 depictions of the ethrog flanking the menorah
> 30 depictions of the incense shovel
> 8 depictions of the hanging lamp

The shofar is the object which most frequently flanks the menorah, and the incense shovel and hanging lamp are rarely rendered.

Comparison with information on distribution of the ritual objects in the Diaspora (table 4) is enlightening. About half of the Roman Jewish catacomb inscriptions are decorated with a solitary menorah, whereas on the other half the menorah is flanked by the ritual objects (Leon 1949: 87-90; 1960: 195). The order of frequency is also different: the lulav is the most common whereas the other three appear less frequently (Leon 1960: 196, note 3).

Chronology

Ritual objects flanking the menorah appear frequently first in Jewish cemeteries of the Diaspora in the Roman catacombs of the second-fourth centuries CE (Goodenough 1953, III: figs. 768, 769, 772, 773, 817, 818, 846, 847) and are dated to the third-fourth centuries. In the Land of Israel they appear on a few objects in the Beth She'arim cemetery: on two marble slabs and on lead sarcophagi (fig. 10: 2, 4, 5) (Avigad 1976: 270, fig. 130: 2, 4, 5). Avigad (1976: 268, 273) maintains that these objects were probably imported from the Diaspora, and thus furnish proof for his theory that these religious emblems were used commonly by the Diaspora Jews who needed to emphasize their identity; and Jews in the Land of Israel may have used these symbols less at this time, probably as they felt less need to differentiate themselves from the non-Jewish population.

From the fourth century on, the use of the ritual objects flanking the menorah is common on all kinds of objects and on synagogue pavements (such as Ḥammath Tiberias of the fourth century, fig. 14a). Their representation, which in funerary art probably indicates Jewish identification, gains profound significance when depicted in synagogal art, where it alludes to the Temple implements used during feasts of the seventh month, and to the function of the ritual objects in the same rituals in the synagogues of the day.

Origins and Symbolism

Representations of ritual objects flanking the menorah are to be explained by their association with the Feast of Tabernacles which during the Second Temple period came to be the most important of the three annual pilgrimage feasts (attested to already by Zechariah, 14: 16-18). The Feast of Tabernacles was referred to as "The Feast" (Jos., *Ant.* VIII, 100) and *'Asif* (= final harvest of the year).

The rituals accompanying the Feast of Tabernacles in the Temple (Safrai 1965: 190-196; 1976: 894-996) were many:

1) The rite of the four species (the lulav, ethrog, willow and myrtle) which were raised up and carried aloft in a procession around the Temple altar during the days of the festival (Jos. *Ant.* III: 244-245). The waving of the lulav and its procession served also during other celebrations to express the people's joy, especially when commemorating the dedication of the Temple, victory celebrations and communal rejoicing in the seventh month (I Kings 8:2-5, 65; II Chron. 5:3-6; 7:8-10; I Macc. 13:51; II Macc. 10:6-9; Jos. *Ant.* VIII:100; John 12:13; *M. Sukkah*, 4-5). After the destruction of the Temple a custom was established in which the lulav was raised and carried around the *bema* in the synagogue during the seven days of the Feast of Tabernacles in memory of the Temple rite.

2) The willow was carried aloft round the altar, and was shaken on the last day of the feast.

3) Water-libation ceremonies were performed during the festival nights in the Court of Women, by the High Priest or another priest, and were connected with the supplicants' desire for rain.

4) A celebration of rejoicing (*Simchat Beth Hashoevah*) was carried out during the nights of the festival in the Temple courtyard. The distinctive features of this revelry consisted of bonfires, torchfires and lights, which were employed to increase the festivity. Men danced throughout the nights in the Court of the Women with the women looking down upon them from the galleries.

5) Once every seven years on the last day of the feast and after the sabbatical year, chapters of the Torah (particularly from Deuteronomy) were read to the communal assembly of the people (Deut. 31: 10-13; *M. Sotah* 7:8).

6) The *Hallel* was sung with flute accompaniment on all eight days of the Tabernacles feast.

It is also suggested (Meshorer 1982, II:117-118) that Tabernacles was the only practical time that the Jewish farming population was able to embark upon the pilgrimage to Jerusalem, and thus it also developed into a celebration of the final harvest of the year. The Tabernacles was further distinguished by additional sacrifices offered on several days of the feast.

A most important element distinguishing this feast from others must be stressed: all the rites and ceremonies performed during Tabernacles at the Temple involved the participation of all the people who came to the Jerusalem Temple. They participated in the offerings, processions and dancing. By comparison, Passover was a more family-oriented feast, and Pentecost, which was only a one-day feast, entailed no popular participation in its rites (Safrai 1965: 181-190).

e) The Hanging (Suspended) Lamp

One other ritual utensil was employed in the synagogue ceremony as can be seen from depictions on mosaic pavements, on objects found in synagogue excavations, and in funerary art: the hanging chandelier or suspended lamp, all of which, with the exception of those at Beth She'arim, are dated to the sixth century. It took two forms: either (a) a single glass lamp (*Kos*) in the form of a cup with a high or pointed base, hanging from a single or triple chain (figs. 18, 19; also Zevulun and Olenik 1978: 80, no. 211); or (b) a polycandelon, a bronze ring with openings for lamps, suspended by chains (figs. 19, 20; Nabratein). This was known as the *Kelilah* (Rahmani 1960: 16, note 20; Naveh 1978: 34-36, no. 16).

Most of these objects and their variations are found in synagogues or on ornamental depictions. For instance, several chains, polycandelons and glass lamps have been found in synagogue excavations. Inside the apse of the Ma'on synagogue remains were found of parts of a bronze polycandelon with circlets (holes) for the oil lamps, iron hooks, chain and fittings and parts of two cone-shaped glass lamps (Rahmani 1960: 16, fig. 9: 3, 4; Pl. II:2, 3, 9). In the Beth She'an synagogue a bronze polycandelon was found (Zori 1967: 163, Pl. 33: 7), as well as some glass cups probably belonging to it (*ibid.*, Pl. 33:5, fig. 11:1-3). In the Reḥov synagogue bronze chains and glass fragments from a polycandelon were found on the floor (Vitto 1980: 217; 1981: 92-93). In the Jericho synagogue a bronze hanger of a glass lamp was found (Baramki 1936: 75, Pl. 22). At the Rimmon synagogue, parts of bronze rings and chains for a polycandelon were found in debris west of the synagogue (Kloner 1983b: 67-68). A complete bronze polycandelon was found at Kefar Macher (now in the Musée Mariemont, Belgium) and has twelve openings for lamps and three chains for suspension (fig. 20). An Aramaic inscription is incised on the ring: "This *Kelilah* (= polycandelon)...for the sacred place at Kefar

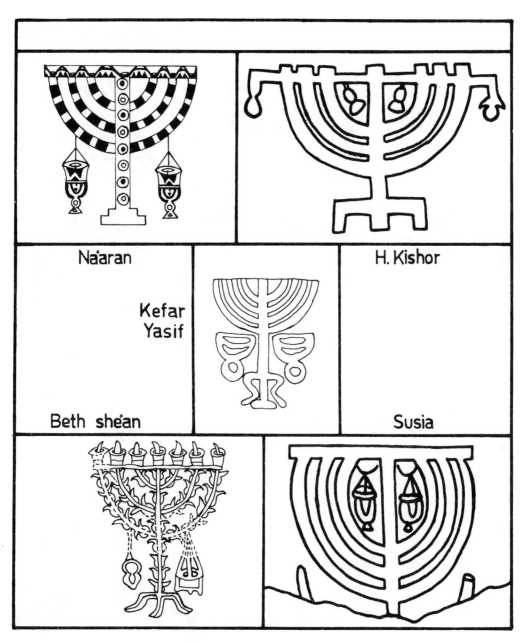

18. Menoroth with Hanging Lamps.

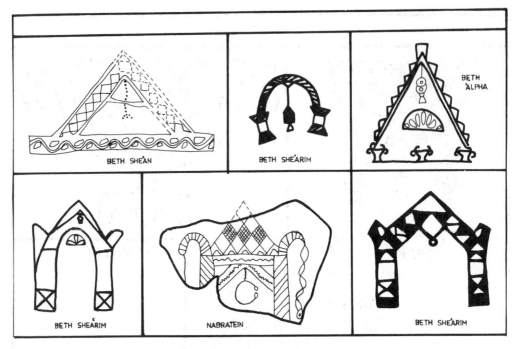

19. Hanging Lamps on Torah Shrine.

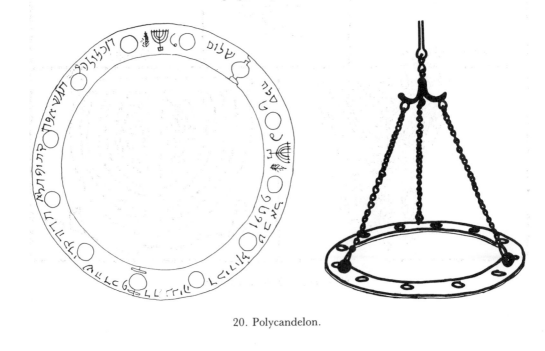

20. Polycandelon.

Ḥananiya'' (Naveh 1978: 34-36, no. 16, and more examples in Zevulun and Olenik 1978: 80-82). (Similar polycandela were found in sites other than synagogues: Beth She'an monastery (Fitzgerald 1939, III: Pl. 37:3), Jericho (Barʿamki 1935: 82, Pl. LIII: 2a, b), and Sardis (Foss 1976: fig. 21c).) In the Jerusalem Temple Mount excavations a bronze chandelier of the Byzantine period was found (Mazar 1975a: 37). The excavations at the Nabratein synagogue yielded a carved stone lintel of the Torah shrine with a vertical slit in the moulding above the conch (fig. VIII.18, Pl. 24). Meyers *et al.* propose (1981a: 239) that from this hole a lamp was suspended in front of the Ark doors.

Depictions of Hanging Lamps
The Lamp on the Torah Shrine (fig. 19)
Most depictions render the hanging glass lamp (*Kos*) form (a). The depictions on the mosaic pavements of the synagogues of Beth 'Alpha and Beth She'an, and the drawing from Beth Sheʿarim show the glass lamp suspended from the centre of the gable of the Torah shrine. A similar rendition appears on a drawing on plaster from the Reḥov synagogue (unpublished). The ceramic bowl (dated to the Byzantine period) found in a house at Nabratein is the only depiction of a polycandelon of form (b) showing a chain suspended from the inner gable and holding a ring, depicted on its side, which probably held glass lamps (Meyers and Meyers 1982: 182 and fig. 3). A lamp suspended from an arch is depicted on a glass plate from Beth Sheʿarim (Avigad 1976: 211 and fig. 100). Similar lamps suspended from building entrances are depicted on a church mosaic floor at Gerasa (Zevulun and Olenik 1978: no. 220) and at the church of S. Maria Maggiore in Rome (Goodenough 1954, IV: fig. 93).

Lamps Hanging from a Menorah (fig. 18)
Several lamps are depicted hanging from a menorah. On the upper panel of the Naʿaran synagogue mosaic pavement, two glass lamps are shown suspended on a triple chain hanging down from each of the two menoroth. Another lamp is depicted hanging on one side of the menorah in the central medallion of the small synagogue mosaic at Beth She'an B. On a stone screen relief from the Susiya synagogue two lamps are carved suspended from the bar of the menorah between the upper branches. A similar depiction of lamps hanging from a bar is possibly rendered on a lintel from Ḥ. Kishor (Kloner 1974: p. 199, note 14, Pl. 39A). Two similar lamps are carved on the Kefar Yasif tomb door, on either side of a menorah (fig. 18 and Pl. 33).

These suspended lamps, whether single light hangings or of the *Kelilah* type, were probably synagogue fixtures, used to light the synagogue during the Late Antiquity period. Few sources remain to explain their use. A later source relates "A custom of ours, the light of the synagogue held in an *ʿashashit* with oil floating on the water, and (the light) burning and the oil wasting till it reaches the water and (the light) goes out" (*Tšuvot Gaonim, Shar, Tshuva* 23a; Zevulun and Olenik 1978: 42). Depictions of hanging lamps in representational art seem to suggest to scholars an additional meaning: Goodenough (1954, IV: 130) asserts that the hanging lamp was "the perpetual light (*Ner HaTamid*) burned before the Torah shrine, as a memory of the function of the same light before the Ark." Meyers, Strange and Meyers (1982: 182) suggest that the hanging *Kelilah* "represents the prototype of the hanging Eternal Light in Jewish synagogues." However, as hanging lamps are shown as suspended not only from Torah shrines, but also from menoroth, the identification of these lamps with the Eternal Light of the Tabernacle becomes suspect.

In conclusion, the hanging lamp is part of the repertoire of ritual objects depicted in connection with either the Ark or the menorah, signifying its use in the synagogue ceremony.

3) The Ark of the Scrolls

The Ark was a chest which housed the Torah (= the Scrolls, the Scriptures), and stood inside the Torah shrine (aedicula, niche or apse). Several inscriptions which mention the "*ʾaron*" (= Ark) presumably refer to the Ark of the Scrolls:

1) An Aramaic inscription on the facade of the niche at the Dura Europos synagogue mentions the "repository of the Ark" (Kraeling 1956: 269), in reference to the niche which housed the Ark.

2) An inscription from the H. ʿAmmudim synagogue refers to "Yoezer the ḥazan and Simeon his brother made this Ark (?) of the Lord of Heaven" (Naveh 1978: 41-42; cf. Avigad, 1960b: 62-63, who reads "Gate of the Lord" instead of "Ark").

3) A basalt stone in secondary use in the mosque at Naveh (Hauran, Syria) bears an inscription probably mentioning "repository of the Ark." Naveh (1978: 64-65) questions the validity of this reading.

The term used for the Ark in the Mishnah is *tevah* (*Taʿanit* 1.1;2.1; *Meg.* 3.1; *Meg.* 4.21). It presumably denotes a chest [portable—ΚΙΒΩΤΟΣ in Greek] (See also Sukenik 1934: 52-53; Wendel 1950: 20-24; Goodenough 1954, IV:115-120).

Scholars suggest that in the early Galilean synagogues no permanent place for the Torah shrine existed, and the congregation used a portable chest (Sukenik 1934: 52; Avi-Yonah 1961a: 172) as depicted on a Bar Kokhba coin (fig. I,7C) and the Capernaum frieze (fig. VIII,56) (which portrays an Ark on wheels). However, recent excavations of Galilean synagogues demonstrate that aediculae already existed as early as the second century (see p. 173).

The form of the Ark and its place can be deduced by: a) Traces of the Ark, which are seldom found, and b) The Ark as depicted on art objects with or without the Torah shrine.

a) Traces found of the Ark:

Only a few pieces of surviving evidence point to the existence of wooden chests in synagogues as, obviously, wood is seldom preserved due to climatological conditions. The finds consist mainly of iron or bronze nails, and bone inlays or plaster impressions, which suggest furniture (also Maoz 1972: 27). In the Maᶜon synagogue (Rahmani 1960: 14), a bronze nail was found which Rahmani suggests was part of a catch to the cornice of the Ark. Also found were bone inlays which may have decorated an Ark (*idem.*, Pls. 3-7). In the Beth Sheᵓan synagogue (Zori 1967: 164), seventy nails (45 iron nails) were found in the main hall close to the apse, as well as a plaster fragment (measuring 1.0 m. × 0.23 m.) in the middle of the apse, close to the back wall. These suggest wooden furniture, that is, an Ark. Excavated sections of the earlier ᶜEn-Gedi synagogue (probably third-fourth centuries) show traces of a wooden Ark (Barag *et al.* 1981: 118-119).

b) Renditions of the Ark in Jewish Art

The Ark of the Scrolls is rendered either inside the Torah shrine facade or is shown independently, usually with a symbolic conch referring to the absent Torah shrine within which the Ark stood (Hachlili 1976; see p. 280ff. for the conch, and Hachlili 1980b: 59-60). The form of the Ark consists of a double door decorated by a geometric ornamentation of several rectangles. Most of the Arks depicted bear from two to four legs (fig. 21), and are surmounted by a gable or round top. All the Ark representations in the Land of Israel, except one on a Beth Sheᶜarim drawing (figs. 23, VIII.30), portray the Ark with its doors closed, and the internal shelves or scrolls not exposed to view, this in direct contrast to the Ark renditions in the Diaspora which show the scrolls on shelves inside an open-door Ark (fig. 9a, b). Taking into consideration, therefore, all finds and artistic renditions of the Ark, it can be conjectured to have been made of wood. The stone fragments found at synagogue sites are parts of the aedicula or niche, which was the location of the wooden Ark of the Scrolls (see p. 184ff.).

There are four types of Ark representations:

1) The gable top, usually depicted as a free standing chest with a double ornamented door and legs: on the Ark on the Capernaum synagogue lintel, on the Naᶜana bronze plate, on the Beth ᵓAlpha mosaic floor, and on the Naᶜaran mosaic floor (fig. 21).

21. Depictions of Independent Arks.

2) The round top, a chest with legs and an arched top sometimes decorated with a conch. These Arks are depicted in very stylized fashion: on the Beth She^{c}arim drawing and relief (figs. 22), on a limestone mirror frame from Shikmona, on a stone plaque, on a lamp, and on the Jericho mosaic floor (figs. 21-22, Pl. 63). This round-top type of Ark probably suited the niche or apse, as it would fit in a round topped structure.

3) The box form, with ornamented double doors, and lacking both top and legs (fig. 23). These depictions show the Ark inside the Torah shrine (not free standing). These Arks are portrayed on the Ḥammath Tiberias and Susiya mosaic floors (Pls. 101, 104), on the Beth She^{c}arim incisions and drawings, on the Pekiin relief and on an unpublished screen from Susiya (fig. 23).

4) A stylized geometric form. In two cases the Ark is depicted inside a Torah shrine in the highly stylized form of a lozenge pattern. This is found on the Kefar Yasif stone tomb door (Pl. 33) and on a clay lamp (fig. VIII.30).

The Beth She$^{\jmath}$an A mosaic portrays a *parochet* (veil) (fig. 22 and Pl. 103), which may indicate an Ark behind it, or only shelves which may have held the scrolls. (See also Zori (1967: 152, 164), referring to fragments of an Ark.)

The free standing Ark is represented by types 1 and 2 (figs. 21, 23) which have gabled and arched top and legs, whereas the other types are usually depicted inside the facade of the Torah shrine. Several scholars suggest a chronological development for these Arks. Wendel (1950: 16) sees the Ark of the Na^{c}ana plate as the earliest, dated to the first century; however this date is questionable. Bar^{c}amki (1936: 73, note 4) suggests a typological sequence from the earlier round topped chest to the later gable topped one. Galling (1956: 171) rightly refutes this and concludes that there is no proof for any preference for one type over another as both these types are rendered in every period.

Due to recent synagogue excavations as well as historical research, knowledge and evidence are now much more extensive than before; it seems reasonable to infer, therefore, that an Ark of the Scrolls in the shape of a wooden chest stood inside the architectural structure of the Torah shrine in the synagogue building.

Representations of the Ark in Jewish art confirm the fact that a wooden Ark of the Scrolls stood inside the Torah shrine in all its forms (aedicula, niche and apse) in the synagogues of Late Antiquity (fig. 24). Nevertheless the Ark was also part of the symbolic repertoire of Jewish art: it represented much deeper connotations, being an integral part of the focal point of Jewish worship, the Torah, and symbolizing also the place of the Scriptures and their study and prayer in the destroyed Temple. Renditions of the Ark are also encountered on tomb walls and doors, and on lamps not found in a synagogue context. On mosaic floors the Torah shrine is com-

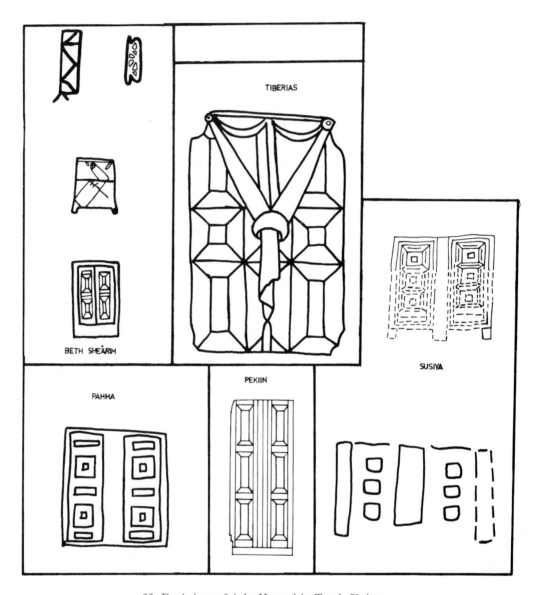

22. Depictions of Arks Housed in Torah Shrines.

23. Depictions of Torah Shrines.

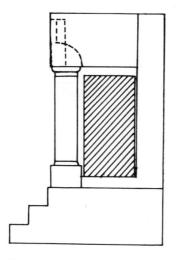

24a. Reconstructions of the Ark housed in the Torah shrine: a) a general example.

24b. Reconstructions of the Ark housed in the Torah shrines. b) reconstruction with the ʿEn Samsam aedicula stone.

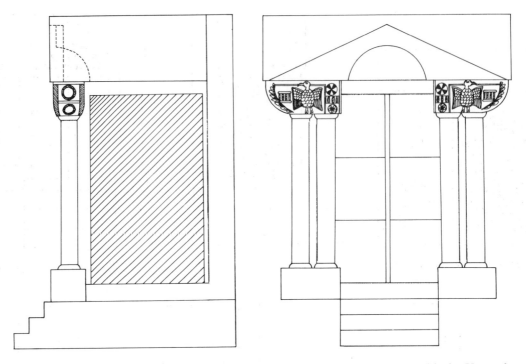

24c. Reconstructions of the Ark housed in the Torah shrines. c) reconstruction with the Umm el-Kanatir aedicula capital.

monly depicted with the two menoroth flanking it; this may very probably represent the actual position of the Torah shrine and menoroth in their prominent place in the synagogue building.

Depictions of the Torah shrine and Ark (fig. 24) had symbolic connotations which were twofold: first, as spiritual and religious symbols of the Torah and the Scriptures. Public Torah reading was a most important element in the life of the synagogue and its ceremonies (see pp. 138-139). Second, they symbolize the actual place of the Torah shrine and the Ark. Their representation in Jewish art (especially on the mosaic pavement of the synagogue) is a rendition of the actual design and position of the Torah shrine in synagogue architecture. The Torah shrine and Ark are represented on various objects in order to symbolize the Torah and its spiritual associations for the community as well as suggesting its actual location in the synagogue. It was a unique Jewish symbol, recognizable wherever encountered.

The Synagogue Ark of Scrolls and the Ark of the Covenant

A confusion has arisen due to inaccuracies of definition of the synagogue Ark and has led to its doubtful identification with the Ark of the Covenant, which had stood in Solomon's Temple in Jerusalem (Goodenough 1954, IV: 115-116, 130; Meyers *et al.* 1981a: 241-242). The Ark of the Covenant was a chest which contained the Tablets of the Law (I Kings 8, 9; II Chronicles ll:5, 10), and which disappeared from the Temple, probably in the time of King Manasseh (see Haran 1959: 31-32; 1963: 58), never again to reappear. *No Ark stood in the Second Temple* (Avi-Yonah 1968: 330; but see Gutman 1971a: 28-29 who suggests that "the Ark described for the Tabernacle in Exodus was in all likelihood an Ark which must actually have stood in the Second Temple"). Torah reading, begun already in the time of ʿEzra, was institutionalized, however, later with the development of the synagogue buildings. A permanent place for the sacred scrolls had, therefore, to be provided. The Ark of the synagogue was the answer and was an entirely different entity to the Ark of the Covenant (also Gutmann 1971a: 22): it was a chest containing the Torah scrolls and was the most prominent feature in the synagogue. Scrolls were continually taken out of the Ark and read in the synagogue all year round.

Some scholars (Goodenough 1954, IV: 115-116, 130; and Meyers *et al.* 1981a: 241-242) maintain that the synagogue Ark became the successor to the Ark of the Covenant both in form and symbol. However, there was no continuation either in purpose or in form. The Ark of the Covenant contained a holy article not meant to be observed or used, whereas the synagogue Ark contained the Scriptures meant to be often taken out and read in public in the synagogue; it was thus an everyday necessity of community life. No continuation of form can be predicated between the *two* Arks, especially as the Ark of the Covenant's design is known solely by the Biblical literary description. (The only depiction of the Ark of the Covenant is the much later painting in the Dura Europos synagogue of the third century.)

The Symbolic Meaning of the Depictions of Torah Shrine and Ark

The Torah shrine had a generally accepted design with recurring elements: an elevated structure and a facade of from two to four columns crowned with an arcuated lintel, with or without a gable, frequently approached by steps (fig. VIII.30). The Ark of the Scrolls is commonly rendered inside this facade, and occasionally the Ark is depicted as free standing, thus representing the Torah shrine itself (figs. 21-23). It is reasonable to infer that it also symbolized the Torah, the spiritual backbone of Judaism, as well as representing the actual form and place of the Torah shrine in the synagogue structure (attested to also by the architectural fragments of the

Torah shrine found in various synagogues (p. 184)). The Torah shrine is similar to other sacred niches and aediculae in the pagan Hellenistic-Roman world (Hachlili 1980b: 57-58). In all likelihood the Torah shrine facade resembled the Jerusalem Temple facade. Meyers and Meyers (1981: 34; also Goodenough 1954, IV: 140-143) contend that the synagogue Torah shrine with its gable-roof and columns represents ''a symbolic merger of Temple and Holy of Holies...'' but this seems far-fetched and cannot be proved.

Altogether, these assumed associations with the Jerusalem Temple are difficult to prove, as no depiction of the Temple facade has ever been found. Attempts to reconstruct the Temple facade are mainly based on later objects from the second century onwards, such as the Bar Kokhba tetradrachme coin, the fresco image above the Dura Europos synagogue niche (fig. I, 7),and on later synagogue Torah shrine images (see also Avi-Yonah 1968; Ben-Dov 1982: fig. on p. 98 for reconstructions of the Temple facade).

4) The Conch

The conch motif (Hachlili 1980b) was employed in Jewish funerary and synagogal art. Long occupying an important place in the art of the Near East, the conch motif was already popular in Egypt during the first millennium BCE in the form of an actual shell which appears to have been worn as an amulet. Great Tridacna shells thought to be of Assyrian origin have been found at many sites, covered with incised floral and animal motifs in a Phoenician style. In the period from the fifth century BCE until late Roman times, the conch often appears in Graeco-Roman art, portrayed naturalistically, and is associated with the myth of Aphrodite, who emerged from a shell (Bratschova 1938:8-14; Goodenough 1958, VIII:95-106). A more stylized version of the conch became a motif in Christian and pagan funerary art. Goodenough declares (1958, VIII:150 fig. 75-77) that it represented ''a coming into new life.'' The conch appears in Jewish art in the form of a stylized scallop with rays extending from the hinge at the base, in the manner of the eastern version of the conch (Hachlili 1980b: note 6).

The conch in synagogal and funerary art can be classified into three groups, according to significance and context: in the first it appears as a stylized ornamentation together with other geometric or floral motifs (figs. 25, VIII.49b). The conch is occasionally placed within a wreath, is occasionally found alone, and is sometimes one of a row of decorative motifs in a meander (see figs. 25, VIII.54). It may also occupy the central roundel of a clay lamp. Other examples appear wreathed in leaves joined by a Hercules knot (fig. X.20; VIII.52b). It may also occur inside a wreath of acan-

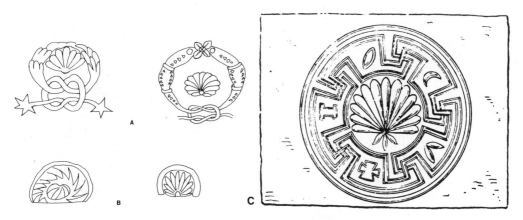

25. Conch in Wreath and in Acanthus Leaves.

thus leaves (fig. 25). Such representations of the conch serve purely ornamental puposes and most probably had no special significance (but see Goodenough 1958, VIII:95).

In the second group of representations the conch is stylized, and appears as an architectural element used to decorate a semicircular space, usually the upper part of a niche or an aedicula (figs. VIII.29,30). It first appears as such in Jewish funerary art in the first century on an ossuary bearing an incised design of a conch over a central fluted column (fig. 26). A conch also decorates the upper part of the central entrance of a first century tomb in Jerusalem (fig. 27). Later examples come from the Beth She‘arim cemetery, where conches decorate aediculae on two sarcophagi (fig. 28). From the third century onward, stylized conches occur in several of the Galilean synagogues, as window lintel decorations (fig. 29), or in the upper parts of the aediculae (fig. VIII.29, 30). The earliest example of a conch in a synagogue niche comes from the Dura Europos synagogue, where it appears painted naturalistically inside the semi-dome (Pl. 27).

The conch's use as an architectural element is not unique to Jewish architecture, for it commonly appears in Nabataean, Syrian and Phoenician temple niches usually occupied by a statue of a deity (Bratschkova 1938: nos. 102-124;127-132;134-135;139-147;149; also Hachlili 1980b: note 19,p. 57).

From the second century onwards, a decorative and non-symbolic, naturalistic representation of the conch appears in the semi-domes of niches and aediculae. Its first appearances in architecture are almost certainly due to its suitability for filling a semicircular space.

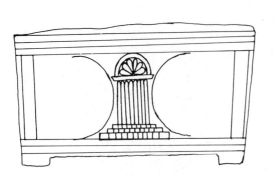

26. Conch on Ossuary, Jerusalem.

27. Tomb Facade, Jerusalem.

28. Conch on Sarcophagi, Beth She‘arim.

When, through constant application, the conch had become an inevitable niche decoration, it seems to have also become conceptually associated with the niche and its inhabitant, the statue of the deity, themselves. By the second century the conch

29. Reconstructed window from Capernaum.

30. Conch on Architectural Fragments, Raphid (Golan).

was already inseparable from the niche or aedicula, and had acquired religious connotations. It thus became a specifically religious motif associated with the sacred niche.

The third group consists of conch designs which appear only in Jewish art from the fourth to the sixth century (figs. VIII.29, 30; IX.21-23). These depictions, found on reliefs and mosaic pavements, are conches shown decorating the represented Torah shrine and forming a part of the facade with two or four columns supporting a Syrian gable. The Ark appears within the Torah shrine as a facade with two doors (see p. 273). In some depictions, the conch decorates an unoccupied Torah shrine (fig. VIII.29). Such designs have been found carved on a wall of the Beth Sheᶜarim necropolis (Pl. 31), on a tomb door (Pl. 33), and on a lamp. The most elaborate depictions of the conch decorating the Torah shrine containing the Ark are to be found in the synagogue mosaic pavements of Ḥammath Tiberias, Susiya and Beth Sheʾan A (Pls. 101, 103, 104). The motif also appears carved on an architectural element which may have belonged originally to a synagogue (fig. 30). The conch appears in two synagogue mosaic pavements of Beth ʾAlpha (fig. 21 and Pl. 102), where a stylized version is shown within the gable of the Ark, and in another at Jericho (fig. 21 and Pl. 63), where, in the central panel of the pavement, a geometric pattern surrounds a stylized Ark surmounted by a conch. The Ark and conch are depicted in a stylized manner on a stone plaque (Pl. 34).

The examples of the third group seem to indicate that the conch had by now become an integral part of the Torah shrine and Ark. Whenever the conch is shown with the Ark only and without the Torah shrine, as in the last three examples, it can be assumed that it was itself seen as a symbolic portrayal of the Torah shrine (aedicula or niche or apse). If this is so, it would explain the occasional appearance of the conch above the menorah, as on a stone fragment from Capernaum (fig. 13), and on a lamp from a tomb in Gezer (Goodenough 1953, III: fig. 268: 4). The conch would here symbolize the niche in which the menorah stood.

To summarize, in Jewish funerary and synagogal art the conch appears initially as a decorative and non-symbolic motif, in order to provide an architectural element in the semi-domes of aediculae and niches. This use can also be observed in pagan temples. The conch is widely employed as an architectural decoration during Late Antiquity, in Nabatean, Syrian and Phoenician architecture, usually lining the semi-circular space at the top of large niches. However, the conch seems to have later become something more than a mere decorative motif in Jewish art. It came to symbolize the synagogal Torah shrine itself, and to have acquired a sacredness of its own. The sacred connotation of the niche or aedicula to Jew and non-Jew alike later attached itself to the conch as being the traditional niche decoration to such an extent that Jews seem to have regarded it as a religious motif. When represented together with depictions of the Torah shrine, Ark or menorah, it was regarded as a symbol of the aedicula, niche, or apse itself. There can be no doubt that the conch developed the characteristics of a religious symbol in Jewish art, and came to represent the sacred Torah shrine which held the holy Ark.

Conclusions

Following the destruction of the Temple, the Torah shrine, like the menorah, developed into one of the most important Jewish symbols (see p. 166). Like the menorah, it satisfied the desires of the Jewish people for a symbol which would, by reminding them of the past, represent both their spiritual and national aspirations. Furthermore, they were chosen as symbols by the Jewish people at a time of conflict with the numerically and powerfully growing Christian community. The Torah shrine, menorah, and ritual objects came to be associated with Judaism and to be recognized as Jewish symbols. This combination of menorah and ritual objects developed as a unified design of Jewish symbols during the third century.

The rites of the Feast of Tabernacles, described above, enable us to explain the origins of the representation of these Jewish symbols, which flank the menorah in post-Temple art. The lulav and ethrog came to symbolize this most important annual feast, thereby serving as a reminder of the Temple rites. The representation of the four species also acted as a means of recollecting and celebrating national, communal and agricultural rejoicings which had been part of the significance of the Feast of Tabernacles. The amphora, depicted mostly on Diaspora objects (fig. 9a,b), replaced the shovel and represented the water libation ceremony. Finally, the ritual objects flanking the menorah together represented the lights and fires used during the nocturnal celebrations of rejoicing at the time of the Tabernacles Feast. The Torah shrine itself, as it appears in post-Temple art, is meant to be an evocation of this rite of the Tabernacles, and a commemoration of the seven year cycle of reading the Torah. Thus, depictions of a menorah flanked by ritual objects, or of the more elaborate Torah shrine flanked by menoroth and ritual objects, came to symbolize participation in the annual pilgrimages, the Feast of the Tabernacles (the most important annual festival), and, by association, the Temple and its eventual rebuilding.

B) FIGURATIVE ART

The art of the Second Temple was aniconic. Hellenistic influences are shown in the adopted decorative and architectural motifs, but no figurative designs are depicted in this period. However, Jewish figurative art is an extensive and essential part of Jewish art in Late Antiquity. A major change occurred at the end

of the second century and particularly during the third century when representational art began to flourish. It was at this time that the barriers within which Judaism
protected itself against foreign influences were being shattered. During this period
the Jews acquired some of the customs and decorative elements of surrounding
cultures and began to develop their own figurative and representational art, using
pagan motifs, figures and animals, for both synagogal and funerary art.

Conflicting opinions and heated arguments have existed in the past century about
the phenomenon of representational art, due to the prohibition of the second of the
Ten Commandments:

> Thou shalt not make unto thee any graven image, or any likeness of anything that is
> in the heaven above, or that is in the earth beneath, or that is in the water under the
> earth: Thou shalt not bow down thyself to them, nor serve them (Exod. 20: 4, 5; Deut.
> 5: 8, 9).

Despite this prohibition figurative art developed and was cultivated from the end of
the second and the start of the third century onwards among the Jewish communities
in the Land of Israel and in the Diaspora.

Figurative art became possible for several reasons:

a) First of all, the attitude of the rabbis changed to one of greater tolerance. Such
changes, reflected in Talmudic literature, were the result of political, economic and
social circumstances (Urbach 1959).

b) The influence of the surrounding cultures, from which certain pagan and
mythological motifs were taken, became much stronger.

c) Jewish literature, legends and Midrashim influenced artistic traditions.

The theory accepted by most scholars (except Goodenough, see p. 235) is that the
pagan motifs used in Jewish representational art became void of their original symbolic (idolatrous) significance (Avi-Yonah 1973: 126), and evolved into merely ornamental motifs (Avigad 1976: 282, 285). However, certain selected mythological
and symbolic motifs were acquired by the Jews because of the influence of Jewish
legends and Midrashic literature (Breslavi 1968). Avigad (1976: 284) maintains that
some of the pagan themes ''are simply graphic representations of values which were
openly accepted by the Judaism of that period...'' Several motifs acquired vague
symbolic significance in Jewish art, such as the lion or the Nikae (pp. 328, 340). The
vast majority, however, of the appropriated pagan motifs were ornamental designs
copied from pattern books (p. 391).

Judaism had no tradition of figurative art. The Jews were influenced by
Hellenistic figurative art and used contemporary pattern books, as well as creating
their own pattern books (see p. 393ff.). The Jewish attitude towards art was basically

decorative, in order to add beauty and ornamentation to their buildings. Even mythological scenes found their way into Jewish buildings (such as the House of Leontis, fig. 37, Pls. 68-70), as did many other pagan motifs in the funerary art of Beth She'arim and synagogal architectural decoration and pavements. At the time, the rabbis emphasized the latter part of the sentence "Thou shalt not worship them," the prohibition concerning the worship of idols. The Jews of this period were indeed unafraid of idolatry (Urbach 1959: 204). Moreover, in Jewish art no law forbids the depiction of religious subjects; on the contrary, they were allowed. Judaism was indifferent to pictures and did not ascribe to them any sanctity, and therefore there was no reason to prevent the depiction of representations on pavements which were trodden upon. Furthermore, walking upon pavements with such depictions insured that no sanctity or sacred quality which would cause their worship could be attached to the scenes. Such a depiction could not be related to as a "graven image" prohibited by the law. This might have been the reason why even pagan elements such as the zodiac were used. Judaism attached much more importance to the written word, as may be deduced from the iconoclastic destruction of the Na'aran synagogue pavement, in which the letters, however, were preserved, and from the synagogues at Reḥov and 'En-Gedi, where the floors paved with long inscriptions were left untouched.

The Jewish figurative repertoire included themes such as Biblical narrative scenes, mythological designs, motifs of animals and human figures which occurred also in Jewish poetry.

The significance of the symbolic and iconographic themes was in contrast to the aniconic Christian art, and was a means of emphasizing the difference between the Jewish and Christian arts (see p. 370f.).

1) Biblical Scenes

Biblical themes on synagogue mosaics were selected from a relatively few Biblical stories: the Sacrifice of Isaac (*Akedah*), Noah's Ark, Daniel in the lion's den, the Twelve Tribes and King David. Noteworthy is the recurrence of Biblical scenes in more than one synagogue mosaic pavement in the Land of Israel and on mosaics and frescoes in the Diaspora: the offering of Isaac—at Beth 'Alpha and Dura Europos; Noah's Ark—at Gerasa and Misis-Mopsuestia in Cilicia; Daniel in the lions' den—at Na'aran and Susiya; David = Orpheus—at Gaza and Dura Europos and David and Goliath's weapons at Marous. They were depicted in simple narratives, although some of the scenes as a whole may have had symbolic meanings (but see Kraeling 1979: 363 and 385, who proposes that the Biblical scenes on the mosaic floors belong to a symbolic tradition of ancient Jewish art). The scenes had in common the illustration of the theme of salvation (Schapiro 1960: 11; Avigad 1969: 68) and were associated with prayers offered in time of drought (Avi-Yonah 1975: 53). All three subjects were part of prayers such as "Remember" and "He that answereth..." (Sukenik 1932: 56 and note 4 ; but see Goodenough I: 253 who suggests symbolic meaning connected with Eastern mystery religions). The choice of themes derived from the religio-cultural climate of the period and was meant to be a reminder of and reference to traditional historical events (Avigad 1968: 68); there was no intention of using these themes for symbolic or didactic purposes, as suggested by some scholars (Goodenough 1953, I: 253 ff.). The style, form and artistic depiction on each of these floors is completely different, and each scene may be traced back to a distinct influence or source. Noah's Ark, for example, (Gerasa) is a realistic scene, derived from lists of animals in pattern books (see p. 392). Many animal renditions occur in other synagogues as a central theme—Maꜥon, Naꜥaran, Gaza, see p. 310ff.; Goodenough connects beasts and their victims to the Dionysus and Mithra cults.

The Sacrifice of Isaac (*Akedah*) in the Beth ʾAlpha synagogue is an example of local, popular art, which at the same time may contain iconographical influences from Alexandria (Sukenik 1932: 42). Daniel at Naꜥaran is very similar to the same scene appearing in Christian iconography. David in Gaza exhibits Hellenistic and Byzantine influences in its depiction and iconography. (See Chapter XIII, pp. 373-374, for a comparative treatment of Biblical scenes in Jewish and Christian art.)

The Sacrifice of Isaac

The third panel of the Beth ʾAlpha synagogue pavement portrays the scene of the sacrifice of Isaac, depicted according to the Biblical source (Gen. 22: 3-14) (fig. 31 and Pl. 64). On the left a donkey carrying wood (cut by the frame) and two young men accompany Abraham and Isaac. One of the youths stands behind the donkey, only his upper body showing while the other youth stands beside the donkey, holding the reins in his right hand and with a whip fastened to his left hand. The centre is occupied by the most dramatic aspect of the story, the Hand of God, which appears from above, emerging out of a cloud emitting rays. Under His hand the ram is caught in a thicket, suspended in the air in very unusual posture. Abraham is depicted on the right side of the panel, the tallest image in the scene, bearded and holding Isaac with one hand while in the other he carries a long knife. Isaac is rendered as a child, with bound hands. The altar is at the far right with flames leaping up (fig. 31).

31. Sacrifice of Isaac, Beth Alpha.

Inscriptions have been worked into the scene, for instance the names "Abraham" and "Isaac" appear above the figures. In the centre parts of Biblical legends are inscribed: "Thou shalt not stretch forth" occurs under the Hand of God, while "And behold a ram" accompanies the ram. A row of stylized palm trees is shown above the scene (Goodenough 1953, I: 246-247, contends that they symbolize sky).

The depiction of the scene is stylized and naive. All the figures are rendered in a frontal posture, whereas the animals are in profile. All are connected only by the narrative. The details accompanying the scene, such as the whip, the knife, and the donkey's bell are anachronisms from the contemporary environment of the artist. The empty space between images is filled in with plants, due to the *horror vacui* element, characteristic to this art.

The sacrifice of Isaac (also depicted in a prominent place in the Dura Europos synagogue (fig. 32)) is an event which held deep religious implications in Judaism and later came to symbolize the covenant between God and the Jewish people. It also became a popular theme in early Christian art (Smith 1922; Grabar 1968: 25-26; Kraeling 1979: 361-363). Gutmann (1984: 120) contends that the Beth 'Alpha sacrifice scene follows "an established early Christian type."

Direction and Organization of the Scene

Details on this panel have been subjected to many iconographical interpretations. Sukenik (1932: 40) maintains that the description of the scene is from left to right,

32. Sacrifice of Isaac, Dura Europos.

although it does not follow the exact narration of the Biblical story. Yeivin (1946: 21-22) remarks that the depiction was constructed from right to left, as proved by the fact that the donkey is incomplete.

The composition is narratively divided into three events: 1) the donkey and the lads, 2) the ram, thicket and the Hand of God, and 3) Abraham, Isaac and the altar. The dramatic centre is stressed by the Hand of God, by the inscriptions, and by the exceptional posture of the ram. Sukenik (1932: 40) maintains that the reason for the position of the ram is simply lack of space whereas Yeivin (1946: 32) suggests that the ram is rendered after naturalistic observation, as well as being a continuation of a prototype in Mesopotamian art. In comparable Christian scenes the ram is seldom tied to a thicket, but usually stands aside (see Ehrenstein 1923: figs. IX.2-4, 8, 11, 13-15, 18; also Gutmann 1984: 117-118). The ram's single horn close to the tree is also exceptional, and seems to illustrate the Biblical sentence "a ram caught in a thicket by his horns" (Gen. 22:13). The Hand symbolizing God is similar in its depiction to that in the Dura Europos scene (see fig. 32) where it also appears in the centre. In Christian art the Hand of God is depicted reaching out of a cloud or the sky (see Ehrenstein 1923: figs. IX.5-8, 11, 18) where it is an important symbol of God's intervention.

Abraham is rendered as the chief figure, by being shown as exceeding all other figures in height; by this device his prominence in the story is shown. Isaac is also depicted in an unusual attitude: he is not bound to the altar but is suspended in the air and seems to be held by Abraham. At Dura Europos he is depicted bound and lying on the altar (fig. 32). In Christian art, Isaac is depicted in either of two poses (proposed by Smith, 1922: 163): 1) on the altar (an Eastern-Hellenistic type), or 2) kneeling near Abraham (usually the position employed on the fresco of the catacombs of Rome, and the western-Hellenistic type). Sukenik (1932: 41) states that Abraham is carrying Isaac on his way to place him on the altar; at Dura Europos the depiction more closely follows the Biblical story. It is possible that at Beth ʾAlpha the end of the story is depicted: after Abraham has seen the substitute ram, he removes Isaac from the altar. Thus, the scene expresses the moment of rescue, of salvation.

Two details bear some similarity to the scene at the Dura Europos synagogue: the altars, with their architectural renditions, and the wood on the altar depicted as triangles (see Kraeling 1979: Pl. 51; Goodenough 1958, IX: 73).

The source for the panel of the sacrifice of Isaac was the written Biblical story. The scene unfolds from left to right, following the action and yet the dramatic climax of the story is shown in its centre. The close relation with the written source is verified by the inscriptions accompanying the depiction which quote exactly and concisely the Biblical source. The ram's single horn caught in the thicket is a direct illustration of the Biblical description. Isaac is portrayed at the very moment of being taken down by Abraham from the altar; this episode is the highlight of the story, determining its purpose and conclusion by expressing the moment of rescue and of salvation. In short, a straightforward narrative depiction of a popular Biblical scene becomes the symbol and expression of the desire for and hope of salvation.

In Early Christian art, where the sacrifice is depicted on catacomb walls and sarcophagi, in a style part realistic and part symbolic, the most typical scenes show a dramatic-symbolic rendering of Abraham with the knife, Isaac, and God's Hand.

Meaning in Judaism and Christianity

The sacrifice of Isaac as the pre-figuration of the life and sacrifice of Jesus was a common feature of Christian art and was related symbolically to death and salvation. In Judaism, however, the sacrifice is a symbol of life and of belief in God's grace, "an example of divine help as well as confirmation of God's covenant with Israel" (Schapiro 1960: 10). Because of this contrast in attitude towards the subject, the Jews felt the appropriate place to portray the scene was the synagogue, whereas the Early Christians preferred to show it in their funerary art, in catacombs and on sarcophagi. Furthermore, the lack of sanctity towards the topic shown by the Jews of Beth ꜃Alpha, where the mosaic was intended to be trodden on, would not have been acceptable to the Christian believers (see also Kraeling 1979: 361-363 for a suggestion of two traditions in Judaism: a symbolic and a narrative, with different sources).

Noah's Ark

The mosaic panel depicting Noah's Ark in the Gerasa synaogogue is dated to the early fifth century (Kraeling 1938: 323; Sukenik 1932: 55-56 suggests a date between the mid-fourth century and 530 CE). This mosaic scene was found under a church apse built over the synagogue structure in 530 CE. The scene is a rendition of the story of Noah's Ark incorporated into an oblong mosaic panel in the East vestibule of the synagogue (fig. 33 and Pl. 65). The Noah's Ark scene could be observed by those entering the East courtyard. In the centre of the East frame is an inscription placed upside down in relation to the entrance of the vestibule. The scene depicts the animals leaving Noah's Ark as described in Genesis 8, 19, each with its own kind. The framed central panel consists of three rows of realistically rendered animals, striding from left to right: the upper row shows the birds, the middle row, the mammals, and the lower, the reptiles (Sukenik 1932: 55, note 4, gives their identification). The south corner of the panel is only partly preserved. A dove holding an olive twig sits on a branch. Under the branch two partly preserved heads are inscribed "Shem" and "Japhet;" originally Noah's family was probably depicted sacrificing or leaving the Ark (Pl. 65). The panel is bordered by a frieze of beasts chasing their victims, with flowers and plants filling the space (fig. 33b) (Sukenik, 1932: 56, proposes that they describe the situation before the flood. Goodenough, 1968, XII: 133, asserts that the beasts in the border symbolize immortality and after life). A Greek inscription around a menorah and ritual implements appears in the centre of the East border frieze. The partly destroyed inscription contains the greeting "Holy place. Amen. Sela. Peace to the Synagogue." (fig. 17) The border frieze scene begins at the inscription with the beasts facing opposite directions.

The Gerasa scene commemorates the moment when the animals leave Noah's Ark, while Noah and his family celebrate the event or sacrifice in its honour, with

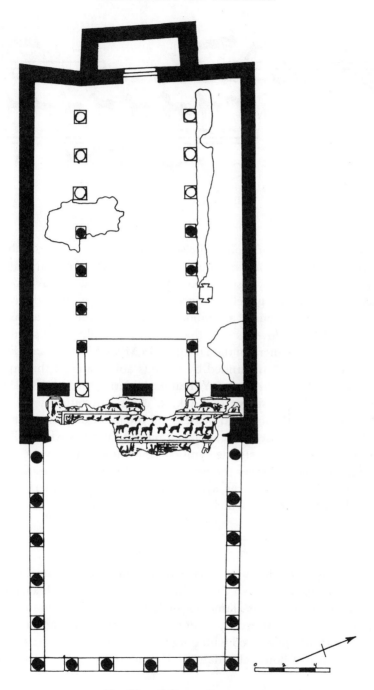

33a. Plan of Gerasa Synagogue.

33b. Noah's Ark, Gerasa.

the dove looking on. The rendition of the scene is very different from the way it appears in Early Christian art on catacombs and sarcophagi. The emphasis in Gerasa is on the animals and the story is depicted in a narrative-illustrative form, with the animals marching along the panel: in contrast to this in the art of the catacombs no depiction of the animals is found, a symbolic rendering of the Ark (a box) with Noah in it, sending off the dove is all that appears. Only one similar scene is depicted on a mosaic pavement in the Diaspora in Misis-Mopsuestia (Cilicia): a central scene of Noah's Ark, surrounded by various animals is all that appears. This is found in a building which Avi-Yonah considers (1981g: 186-190) to be a synagogue. The depiction shows the Ark, a chest, surrounded by two rows of animals. The outer row depicts wild beasts, and the inner depicts a variety of birds. At Gerasa the artist has chosen to render that part of the story where all are quitting the Ark: in this way he suggests the symbolic meaning of the event, which is that God has promised not to destroy the world again. By comparison, Early Christian art sees the Noah's Ark story as symbolizing death and resurrection: the Ark represents faith in the Church which will bring salvation to the believer.

Daniel in the Lions' Den

The Na'aran synagogue is dated to the sixth century and the panel containing the Biblical scene is depicted between the zodiac panel and the Torah shrine panel (fig. 34 and fig. XI.11). Its theme is Daniel in the lions' den. The human figures on this mosaic pavement were destroyed by iconoclasts sometime during the sixth century. Daniel himself is poorly preserved with only his arms remaining in an *orans* posture. He stands between two lions, also damaged, rendered in schematic style. Next to

34. Daniel in the Lions' Den, Naaran.

Daniel's head is the inscription "Daniel, shalom," and next to the lion's legs are more inscriptions.

A similar theme may be portrayed on the mosaic pavement of Susiya, in the westernmost panel. However, as it is almost completely destroyed, and only the end of the word [Dani]*el* is preserved (Gutman *et al.* 1981: 126) it is difficult to make a positive identification. The theme of Daniel in the lions' den is also popular in Early Christian art, appearing on catacombs and sarcophagi in Rome (Ehrenstein 1923: chap. XXXVI: figs. 1-3). Scholars relate this theme to a death cult and think that the scene symbolizes a person who is saved because of his belief. Goodenough (1953, II: 129) relates it to the Beth ʾAlpha mosaic and maintains that Daniel's scene symbolizes victory over death, as illustrated by the word *shalom*.

This scene, by contrast to the previously discussed Biblical scenes found on synagogue pavements, is depicted symbolically and not in the narrative style used elsewhere. This, however, may be due to the fact that a representation of a figure flanked by lions would be enough to suggest the theme to observers, because the story only concerns Daniel himself and the lions.

The Twelve Tribes

The Japhiʿa pavement's central westernmost panel depicts a square containing a large circle within which another, smaller circle is inscribed. In the space between the two circles twelve small interlacing circles appear. Unfortunately only two of these circles survive (fig. 35; Sukenik 1951a: 17). The central circle contains a bull facing right, and the other circle, which is badly damaged, depicts the head of a horned animal facing left and with two feet. Above its head are three Hebrew letter: *RIM*. Presumably this is Ephraim, one of the twelve tribes, whose symbol is *reʾem*

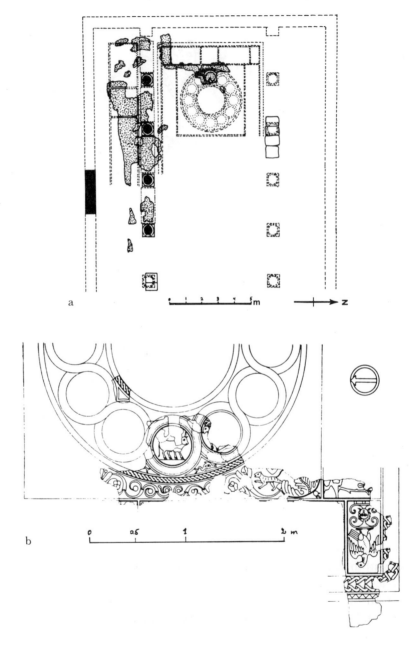

35. Japhiᶜa: a) Plan; b) Mosaic Floor.

(= wild ox). The other bull probably represents Manasseh. Sukenik (1951a: 18) maintains that the circles contain the symbols of the twelve tribes. This, he asserts, is illustrated by a passage in *Midrash Rabba* (*BaMidbar* 82), which says, regarding the two surviving circles "...On the flag of Ephraim was embroidered a bull (or "ox")...", "...On the flag of the tribe of Manasseh was embroidered a wild ox...." However, a discrepancy exists here, as the sign of Ephraim in the mosaic is *re'em* (the wild ox), and the sign of Manasseh is the bull (Sukenik 1951a: 20-23; cf. Goodenough, 1953, I: 217-218; 1964, VIII: 168, who suggests that this mosaic portrays a zodiac). The Japhiᶜa circle design however is a different scheme from that of the Jewish zodiac (see p. 305) (see also Naveh 1978: 70). This design is unique and has not been found in any other symbolic or iconographical portrayals in ancient Jewish art. Moreover, its theme probably is not taken from the Bible, but from Rabbinical literature.

King David

A synagogue decorated with figurative art was discovered on the Gaza seashore. An inscription dates its pavement to the years 508-509 CE (see p. 396; Avi-Yonah 1966: 221-223; Ovadiah 1969.). The floor of the synagogue is paved with mosaics consisting of an inhabited scroll design in a side aisle (see p. 312, Pl. 86.a-c) while the section of the western end of the central nave is depicted with a fragmentary representation of King David, crowned and dressed in a Byzantine emperor's robes. He sits on a throne playing the lyre and faced by animals, of which only the lion, serpent and giraffe survive (Pls. 66, 67). (Barash, 1980: 17-20, maintains that the giraffe depiction is highly unusual in connection with King David, but appears in renditions of scenes containing Orpheus.) This Gaza depiction represents King David as Orpheus charming wild beasts. The pagan world saw Orpheus as a symbol of heavenly peace, whereas Early Christian art depicted Orpheus as symbolizing Jesus, the good shepherd. Barash, in his comprehensive article (1980), proposes that the David of Gaza is a combination of two different iconographic themes: of the royal David, on the one hand, and of Orpheus charming beasts, on the other. Complete harmony of style has not been achieved in this allegorical combination probably because it had no earlier model on which to draw. Its uniqueness suggests it was the artist's own invention. The crown and throne are emphasized, as ceremonial motifs expressing royal images; they are unknown in renditions of Orpheus.

An earlier example of the same theme in Jewish art is the depiction in the Dura Europos synagogue. A figure, Orpheus, attired in Persian dress, plays the lyre. Next to him stands a lion and behind him perches an eagle (fig. 36) (Kraeling 1979: 223-

36. Orpheus, Dura Europos.

225; Goodenough 1965, IX: 89ff.). This theme of King David as Orpheus could hardly have been taken from a Biblical story, although stress is laid on the royal image. It clearly belongs to the adoption of a mythological pagan figure with iconographic affinities to the image of David as poet, psalmist, and charmer with music. The David-Orpheus motif was probably appropriated by Jewish iconography from the pagan world at the same time retaining its original meaning of the charming of beasts by music, and combining it with the royal image of David. David, as the Biblical psalmist king, in this composition, is represented by Orpheus playing the lyre before the wild beasts.

Gaza was an ancient Hellenistic town which had a Hellenistic-Byzantine tradition; this may have influenced the Jewish community to choose for their synagogue pavement a Biblical figure represented in its original pagan mythological image.

David with Goliath's weapons

A fragment of a mosaic floor was found recently in the Galilean synagogue of Marous (Ilan and Damati 1984-85). The remains of the mosaic floor were found at the northern edge of the eastern aisle (Ilan and Damati 1985: fig. 2); it measures 1.80 m × 3.00 m and is dated by the excavators to the fifth century. The mosaic (fig. VIII, 57, Pl. 48) depicts the figure of a man, probably crowned, wearing a short white tunic with a red cloak over his left shoulder, fastened by a fibula. On his arm and hip are symbolic designs (Ilan and Damati 1985:52 and fig. 3). The figure is surrounded by weapons: a shield on which he leans, a helmet and a sword in its sheath with an attached sling. On the corner of the mosaic along the frame beside the weapons is an inscription: "Yudan Son of Shimeon Mani" which may refer to a donor, it may be the artist's signature, or it may be the name of the figure itself (Ilan and Damati 1985:54-55). Most likely David is represented, surrounded by the weapons taken from Goliath, after his victory (as suggested by the late Prof. Yadin and followed by the excavators Ilan and Damati 1985:55 and note 12). This would be the most likely interpretation because depictions on synagogue mosaic pavements show Biblical (or mythological) personalities, whereas local individuals have never yet been found portrayed on a mosaic.

The Origin of the Biblical Scene Theme

Most scholars maintain that the Biblical scenes appearing in Jewish art such as in the Dura Europos frescoes, on the synagogue mosaic floors, as well as Old Testament scenes present in Christian art, catacomb paintings and church mosaics, originated in illuminated Biblical manuscripts first created by Alexandrian Jews in imitation of the rolls of classical antiquity (Roth 1953: 29, 32, 40, 44; Weitzman 1957: 89; 1971a: 227-231; 1971b; Kraeling 1979: 395-397; Avi-Yonah 1973: 128; 1975a: 65). These manuscripts may have been written for gentiles, in Greek translations of the Jewish Bible (Avi-Yonah 1973: 128). This theory seems highly doubtful for several reasons: 1) No proof exists as no ancient illuminated manuscripts dating to or before the sixth century have ever been found; 2) Sages' rules about illustration would have forbidden illuminated manuscripts of the Bible (also Kraeling 1979: 396); 3) The Bible because it is considered so sacred, especially the writing itself, has never been illustrated in any period, therefore it is highly unlikely that the Bible would have been illuminated by or for Jews at this time; 4) The Dead Sea scrolls, ranging in time from the second century BCE to the second century CE, do not contain even a single illustration; 5) If illustrated manuscripts had actually existed, and had been the origins for Biblical scene themes, then a uniformity of pattern and design would be seen in the later Jewish art. This, however, is not the case and each Biblical scene portrayed is fundamentally different. At the same time it may reasonably be inferred that pattern books of Jewish motifs and themes existed in antiquity and were used by the Jewish communities, by donors, artists and artisans (see p. 394). Biblical stories would naturally be included as subject matter for the decoration of synagogues. [Thompson (1973: 46) proposes that pattern books, panels and cartoons were copied and served wall painters in Dura as they had in Pompeii.]

Conclusions

A certain changing attitude is discernible in these Biblical scenes which may help to determine the development of the Biblical scene depictions from highly-detailed narrative stories to concise symbolic depictions. For instance, the rendition of Noah's Ark at Gerasa is executed in a narrative mode which is stressed by the many details. This style suggests an earlier date for Gerasa than at Beth ʾAlpha where there is already a tendency towards the symbolic in the narrative of Isaac's sacrifice. Daniel, at Naᶜaran, is concisely and completely symbolically rendered in the *orans* posture, similar to Early Christian art depictions. At Marous David is depicted as a Byzantine warrior or prominent figure. Finally, David of Gaza is shown as a Biblical monarch but in the Hellenistic attitude used for the mythological figure of Orpheus, as is the Christian figure of Jesus the Shepherd.

The narrative-historical style in Jewish art appears by the mid-third century in the fresco paintings at the Dura Europos synagogue. Synagogal art therefore, as Grabar maintains (1968: 95) anticipates Christian catacomb art of the fourth century.

The Biblical scenes found so far do not seem to have a common denominator as regards style or origins. However, some similarity does exist in the arrangement of interconnecting panels and subject matter found both at Beth ʾAlpha and Naᶜaran as to suggest mutual intercourse or social affinities.

Biblical scenes were considered appropriate subject matter for the synagogue pavements. They appear to exhibit disregard, however, for the second commandment of "no graven image." Furthermore, they were trodden upon (even when the pavements included the Hand of God and the ritual objects). This was intentionally done: if these depictions were stepped upon, they could not then be considered sacred, and no danger of worshipping graven images could arise (see p. 379).

2) Mythological Scenes

The House of Leontis

The sole example of a Jewish pavement depicting several mythological scenes oc-curs in a house adjoining the small synagogue of Beth She'an (B) (Zori 1966). This Jewish house belonged, according to the inscription, to Kyrios Leontis, and is dated to the sixth century. Its pavement is divided into three panels (fig. 37): the upper panel shows two scenes from the Odyssey: 1) Odysseus fighting the monster Scylla, and 2) Odysseus and the Sirens (Pl. 68). The central panel is occupied by a Greek inscription within a circle which may be a wreath, surrounded by birds (Pl. 69). On the right side of the inscription a now mutilated five-branched menorah is depicted. A rendition of a Nilotic landscape is shown on the lower panel of the pavements, including a nilometer, a representation of "Alexandria," a personification of the Nile, a crocodile attacking a cow, and a sailor in a boat (Pl. 70). Nilotic scenes have a tradition going back to the Hellenistic period, with many Nilotic scenes being depicted in churches at the time of the Leontis house. Avi-Yonah (1972: 121-122) explains the attraction of these scenes for Christian art in their representation of the "earth-bound" world. A favourite Nilotic subject is that of the crocodile attacking the cow, which also appears in Nilotic scenes on church floors in Cyrenaica. Alföldi-Rosenbaum (1975: 150-151) contends that these motifs were included in the pattern books of mosaic workshops. They probably did not have any significance on the church floor, but they may have been considered suitable as an expression of the idea of paradise: the Nile was considered one of the rivers of Paradise. Avi-Yonah pro-poses (1975a: 54) that this pavement indicates that Jews knew and appreciated Greek mythology and the Homeric poems. [Roussin (1981: 6-9) suggests a Jewish meaning for the crocodile-cow scene, interpreting them as *Behemoth* and *Leviatan*, with eschatological connotations.] Finally, it is just as probable that Kyrios Leontis chose this particular Nilotic scene simply because, among all the patterns in the pattern book (p. 393) through which he looked, this scene seemed the most attractive and appropriate to him.

3) The Zodiac Panel

An interesting phenomenon is found in four of the ancient synagogues discovered so far in Israel. These synagogues, ranging in date from the fourth to sixth centuries, contain mosaics showing the zodiac cycle (fig. 38) (Hachlili 1977 and bibliography there, also Avi-Yonah 1981e). This is surprising in view of the pagan origin of the zodiac, and all the more so, since the mosaic would have been immediately visible

37. House of Leontis, Beth Sheʾan.

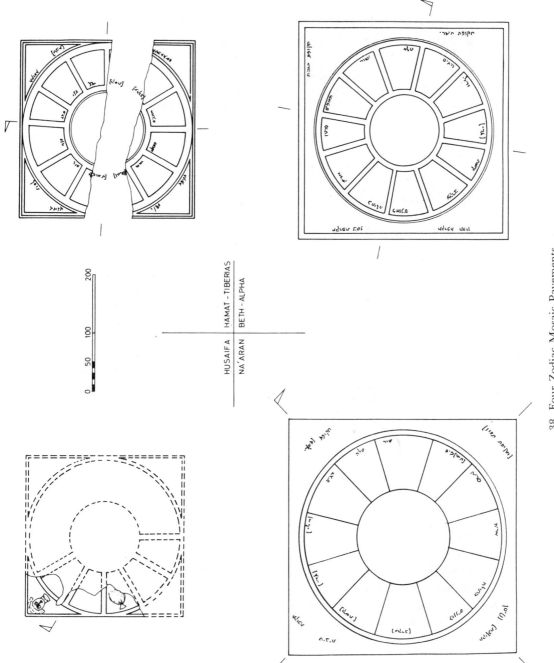

38. Four Zodiac Mosaic Pavements.

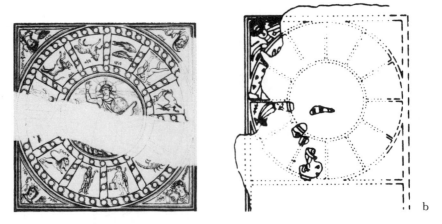

39. Zodiacs: a) Ḥammath Tiberias; b) Ḥuseifa.

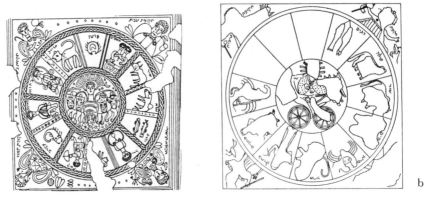

40. Zodiacs: a) Beth ʾAlpha; b) Naʿaran.

to all who entered the synagogue as it lay inside the main entrances. This widespread use, over two centuries, of a "pagan" motif, invites many questions as to its function in the synagogue.

One zodiac mosaic was found at Ḥammath Tiberias (fig. 39a, Pl. 71) (Dothan 1982). At that time, Tiberias was an important Jewish centre, being the seat of the Sanhedrin, or Patriarchate, from the end of the third until the fourth centuries. Another mosaic was found at Ḥuseifa (fig. 39b and Pl. 72) (Avi-Yonah 1934). The third mosaic comes from Beth ʾAlpha (fig. 40a, Pl. 73), and dates from the time of Justin

I, 518-527 CE (Sukenik 1932). The fourth mosaic floor was found at Naᶜaran (fig. 40b and Pl. 74; Vincent 1961). A fifth synagogue, that of Susiya near Hebron (Pl. 75, left corner; see Gutman *et al.* 1981: 126) did contain at one time a zodiac mosaic floor, but it was later changed into a geometric pattern. This recurrence of the zodiac design in a number of synagogue mosaics, indicates its relevance to religious thought, and makes it necessary to analyse its place and importance in synagogal art.

The Design: Form and Composition

The zodiac cycle in all four synagogues occupies the centre of a three-panel mosaic floor (figs. XI, 1, 3, 4, 5); another panel below it contains various designs. The zodiac design cycle consists of a square frame containing two concentric circles. The innermost circle contains a portrayal of the sun-god in a chariot. The outer, larger, circle depicts the zodiac divided into twelve radial units, each one containing one of the signs and bearing its Hebrew name. Outside the zodiac circle and within the square frame in its corners, are portrayed symbolically represented busts of the four seasons. These are named in Hebrew, after the month with which the season begins. The composition of each mosaic is harmoniously balanced, each section having a significant and integral place in the design (fig. 38).

Although there are differences in the four Jewish zodiac designs in the depiction and execution of the figures the development of a distinctive Jewish design is discernible. Moreover, the exceptional and unmistakable style of conception of the figures, in the three parts of the design, the sun god in the central circle, the zodiac signs in the outer circle and the seasons in the square corners, point to the meaning and significance for the Jewish worshippers.

The sun god is shown frontally (*en-face*) and occupies the centre of the zodiac. He is crowned; a halo radiating light appears above his head. His chariot has two wheels in front, and is pulled by four horses, two on either side. The background shows a crescent moon and several stars, at Beth ʾAlpha (Pl. 76); in Naᶜaran this is depicted on the front of the sun god's dress (Pl. 77), and in Ḥammath Tiberias the sun god is shown riding his chariot and holding a globe and whip in his hand (Pl. 78).

The zodiac circle contains the twelve signs of the zodiac (which are identical to the twelve months of the Jewish year). The circles at Naᶜaran and Ḥuseifa run clockwise, whereas at Beth ʾAlpha and Ḥammath Tiberias counter-clockwise. The signs do not correspond to the seasons, except at Ḥammath Tiberias where they are coordinated. At Beth ʾAlpha and Naʿaran the zodiac figures are directed outwards with their feet toward the central circle. At Ḥammath Tiberias and Ḥuseifa the figures are directed inwards, with their heads towards the central circle (figs. 39a-b, Pls.71-72). The human figures in the mosaic pavement at Ḥammath Tiberias are shown in movement and all the males are portrayed nude. The figures at Beth ʾAlpha and Naʿaran (figs. 40a-b, Pls.73-74), however, are shown as static portraits and are fully clothed. In all the zodiacs the animals are depicted in profile, facing forward.

The signs themselves are portrayed with individuality, as illustrated in Pls. 79-82. Several deserve special attention because of the wide range of styles from synagogue to synagogue.

Virgo: (*Virgin, Bethulah*): In the Ḥammath Tiberias mosaic, Virgo is shown as a robed Greek Kore with a covered head, holding a torch (Pl. 80c). In Beth ʾAlpha, the figure of Virgo resembles a Byzantine queen and is shown seated on a throne (Pl. 80c) (Sukenik 1932: 37).

Libra (*Scales, Moznayim*): In three synagogue mosaics, the sign of Libra is shown as a human figure holding a pair of scales. At Ḥammath Tiberias, however, the figure of Libra represents Greek mythological depictions of the sign but with the addition of a sceptre (Pl. 81a). In the Beth ʾAlpha mosaic the figure of Libra holds the scales in a very akward position, standing on one leg. The second leg has been omitted by the artist in order to allow enough room for the scales (Pl. 81a).

Sagittarius (*Archer, Kashat*): Pagan representations of Sagittarius usually show a half human-half animal figure, a centaur, shooting a bow and arrow. Depictions of Sagittarius survive on only two of the mosaic floors, those of Beth ʾAlpha and Ḥuseifa (Pl. 81c), and show it in human form, holding a bow and arrow in its left hand (for Ḥuseifa see Avi-Yonah's description, 1934: 125). Jews were probably very reluctant to depict Sagittarius in its pagan hybrid form, and preferred a human archer, which would have been sufficient to symbolize the Hebrew name of Sagittarius: *Kashat*—the archer.

Capricorn (*Goat, Gedi*): In the Ḥammath Tiberias mosaic, Capricorn takes its common pagan form of a horned goat with a fish's tail (Pl. 82a). In the Ḥuseifa mosaic, only the horns of Capricorn remain (Pl. 72) and at Beth ʾAlpha, where the sign is partially destroyed, it appears that a kid is depicted (Pl. 82a).

Aquarius (*Water-bearer, Deli*): The sign is differently depicted in each of the zodiac mosaics. At Ḥammath Tiberias a figure pours water from an amphora (Pl. 82b), which is also the common depiction of Aquarius in Roman art (Hachlili 1977: 69; fig. 14). The Ḥuseifa zodiac portrays Aquarius as an amphora with water pouring from it (Pl. 72 and fig. 39b). The Beth ʾAlpha sign is unique in that Aquarius is shown as a figure drawing water from a well with a bucket (Pl. 82b) (bucket is the translation of the Hebrew word *deli*).

The Seasons (*Tekufoth*)

These are diagonally placed in the four corners of the outer square. They are each represented by the bust of a woman wearing jewellery and equipped with identifying attributes, such as the Jewish symbol of the shofar, and accompanied by the Jewish name of the first month of each season, except at Ḥuseifa (Pls. 71-74, 83-84). The Beth ʾAlpha winged figures of the seasons are exceptional because of their richly coloured jewellery and decorations (Pls. 83-84). A comparison of the seasons in the Jewish depictions with those appearing in pagan mosaics dating to the fourth-fifth centuries reveals similarities in their attributes: most of the figures are represented by crowned, winged busts. However, there is no consistent similarity (Hachlili 1977: 70-72, figs. 16, 18).

At Ḥammath Tiberias and Beth ʾAlpha the bust of the season *Nisan* (Spring) is placed in the upper left corner with *Tammuz* (Summer) and *Tebeth* (Winter) running counterclockwise. At Naʿaran *Nisan* (Spring) is in the lower left corner with the other seasons running in a counterclockwise direction. In Ḥuseifa the only remaining representation of the seasons is *Tishri* (Autumn) which is located in the upper left corner (Avi-Yonah 1934: 126-127). The following descriptions of the seasons underline the contrasts and comparisons between them and their attributes:

Spring (*Nisan*) (Pl. 83a): The figures at both Beth ʾAlpha and Ḥammath Tiberias are adorned with bracelets, earrings, and necklaces. The Ḥammath Tiberias figure is crowned with flowers and holds a bowl of fruit in her right hand whereas the Beth ʾAlpha figure includes a shepherd's crook (pedum) and a bird (Sukenik 1932: 42). At Naʿaran the figure holds a shepherd's crook, with a sheaf of corn and bird placed on either side of the image (Sukenik 1932: 42).

Summer (*Tammuz*) (Pl. 83b): The representation of Summer in the mosaic of Ḥammath Tiberias is of a jewelled female bust crowned with olive branches, holding a sickle in her right hand and with a sheaf of corn at her left. The Beth ʾAlpha figure is also of a jewelled female bust, with fruits and field produce in front of it and to its sides. The remains of the mosaic at Naʿaran show a cluster of grapes and a wand at the figure's right and a bird at its left.

Autumn (*Tishri*) (Pl. 84a): The Ḥammath Tiberias mosaic portrays a jewelled figure crowned with pomegranates and an olive branch, holding a cluster of grapes. At Beth ʾAlpha, the bust is jewelled and crowned, surrounded by pomegranates, figs, apples, a cluster of grapes, a palm tree, and a bird. The Naʿaran bust holds a crook and shofar in her right hand and has a bird at her side. At Ḥuseifa, where the representation of Autumn is the only remaining figure, we find a bust with pomegranates, a palm tree, and a shofar at the right of the figure.

Winter (Tebeth) (Pl. 84b): The bust of Winter in Ḥammath Tiberias is draped with a scarf over the head, and has an amphora with water flowing from it at its left. The Beth ᵓAlpha figure has only a branch with two leaves and a cylindrical object (Sukenik 1932: 39; Goodenough 1953, I: 249, n. 499).

The zodiac is known also in pagan art, at first depicted on ceilings, and only later worked into mosaic pavements (Hachlili 1977: 61-65, figs. 8-12, 17). However, important differences exist between the Jewish and pagan portrayals. It is only in the Jewish versions of the zodiac that the triple depiction of the sun god, the zodiac signs and the four seasons appear in the same composition. Outside of Jewish sources the three elements never appear in the same mosaic. One or two of the elements are always missing, or are replaced by other motifs, such as seven planets in place of the sun god. Decorative patterns in addition replace the four seasons in the corners, or, as on the Antioch mosaic (Hachlili 1977: fig. 12) or in the Beth Sheᵓan monastery (Hachlili 1977: fig. 17), the work performed during each month, the labours of the month, replaces the signs of the zodiac.

Style

The Jewish version of the zodiac, unlike its pagan equivalent, has a specific standard design which is repeated in all four of the mosaic floors discussed above. The diverging styles of the synagogue zodiac panels are best explained by a comparison between the earliest floor at Ḥammath Tiberias, of the fourth century (Pl. 71), and the sixth century Beth ᵓAlpha mosaic (Pl. 73). The earlier mosaic contains three dimensional, naturalistically portrayed and animated figures, showing a marked Hellenistic style, whereas the Beth ᵓAlpha floor is in a stiffer, rustic style, with distorted and anatomically disproportionate figures without indication of sex, except through jewellery in the case of the women. Colour is used to emphasize different parts of the body. The later floor gives a linear, two dimensional impression, the flat figures being shown frontally.

Meaning and Significance

Scholars have attempted to explain the significance and meaning of the Jewish zodiac panel in various ways (Hachlili 1977: 72). Goodenough (1958, XII: 214-215) claims that the zodiac containing a portrayal of the sun god Helios symbolized for the pagans the supremacy of the law of nature, of the cosmic order under the sovereignty of *Sol Invictus*. He further claims that for the Jews, "Helios and the chariot symbolized the divine charioteer of Hellenistic Judaism, God himself." Avigad, on the other hand (1976: 283), proposes that "the figure in the chariot was the sun, itself a component of the cycle of cosmic forces depicted in the zodiac." The most logical explanation, however, seems to be that the Jewish zodiac mosaic functioned as a calendar (suggested first in connection with the list of the priestly courses by Avi-Yonah, 1964: 56-57; also Hachlili 1977: 76), consisting as it does of three compulsory sections: 1) the four seasons which represent the year; 2) the twelve signs of the zodiac representing the months, and 3) the sun god symbolizing the day, the night being denoted by the background of the crescent moon and stars. Additional support for this interpretation is provided by the discovery of a mosaic inscription in the ʿEn-Gedi synagogue floor, dating to the late sixth century (Pl. 51), which includes the names of the zodiac signs followed by the names of the corresponding Jewish months. The written inscription must have replaced the illustrated zodiac mosaic during this later period, and it may have been that the images of the Naʿaran floor were torn up at this same time. This change in the Jewish attitude towards figurative art produced a general prohibition against representing human and animal forms.

It is highly characteristic of Jewish art that a pagan subject, in this case the zodiac, should be adapted to express a Jewish idea such as an annual calendar. In the Roman world zodiac signs are of solely cosmic and astronomical significance; moreover in Christian, as in Roman art, the calendar is represented by the labours of the months (Hachlili 1977: fig. 17). Jewish art preferred an abstract and symbolic zodiac, rather than the naturalistic representation of human activity depicted on the Christian examples, in order to assure the religious nature of the calendar. The fact that the zodiac was used many times makes it clear that the Jewish community was not interested merely in a strictly decorative design for its floors. There must have been something unique about this particular design that caused the community to wish to adopt it. Probably it regarded the zodiac as a suitable vehicle for expressing conceptual needs. The community's intent was not only to portray a decorative design but also to express a deeper import; in this balanced representation of the three elements, sun god, zodiac and seasons, a two-fold purpose, of significance and design, could be achieved. Annual religious rituals consequently could be graphically portrayed in the synagogue's interior decoration itself. From this it can be seen that the fundamentally pagan zodiac cycle came to serve the Jewish community as a popular, symbolic calendar, and was employed as a significant framework for the annual synagogue rituals.

4) Inhabited Scrolls

The "inhabited scroll" composition was popular and fashionable during the sixth century and is one of the most common patterns found on church pavements (Avi-Yonah 1981b: 364; Kitzinger 1965: 347-348). It also appears on three synagogue pavements as complete carpets: Maꜥon, Gaza and the Beth Sheʾan B small synagogue (figs. 41-42 and Pls. 85-87). Two of these, Maꜥon and Gaza, are situated in the southern part of the Land of Israel and their design is also common to church pavements in the same area, such as Shellal, ꜤEn Ḥanniya, ꜤAsida, and Ḥazor, as well as the "Armenian" church at Jerusalem, which Avi-Yonah (1981d) relates to a school at Gaza (cf. Hachlili 1986). (Recently several other churches with "inhabited scroll patterns" have been unearthed in Israel—at Herodium, Ḥevel Habsor and Beth Guvrin.) The inhabited scroll design was usually executed on the mosaic pavement in long- and narrow rooms. The pavement is divided into three to five vertical columns of medallions, generally filled by antithetic groups of animals symmetrically flanking the central axial column which usually contains objects. Vine branches forming the medallions issue from an amphora flanked by peacocks or horned animals at the base edge of the pavement.

The Moꜥan Pavement (Avi-Yonah 1960b: 25-35).

The mosaic pavement fills the entire width of the nave, originally 10.20 m. × 5.40 m., and is now partially damaged and lost. The composition is divided into 55 circular medallions in five vertical columns with eleven horizontal rows. Vine branches issuing from an amphora in place of the lowest central medallion form the medallions (fig. 41). The medallions of the central axial column contain objects, flanked by columns symmetrically containing alternated birds and beasts in antithetic positions. A symbolically decorated panel is inserted into the upper part of the pavement in front of the apse. This panel contains: a menorah in its centre flanked by two lions, with four other medallions below which are filled with symbolic palm trees and pairs of doves. The menorah is flanked by a pair of lions, a pair of ethrogs, a shofar and a lulav (Pl. 87). This "symbolic" panel suggests that the Jewish community who ordered this common inhabited scroll design wanted even so to be mindful of the important point that the floor was situated in a synagogue. Avi-Yonah (1960b: 32) maintains that the vine branch pattern serves merely as a pleasing design and that the contents of the upper panel are the real symbols meant to lead one up spiritually towards the apse.

Renditions on the pavement are sometimes formalized. Beasts are depicted realistically in quite naturalistic poses. The artists show a fine sense of humour, for

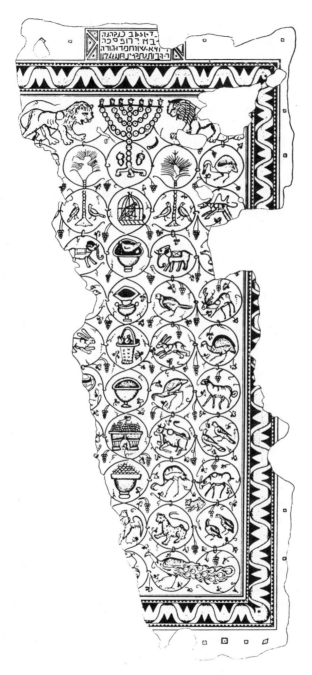

41. Inhabited Scrolls, Maꜥon.

example in the hen laying an egg, the depiction of the hunting dog, the elephants and the leopard cub playing outside the leopard medallion.

The Gaza Pavement (Pl. 86a-c).

The inhabited scroll pavement is situated in the southernmost aisle of the Gaza synagogue (Ovadiah 1981: 130). The composition is divided into more than thirty circular medallions in three vertical columns; as it is partly damaged, only ten rows survive: the lower part is missing, and it is difficult to determine if the vine branches forming the medallions issue from an amphora or an acanthus head (Avi-Yonah 1981d: 389). Most of the medallions contain beasts and birds. The arrangement is of three animals in the medallions of each row, connected horizontally, especially the animal chase scenes in rows 3, 7, and 9 (Pl. 86a-c). In the other rows either a bird or a beast in the centre is flanked symmetrically by two animals facing each other in an antithetic composition. Opposing this arrangement is row 2, where peacocks flank an inscription (commemorating the donors Menachem and Yeshuᶜa, sons of Jesse); and row 6, in which a bird cage flanked by partridges is depicted in the central medallion (Pl. 86b). The rendition of the animals, which is sometimes impressionistic, sometimes naturalistic and full of life, includes a lioness and cub, a giraffe, a tigress, a zebra, and a donkey (Pl. 86).

The Beth Sheʾan B Pavement (fig. 42 and Pl. 85) (Bahat 1981a: 82-85).

A variation of the inhabited scroll pattern is to be found on this pavement. Attached to the House of Leontis (see p. 301), the synagogue has a mosaic pavement with a wide, ornate border, and a central panel consisting of nine medallions (three columns and three rows). An amphora at its base edge is flanked by two horned animals, either rams or goats. A menorah occupies the central medallion with an ethrog flanking it and a lamp suspended from it, and the word shalom written above it (fig. 6). A peacock, en face fills the upper central medallion. Two medallions are lost, so it is impossible to determine whether the scene was symmetrical (Bahat 1981a) , or whether each medallion contained a different animal, like the Beth Guvrin church floor (Hachlili 1986).

A border design surrounds the central panel, and consists of four corner amphorae with vines issuing from them, and intertwining animal chase scenes. Among the depicted animals are a bear, fox, hare, dog, deer, hen, and also an elephant which appears in only one other site, at the Maᶜon synagogue. The chase scenes show a fox chasing a hare, and a bear chasing a deer (fig. 42 and Pl. 85). Birds fill

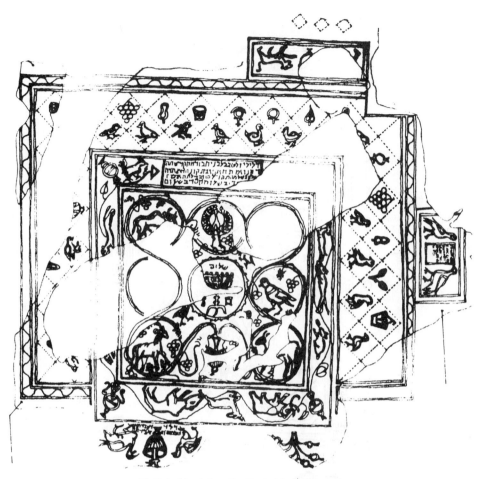

42. Inhabited Scrolls, Beth Sheʾan B.

the space around and outside the menorah medallion. In the centre of the upper part of this border is a dedicatory inscription in a *tabula ansata* (fig. 42 and Pl. 85). The style of this pavement is fairly similar to the style of the inhabited scroll pavement in the monastery at Beth Sheʾan, room L (Pl. 107). Probably both were executed by a common workshop or by the same artist (see p. 390).

Differences in execution and composition exist among the synagogue pavements. At Gaza the design includes at least three columns of medallions, each consisting of at least eleven rows. The Beth Shʾan B pavement is a square composition of three

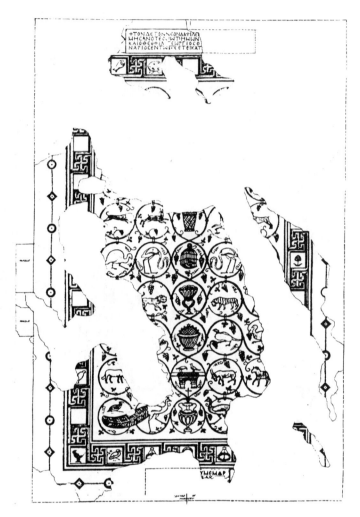

43. Inhabited Scrolls, Shellal Church.

columns, each having three medallions in the centre of the pavement. At Maᶜon are eleven rows of five medallions each. The arrangement here (and at the Shellal (fig. 43) and ''Armenian'' church of Jerusalem, fig. 43) emphasises the central axial column which contains objects flanked by symmetrical antithetic animals. On the other hand, the Gaza synagogue depicts no objects, except for a bird cage and inscription. The arrangement here is horizontal, each row having a group of three animals, connected by a chase scene or by a symmetrical composition of animals facing towards the central medallion.

Thematic structure in each of these synagogue pavements is different: at Maᶜon, objects only are depicted in the central axial column; chase scenes connecting from two to three medallions are found only at Gaza; Beth Sheᵓan B, on the other hand, has a central axial emphasis on the Jewish symbol.

Naturalistic and impressionistic renditions characterize the Gaza pavement, and are also apparent in the animals which break out from the bounds of the medallions (Pl. 86). The design at Maᶜon is realistic but more stylized (fig. 41 and Pl. 87). Both pavements exhibit a rustic sense of humour. Gaza has a donors' commemoratory inscription placed in the central axial medallion flanked by peacocks (Pl. 86b), whereas Maᶜon has a panel of Jewish symbols in its upper section (Pl. 87). Beth Shᵓan B has a medallion filled with Jewish symbols in the centre of the design (Pl. 85).

The inhabited scroll pattern constitutes a design commonly used during the sixth century in the Levant, both in church and synagogue pavements. This pattern took the place of a geometrically-patterned carpet, and evenly covers the entire floor (Kitzinger 1965b: 24). The animals, birds and objects which occupy the medallions add their part to the harmonious and integrated impression these carpets give. (See the border of the Beth ᵓAlpha mosaic floor which portrays an inhabited scroll frame, filled with animals, objects and genre scenes (fig. X, 33).

The following characteristics of the inhabited scroll pattern are shared by sixth century pavements of both churches and synagogues, according to Avi-Yonah (1960b: 31; 1981d: 394; also Hachlili 1986):

1) A pattern of an all-over and aesthetically pleasing composition.

2) A formalized geometric motif of vine branches dividing the floor into circular medallions.

3) Stylization of fauna and flora.

4) Rhythmic, symmetrical groups arranged horizontally in antithetic groups on both sides of a central axial column.

5) Proportions according to the size of the medallions, thus no difference made in the size of the animals or birds.

6) *Horror vacui.*

7) Descriptive isolation.

To these common characteristics should be added another which occurs exclusively on synagogue pavements, that is, the Jewish symbols depicted in a central position on the Maᶜon and Beth Sheᵓan B pavements.

Most of the motifs used in these mosaics are not exclusive to the inhabited scroll pavements, but also occur on other types of all-over geometric patterned pavements (see for instance the Naᶜaran synagogue's front panel (fig. XI.4), and the church mosaics of Gerasa, Madeba, and Mount Nebo). The appearance in both contexts infers that its designs and motifs are simply decorative. Furthermore, the addition of the symbolic panel to the synagogue mosaic by the Jews supports this inference as it is clear that there was a need to differentiate the building of the synagogue from the neighbouring churches also decorated with inhabited scrolls (Avi-Yonah 1960b: 32).

All the details of the pavement, both the general composition of the floor, the individual patterns and motifs, and especially the Jewish symbolic objects, were taken from pattern books according to individual or communal taste. This can be deduced from the uniformity of and similarity in composition and motif. As the individual styles are obviously dissimilar, however, there must have been many artists and workshops producing mosaics in different parts of the country (see p. 390). It is also possible that certain combinations of motifs recurring in synagogues may have been preferred by the Jewish community without specific significance attached to it as, for instance, the motif of the bird cage (see p. 337).

Finally it is important to emphasize that Jewish inhabited scroll mosaics are distinctive for two reasons. First, because of the addition of Jewish symbols to the composition in the synagogues of Maᶜon and Beth Sheʾan B; second, because no human figures are depicted in the medallions, although genre and vintage scenes are depicted in many of the church mosaics.

CHAPTER TEN

MOTIFS OF JEWISH ARTS

The discussion of the motifs in the following pages concentrates on popular and common motifs in Jewish art which will be shown to indicate a persistent preference for particular themes in Jewish ornamentation.

Several sources are posited for the motifs used in Jewish art. 1) Tradition and the continuation of popular motifs descending from Jewish art of the Second Temple period (p. 79ff.). 2) Selected decorative patterns and motifs taken from contemporary arts (Graeco-Roman, Syrian and Nabatean), but devoid of their symbolic context and significance. 3) Chosen motifs from pattern books. 4) Motifs of symbolic significance for Judaism (discussed in Chapter IV, pp. 79-83). A motif either consists of a combination of several antithetic or heraldic elements such as lions flanking a menorah or Nikae flanking a wreath, or of a single image or object such as a rosette. The motifs discussed include:

A) Flora, plant ornaments; B) Geometric motifs; C) Fauna, animal motifs; D) Human figures; E) Mythological motifs; F) Genre motifs.

Definite tendencies betray themselves in the persistent selection by the Jews of Late Antiquity of heraldic and antithetic symmetrical designs, such as lions, eagles, bulls, Nikae, peacocks, birds, horned animals, dolphins, and rosettes, which are depicted on sarcophagi, synagogue lintels, friezes, and mosaic floors.

A common source for the motifs in Jewish art, most probably a pattern book, is indicated by the stylization of pose and posture as well as the patterning, for the representations of animals, plants and other ornaments; it is less likely that the motifs were directly copied from nature.

A) Flora, Plant Ornaments

Plant ornaments were popular and widespread in Jewish synagogal and funerary art, occurring on sarcophagi, on architectural decoration as well as on mosaic pavements. The repertoire of plant ornaments includes independent and recognizable species as well as decorative compositions, and repetitive all-over motifs which sometimes change into geometric patterns (Avi-Yonah 1981a:66 ff.).

The Vine

Most popular among the plant motifs is the vine which appears in Jewish art already in the Second Temple period (figs. IV, 16, 21, Hachlili 1985:119-123). The vine is presented stylized; the bunches of grapes and leaves are arranged unnaturally in various geometric forms, sometimes so regularly rendered that the effect is of an abstract pattern. One type of grape cluster is typical of Jewish art: a central bunch flanked by two smaller bunches—see fig. IV, 8 (Avi-Yonah 1981a:70). The most common motif is the vine scroll either carved or depicted on mosaic (Avi-Yonah 1981a:79-82). A vine scroll is carved on the Beth Sheᶜarim "Shell" sarcophagus (Pl. 30). Examples occur on synagogue lintels such as at Naveh, Chorazin, Nabratein, ᶜAhmadieh, Kanef and Bathra (fig. VIII, 52). The Kanef entrance frame has a stylized all-over vine scroll pattern (fig. VIII.41). On mosaic floors the vine scroll is found on borders, and the inhabited scroll pavements in particular use vine scroll medallions (figs. IX.41, 42 and Pl. 87). Avi-Yonah (1960b: 32) maintains that the vine branch pattern served as a carpet design, meant to lead up to the symbols, as at Maᶜon. The vine in Jewish art is plainly an ornamental design used to decorate confined spaces or to cover complete floors. Its only symbolic connotation might be due to the fact that it is one of the "seven species" (Deut. 8:8; Avigad 1976: 2; but see Goodenough, 1956, VI: 126 ff., who associates the vine with mystic Dionysian cults).

The Wreath

The wreath in antiquity symbolized victory and peace. In Hellenistic funerary paintings and reliefs the wreath was a common motif which signified immortality. The wreath was also one of the most common motifs in Jewish decorative art, used already in the Second Temple period (figs. IV, 7, 8, p. 80: Hachlili 1985: 123-124). In early depictions the wreath is found alone (Avi-Yonah 1981a: 76-77) whereas in later renditions it is usually depicted as a central motif flanked by figures such as Nikae, dolphins, eagles, bull heads, and vine scrolls; other motifs are also shown inside it: lion head, menorah, conch, and geometric designs; see, for instance, the Beth Sheᶜarim "Nikae" (fig. 1) and "Daughters" sarcophagi (Avigad 1967: Pl. XXXIX), and the frieze fragment from Chorazin (Pl. 45). Carved lintels include wreaths flanked by eagles (fig. VIII.46), by Nikae (figs. VIII.45), or by amphorae and pomegranates, and by rosettes at Kazrin, and Tybe (fig. VIII, 53a, c).

1. "Nikae" Sarcophagus, Beth She͑arim.

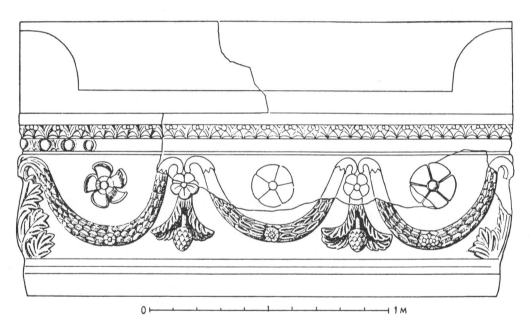

2. "Acanthus A" Sarcophagus, Beth She͑arim.

3. Bar͑am, Relief.

Garlands

A common decorative pattern in Graeco-Roman art, the garland, is used sporadically in Jewish art. It is found in Beth She'arim on several sarcophagi: the "eagles," "Bucrania," "mask," "Acanthus A" and "B" and others (fig. 2; Avigad 1976: Pls. XLI, XLII, XLV, XLVII, XLVIII, LI). On the soffit of the Gush Ḥalav synagogue lintel an eagle is flanked by garlands (fig. 20a).

B) Selected Geometric Ornaments

The Rosette

The rosette was a most frequently used motif in Jewish art of the Second Temple period (figs. II,9; IV,16). Several synagogue lintels are decorated with carved rosettes, at 'Ammudim (KW 1916: figs. 140-131) and Tybe (Golan) (fig. VIII.53b) and sarcophagi from Beth Shearim also carry carved rosettes (fig. 2). Significantly, the rosette is an exclusively Jewish ornament in the Second Temple period and persists in later periods. It seems to be a strictly decorative design, devoid of any ancient symbolism (Avi-Yonah 1981a:97-99).

Inhabited Double Meander

This motif was popular in carved architectural decorations on lintels, capitals, and architraves, in the Galilee and Golan, as well as in Syrian Roman art. It is to be seen in the synagogues of Bar'am (fig. 3), and on the Naveh lintels (fig. VIII.54). In the Golan it is found on an architrave at Dikke (KW 1916: figs. 235, 236), on a door-post stone at Dabbura (Maoz 1981b: 109), in the circular design on the side of the Kanef doorpost (fig. IX.25b), and is carved on a capital from the Gamla synagogue (Maoz 1981b: 36). The inhabited double meander is common on border designs of mosaic pavements, such as Susiya and Ma'oz Ḥayim (Pls. 75, 95).

C) Fauna, Animal Motifs

Animal motifs appear frequently in Jewish art, and sometimes display Oriental influences. Some of these animals, such as the lion, bull and eagle, possess religious symbolism in pagan arts as astral and solar symbols. In Jewish art they occur as motifs deprived of their pagan religious symbolism (Avi-Yonah 1981a:65).

Lions

The depiction of lions in association with the Jewish symbols of the Torah shrine and the menorah does suggest a certain contextual significance for these animals. A pair of lions flanks the Torah shrine in the Beth ʾAlpha mosaic pavement (Pl. 102), and flank the menorah on the Maʿon floor (Pl. 87). Lions are also found carved on stone aediculae lintel at Nabratein (fig. VIII.18, Pl. 24 and p. 184). These finds seem to indicate that the lions were persistently selected in their capacity as power motifs or images of vigil to adorn synagogues; some hint of the tradition of the lion symbolizing Judah, however, remains in these representations. Lions are a common motif in Jewish art, and appear in sculpture and mosaics depicted in several standard types of ornamentation:

a) A symmetrical heraldic motif of lions flanking objects, such as a vase, a menorah, tree, bull's head or a human figure, is a frequent occurrence in Jewish synagogal and funerary art. Lions flanking a vase or trees are carved on lintels from H. ʿAmmudim, Capernaum, H. Summaqe (fig. 4), and are seen on the mosaic floor of Beth Sheʾan B (fig. 5). The Beth Sheʿarim "Lion" sarcophagus depicts a lion and lioness flanking a vase (fig. 6a). A lintel found near Tiberias probably belongs to a synagogue. It is carved with flanking lions placing their paws on bulls' heads (Pl. 91). This lintel resembles the H. ʿAmmudim lintel.

A symmetrical repetition of representations of lions in an antithetic compostion is also common on mosaic floors. Lions flank various objects and figures:

i) the Torah shrine scene at Beth ʾAlpha (fig. IX.8b; Pl. 102) (similar depictions are found on gold glasses from catacombs in Rome, fig. IX.9),

ii) a menorah at Maʿon (Pl. 87);

iii) an inscription at Hammath Tiberias and Hammath Gader (fig. 7a, b). At Beth ʾAlpha an inscription is flanked by a lion and a bull (fig. 7c);

iv) a human figure in the Daniel scene at Naʿaran (fig. IX.34), and probably also at Susiya.

On the lion stone from ʿEn Samsam a lion and lioness suckling her cub flank a human figure (Pl. 88). Two of the Beth Sheʿarim sarcophagi depict lions flanking a bull's head, as on both sides of the "Eagles" sarcophagus (fig. 6b, c). Another similar scene of a lion and lioness flanking a bull's head is rendered on the "Shell" sarcophagus (fig. 6d) (also Avigad 1976: 142, Pl. XLIIIA). A lion and lioness flank a gazelle on the narrow side of the "Shell" sarcophagus (Avigad 1976: Pl. XLIII:2). On a stone plaque (Goodenough 1953 III: fig. 44), are carved two heraldic fighting lions with a bird perched on each back. (Pl. 89b). Avigad (1976: 140) proposes that the flanking lions motif originates in decorative funerary art.

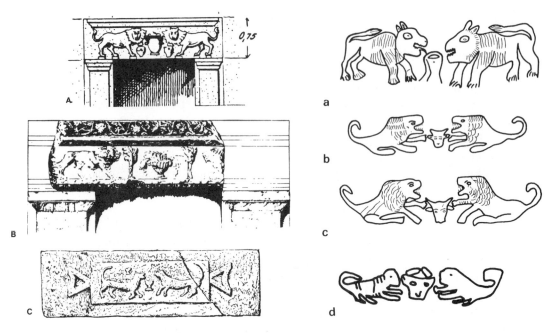

4. Lions on Lintels from: a) H. ʿAmmudim; b) Capernaum; c) Summaqa.

6. Lions on "Lion" and "Eagle" Sarcophagi,
Beth Sheʿarim.

5. Lion from Beth Sheʾan B Mosaic.

b) The most prevalent and important depiction is that of lions flanking a Torah shrine and becoming an integral part of its structure, for instance, as ornamentation on an aedicula lintel (Nabratein) or as three-dimensional lion sculptures which presumably flanked the Torah shrine.

Several lion reliefs probably belong to Torah shrine ornamentation:

i) The ʿEn Samsam stone from the Golan may have been the base of the side wall of an aedicula (fig. IX.24b). This stone is probably from the ʿEn Neshut synagogue (Pls. 26, 88, and p. 184; Maoz 1981b: 112). Its front extremity takes the shape of a

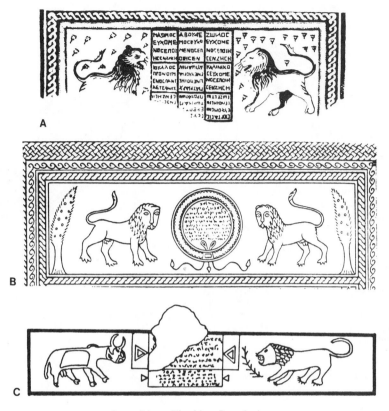

7a-c. Lions Flanking Inscriptions.

three-dimensional torso of a lion; on one side of the stone a carved scene depicts a lion and lioness suckling her cub flanking a figure (Pl. 88). Another relief of a lioness, with only her head carved three-dimensionally, similar to the front end of the ʿEn Samsam stone, was found at ʿEn Neshut. In Umm el-Kanatir two lion reliefs, each with a three-dimensional head, may have belonged to the side of an aedicula (figs. 8, 9) (KW, 1916: 259, 272, reconstructs these lions flanking the upper window in the synagogue facade). An aedicula lintel, found at Nabratein (fig. VIII.18 and Pl. 24) depicts a pair of carved rampant lions facing each other (Meyers *et al.* 1981a). A similar rendering of lions is carved on a lintel from Raphid (fig. IX.30a). A relief from Zumimra renders a lion beside a pilaster (Pl. 35) which may have been part of an aedicula decoration. A representation of a lion decorating a Torah shrine can be seen in a carving on a catacomb wall at Beth Sheʿarim (Pl.31).

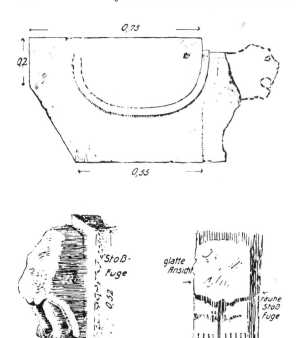

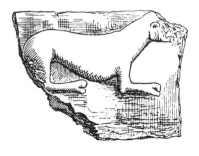

9. Lion Relief from Umm el-
Kanatir.

8. Lion from Umm el-Kanatir.

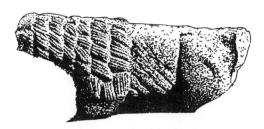

10. Three-dimensional lion from Chorazin.

ii) Several examples of three-dimensional sculptures of lions have survived: a torso
of a lion in profile from Chorazin, a fragment from Capernaum, and a head from
the Barᶜam synagogue (figs. 10, 11). Sukenik (1949: 21, fig. 5) proposes that the

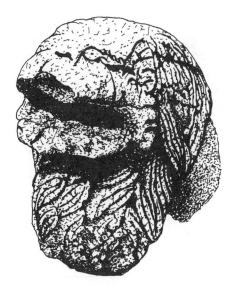

11. Three-Dimensional Lion from Barᶜam.

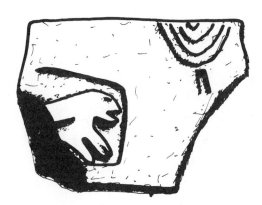

12. Lion from ᶜEn Neshut.

13. Lintel Fragment from Reḥov.

Capernaum lions may have flanked the facade of the synagogue as acroteria. Note also the lion found at Mishrafawi in the Golan; a carved basalt three dimensional lion, missing its lower part, has its right side covered with stylized geometric decoration (Pl. 92).

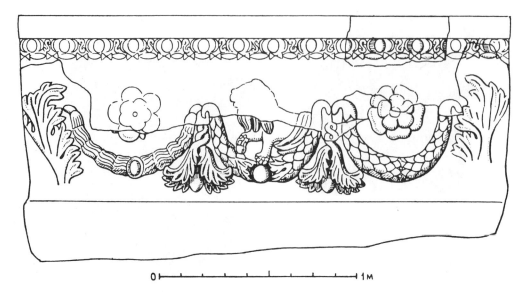

0 |⊢————————————————| 1 M

14. "Acanthus B" Sarcophagus, Beth Shecarim

15. "Hunt" Sarcophagus, Beth Shecarim .

c) The lion is also encountered as a single motif decorating friezes, lintels, or sar-cophagi:

i) Lions carved in stone, on friezes and reliefs come mostly from Golan synagogues, such as Umm el-Kanatir (figs. 8,9) and ʿEn Neshut (fig. 12). Un-published lion reliefs come from Beth Lavi, Kasabieh (here, a lioness who suckles her cub has a face similar to that seen on the Ḥ. ʿAmmudim lintel), and Misraʿat

Kanef (all of these now on exhibition in the Kazrin museum). Mutilated lions are carved on two frieze fragments from Chorazin (Goodenough 1953, III: figs. 492, 494) and Capernaum (Orfali 1922: fig. 80, p. 47).

ii) Lions emerging from leaf patterns and acanthus are carved on a lintel from Reḥov (fig. 13), on "Acanthus" sarcophagus A (fig. 14) and at Capernaum (Orfali 1922: 39, 47). In one case, on the lintel from Safed, a lion head (probably a mask) is carved inside a wreath (fig. VIII.46a).

iii) Lions are shown in hunting scenes, in the Gerasa mosaic (fig. IX.33), and on the Beth Sheᶜarim "Hunt" sarcophagus (fig. 15).

iv) A lion is depicted listening to King David's music in the Gaza mosaic pavement (Pls. 66, 67).

v) Lions appear on the zodiac panel representing the Leo sign in Ḥammath Tiberias, Beth ᵓAlpha and Naᶜaran (figs. IX 39a, 40 and Pl. 80b).

d) Lionesses are encountered in heraldic scenes where they are shown either facing a lion, or standing alone. The popularity of the lioness in Jewish art should be noted. A lioness is depicted in heraldic scenes as the lion's mate on the "Lions" and "Shell" sarcophagi from Beth Sheᶜarim (fig. 6). A lioness is included on the Gerasa mosaic border (fig. IX.33). Popular is the motif of a lioness suckling her cub, encountered on carved basalt stones, such as the mutilated Chorazin frieze fragment (Goodenough 1953, III: fig. 492), the carved stone from ᶜEn Samsam which depicts a lioness and her cub flanking a figure (Pl. 88), and an unpublished basalt fragment from Kasabieh in the Golan. On the Gaza mosaic pavement a lioness suckling her cub is portrayed (Pl. 86a).

Depictions of lions are portrayed both in stylized and detailed manners (Avi-Yonah 1981a:53-54). Stylization is achieved by two methods: 1) By the adoption of a selected pose, the most common Oriental pose, that is, body in profile with head and face turned toward the spectator (examples come from ᶜAmmudim and Kasabieh, fig. 4a). Many lions are depicted in the Assyrian convention of the left and right limbs moving simultaneously (ᶜAmmudim, Ḥammath Gader, Beth ᵓAlpha, Beth Sheᶜarim (figs. 4a, 7, and Pl. 102). 2) By the method of showing the details of the lion's body covered by a pattern. The carved mane is depicted schematically in a pattern of curls in regular groups of rows (Chorazin, Barᶜam, ᶜEn Samsam, figs. 10, 11 and Pl. 88). Mane and ribs are depicted in carved parallel lines on the Beth Sheᶜarim "Lions" and "Eagle" sarcophagi and the carved lion from Mishrafawi (fig. 6 and Pl. 92). The Nabratein relief lion has his mane rendered in curls (Goodenough 1953, III: fig. 523). The style of the ᶜEn Samsam carving (Pl. 88) is unusual: the lions have proportionally very small heads, large bodies and paws, long tails, and manes portrayed by several carved lines.

Most of the lions are depicted with their tails in an upcurving posture. Exceptions are the left-hand lion at Naʿaran whose tail is held down (fig. IX, 34), the left-hand lion on the ʿEn Samsam relief (Pl. 88) and the lioness on the relief of ʿEn Neshut (fig. 12).

The lion in all its various portrayals is an important motif in the repertoire of Jewish art. A motif evolved from ancient Oriental art is that of the lion flanking various objects such as the common representation of lions subduing bulls, also prevalent in Hellenistic tombs. There, the lion symbolically signifies death claiming its victim (Avigad 1976: 140). A similar motif of lions flanking a bull's head may have been a stylized version of this same motif (Avigad 1976: 142). Avi-Yonah (1960a: 23; 1960b: 30 note 19) contends that the lion is the symbol of Judah, the guardian and protector. This may explain the significance of lions flanking the Torah Ark in Beth ʾAlpha (Pl. 102), and the menorah at Maʿon (Pl. 87), as well as gold glasses from Jewish catacombs in Rome (fig. IX.9). Possibly the lions flanking inscriptions at Ḥammath Tiberias, Ḥammath Gader and Beth ʾAlpha (fig. 7) have the same significance as protectors (Goodenough, 1958, VII: 29-37, 78-86, proposes that the lion is meant as a protector and indicates "the ferocious but saving power of the God of the Torah").

Lions flanking Jewish symbols such as the menorah or the Torah shrine may have had significance beyond their decorative function, a significance in which the attributions of guardian and protector are attached to the lions.

The Bull

The bull appears in both synagogal and funerary art as an independent animal motif or as a bull's head.

a) A bull as a flanking animal is often paired with a lion (Beth ʾAlpha, fig. 7c). A bull is portrayed in the upper right medallion of the Beth Sheʾan B synagogue (fig. IX.42). On zodiac panels, the bull is encountered at Beth ʾAlpha, Naʿaran and Ḥammath Tiberias (Pl. 79).

b) A further motif consists of the head of a bull, under a lion's paws, as on the ʿAmmudim lintel (fig. 4a) and the Tiberias lintel (Pl. 91) or between flanking lions, as on the Beth Sheʿarim "Eagle" and "Shell" sarcophagi (fig. 6). Avigad (1976: 141) maintains that the lion laying his paw on a bull's head evolved into an abstract motif from a prototype animal chase motif.

c) A bull's head is used as an independent motif in the "Eagle" and "Bull" sarcophagi at Beth Sheʿarim (fig. 16).

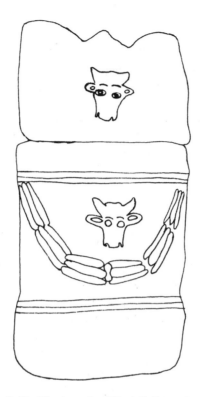

16. Bull's Head on the ''Eagle'' Sarcophagus,
Beth She‘arim.

The bucranium is depicted in heraldic fashion flanking a wreath on a lintel from Safsaf (fig. VIII.51e). A lintel from ʾAḥmadieh (Golan) which was drawn by Schumacher has a bull's head on its side. (Maoz (1981b: 111, note 1) reports lintels from Ahmadieh and Kasabieh which portray bulls' heads flanking eagles.) The artists who portrayed bulls emphasized their heaviness in the usual Oriental fashion which stressed animal qualities (Avi-Yonah 1981a: 63). The bull is a lunar symbol in pagan art, and in Syrian and Nabatean art it is associated with Hadad or Jupiter Heliopolitanus (Avi-Yonah 1981a: 65, see the symbolic association of the bull illuminating the hope of immortality in Goodenough VII, 1958: 1-28). The appearance of the bull in Jewish synagogal and funerary art is without these pagan symbolisms, and was probably a motif in a pattern book used as a decorative design.

Horned Animals

A popular motif on mosaic pavements of both synagogues and churches consists of horned animals flanking objects such as vases and trees. The Beth She'an B synagogue inhabited scroll pavement depicts goats flanking a vase (Pl. 85). At Na'aran a repaired panel at the entrance of the nave mosaic pavement depicts two unidentical stags facing each other among flowers (fig. 17). Sheep flank the Torah shrine panel on the Susiya mosaic pavement (Pl. 104—the flower behind the sheep is similar to the Na'aran flowers behind the stags). Deer also appear in animal chase friezes (Beth She'an B, fig. IX.42).

Fish

Several fish occur in Jewish art, in both synagogal and funerary depictions. In Christian art the fish is a very common motif. On Beth She'arim sarcophagi several fish are carved. On the "Shell" sarcophagus (Avigad 1976: 144, Pl. 43:2) five fish of various sizes and facing various directions are depicted above the lions. Fish are carved on some reliefs from the Golan: on the Dabbura lintel a fish is carved in profile beside an eagle (fig. 18a); another is carved on a stone (fig. 18b), two fish are portrayed on a stone from Rafid (fig. 18a); and fish tails flank an eagle on a lintel from 'Ahmadieh (Maoz 1980:36, as drawn by Schumacher). Fish are also portrayed as the sign of Pisces in the zodiac mosaics (Pl. 82c). A fish is depicted in the border of the Beth 'Alpha mosaic pavement (fig. 33a).

Dolphins

Dolphins are portrayed in heraldic fashion, flanking a wreath, in a similar manner on two sarcophagi: on the narrow side of the "Menorah" and the "Nikae" sarcophagi (fig. 19). The mosaic floor in front of Beth She'arim catacomb 11 depicts four dolphins which fill the corners of a square (Goodenough 1953: figs. 84-85). On the Japhi'a mosaic floor, dolphins fill the space between the circles of the tribal symbols (fig. IX.35b). Dolphins are a widespread motif in Greek and Roman art. They are also popular in Nabatean reliefs.

Scholars are divided as to the meaning of the fish and dolphin depictions. Goodenough (1956, V: 11) maintains that the fish is a sacred or magical symbol. The dolphin, he contends (*ibid*: 26) in pagan art suggests the loving concern of the deity to bring one into a happy life after death. The Jews, Goodenough proposes (1956, V: 27) see the dolphin as "a symbol of hope for themselves and their loved ones" and may have called it *Leviathan*; one explanation of a Talmudic reference is

17. Na'aran Stags Mosaic.

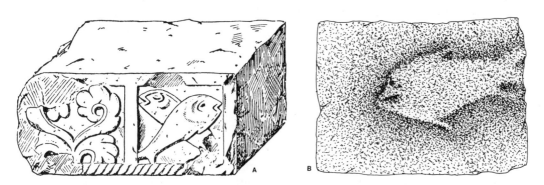

18. a) Raphid fishes; b) A fish carved on stone from Dabbura.

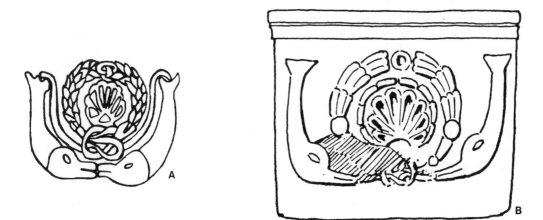

19. Dolphins Flanking a Wreath on: a) ''Menorah'' Sarcophagus; b) ''Nikae'' Sarcophagus.

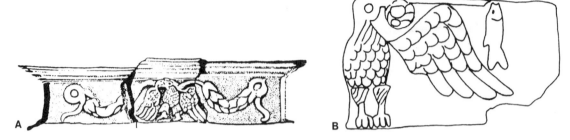

20. a)Lintel Soffit, Gush Halav; b) Dabbura Lintel Fragment.

that the dolphin represents fertility. Fish and dolphins symbolize the sea (Avigad 1976: 149) and could be also apotropaic. They are employed as decorative motifs, especially for filling empty spaces, and are probably taken from patterns in sketch books of motifs used in antiquity.

Eagle

The eagle is a well known motif in ancient art and is prevalent in Jewish art, decorating different artefacts: lintels, windows, Torah shrines, as well as various examples of funerary art.

Aa) In synagogal art the eagle is encountered on synagogue lintels as the central figure, or two eagles are shown facing each other and flanking a wreath.

i) An eagle as the central figure is carved on the Capernaum lintel (fig. VIII.46), now nearly obliterated. An eagle and garlands are seen on the lintel soffit of Gush Ḥalav (fig. 20a) and on the soffit of the central lintel of the Roman temple at Kadesh in the Galilee. Two lintel fragments from Dabbura (Golan) depict eagles glancing aside. One fragment is made in shallow relief (fig. 20b), and the other is richly carved, stylized, and depicts an eagle holding a wreath in his beak (fig. 20c). Two lintel fragments drawn by Schumacher depict eagles. A lintel with an eagle is reported from Ḥ. Weradim (Huttenmeister 1977: 477), and Maoz reports (1981b: 111) a lintel from Kasbieh which depicts a eagle flanked by bulls' heads.

ii) Several lintels depict eagles flanking a wreath: a lintel from Safed (fig. VIII.46a) has a naturalistic eagle and wreath framing a lion's head. A lintel from Japhiᶜa (fig. VIII.46d) has flanking eagles and a wreath, each separate within a metope. Two lintels from Dabbura (Golan, fig. VIII.46b, c) depict short-toed eagles, one of which holds a snake in its beak, and the other of which probably holds the end of a ribbon, as on the Safed lintel (fig. VIII, 46a).

b) Eagles appear as Torah shrine ornamentation: a stylized eagle is carved on the Umm el-Kanatir double column (Pl. 23). The ᶜEn Samsam lion stone has two eagles carved on both ends, flanking the heraldic scene of a figure and lions (Pl. 26 and p. 322). The eagles in both these reliefs are stylistically similar, and may have been carved by the same workshop, although the capital from Umm el-Kanatir is of a better quality work.

c) Eagles are carved on the tip of the front gable in the synagogues of Chorazin (Pl. 93) and Umm el-Kanatir (Golan) (Goodenough 1953, III: fig. 531). A similar eagle is carved on fragments of an arch which was found at ᶜEn Neshut (Maoz 1980: 23). Two eagles are probably carved on the mutilated key stone of the arch at Capernaum (Goodenough 1953, III: fig. 465).

d) A pair of back-to-back eagles holding a garland is carved on a frieze at Capernaum (fig. 21).

e) A stone window fragment from the Dikke synagogue has a small eagle carved on the side (Pl. 94).

f) A carved eagle decorates one of the west door jambs of the second southwest entrance at H. Shemᶜa (fig. 22) (Meyers 1981a: 71).

It should be noted that all these reported reliefs depicting eagles are encountered in the Golan and the Galilean synagogues, with the exception of the one found in Japhiᶜa.

Ba) In funerary art, eagles appear on the "Eagle," "Shell," and "Gable" sarcophagi of Beth Sheᶜarim (fig. 23a) (Avigad 1976: 141, 142, Pls. XLII:2, XLI:1) above garlands on the sarcophagus lid and on one of the narrow sides.

b) An eagle is carved at the centre of the top of the arch of the facade of the mausoleum at Beth Sheᶜarim (fig. 23b).

The eagles depicted in Jewish art are rendered according to Oriental stylization (Avi-Yonah 1981a: 56-59). Carved in an inveterate pose, with its body turned towards the spectator, the eagle's head is turned aside, the wings are spread and the legs stay apart. The body, wings and upper part of the legs are patterned by either cross-hatching or carved dots so that the body features become a geometric pattern. Only the two Safed eagles are more naturalistically depicted (fig. VIII.46a). On mosaic floors, the eagle is depicted only once—on the Maᶜon inhabited scroll mosaic pavement (fig. 24). Here the eagle is rendered in frontal pose, its head turned towards the left, wings spread and legs apart. A ring with a bulla hangs around its neck. Similar eagles are depicted on other mosaic pavements (Avi-Yonah 1960b: 26 and note 4).

The eagle is an Oriental religious symbol, a well-known astral and solar symbol depicted on many pagan monuments. In the synagogue adornment the eagle motif

21. Capernaum Frieze.

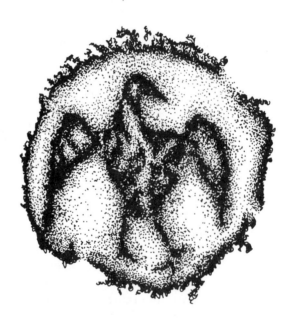

22. An Eagle on the H. Shemᶜa Synagogue, West Entrance.

is deprived of its religious symbolism (Avi-Yonah 1981a: 65; cf. Goodenough, 1958, VIII: 121-142, who maintains that the eagle is a symbol of immortality). In pagan tombs the eagle has symbolic connotations—it is responsible for carrying the soul of the deceased to heaven. However in funerary art at Beth Sheᶜarim the eagles are simply decorative motifs (Avigad 1976: 142).

23a. Eagle on "Eagle" Sarcophagus, Beth She‘arim.

24. Eagle on the Ma‘on
Mosaic.

23b. Mausoleum Facade, Beth She‘arim.

Birds

Birds comprise a widespread motif in ancient art, and Jewish artists commonly use them. In fact they appear to be one of the artists' favourite motifs (Avigad 1976: 144-145, Pls. 33:1, 2, 3; 44:4).

On the "Shell" sarcophagus of Beth She‘arim several birds are carved. By the Second Temple period (fig. IV.21, p. 81) birds were already being used in Jewish art. One of the birds on the "Shell" sarcophagus is very similar to a bird on the "Gable" sarcophagus (fig. 25). [Saller and Bagatti (1949: Pl. 28: 2) call a similar bird—depicted on the Lot and Procopius church mosaic pavement—an eagle.] Birds are depicted in heraldic scenes, flanking a menorah, on two lintels from Tiberias and

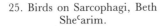

25. Birds on Sarcophagi, Beth
She'arim.

26. Birds on Mosaic, Beth She'an B.

27. Birds Pecking Grapes,
"Shell" Sarcophagus, Beth
She'arim.

Sarona (fig. VIII.50e; Pl. 36). On the Torah shrine panel at Beth ʾAlpha birds flank the Ark (Pl. 102). On three stone plaques (mirror frames) they appear flanking a menorah and two Torah shrines, drinking from a vase (Pl. 89), perched on the backs of fighting lions and situated above a Torah shrine . Similar depictions occur in the catacombs of Rome (fig. IX 9a). A sculptured stone depicting a bird's head was found at the Nabratein synagogue (Meyers *et al.* 1982: fig. 10a). On the Beth She'an B mosaic floor birds flank an inscription and a vase (fig. 26). Here, also, birds depicted with ribbons around their necks fill the spaces between the medallions and the inner row of the border of the mosaic (the outer row is filled with objects (fig. IX.42; Pl. 85)). The same rendering of birds is encountered in the House of Leontis (fig. IX.37; Pl. 69), which is in the same building as the synagogue. On mosaic pavements with inhabited scroll designs, birds fill many of the medallions. Several birds fill the border medallion of the Beth ʾAlpha mosaic pavements (fig. XI.10), and a bird fills one square in the border fret pattern of the Maʿoz Ḥayim mosaic pavement (Pl. 95). On the Noah's Ark pavement at Gerasa, a row of birds is shown leaving the Ark (fig. IX.33). Birds are portrayed inside the octagons of a geometric mosaic in the Susiya synagogue (Gutman *et al.* 1981: 126). The ʿEn-Gedi mosaic pavements display groups of birds in pairs on the emblem of the main mosaic, and a single bird is depicted in the centre of the small mosaic (Pl. 96a, b).

The motif of a bird pecking grapes was popular in Syrian and Nabatean art (Butler 1916, II: figs. 326, 327, 330). In Jewish art it is found on the Beth She^carim "Shell" sarcophagus, where two birds pecking grapes are carved (fig. 27). On a Chorazin lintel (fig. VIII.52j), on the Delta lintel (Goodenough 1953, III: fig. 588), and on two Golan lintels from Kanef and ^cEn Neshut (fig. VIII.52i) birds peck grapes. This motif also appears in a medallion on the Beth She^ɔan B synagogue pavement (fig. IX.42). Depiction of birds is usually in the Oriental style. When carved the body is circular in shape and is shown from the side. Stylization is represented by patterning of body and wings (Avi-Yonah 1981a: 56-58). The bird motif was taken from a catalogue sketch book used by artists in antiquity (see p. 392).

Symbolic connotations and figurative significance have been conferred on the bird motif by several scholars. Goodenough (1958, VII: 24, 41, 42) and Avi-Yonah (1960b: 29 note 16) maintain that the bird is associated with the soul of the deceased (also Hachlili 1985:123). However, birds appear in every kind of combination, both in heraldic fashion and as a single motif on lintels and mosaic floors, which would seem to rule out the idea of its symbolic significance.

Birds serve as decorative motifs taken from pattern books, filling spaces of lintels and medallions, and are also part of symbolic Jewish scenes portraying menoroth and Torah shrines.

The Bird Cage

This motif appears on the Ma^con and Gaza synagogues (fig. 28; Pls. 86a, 87) and on some church inhabited scroll pavements (fig. IX.43), and is one of the motifs attributed by Avi-Yonah (1981d: 393) to the "Gaza school." However, this motif also appears in the centre of an hexagonal medallion in the geometric "carpet" of the Na^caran synagogue pavement (Pl. 100). It also occurs in some churches on carpets such as at Madaba and Gerasa, as well as Sabrath in North Africa and in the synagogue at Misis-Mopsuestis in Cilicia. Iconographic interpretations differ: Grabar proposes (1966: 9-16) a symbolic meaning for this motif, that the bird in the cage is "the human soul imprisoned in a body yearning for delivery." Avi-Yonah (1960b: note 16 p. 29) maintains that the partridge in the cage is being used as a decoy, which may reflect a hunting custom, possibly also attested to by the fact that the cage is usually flanked by birds, thus indicating that this motif is part of the birds' repertoire.

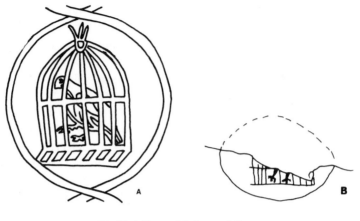

28. Bird Cages, Maᶜon and Gaza.

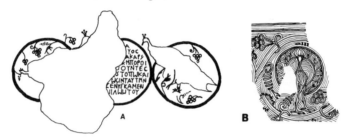

29a,b. Peacocks, Gaza and Beth
She'an B Mosaics.

Peacocks

The peacock as a motif usually appears either a) flanking amphorae or acanthus issuing from a winding vine and forming a medallion (very popular on church pavements and also on some synagogue floors) (Avi-Yonah 1960b: 26, note 3; Dauphin 1976a: 120); or b) *en face*.

a) The inhabited scroll mosaic pavements are characterized by medallions formed by a winding vine issuing from an amphora, situated in the lowest central medallion, and flanked by peacocks (Maᶜon, fig. IX, 41), and the comparable church mosaics of Shellal and the Armenian Church of Jerusalem (fig. IX.43). In the Gaza inhabited scrolls, peacocks flank the inscription (fig. 29a; Pl. 86a). The peacock is rendered walking forward, its long tail folded, extending into the second medallion (Maᶜon, fig. IX.41) or partly protruding from the medallion (Gaza, fig. 29a; Pl. 86a). Two feathers are shown on its head. The synagogue pavement of Ḥuseifa has,

MOTIFS OF JEWISH ART

in its lower, damaged panel, a depiction of vine branches with grapes, and in its lower remaining corner two peacock heads face each other (fig. IX.39b). Peacocks are also depicted in the Diaspora, on catacomb ceilings, on the Dura Europos synagogue ceiling, and on the pavement of the Hammam-Lif synagogue.

b) A variation of this motif is the peacock *en face* with an open tail spread out behind, depicted in the central medallion of the upper row on the Beth She'an B pavement, above the menorah medallion (fig. 29b; Pl. 85). This peacock is similar to depictions on several mosaic pavements at Gerasa and in Syria at Antioch and Apamea, as well as in North Africa. The Beth She'an B peacock is a stylized representation of the motif.

The significance of the peacock and its symbolism is explained by Goodenough (1958, VIII: 52-58): peacock motifs were utilized as flanking objects, having been taken from a pattern book of heraldic sketches (p. 393); the *en face* peacock was probably a space filling (medallion) device only.

Animal chase friezes

Animal friezes including chase scenes are few and not usually represented in Jewish art. Scenes of humans hunting animals are never found. Hunting and chase scenes are usually popular in Roman and Byzantine art (see Lavin 1963). They are also depicted during the latter part of the sixth century on mosaic floors of Christian churches in the Land of Israel and in surrounding areas. At Kissufim (Cohen 1980: 16) several elaborate hunting scenes (two of which depict animal combats) are portrayed: a hound chasing a hare and an antelope, a lion attacking a bull, and a griffin seizing a swan.

An animal chase is portrayed on the Beth She'arim mausoleum (fig. 23b) and on the Beth She'arim "Hunt" sarcophagus (fig. 15). Avigad proposes (1976: 141) that this scene of a lion chasing a gazelle is a later addition at the request of a customer. Animal chase scenes are depicted in animal frieze borders of mosaic pavements of the Beth She'an B small synagogue and the Gerasa synagogue. The animal frieze at Beth She'an B is shown issuing from four corner vases, and includes chase scenes of a dog chasing a hare, and what seems to be a bear chasing a deer; in both cases the hunting beast catches its victim by the legs (fig. IX.42). (See also the crocodile catching a cow on the pavement in the House of Leontis (fig. IX.37; Pl. 68).) At Gerasa the beasts are depicted chasing after their victims (Avi-Yonah, 1981a: 7, maintains that Assyrian friezes influence the art of the Roman period). On the Gaza inhabited scroll pavement several hunting scenes occur (Pl. 86): a tigress chases a donkey in row three; dogs chase a deer in row seven, and in row nine two leopards chase a horse. Although each of the animals is rendered in a separate medallion, the scene is lively, naturalistic, and full of movement. It is very interesting to note that the elephant and buffalo seldom appear on mosaic floors in antiquity; they do appear, though, in the synagogues with inhabited scroll pavements, Maʿon and Beth Sheʾan B (figs. IX.41, 42); the buffalo may also appear at Naʿaran.

D) The Human Figure Motifs

The Oriental artist portrayed human figures in a stylized manner: each part of the body was considered as a discrete element; body proportions were disregarded; and each limb was rendered separately.

a) On carved reliefs (lintels and friezes) human figures are portrayed (Avi-Yonah 1981a: 8-9, 26-31). All the carved figures exhibit the characteristic conventions of Oriental art: a head exaggerated in size, body and face portrayed *en face*, legs in profile, arms attached unnaturally to the body, and few details depicted. The reliefs are flatly, schematically and crudely carved.

On the Beth Sheʿarim ''Column'' sarcophagus a human figure and a dog are portrayed (fig. 30). Avigad (1976: 155) proposes that these represent a mythological hunting scene. The Chorazin frieze (Pl. 47), although mutilated, clearly shows four vine medallions, one filled with a figure with a staff, and three vintage scenes which each depict a pair of figures either holding or picking grapes; the third couple from the left treads grapes. The ʿEn Samsam stone depicts a crudely carved figure in the centre, flanked by lions and eagles (Pl. 26). Its head is disproportionately small, as are the animal heads, and its left hand is disproportionately large. A relief from Dabbura depicts a crudely stylized figure holding objects in its hands (Pl. 98).

Another motif depicting human figures consists of the Nikae, flying winged Victories, portrayed flanking a wreath on lintels and on a sarcophagus (figs. 1; VIII.45; p. 205). The Nikae are carved *en face*, wings spread out behind, and feet in profile. They are rendered angularly, with faces depicted schematically and hands holding wreaths. The uniformity of their portrayal on the lintels of Rama and Dikke (fig. VIII.45), and on the Beth Sheʿarim sarcophagus (fig. 1) (and probably also on the Barʿam lintels) proves that this motif must have existed in a pattern book (see p. 393). They are identical in form to similar pagan motifs, but are completely different in meaning. The Victories in Jewish art may have been associated with angels or cherubim (Avigad 1976: 285), or, as Avi-Yonah maintains (1973: 127) may have represented the triumph of the faith, evoked by the Triumph of the Emperor as depicted on Roman arches.

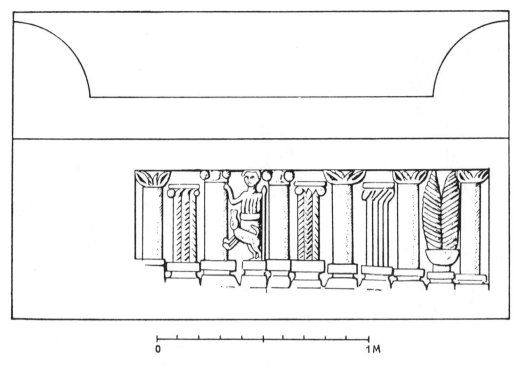

30. "Column" Sarcophagus,
Beth She‘arim .

The Beth She‘arim cemetery yields another important relief which represents a carved figure in military dress, supporting a menorah on its head (fig. 31a). Several other figures, including horsemen fighting gladiators (fig. 31b, c), are carved or incised on some of the catacomb walls here (Mazar 1973: Pls. XIV:2; XV:2; XXIX:5)). A bearded head is crudely carved on the "Mask" sarcophagus (fig. 32). The hair is curly and the eyes expressive. Avigad (1976: 146-147) asserts that a head on an imported coffin was used as a model. On a stone plaque (mirror frame) (Pl. 89a) two figures are represented, one with raised arms (below the top gable), and the other, a carved female bust, with jewellery around its neck and what seems to be a bird held in one hand. A bust is also carved on the Bar‘am stone relief (fig. 3). b) Mosaic floors portray several human figures, in the Biblical scenes and zodiac panels. On the zodiac panel, human figures and protomes are used for depicting the seasons, the signs of the zodiac and the sun god. The four season protomes in Ḥammath Tiberias (Pls. 83, 84) have exactly the same face, differing only in clothing,

31. Beth She'arim Relief and
Graffiti: a) Figure with menorah
on its head; b) Rider; c) Man and
horse.

32. Head on ''Mask'' Sar-
cophagus, Beth She'arim.

hair style and attributes, as do the figures in Beth ʾAlpha (Pls. 83, 84). The personification of the seasons is a frequent motif in ancient art (see Hachlili 1977: 69-72 and p. 307-308). Signs of the zodiac which depict human figures are Gemini, Virgo, Libra, Sagittarius and Aquarius (Pls. 79, 81, 82). The Ḥammath Tiberias zodiac (Pl. 71) is depicted in a Hellenistic-naturalistic style: the bodies are rendered in natural postures, the head turned freely to the side, the faces contain expression, the folds of the dress falling naturally and the jewellery representative of the fashion of the period. By comparison, the unique Beth ʾAlpha mosaic with its zodiac and Biblical scenes renders the figures according to the Oriental perception (Pl. 73; fig. IX.31): the bodies are shown in front view, the legs and feet in profile, the face round, the eyes enlarged, the hair not shown as an intrinsic part of the head which is large in proportion to the body, the arms shown sideways and attached unnaturally to the bodies (Avi-Yonah 1981a: 34-35). There is no difference in the portrayals of men, women or youths.

King David in Gaza (Pls. 66, 67) is shown in a conventional depiction of Orpheus stylized as a Byzantine emperor; David in Marous is shown as a Byzantine warrior. A human head is depicted on the Japhiʿa mosaic (fig. IX.35b) where it is used purely as a decorative and stylized motif. In the House of Leontis several figures are depicted: Odysseus, the Sirens and a personification of the Nile (fig. IX.37; Pls. 68, 70). The human figures are similar to the figures depicted in room L of the Beth Sheʾan Christian monastery of the sixth century (p. 390). They have the same face and hair, all glance sideways, and all are portrayed in quite naturalistic postures which convey their actions.

It is important to call attention to the phenomenon that the inhabited scrolls or geometric sections in synagogue pavements never contain any human images, although human figures appear on the same pavements but in other panels in the contexts of Biblical scenes and zodiacs (see Naʿaran, or the nave floor at Gaza, fig. XI.11; Pl. 86). During the same period, inhabited scroll church pavements depict humans, although most of the so-called "Gaza school" pavements do not depict human figures.

The human figure is one of the best examples of the Oriental conception in Jewish art, and represents some of the characteristic elements of Oriental art of the period (see p. 367). Avi-Yonah (1981a:9) maintains that this "can be perhaps explained by the predominantly religious character of Oriental art and its consequent conservatism."

E) Mythological Motifs

Few examples of mythological motifs occur in synagogue ornamentation. Several carved motifs, sea goats, centaurs and medusa heads are encountered:

Sea Goats

A sea goat is depicted on a frieze fragment from Capernaum (fig. 21).

Centaurs

A Capernaum lintel has carved on it what are considered to be centaurs, now mutilated (fig. VIII.48b). Several centaurs are depicted on the frieze fragments at Chorazin (Goodenough 1953, III: figs. 489, 494, 497). On a stone fragment from Bar'am (fig. 3) a centaur is depicted on its lower left edge.

Medusa

A medusa head is encountered on a Chorazin frieze fragment (Pl. 46). Goodenough (1953, I: 217) contends that the Japhi'a head is also of a medusa (fig. IX, 35b).

The mosaic floor in the House of Leontis at Beth She'an portrays mythological scenes of Odysseus and Nilotic scenes (fig. IX.37, p. 301) copied from Hellenistic pagan art. Goodenough (1958, VIII: 115-116; 1968, XII: 148) contends that mythological motifs symbolize mystical and eschatological hopes in Judaism, as well as signifying immortality. However, it seems more probable that these mythological images, borrowed from pagan art, are being used often as decorative patterns which have lost their symbolic content; these representations were simply copied from pattern books. Also, some of the mythological motifs penetrated into Jewish imagery through the influence of Midrashic literature (Breslavi 1967: 120-129).

F) Genre Motifs

Only few genre motifs are depicted in synagogue reliefs and pavements:
a) The vintage scene of the Chorazin frieze (Pl. 47) is a carved frieze of vine scrolls within which three vintage scenes are depicted. This is the only such scene in Jewish art, whereas in Christian art it appears regularly on mosaic floors in churches and monasteries.
b) A figure holding a goose is depicted in one of the medallions in the single running border of the Beth 'Alpha mosaic pavement (fig. 33b). This motif is unique.

33a-c. Genre Scenes. a,b. Beth ʾAlpha Mosaic. c. Maʿon Mosaic.

Two more humorous and realistic genre subjects are depicted on synagogue mosaic floors:

c) A hen strutting along with her four chicks behind her, in the Beth ʾAlpha lozenge medallion in the border (fig. 33a).

d) In the centre of the eighth row of the Maʿon synagogue mosaic pavement, a hen lays an egg into a water vessel (fig. 33c).

These last three motifs are unique, and may represent the various artists' own initiative and imaginative contribution to these mosaic floors. These refreshing innovations contrast sharply with the conventional motifs taken from pattern books and used many times.

The motifs most frequently encountered in Jewish art are those of the lion, the eagle and the bull. These animal motifs appear both on sculpture and in mosaics, where they are usually depicted in a prominent position. The following commentary may explain part of the reason for the prominence of these particular motifs:

Midrash Rabba. Exodus 23, 13:

> R. Abin said: four kinds of exalted beings have been created in the world. The most exalted of all living creatures is man; of birds, the eagle; of cattle the ox; and of wild beasts, the lion. All of these received royalty and had greatness bestowed upon them, and they set under the chariot of God as... This is the meaning of ''For he is highly exalted.

These prominent animal images in Jewish art, although they were sometimes transferred from pagan art, lost their pagan meaning and acquired new values by the influence of Biblical and Midrashic literature.

CHAPTER ELEVEN

COMPOSITION AND STYLE

A) Mosaic Floor Composition and Style

Between the fourth and seventh centuries synagogue adornment is concentrated entirely in the interior of the building; the exterior is left unornamented. Because of this innovation, the floor of the synagogue becomes an important location for elaborate decorations. Each floor is planned as one framed unit but is divided geometrically into panels or medallions. Principles of depth and perspective are ignored. Like the changes in the Byzantine mosaic pavements, a marked evolution of style occurred in synagogue mosaics during this period (Avi-Yonah 1975: 41).

The surface of the synagogue floor which is exploited for adornment is termed the field. This field is divided into smaller areas which correspond to the structural entities such as the nave and aisle. The aisle is usually paved with one complete carpet (which is one particular design unit), for instance like that in the eastern aisle at Ḥammath Tiberias (fig. 1), or with various carpets, for instance at Beth ʾAlpha (fig. 3). These aisle carpets are usually geometric. The most important and outstanding designs always appear on the nave carpets; moreover, they are always clearly and intentionally separated from the aisles by ornate, elaborately decorated borders (see Ḥammath Tiberias, Beth ʾAlpha, Beth Sheʾan A, Naʿaran, Jericho, Ḥammath Gader (figs. 1-4, VIII.7) and Ḥuseifa (fig. 5).

Three distinctive systematic schemes of nave carpet design can be recognized:

Scheme A, which is the most common and is found on several synagogue floors, has a field which is divided into three rectangular carpets, each thematically distinct and appropriate to its position in the construction. A frame encloses each panel (fig. 6) (Ḥammath Tiberias, Beth ʾAlpha, Beth Sheʾan A, Ḥuseifa, Ḥammath Gader, probably Japhiʿa, Naʿaran, and Susiya, figs. 1-5; VIII.6, 7; IX.35a).

Scheme B has a field of an even and harmonious design paved on the complete nave floor—inhabited scroll carpets (fig. 7). This carpet was in vogue during the sixth century both in synagogues and churches (see Avi-Yonah 1960b: 31). (See the synagogues of Beth Sheʾan B, Gaza and Maʿon (figs. 7; IX.41, 42; Pls. 85-87).)

Scheme C consists of a geometric carpet design with an emblem as the central focus (fig. 8). It sometimes also appears on church floors (see ʿEn-Gedi and Jericho, Pl. 96 and fig. 13). It sometimes also appears on church floors.

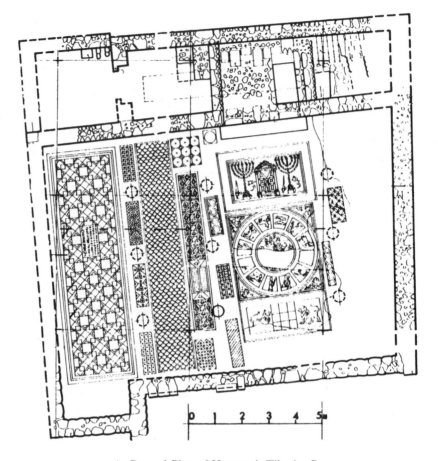

1. General Plan of Ḥammath Tiberias B.

    These three designs avoid free composition and also portray several typical char-
acteristics of Oriental art: first, the principle of *horror vacui*, second, representations
are depicted by the conceptual method instead of in the visual illusionistic Graeco-
Roman manner (Avi-Yonah 1960a: 20-21; 1975: 41) (pp. 366-367). Compositions
include figurative art, and iconic and mythological themes which are depicted in sections, rhythmically and antithetically united.

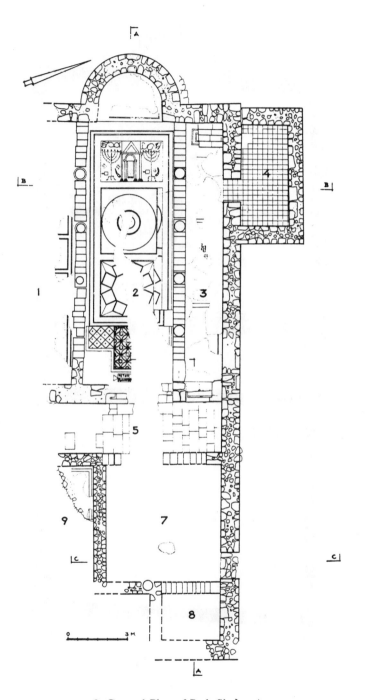

2. General Plan of Beth She'an A.

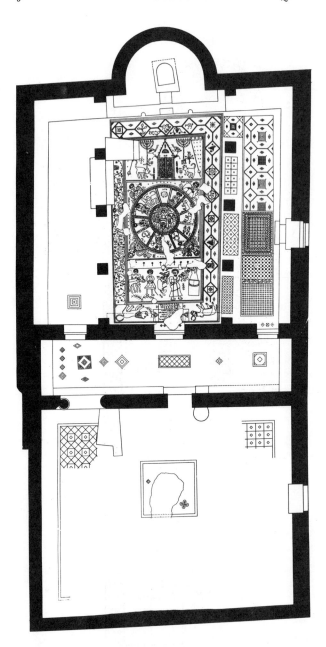

3. General Plan of Beth ʾAlpha.

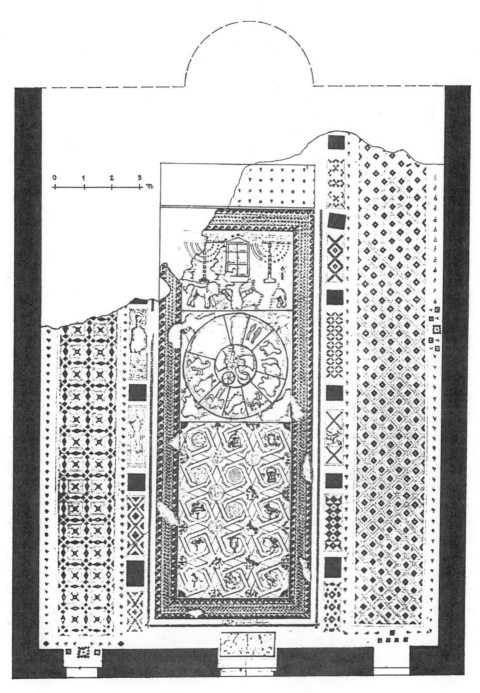

4. General Plan of Na'aran.

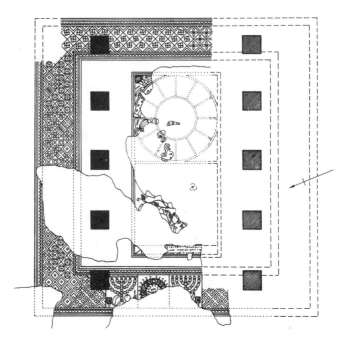

5. General Plan of Ḥuseifa.

Scheme A Carpets

This carpet is usually divided into three panels (fig. 6) in a recurring design and theme which is repeated on different synagogue floors, for instance at Ḥammath Tiberias, Beth ᵓAlpha, Naᶜaran, Susiya, and Beth Sheᵓan A (figs. 2, 6; 9-11; VIII.6). The panels in scheme A are divided into: 1) a Jewish symbols panel which is situated in front of the Torah shrine; 2) a middle panel with a zodiac scheme; and 3) a panel with a Biblical scene: at Beth ᵓAlpha it is the first panel close to the entrance (fig. 10) and at Naᶜaran this is situated between the zodiac and Jewish symbols panels (fig. 11). The third panel at Ḥammath Tiberias has a depiction of heraldic lions guarding an inscription, whereas in Naᶜaran and Susiya the third panel shows a geometric carpet (figs. 9, 11; VIII.6). The Susiya pavement, which is only partly preserved, is slightly different, mainly because of an additional panel depicting Jewish symbols located in front of the Torah shrine (fig. VIII.6). A radical change in attitudes towards figurative art during the sixth century is the cause of the redesign and restoration of the pavements at Beth Sheᵓan A and Susiya (fig. 2, Pls. 75, 104). Zodiac and Biblical panels are replaced by geometric designs which, how-

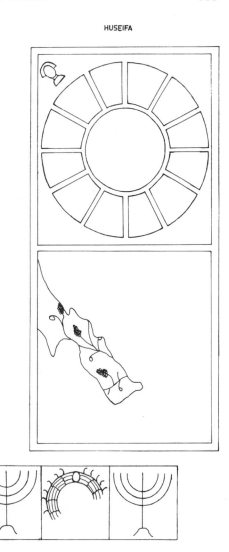

6. Scheme A.

ever, are inserted into the original panels. Other synagogue pavements are divided into less than three panels, for example, Ḥuseifa (fig. 5), which has two panels in the nave, a similar zodiac scheme and a vine-branch panel. Incorporated into the wide and ornate border in front of the main entrance is a heraldic panel of Jewish symbols consisting of a pair of menoroth flanking an inscription inside a wreath. A similar scheme of two panels may have existed in Japhiᶜa (see fig. IX.35a and p. 295). The Ḥammath Gader synagogue pavement is divided into three panels consisting of two geometric carpets with a third in front of the apse which shows two heraldic lions flanking an inscription enclosed by a wreath (figs. 6; 12). The division of large rooms into panels has comparisons in the fourth century Antioch mosaics (Levi 1947, I: fig. 85).

The popularity of scheme A panel divisions on synagogue floors probably derives from the iconography and symbols the Jewish community wanted to incorporate into their synagogue decoration. It enabled them to group together different themes including the special panels of inscriptions and heraldic lions (as at Ḥammath Tiberias and Ḥammath Gader). Kitzinger (1965a: 348-349) expresses this tendency very accurately:

> It is, I believe, this tendency to organize, to articulate, to keep things within bounds and in harmonious relationships and proportions, which in due course [early years of Justinian era] brings about a return to a natural arrangement of figures and landscape elements in panels of limited size.

Scheme B Carpets (fig. 7)

The composition of the inhabited scroll is an all-over pattern effecting an abstract, unified carpet design which is a characteristic development of sixth century mosaic floors (Avi-Yonah 1981d: 377-382; Kitzinger 1965a: 347- 348; 1965b: 24; Hachlili 1987). This scheme occurs in the synagogues of Gaza, Maᶜon and Beth Sheʾan B (figs. 7; IX.41, 42; Pl. 85-87). The composition covers the entire floor, and the design consists of vine branches issuing from an amphora and forming circular medallions within which beasts, birds and various objects are portrayed. The design is divided into vertical columns of medallions. The central axial column usually contains objects and the columns of medallions on each side usually contain birds and beasts facing the axial column in an antithetic pattern (see p. 310ff.). The amphora is usually flanked by peacocks (Maᶜon), which at Gaza however flank the inscription. The amphora at the Beth Sheʾan B synagogue is flanked by goats. This scheme B design, because it was very much in vogue on contemporary church floors, always has Jewish symbols added to the medallion pattern. In this way the synagogue floor could be differentiated from the neighbouring church floors. At Maᶜon two lions flank a menorah and at Beth Sheʾan a central medallion depicts a menorah with ritual objects (see p. 316). No symbols have survived at Gaza, but possibly they were not considered necessary, as the design covers an aisle carpet and not that of the central nave.

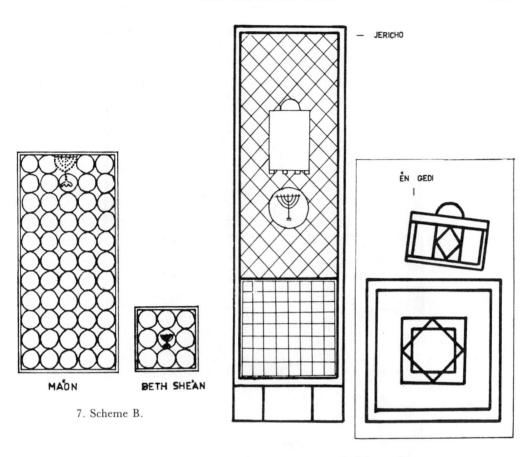

7. Scheme B.

8. Scheme C.

Scheme C Carpets (fig. 8)

These floors depict geometric carpets which cover the entire nave and include Jewish emblems. At Jericho emblems of two groups of Jewish symbols are added (figs. 8; 13). A geometric emblem with birds is depicted in the centre of the ʿEn-Gedi square carpet (fig. 8 and Pl. 96b). The same scheme design is depicted on the niche floor at ʿEn-Gedi (Pl. 96c), with the addition of three menoroth portrayed on the mosaic close to the main carpet and in front of the niche. The emblems are clearly emphasized by the even and harmonious geometric carpet surrounding them, giving the design a central focus which is probably their purpose.

9. Nave Mosaic, Ḥammath Tiberias B.

10. Nave Mosaic, Beth ᵓAlpha.

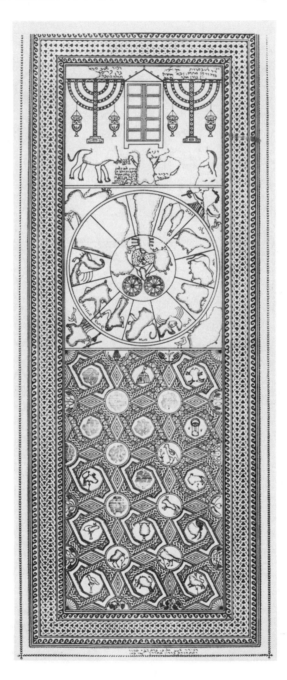

11. Nave Mosaic, Naᶜaran.

12. Nave Mosaic, Ḥammath Gader.

The three schemes of design have chronological significance. Scheme A is the most common and popular design on synagogue floors, beginning already in the fourth century synagogue of Ḥammath Tiberias, and continuing through the fifth and sixth centuries. Scheme B is common in the sixth century, appearing also on church floors. Scheme C is the preferred design during the latter part of the sixth century, probably after figurative art was forbidden on synagogue floors.

The most remarkable element of the synagogue pavement field is its division into *three*: for example, Scheme A carpets are divided into three panels; panels themselves consist of three elements: a central design with antithetical designs flanking it (fig.

13. Nave Mosaic, Jericho.

6); inscription panels are divided into the inscription which is flanked by antithetical objects or animals (fig. 14); panels are sometimes divided narratively into three events, for example Isaac's Sacrifice at Beth ʾAlpha (fig. IX.31); the zodiac panel is always divided into three constituents: a square enclosing an outer and inner circle (figs. IX. 39-40); the Noah's Ark panel at Gerasa is divided into three horizontal rows of animals (fig. IX.33a); Scheme B design is also divided into three parts: a central column flanked by antithetical columns (fig. 7). This division into three is mainly a result of a tendency towards and preference for symmetry and heraldic patterns, which are traditional Oriental elements (Avi-Yonah 1981a: 48, 114). A totally organized and systematic composition results in a harmonious, rhythmic and aesthetic design.

A further useful way of categorizing field organization of synagogue mosaic floors is by analysis of the different types of panels. Each panel contains a composition appropriate both thematically and functionally.
The following panels will be discussed:
1) The Jewish symbols panel.
2) The panel depicting inscriptions flanked by figurative or symbolic elements.
3) Panels depicting Biblical scenes.
4) The zodiac panel prominent in the synagogue pavement arrangements (discussed on p. 305).

1) The most prominent panel is that containing Jewish ritual symbols which are depicted on the upper panel of the mosaic floors of five synagogues (fig. IX.8), Ḥammath Tiberias (Pl. 101), Beth ʾAlpha (Pl. 102), Beth Sheʾan A (Pl. 103), Naʿaran (Pl. 105) and Susiya (Pl. 104), and which is situated near the apse or niche which probably contained these same objects of synagogue cult.

The panel is composed of a symbolic, antithetic design, symmetrically arranged: a pair of menoroth flank a Torah shrine, each menorah in turn being flanked by four ritual objects—the lulav, ethrog, shofar and incense shovel—twice in exactly the same formation (Pls. 101-104). In Beth Sheʾan A, only two of the ritual objects—the shofar and the incense shovel—are depicted flanking the menorah (Pl. 103). At Ḥammath Tiberias and Beth Sheʾan A the menorah and objects are depicted twice in the same attitude on either side of the Torah shrine, and do not face each other. The Naʿaran panel is different in that two hanging lamps are suspended from either side of each menorah (Pl. 105). Similar objects suspended from the Torah shrine gable are depicted in Beth ʾAlpha and Beth Sheʾan A (fig. IX.19, p. 271).

The composition of these panels is generally very similar, suggesting that they derive from a common pattern. The style of each mosaic pavement, however, is completely different as each synagogue's artist added to and changed the basic pattern. Beth ʾAlpha has the most elaborate additional images, its menoroth, animals and objects being symmetrical but not identical (see p. 377).

This same design is also portrayed on other objects, for instance, on four drawings at Beth Sheʿarim (fig. IX.7); and on a limestone plaque (Pl. 34) a Torah shrine is rendered flanked by two menoroth, without ritual objects. On a lintel from Kochav HaYarden and on a limestone plaque, a menorah is flanked by two Torah shrines (figs. VIII.27; Pl. 89). This design also occurs in the Diaspora, in catacomb drawings and on gold glasses (fig. IX.9). Regularly used for mosaic floors, this panel was one of the designs appearing in the Jewish pattern book (p. 394). Furthermore, its proximity to the Torah shrine reinforces the hypothesis that the Ark and menoroth were actually placed in the niche or apse of these synagogues (see for instance the reconstruction of the Beth ʾAlpha interior in Sukenik 1932: fig. 17). Synagogue mosaics which show these objects have a twofold function, both to show the actual use as well as to suggest the symbolic connotations. As these objects had been previously connected to the Temple, they probably expressed a longing for the Temple rites and ceremonies which could be gratified by the depiction of the objects on the synagogue floor.

2) Several mosaic panels which are much less common depict antithetic designs of lions flanking inscriptions (fig. 14), as in Ḥammath Gader and Ḥammath Tiberias B (figs. 6; X.7a, b). A similar panel at Beth ʾAlpha depicts an inscription flanked by a lion and a bull, on the panel in front of the entrance (fig. X.7c). Another panel in Ḥuseifa portrays two menoroth and ritual objects flanking the inscription (fig. 5). The Ḥammath Gader design is depicted on the upper panel close to the apse, the usual place for the Ark and menoroth panel (fig. 12). The designs of Ḥammath Tiberias and Ḥuseifa are depicted on the third panel near the entrance (figs. 1; 5). The Gaza inscription flanked by peacocks (fig. 14f, Pl. 86a) possibly derives from the same pattern.

3) The composition of Biblical scenes was adapted to the shape of the panel, which is divided into three, in rhythmic groupings of two figures each, such as in the sacrifice of Isaac at Beth ʾAlpha (fig. IX.31); an antithetical design of Daniel flanked by two lions at Naʿaran (fig. IX.34) David of Gaza is also divided compositionally into three: David sits on one side with the animals on the other side, and the lyre in the centre (Pls. 66, 67). The panel of Noah's Ark at Gerasa is divided horizontally into three rows of different types of animals (fig. IX.33b).

This panel composition, with its three parts, is similar in spatial conception to the Jewish symbol panel, which suggests that the most prevalent composition on synagogue pavements is a rhythmic, antithetic design whose emphasis lies in its centre by the method of depicting flanking symmetrical objects or figures.

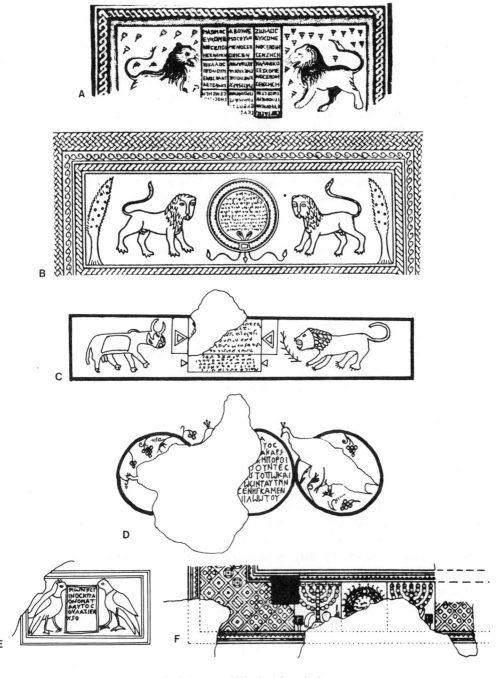

14a-f. Panels of Flanked Inscriptions.

The stylistic depiction of Biblical scenes shows a development from more or less realistic and lifelike modelling of images to a very schematic imitation. A chronological progression can be observed if the rendition of animals is analyzed. For example, the Noah's Ark mosaic of Gerasa is the closest to a realistic representation and possibly also the earliest. The animals are depicted within a geometric composition which is enclosed by a frame of beasts among plants, arranged in a frieze. Consider also the Noah's Ark depiction at Misis-Mopsuestia (presumed synagogue in Cilicia, Turkey—see Avi-Yonah 1981g: 186) which includes a row each of birds and beasts surrounding the Ark (Budde 1969: Pls. 26-28, 45-49).

By comparison, the composition of the David mosaic at Gaza is depicted in a schematic and stylized manner, probably in accordance with a contemporary pattern in use. The animals however still exhibit individual expressions: the lion, for instance, is rendered with a bowed head and submissive stance. David shows Byzantine influence by his *en-face* posture and his style of dress.

The Beth ʾAlpha mosaic shows a local and naive portrayal of the figures, making classification difficult (see comparable scenes in Misis-Mopsuestia—Budde 1969: Pl. 113).

B) Relief and Sculpture Composition and Style

Jewish synagogal and funerary reliefs and sculpture are Oriental in their style; this is visible in the richness of ornament, and in the tendency to stylization in the detailed, patterned motifs and designs. The artists show a highly skilled technique in stone and basalt relief execution. Architectural decoration reveals a square, heavy, plastic perception. The following stylistic features are worthy of note (also Avi-Yonah 1960b: 34-36):

1) The most important attitude of Oriental art, frontality, is a major element in synagogue and funerary sculpture. Humans and animals all face the spectator (Beth Sheʿarim, Chorazin, ʿAmmudim, Reḥov, figs. X.4, 13, 16, 32).

2) Organic and natural forms are stylized to the point where they become abstract patterns, such as happens with the acanthus leaves of the Chorazin medallions (Pls. 45-47) and the laurel leaf pattern on some lintels at Barʿam, Gush Ḥalav, and Nabratein (fig. VIII.43, Pl. 40). Stylization of framed patterns which turn into geometric forms is seen in the leaves of the vintage scene at Chorazin (Pl. 47).

3) The deep carving produces alternating and sharply defined light and dark areas, especially in basalt carvings, as for example at Chorazin (Pls. 45-47), and on the Umm el-Kanatir aedicula capital (Pl. 23).

4) A further stylistic feature is a tendency to a heavy execution at the same time as flat relief and shallow incisions (ʿEn Samsam relief, Pls. 26, 88).

5) The proportions of most of the figures in these reliefs are effected in the Oriental style, with the head exaggerated in size: at Chorazin the men in the vintage scene and the armed men have over-sized heads (Pl. 47). The best example of this lack of proportion is the ʿEn Samsam relief, on which both the figure and lions have under-sized heads (Pl. 26, 88).

The composition of lintel reliefs is different to that of friezes. Lintels are generally ornamented in antithetic compositions, in which a central object is flanked by two symmetrical motifs (see Barʿam, ʿAmmudim, Rama, Dabbura, Japhiʿa, figs. VIII.45a,c 46b, d; X,4a; Pl. 40), or, if the central object is a vase or wreath, it has vine branches issuing from it (fig. VIII.52, p. 212). Friezes, on the other hand, are executed in an overall design divided into several sections, each design consisting of a central motif framed in an acanthus leaf (see Chorazin, Capernaum, Pls. 43-47). Exceptional compositions are the Capernaum frieze, with two eagles and sea-goat figure (fig. X.21), and the Chorazin vintage scene (Pl. 47, p. 219).

Compositions similar to those found on synagogue architecture also appear on the majority of sarcophagi, as, for example, the antithetic arrangements at Beth Sheʿarim (figs. X.6, 25).

Architectural decoration of the synagogue was influenced by local, Nabatean and Roman-Syrian art, which had transformed Classical architectural elements into ornamental motifs. Architectural ornamentation was also, in some ways, a continuation of the art of the previous Second Temple period.

CHAPTER TWELVE

ORIGINS AND SOURCES OF JEWISH ART

A) Oriental Elements in Jewish Art

The discussion below is based on Avi-Yonah's comprehensive research on Oriental elements in the arts of the Land of Israel during the Roman and Byzantine periods (1961b: 33-36; 1981a: 1-117).

Jewish art is one of the best examples of an Oriental art in Late Antiquity. The essential Oriental elements can be defined by reference to two conceptions. The first conception, which dominates the representational branch of Oriental art, is *expressionism*. This is "a tendency to prefer a mental, spiritual view of things as opposed to a visual aspect [characteristic of classical art]" (Avi-Yonah 1981a: 35). "The artist showed things as he felt or thought them to be," he uses the "expressionistic element to project the spiritual value of his subject, contrary to a realistic conception" (Avi-Yonah 1981a: 113). This expressionistic conception is composed of a pair of antithetic tendencies:

1) The *conceptual* aspect is expressed by a clarification of presentation of the subject, thus stressing its spiritual value. This can be seen in the Beth ʾAlpha sacrifice of Isaac (fig. IX.31 and Pl. 64), where a spiritual view is preferred to a visual aspect. Moreover, by representing the details of a subject schematically in an abstract outline, the conceptual aspect of Oriental expressionism is emphasized, for example, by placing objects in full view even though they are meant to be hidden: the hands of figures at Beth ʾAlpha (fig. IX.31 and Pl. 64) are placed in front of the objects they are supposed to be holding, in complete defiance of the laws of perspective (Avi-Yonah 1981a: 11, 28); or by setting objects one above the other without regard for distance (Beth ʾAlpha, the House of Leontis at Beth Sheʾan, a menorah set above a human figure as depicted at Beth Sheʿarim, and an eagle above a human head in the Japhiʿa mosaic, figs. IX.31, 35, 37; X.31a; Pls. 64, 68-70).

2) A tendency towards *emotionalism* counterbalances the above *conceptual* aspect and is expressed by an emphasis laid on the features of an image, an exaggeration of the dimensions of selected features or patterns, or a stress on characteristics to express the dominant quality of a subject (Avi-Yonah 1981a:15). A distinctive Oriental element is the absence of individual characterization which results in a typological representation of humans (Hammath Tiberias, Beth ʾAlpha, Pls. 64, 71, 73) (Avi-

Yonah 1981a: 15). Emotionalism is also expressed by placing an image or motif within a border, and by depicting it in high relief in order to stress its importance. An exaggeration of the dimensions of head and eyes in sculptured human figures is a further feature of emotionalism: the Nikae in Beth She°arim and Dikke (figs. VIII.45b; X.1), the mask with hair arranged in curls on a sarcophagus, and the figure on the "Column" sarcophagus, both from Beth She°arim (fig. X.31, 34), the °En Samsam relief (Pl. 26—note here the figures' exaggerated palms and the small lion heads), and mask or Medusa head from Chorazin (Pl. 46) are all examples of this feature. Emotionalism is also found in mosaics: all the human figures of the Beth ºAlpha mosaic as well as David on the Gaza mosaic show this aspect. Emotionalism is also represented by postures such as frontality, to be seen, for instance, in the vintage relief of Chorazin, in the lion pose in the Nabratein aedicula lintel, on the Ḥ. °Ammudim lintel, on the Ḥammath Gader mosaic, in the Beth ºAlpha symbol panels, and the Gaza inhabited scroll mosaic (figs. VIII.18; X.4a,7; Pls. 47, 86, 102). The exaggerated poses of these animals express strength, speed, massiveness and ferocity.

The second essential concept in Oriental art is *stylization*. Avi-Yonah (1981a: 53) defines it thus: "Stylization is an effort to press artificially the picture of a living being into a pattern, so that it becomes a part of a decorative design." Stylization is also composed of two antithetic tendencies:

1) A tendency of *patterning* by a symmetrical repetition of the design. Symmetrical design is one of the most characteristic elements in ancient Jewish art, and is portrayed in heraldic composition in sculpture and in mosaic; on sarcophagi from Beth She°arim (fig. X.6) (Avigad 1976: 139), on lintels of synagogues such as °Ammudim (fig. X.4a), Japhi°a (fig. VIII.46d) and on others (see p. 206ff.). The lintels of Bar°am and Capernaum (figs. VIII.45a, 49a, b, 51a-c), although disfigured, probably also have a symmetrical antithetic design. In the Golan synagogues this composition is encountered in the lintels of Kazrin, °Assalieh and Dabbura (figs. VIII.46b,c, 53), and in the °En Samsam relief (Pl. 26). Several sarcophagi at Beth She°arim are carved with repetitive heraldic designs: Nikae flanking a wreath, lions flanking a bull's head (figs. X.1, 6) (see also the Safsaf lintel (fig. VIII,51e), and an amphora flanked by lions (fig. X.6). Many mosaic pavement panels and scenes are rendered in this symmetrical patterning (figs. IX.8; 40-42). A further feature of patterning is the reduction of figures, whether human or animal, and plants into abstract shapes and geometric forms, for instance, in the °En Samsam relief (Pl. 26) and on the "Nikae" sarcophagus from Beth She°arim (fig. X.1), on the vine scroll geometrification at Chorazin, Capernaum and Beth She°arim (Pls. 43-47), in the inhabited scroll mosaic pavements (figs. IX.41, 42; Pls. 85-87).

2) A second antithetic tendency is *richness of effect*. This is expressed in 'all-over' or 'endless' patterns formed by repetitive designs filling long and narrow spaces, for example on ossuary decorations (figs. IV.15-17; Pl. 18), and on architectural ornamentation at Chorazin and Capernaum (figs. VIII.47-50). It is also expressed by *horror vacui*, the filling of all space with ornament, and is seen in a preference for optical patterns created by the play of light and shade in sculpture.

Another component of Oriental art, symbolism, had an influence on Jewish art. Because it was important both to the artists and to their employers, appearance is often sacrificed for the sake of symbolism (Avi-Yonah 1981a: 65), for instance, in the preference for the lion and the bull (figs. X.4-11, 16), and especially in the synagogue portrayals of religious symbols such as the menorah and the Ark (fig. IX.8; Pls. 101-105).

The origins of some Oriental features can be discerned in inherited elements of ancient Assyrian and Hittite art and contemporary Parthian art, which strongly influenced Jewish art as well as other ethnic arts in the area, such as Nabatean art. In Avi-Yonah's words (1981a: 115) the native artist

> expressed a Western subject with an Oriental context by using (voluntarily or involuntarily) the motifs of his ancestral inheritance; the resulting 'form' showing... a more or less manifest tendency to expressionism and stylization.

B) Hellenistic-Roman Elements and Sources of Jewish Art

Two main centres, Alexandria and Antioch, are responsible for the Hellenistic influence on Jewish art as regards both iconography and themes, composition and style. Even though little Alexandrian art has itself survived, its authority is felt in works of art, for instance in the iconography of the Nilotic scenes such as in the House of Leontis (fig. IX.37; Pls. 68-70), and on church floors at Tabha and Haditha (Avi-Yonah 1960a: 16, 17; 1972). Scholars maintain that the Biblical pictorial representations may have been based on illuminated manuscripts created, by Alexandrian Jews, as illustrations for the Scriptures translated for foreigners (Avi-Yonah 1973: 128; 1975: 65; 1981c). Thus, an indirect influence of Alexandrian Hellenistic art on Biblical mosaics in the Roman-Byzantine period can be posited.

The selection of objects including floral and faunal motifs presumed to have existed in the Jewish pattern books, also reflects a Hellenistic thematic influence. In Ptolemaic times, interest in the natural sciences was strong: zoological gardens were constructed, and artists probably used catalogues and sketch books of beasts, birds and floral motifs which were based on a study of the creatures themselves (see also p. 392 and Avi-Yonah 1960a:21). The composition of pavement carpets was probably influenced slightly by the Antioch mosaic floors (Levi 1947: 156 ff., 606 ff.), and the depiction of several motifs is similar to their rendition in Antioch mosaics. Hellenistic influence is seen in the movement, the organic forms and in the anatomic emphasis of motifs. Furthermore, Hellenistic impressionism is felt in the highlighting of the centre of bodies, limbs, or trees, although the sides are left in shadow (Avi-Yonah 1960a: 21).

C) Byzantine Elements in Jewish Art

Typical features of Byzantine art, encountered on synagogue mosaic pavements (Avi-Yonah 1960a: 21-22), include: 1) Rhythmic grouping and descriptive isolation (Beth ᵓAlpha Biblical panel, fig. IX.31, Pl. 64); 2) A combination of realistic details with a conceptual isolation of images (see the bird in the cage, the hen laying eggs in the Maᶜon pavement, fig. X. 34); 3) Complete disregard for true proportions of animals and objects in relation to each other; 4) *Horror vacui*—typical of Oriental art. In execution, typical Byzantine methods are noticeable such as a stylization of figures, by the use of a single or double outline. These Byzantine features are based on Oriental elements which can be defined as monumental, static and conceptual attitudes.

The encounter between the different artistic attitudes resulted in an art style, which included integrated Oriental and Hellenistic-Roman elements of ornamentation. The traditional repertoire inherited from the Hellenistic-Roman world contained natural and everyday motifs taken from pattern books which were combined with traditional Jewish geometric and floral motifs based on art of the Second Temple period, and combined with the conceptual and stylized Oriental art; these constituted the main sources of Jewish art during Late Antiquity in the Land of Israel and in the Diaspora.

CHAPTER THIRTEEN

A COMPARISON BETWEEN JEWISH AND CHRISTIAN ART

A) THE PARALLEL BUT SEPARATE DEVELOPMENT OF SYNAGOGUE AND CHURCH

Mosaic Pavements

The number of churches in the Land of Israel constructed during the period is close to three hundred, whereas only a few score synagogues were built at that time. Nevertheless it is still interesting to compare the two groups, as the development of synagogue and church pavement decoration shows interesting comparisons and contrasts which were determined by the religious convictions of the Jewish and Christian communities.

1) Characteristic Features of Synagogue Pavements

a) Synagogue pavements in the fourth century at Ḥammath Tiberias (figs. XI.1, 9) are the first to be designed to include prototypical themes and subjects proving that their iconography developed earlier than that of the churches.

b) The Jews chose figurative subjects and symbolic motifs, such as the menorah and other ritual utensils, Biblical scenes and the zodiac panel, for their synagogue pavements. This deliberate choice of symbolic elements was meant to emphasize the distinct and independent quality of Judaism.

c) Synagogue pavements contain conventionalized designs and schemes such as panels of symbolic and ritual motifs integrated with varied subjects such as the zodiac, and heraldic scenes with inscriptions (Pls. 71-74; figs. XI. 9-14).

d) To floors containing designs of medallions filled with beasts and birds was added a symbolic panel or motif (Maᶜon and Beth Sheʾan B (small) synagogues (figs. IX.41, 42).

e) Artists working on synagogue floors show a humorous inclination in their art when depicting scenes such as the Beth ʾAlpha hen and her chicks (fig. X.33b), or the Maᶜon hen laying an egg (fig. X.34a); Avi-Yonah (1960a:20) proposes that this inclination is due to the agricultural character of the Jewish community.

f) A tendency towards realism is encountered in the menoroth of Maᶜon and Ḥulda which are rendered in detailed naturalism (Pls. 60, 87).

g) Oriental art elements predominate in the decoration of most synagogue pavements.

2) *Characteristic Features of Church Pavements*

a) Figurative subjects on church pavements begin to appear only in the sixth century and are completely different from those of synagogues, taking the form of genre subjects which represented "the world as it is," vintage and village life (for example, see Beth She'an and Haditha churches and monastery (Avi-Yonah 1981b: 364; 1972:122), and the sixth century church of Kissufim (Cohen 1980)).

b) Mythological and pagan themes are absent, except for some specific subjects such as Orpheus (Avi-Yonah 1981b:364). It was forbidden to depict Biblical scenes on church pavements in view of the danger of their being trodden upon. Symbolic motifs and religious elements are rarely depicted on church floors for the same reason.

c) The organization of the church's field is also different to that of the synagogue: floors are divided into geometric or organic carpets, and sometimes sub-divided into sections by vine branches or geometric patterns such as squares, circles, and hexagons, all of which are filled with beasts, birds, and plants (Kursi, Kurnub, Shellal, Beth She'an, fig. IX.43; Pl. 107).

d) The decoration of carpets by the inhabited scroll method is very common on church floors of the sixth century.

3) *Chronological and Stylistic Development of Synagogue and Church Mosaic Pavements*

A very curious phenomenon is revealed when the development of synagogue pavement design is compared to that of church pavements: the growth and evolution of each is always conceptually and consciously in an opposite direction. In other words, whenever one religion chooses to represent figurative art, the other refrains, and *vice versa*. Figurative art, iconography and symbolism, religious themes and calendars (zodiacs) as well as mythology and pagan subjects are introduced into the designs on synagogue floors from the fourth century on; Biblical scenes start being used from the fifth century on; and during the sixth century the presence of carpets with inhabited scrolls becomes common. Synagogue pavements turn to an aniconic style in the mid-sixth century. This style represents the result of the trend away from the depiction of human figures (Ma'on, fig. IX.41); at the same time the zodiac figurative depiction is replaced by an inscribed panel ('En-Gedi, Pl. 51). At Susiya the mosaic figurative zodiac and Biblical scenes are intentionally replaced by geometric and floral carpets (Pl. 75), and at Naᶜaran iconoclasts remove all the figurative depictions (fig. XI.11; Pl. 74). From the mid-sixth century onwards, synagogue pavements comprise geometric and floral carpets, sometimes with an emblem decorating a part of the carpet, as at Jericho, ᶜEn-Gedi and Maᶜoz Ḥayim (fig. XI.13; Pls. 95-96). It should be noted that throughout this development most of the synagogue pavements have some symbolic element depicted, usually the menorah, either in a prominent place (Ḥammath Tiberias, Beth ᵓAlpha, Maᶜon, Susiya, Pls. 87, 101, 103, 104); but occasionally in the border (ᶜEn-Gedi, Maᶜoz Ḥayim, or in an inscription in the House of Leontis in Beth Sheᵓan, Pls. 69, 95, 96b). In conclusion, it seems that synagogue pavement decoration altered from carpets with figurative representations into aniconic geometric and floral patterned carpets which integrated symbolic elements (also Avi-Yonah 1975: 56).

Early churches (early fifth century) are decorated solely with geometric carpets, and no figurative art appears (Shavei Zion, Evron; Kitzinger 1965b: Pls. 6, 7). Floral and faunal subjects begin to appear only in the mid-fifth century at Tabgha and the Church of the Nativity in Bethlehem (Avi-Yonah 1960a; Kitzinger 1965b: Pls. 1-3). In Christian art, representations of sacred symbols on pavements is forbidden by imperial decree in 427 CE (*Theodosian Code*, I tit. VIII). This decree causes the development of a tendency towards hidden Christian symbols, particularly in the sixth century. At the same time, church pavements again begin to employ figurative ornamentation consisting mostly of genre subjects such as natural history, vintage, village and hunting scenes, which are considered inoffensive. Inhabited scroll patterns also become popular. Even though figurative designs are now employed, the negative attitude towards depictions of symbolic subjects is retained. Although village life and labours of the months may seem to be realistic depictions, they probably hide the symbolic meaning of earthly paradise, a very common notion in this period (for this see Avi-Yonah 1972: 122).

The total impression produced by the above analysis, therefore, can be summarized as follows: whereas, in the fourth to sixth centuries synagogue art accepts and uses figurative representations, church art is strictly aniconic. In the mid-sixth century, church pavements begin to show figurative scenes, which simultaneously slowly disappear from synagogue floors: instead, they are replaced by overall geometric carpets including emblems (the Jericho synagogue, fig. XI.13), or by geometric motifs and written inscriptions (Susiya, ᶜEn-Gedi, Reḥov, Pls. 51, 52, 75). One of the causes for this separate and opposite development may have been due to the desire on the part of the Jews to intentionally distinguish their art and architecture from that of Christianity: they did this by an emphatic affirmation of Jewish spiritual values, which they symbolically expressed by the specific ornamentation of their synagogues.

B) A Comparison of Biblical Scenes in both Jewish and Christian Art

Similar themes occur in both Jewish and Christian art, with entirely different interpretations being given by the different religions. Early Christian catacomb art uses Biblical scenes in an abbreviated and summarized manner (Grabar 1968: 25, 94-95, describes them as image-signs). From the beginning, there is a tendency towards a symbolism which would disguise the true meaning of the stories by the use of allegory and proverb; thus only the faithful (Christians) who would be acquainted with the symbols would have the truth revealed to them. Likewise, the Old Testament was also used as a pre-figuration of the New Testament. The cult in early Christianity was centred around death and the after-life. For this reason Christian art most frequently took from the Bible stories which would emphasize a promise of individual salvation, such as Jonah, Moses, Daniel in the lion's den, Noah's Ark and the sacrifice of Isaac.

(In Christian art no Biblical scenes are depicted on pavements except one—Aquileia, which tells the Jonah story, and is dated to the fourth century, see Testini 1958.)

Differences between Jewish and Christian depictions of Biblical scenes are, in sum:

1) In Jewish art the form is descriptive-narrative whereas in early Christian art the scenes are depicted in a symbolic and allegorical form (also Grabar 1968: 94-95). In later Christian monumental art the tendency is also toward the descriptive-narrative form, but different aspects of the story are emphasized.

2) The scenes are depicted on synagogue pavements, that is they are part of synagogal art. Early Christian Biblical scenes are rendered only on catacomb frescoes and sarcophagi, that is, they were considered fit subjects for funerary art.

3) The meaning of the Jewish depictions is connected with the belief in divine salvation for His chosen people. In Christianity the meaning is associated with man's individual salvation, his death, and after-life (also Grabar 1968: 25-26).

4) The Jewish scenes are fully descriptive and include intricate details, as on the synagogue pavements of Gerasa and Beth 'Alpha, whereas in early Christian funerary art the scenes are summarized and abbreviated.

5) The Jewish synagogue scenes are part of the synagogue pavement programme (see p. 347f.), which is not the case in Christian art which probably follows a Hellenistic form.

6) The primary purpose of figurative representation in Jewish scenes was as a reminder of the traditional Biblical stories; the use of symbolism, prevalent in Christian art, was of minor interest.

The iconographical similarity of the Jewish scenes and the early Christian funerary art derives not from a common figurative origin, but rather from a common literary origin, from the Biblical text itself (cf. Weitzman 1971a; 1971b; and see pp. 287-300).

C) Architectural Comparisons

Religious buildings of both Jews and Christians were constructed during the early centuries of this millenium. A new type of worship inside a communal prayer house demanded a new kind of structure, a large hall with a focal point, which had to conform to the requirements of the community in terms of function, ritual and ornament. Jewish ritual influenced early Church liturgy. Thus, the development of the synagogue building from the third century on influenced the architectural design of churches built during the fourth century (Grabar 1967: 171-173).

Churches were the predominant and most numerous religious edifices in the Land of Israel during Late Antiquity so that it follows that the variety of church types is much greater than that of synagogues. Church types included the common basilica, both round and octagonal, as well as cross-shaped structures. Synagogues, in general, were of either the basilica type or were broad-house structures (figs. VIII.1-4).

Several aspects of architectural comparison between churches and synagogues can be documented (also Avi-Yonah 1957: 264-270):

1) *Provenance*—Synagogues were erected on high places, in the centre of a town or village, or on the seashore. The synagogue in the village of Chorazin is more or less in its centre (fig. VII.2) and the same is true of the synagogues of Meiron and Kazrin. The Caesarea synagogue is positioned in the Jewish quarter north of the harbour. Churches, too, were set usually in the centre of a town or village.

2) *Plan*—Synagogues have three main architectural features: the Torah shrine on the Jerusalem-oriented wall, the triple entrance (sometimes only a single entrance), and the gallery (see pp. 232-233). In the fifth century the plan of the synagogue included an apse which became the Torah shrine. In the church, the area in front of the altar and apse was accessible only to the clergy, and was separated from the remainder of the hall by a chancel screen. The two rooms (the *prothasis* and the *diakonikon*) which flank the central apse were added to the church structure at the end of the fifth century.

3) *Orientation*—Synagogue orientation is determined by the Torah shrine erected on the Jerusalem-oriented wall (see p. 231ff.). The church, by comparison, has its apse on the eastern wall, pointing towards the rising sun.

The differences between synagogue and church architecture is the result of the liturgy and the types of worship each religion developed. However, contacts and influences upon the art and architecture of both religions were quite considerable, especially because of the fact that the same craftsmen and artists worked for both Jewish synagogues and Christian churches (see pp. 388-391). Jews, due to a desire to assert their identity, depicted their Jewish symbols or added them to a popular form or design, such as the menorah added to the Corinthian capitals of Capernaum and Caesarea (Pl. 42a, b). This need for identification by the Jews was probably due partly to the fact that synagogues were fewer in number than churches.

CHAPTER FOURTEEN

DISTINGUISHING FEATURES OF JEWISH ART

A) Unidentical Symmetrical Composition

A distinctive feature of Jewish art is the antithetic symmetrical composition, which occurs in almost all figurative and decorative subjects, and which is one of the basic elements of Oriental art (p. 367). This composition is unconventional however in the manner in which it is represented: either 1) in an unsymmetrical design caused by the depiction of different flanking motifs, or 2) rendered in an *unidentical* symmetry:

1) The first group of representations includes heraldic designs of motifs on carved synagogue lintels: for instance, lintels from Capernaum (figs. VIII, 47; 49a,b; 51a). A central motif such as a wreath, conch, or an Ark of the Scrolls is flanked by two dissimilar floral motifs which differ either in size or in actual design. The same unsymmetrical pattern may be observed in funerary art, for instance the "Acanthus" sarcophagus A at Beth She῾arim (fig. X.2). On this sarcophagus are carved three garlands, the central garland containing a lion which is depicted flanked by remnants of two different whorls of leaves. "Acanthus" sarcophagus B (fig. X.14) has two different rosettes depicted above the two lateral garlands. The most outstanding example of this feature is found in the entrance panel of the mosaic pavement of the Beth ᾽Alpha synagogue where the inscription is flanked by a lion on one side and by a bull on the other (fig. X.7c). Avi-Yonah (1981a: 51) maintains that the animals were selected for their symbolic value.

2) Most frequently antithetic designs are composed symmetrically, but in some cases aesthetic symmetry is realised even though some objects or animals are clearly *not identical, and are intentionally represented dissimilarly*. This characteristic is mostly found on synagogue mosaic pavements. By the third and fourth centuries this tendency appears, and its popularity increases during later periods. Examples are encountered on some of the synagogue lintels, such as the Gush Ḥalav lintel suffit where an eagle is flanked by two unidentical garlands (fig. X.20a). The relief from ῾En Samsam (Pl. 26) portrays a figure flanked symmetrically by a lion and a lioness differing from each other in sex, size, and tail position. The eagles flanking the scene at each end are also unidentical.

In funerary art at Beth She'arim, the same tendency is encountered. Menoroth painted in red on sealing stones are unidentical (fig. IX.7): the left menorah has a horizontal bar with lamps, whereas the right menorah lacks this feature. On the other drawing only the left menorah shows lamps on its bar. The left menorah has five branches only, although the right has seven. The carvings of the aediculae flanking the arcosole (fig. VIII.27) are executed symmetrically, but are different and unidentical: the left depicts an Ark inside the aedicula, whereas the right aedicula contains a menorah. Some of the Beth She'arim sarcophagi also exhibit this tendency to unidentical symmetry: the "Shell" sarcophagus shows two aediculae asymmetrically depicted on the panel of the facade. Each aedicula has a different figure, one a lion, the other a bird (Pl. 30). The "Eagle" sarcophagus (fig. X.6b) has lions on the front and back which are symmetrical, but have different tails and leg-execution. The "Lion" sarcophagus is distinguished by its heraldic scene of a lion and a lioness flanking an unfinished vase (fig. X.6a). The lioness is shorter, has a larger, extended tongue, and her ears and hind legs differ from those of the lion. The lion is larger than his mate. The same dimensional difference is seen on the sides of the "Nikae" and "Menorah" sarcophagi (fig. X.19) where symmetrical heraldic dolphins are represented: one is larger than the other. A further unidentical scene is carved on the narrow side of the "Shell" sarcophagus: a lion and lioness flank an animal, probably a gazelle (Avigad 1976: Pl. XLIII:2).

Impressive examples of this tendency are found in the representations on synagogue mosaic pavements:

a) Several panels depict a Torah shrine flanked by menoroth and ritual objects in a symmetrical composition which contains varied flanking objects. For example, the Beth 'Alpha Torah shrine panel is unidentical in almost all its heraldic elements (Pl. 102): the menoroth flanking the Ark are unidentical in their bases and in the lamps on the bar; the four ritual objects are each depicted differently; the two lions appear similar but have different tails; and the birds are each rendered differently. The Hammath Tiberias upper panel shows a symmetrical rendition (Pl. 101), but even here the two shofaroth and incense shovels are dissimilar in their details. The menoroth in the Susiya pavement (Pl. 104) differ completely from each other, particularly in their branches, and bases. The shofaroth and the incense shovels depicted on the synagogue pavement of Beth She'an are each different (Pl. 103). The entrance panel at Huseifa (Pl. 56 and fig. XI.5) shows two menoroth each depicted in a completely different manner: one has pottery lamps whereas glass lamps are shown on the other; furthermore, the branches are rendered dissimilarly. In the centre of the Beth 'Alpha zodiac panel (Pl. 76) the horses, two on each side of the sun god, are rendered symmetrically, but are portrayed differently, particularly in their head decoration.

b) Animals flank inscriptions, menoroth, as well as the Ark on several synagogue mosaic pavements. These animals are usually similar, although differences in details can be distinguished. The Ḥammath Tiberias pavement shows lions facing each other across the inscription (fig. X.7a). These lions differ in facial details such as their ears. The Beth Sheʾan B small synagogue has an inscription flanked by birds (fig. X.26) which differ in size, the left being the larger. The Naʿaran Biblical scene of Daniel flanked by lions depicts the lions symmetrically, but each with a different tail position (fig. IX.34): the left lion has an upward-turned tail, whereas the right lion has his tail between his hind legs. The entrance panel at Naʿaran depicts two unidentical (repaired) stags facing each other (fig. X.17). The ʿEn-Gedi central emblem shows birds symmetrically placed, but with differences in size and stance (Pl. 96b).

c) Inhabited scroll pavements themselves sometimes contain antithetic designs with unidentical details. At Gaza some of the medallions are inhabited by similar heraldic animals (Pl. 86, rows 5, 7, and 9); even these, however, show differences: the leopards in row 9 have unidentical tails. In row 3, different animals flank a dog; a lioness and her cub on one side and a tigress on the other (Pl. 86a). On the upper part of the Maʿon synagogue pavement the lions flanking the menorah differ in mane and heads (Pl. 87). The two elephants in row 8 are rendered differently to each other, particularly their trunks.

Heraldic symmetry with unidentical elements is only seldom encountered on pagan reliefs of Nabatean temples and tombs (Glueck 1965: Pls. 12, 38a,b, 54a,b, 167a,b,c, 177), as well as on mosaic pavements in churches, such as Shellal, and the town of Nebo (Saller and Bagatti 1949: Pls. 14:1, 20:1-4, 21:1, 28:1, 3, 30:1, 34:3, 37:3, 39:2, etc.).

A particularly common method of stressing the unidentical character of these designs is by the varied manner of depicting animal tails (figs. X.6, 7).

The antithetic symmetrical design was an integral part of both Jewish synagogal as well as funerary art. The inclination to depict unidentical objects or animals within the heraldic design must have been intentional as it would have been just as easy to portray completely identical designs. Furthermore, it need not be related to unskillful artistic treatment as some designs do use symmetrical patterns. Unidentical symmetry was a style intentionally adopted by the Jews in particular. One may conjecture that it is associated with a desire to avoid competition with a perfection only God could achieve. On the other hand, this trend may have been due to the character of Jewish popular art, and to the artists' standards of composition and their cultural environment, which did not traditionally demand perfection.

B) Iconographically-decorated mosaic floors

Mosaic floor decorations include iconographic and symbolic elements, a paradoxical fact which needs emphasizing; even Biblical scenes which contain a representation of the Hand of God, as in Isaac's Sacrifice at Beth ʾAlpha (fig. IX.31 and Pl. 64), were considered fit subjects for a floor *which was continually being trodden upon*: Torah shrines, menoroth and other ritual objects were also regarded as suitable for the pavements of Ḥammath Tiberias, Beth ʾAlpha, Naʿaran and Susiya (Pls. 101-105). (For the reason why church floors excluded iconography and symbols, see p. 373). Equally important is the fact that even the inscriptions depicted on mosaic floors were allowed to be stepped upon. Although the word was much more respected than the image, as proved by the iconoclastic treatment given to some pavements such as at Naʿaran (fig. XI.11; Pl. 74), inscriptions were an integral part of the synagogue floor, and probably replaced figurative art as indicated by the inscription at ʿEn-Gedi (Pl. 51) where a list of zodiac signs followed by the twelve months replaces the earlier representational zodiacs as see in other synagogues (p. 309). The first part of the ʿEn-Gedi inscription names the thirteen ancestors of the world, (taken from I Chron. 1: 1-4). On the second part of the inscription following the list of the twelve zodiac signs and twelve months, are depicted the three patriarchs. Amazingly this representation did not prevent the Jewish community of ʿEn-Gedi from treading upon this floor.

The inscription of the Reḥov synagogue is noteworthy not only because of its being the longest synagogue mosaic inscription found up to now but also because of its being devoted to matters of Halakha mentioned also in the Jerusalem Talmud (Pl. 52). Both this and the ʿEn-Gedi inscriptions are dated as late as the seventh century. Their prominent place on the synagogue pavements was the result of the change in the sixth century when figurative art was once again forbidden and was replaced by geometric and floral composition.

Why did Jews intentionally include Biblical scenes and religious symbols among the subject matter used to adorn synagogue mosaic floors? Avi-Yonah (1960b: 32) maintains that Jews of the Talmudic period were "notoriously insensitive to images, whether symbolic or Biblical." However, it seems more likely that this reflects the Jewish avoidance of the worship of images of idolatry, mentioned at the end of the Second of the Ten Commandments (Ex. 20: 15; Deut. 5: 1-9): "Thou shalt not bow down thyself to them, nor serve them." Stepping on an image must have removed its sacrosanct quality. In this way the Jews struggled against idolatry, acting on the principle that as long as the "graven image" would be widely represented on synagogue mosaic floors and would be trodden upon the pernicious influence of idolatry could be neutralized.

C) Intentional Imperfection in Jewish Funerary Art

The phenomenon of the incomplete ornamentation is encountered in the funerary art of the Second Temple period on tomb facades, sarcophagi, and ossuaries in Jerusalem. In the Beth She'arim cemetery the same idiosyncrasy occurs in carvings which are half-finished on tomb walls and in sarcophagi ornamentation.

1) The facade of the "Tomb of the Kings" in Jerusalem dated to the Second Temple period is unfinished: the lintel is complete, but the carved ornament on each side of the door jamb is left incomplete (fig. IV.8).

2) In the same tomb, a sarcophagus was found with an inscription mentioning Queen Saddah, identified as Helena of Adiabene (Avigad 1956, fig. 21). Two discs only flank the inscription. Goodenough (1953, I: 134) maintains that the artisan left these discs to be carved later with rosettes, at the discretion of the client.

3) South of the "Tomb of Zechariah" in the Kidron Valley of Jerusalem, an unfinished entrance is carved with two columns (fig. IV.12).

4) Several ossuaries exhibit the same phenomenon of half-finished carved ornamentation. Many of the motifs, the rosette in particular, are incomplete. Occasionally two rosettes are depicted on the ossuary; one is beautifully chip-carved, whereas the other is only schematically outlined (fig. 1a). Another ossuary has completely carved rosettes; one of them however shows a rudimentary ornamental element between the rosette leaves, never finished (fig. 1b). On another ossuary, ashlar stones, probably meant to cover the whole front of the ossuary, are carved, but are uncompleted (fig. 1c) (Rahmani 1967: ossuary 17, Pl. 39:1, p. 189). On a Jericho ossuary one rosette and the corner patterns are unfinished (Pl. 19).

5) In the Beth She'arim cemetery several of the sarcophagi have incomplete decorations:

a) Sarcophagus no. 25, the "Daughters" sarcophagus (fig. 2a), has an incomplete left wreath.

b) On the "Shell" sarcophagus (Pl. 30), the left wreath adjacent to the eagle aedicula is unfinished.

c) On sarcophagus no. 87 (fig. 2b) the rosette is outlined by a circle only and was never completed.

d) Only the first few eggs of the egg and dart patterns on the rim of the "Acanthus B" sarcophagus are carved (fig. X.14) (Avigad 1976: 152, Pl. 48,1).

e) The "Menorah" sarcophagus has a plain front with two columns, on which two thin red painted lines are marked. Avigad (1976: 149) contends that this was in preparation for carving.

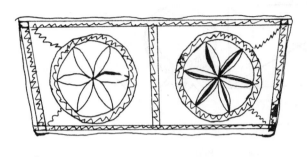

a

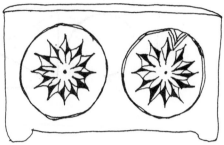

b

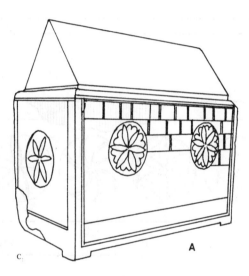

c.   A

1a-c. Ossuaries.

Rahmani contends (1977: 25) that the ossuary work shows indifference on the part of the artists and their clients towards the quality of the finished product (the ossuary). This is explained further by the civil strife and the exigency of the time, which was during the war against the Romans when many of the workshops were either completely closed down or were operating at a reduced level of workmanship. Both demand and quality consequently were affected.

2a. ''Daughters'' Sarcophagus, Beth
She'arim.

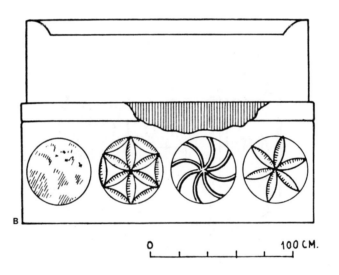

2b. Sarcophagus 87, Beth She'arim.

    This unusual trait of partly incomplete ornamentation recurs often in funerary art and it seems to suggest more than mere negligence in craftsmanship, or indifference on the part of the clientele, but rather that it was done intentionally and also had some significance.

CHAPTER FIFTEEN

ARTISTS AND PATTERN BOOKS

A) Artists, Craftsmen and Workshops

The identity of artists and their workshops is an important topic. Artists and workshops supplied their products indiscriminately to Jews, Christians and pagans alike. However, some Jewish artists produced their works only for Jewish funerary and synagogal purposes.

Schools, workshops and artists can be identified by the following means (also Dauphin 1976: 145-146; 1978: 409-410):

By the means of inscriptions mentioning artists, craftsmen or builders and their works.

By an analysis of stylistic and technical idiosyncrasy which may characterize an artist or workshop.

By an examination of the motifs and patterns which may contribute to the identification of artists and workshops.

Dauphin (1976a: 145) proposes two groups of mosaic artists: 1) mosaicist workshops—groups of artisans and craftsmen working within schools and based in large cities such as Antioch, Hama and Beth She³an, and 2) travelling groups of artists consisting of a master craftsman and his assistants.

An answer to the question of the identity of the artists and craftsmen can be deduced partly from *inscriptions* accompanying some of the architectural decorative elements as well as from inscriptions on synagogue mosaic pavements which sometimes mention the craftsmen by both name and deed. The following examples come from the Galilee and the Golan:

1) An inscribed Hebrew-Aramaic lintel found at ³Alma (near Safed) reads "Amen Selah, I Jose, son of Levi the Levite, the craftsman who made...." (fig. 1a) (Hestrin 1960: 65; Naveh 1978: 22-23).

2) The same artist is mentioned on a Hebrew lintel inscription on the small synagogue at Bar³am (fig. VIII.45a) (Naveh 1960: 19, 23). It seems that both this and the above-mentioned lintel inscription were executed by the same Jewish artisan, "Jose the Levite, son of Levi," during the same period.

3) An Aramaic inscription on a stone from the ³Ammudim synagogue reads "Yoezer the *Ḥazan* and Simeon his brother made this Gate to the Lord of Heaven"

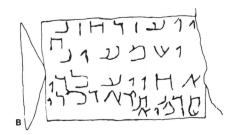

יועזר חזנה
ושמעון
אחוי עבדו
4 הדן תקא דמרי
שומיא

דיכר לטב יוסה בר
תנחום בר בוטה ובנוי
דעבדון הדה טבלה
4 תהי להון ברכתה
אמן

1. Inscriptions: a) ʿAlma; b) H. ʿAmmudim; c) Dabbura; d) Kefar Kana; e) Sepphoris.

(fig. 1b) (Avigad 1960b: 62, 63; See Naveh, 1978: 41-42, who reads not "Gate" but rather "Ark;" see p. 272).

4) On an architrave found at Dabbura (Golan) an otherwise Aramaic inscription mentions in Greek the name of the builder: "Stykos" (fig. 1c) (Naveh 1978: 26-27).

5) In the Beth ʾAlpha synagogue Greek inscription the craftsmen Marianos and Hanina are commemorated (fig. X.7c). Sukenik (1932: 47) maintains that they laid the mosaic.

6) The same artisans are also mentioned in the Beth Sheʾan A synagogue Greek inscription on a small room(7) pavement (fig. XI.2) (Zori 1967: 159).

7) An Aramaic inscription on the Beth Sheʾan B synagogue mosaic reads "Remembered be for good the artisan who made this work" (fig. X.26; Pl. 106) (Bahat 1981a 85; Naveh 1978:78-79).

All these inscriptions use either the Aramaic or the Greek term for craftsman. 8, 9) Two related Aramaic inscriptions record artists who "made" mosaic floors. Both the first, from Kefar Kana (fig. 1d), and the second, from Sepphoris (fig. 1e) (Naveh 1978: 51-53), mention a family of three generations: Yose and Yudan, sons of Tanhum, son of Buta, who "made" mosaic pavements. Avi-Yonah (1981b: 375, after Klein) proposes that these inscriptions attest to a family of artists with an in-herited craft (but see Naveh, 1978: 52, who suggests that they were donors). The terms used in these inscriptions are *omna*, and *oman* in Aramaic and Hebrew respect-ively, and τεχνίτης in Greek.

In Talmudic literature the Aramaic term *omna* means artisan or skilled builder (*M. Berachot* II, 4; *J., Hag.* II, 1, 77b, line 15). The Greek term used at Beth ʾAlpha is τεχνίτες (artists) (Sukenik 1932: 47). Hestrin (1960: 66) proposes the possibility that these artisans or artists were responsible not only for the mosaic but also for the building, for two reasons: 1) the same term also appears in Syria carved on lintels, and tomb walls, and is used there for both artisan and builder; and 2) the inscrip-tions on mosaic pavements could commemorate the mosaicist as well as the builder, because the only ornaments are inside, on the mosaic floors, which were then the only places for inscriptions. In other words the Aramaic, Hebrew and Greek terms can be explained as meaning artisan, craftsman or builder. This is also attested to by Butler (1929: 254) who says:

> There was no great difference in the function of designer and builder. One must assume that in most cases the architect was also the builder or contractor and may have been himself an artisan as well.

1. Jewish Artists

Most of the inscriptions discussed above (with the exception of Dabbura, no. 4) mention Jewish names, which implies that there were many Jewish artists employed in synagogue building. The craft was an inherited skill, traditionally a family occupation, as attested to by the inscriptions. Two generations of a family, Marianos and his son, together made the mosaic pavement of Beth ʾAlpha (inscription no. 5) which is unique in style and execution; and also the pavement in one room of Beth Sheʾan synagogue A (room 7, inscription no. 6). The three-generation family of Buta, Tanḥum, Yose and Yudan were mosaicists in the Galilee. Avi-Yonah (1961b: 32) maintains that the builders of the Galilean synagogues had to be Jewish, as it would be unlikely that the Galilean Jews "would entrust the construction of their synagogue to non-Jews" although the actual execution may have been carried out by local craftsmen, all Galileans (who might also have been Jews). These builders were trained, according to Avi-Yonah, in a Gentile school, because of the conformity of the Galilean synagogues to those of the Graeco-Syrian buildings in the Hauran. Furthermore, Avi-Yonah maintains (1960b: 34) that the mosaicist who made the Maʿon synagogue pavement was possibly a Greek-speaking Jew from the Diaspora, because, on the one hand, the menorah and the ritual objects are rendered faithfully and yet, on the other the artist shows an ignorance of the Hebrew script. Barash (1980: 30-32) proposes that a travelling, foreign mosaicist having connections with Egypt and Syria, produced the David mosaic at Gaza.

Jewish literature of the time, the Mishna and the Talmud, mention the existence of Jewish artists and craftsmen who also worked for Christians and pagans, as well as the attitude of Jews towards artists and craftsmen . Among the various crafts the builders are mentioned first; they were highly appreciated (*B., Sanhedrin* 29a). Hestrin (1960: 66) maintains that the prominent place of the inscription on the ʿAlma lintel was probably related to the high esteem in which the artist was held.

Geometric and floral motifs are frequently rendered in a much higher quality than figurative representations in the same mosaic pavement. A long tradition existed among Jewish artists in the depiction of decorative patterns, that is, floral and geometric motifs, whereas no such tradition is known for figurative representations. This may be the reason for the qualitative differences in renditions.

Clearly, Jewish artists created the mosaic pavements of Beth ʾAlpha. Although pattern books were used for the panel themes as in Ḥammath Tiberias and Naʿaran, the style and execution of these pavements is unique in both Jewish art and in the art of Late Antiquity.

2. *Beth She'arim Workshops*

Several local artists or workshops are responsible for the carving of most of the stone sarcophagi found in catacomb 20. Even though they were influenced by the styles of imported marble sarcophagi, their work testifies to a local style which employs motifs of Jewish art (Avigad 1976: 163-165). These decorated sarcophagi can probably be related to at least four workshops or artists:

a) Two sarcophagi, the "Shell" (no. 117) and the "Gable" (no. 103) sarcophagi (Pl. 30) were probably manufactured in the same workshop and display a combination of Jewish art motifs. This is attested to by i) the shell being a common central motif, ii) the bird motif inside the frames (Avigad 1976: Pls. XLIIIA:2; XLIV:4), iii) the moulding below the frames of the narrow sides, and iv) the cornice of the facades (Avigad 1975: 145).

b) The "Eagle" and "Bull" sarcophagi (fig. X.16) exhibit similarities, confirming that they were made in the same workshop (Avigad 1976: 143), in i) the style of the bulls' heads, ii) the stylized leaves of the garlands, and iii) the rim of the sarcophagi. It should be noted that several similarities can be observed between the "Eagle" and the "Shell" sarcophagi: note the lions with three legs flanking a bull's head (fig. X.6). It is possible that these four sarcophagi come from the same workshop, but were carved by different artists.

c) The two "Acanthus" sarcophagi (nos. 97 and 101) (figs. X.2, 14) were carved by different artists to those who produced the sarcophagi mentioned above. These two resemble marble garland sarcophagi manufactured in Asia Minor, and were carved by artists better qualified than the others. Avigad (1976: 152-153 and note 3) maintains that these two sarcophagi are products of a Beth She'arim workshop or of one in the vicinity.

d) The "Nikae" (no. 125) and the "Menorah" (no. 122) (fig. X.19) sarcophagi display exactly the same motif of dolphins with a wreath on their narrow sides. These may have been executed by the same artists, or it may be possible that the motif was taken from a pattern book.

Further indications of the existence of Jewish artists and/or workshops at Beth She'arim can be seen in the three sarcophagi with unfinished decoration (see also pp. 380-382): sarcophagus no. 87 (fig. XIV.2b) has an incomplete rosette, the "Daughters" sarcophagus (fig. XIV.2a) and the "Shell" sarcophagus have unfinished wreaths (Pl. 30). In all cases the unfinished part is on the left, demonstrating that the artists worked from right to left (Avigad 1976: 158); this suggests that the Jewish artists working at Beth She'arim followed, in their carving, the direction of Hebrew and Aramaic writing, that is, from right to left. Avigad (1976: 162-164) contends that the Jewish artists who carved the Beth Shearim sarcophagi (dated approximately to the third century) "display low standards and inferior talent...limited technical and artistic ability." The artists, he maintains, are "provincial and inexperienced craftsmen." Relatively high standards and artistic ability are displayed only on the two "Acanthus" sarcophagi (figs. X.2, 14), the animal frieze of the mausoleum, and the lion and gazelle on the hunt sarcophagus (figs. X.15, 24).

The Jewish Beth She'arim workshops produced some of the sarcophagi placed afterwards in the catacombs. The patterns they used are a blend of Hellenistic and Oriental elements, with the occasional creation of a new motif. The style in which they worked is similar to that used in contemporary Jewish synagogal art.

Local craftsmen, probably Jewish, worked in Galilean and Golan synagogues and were responsible for the distinctive features in the architectural decoration, such as the Galilean/Golan synagogue architectural plan, the facade, the frame ornamentation of the portals, the Torah shrine structure and decoration (see also pp. 230-231). It may be reasonably inferred that these Jewish artists coming from families with long traditions of inherited craftsmanship worked primarily for Jews, but were also employed by Christians and pagans. This may be deduced from the similarities among stylistic features of synagogues, churches and temples in the Galilee and Syria, and also by synagogal and church architecture and art, particularly during the sixth century (see p. 374). A comprehensive research outside the scope of this book on the comparable style and composition of mosaics and architecture of both synagogues and churches would be able to prove this contention.

3. Craftsmen and workshops

These existed for clientele from all religions who patronized the workshops which produced stone and lead sarcophagi and coffins, as well as ornamented stone chancel screens. There were also mosaicists who executed pavements. These workshops produced uniform or conventional designs which would be acceptable to the various ethnic clientele. Special decorative designs or religious symbols would be added at the request of the customer; they include Jewish symbols for Jews, Christian symbols for Christians, and mythological depictions for pagans.

The following discussion is meant to substantiate the premise that workshops did, in fact, exist:

a) The lead coffins at Beth She'arim are products of a Sidonian workshop (Avigad 1976: 173-182). Similar lead coffins with Christian symbols have also been found.

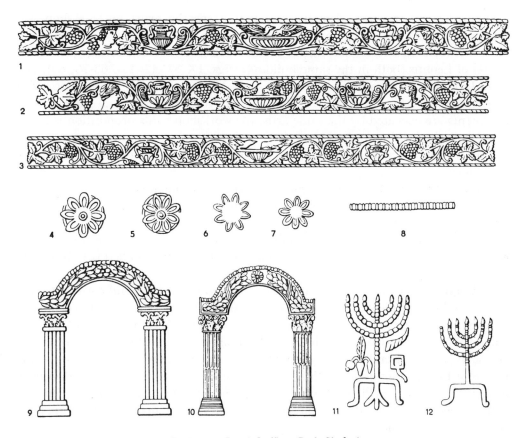

2. Design on Lead Coffins, Beth She‘arim.

The Jewish symbols were added before the casting (fig. 2). These coffins were brought from Tyre or from Sidon for burial use in Beth She‘arim (during the early fourth century).

b) A workshop producing chancel screens for both synagogues and churches is confirmed by finds in the Land of Israel. These screens are ornamented with stylized wreaths with flowing ribbons. A menorah, either with or without flanking ritual objects, is depicted inside the wreath of the synagogue chancel screen (fig. VIII.32), whereas the church screen usually portrays a cross inside the wreath. The similarity of these screens seems to indicate that they are from the same workshop; for example, the Ḥammath Gader synagogue screen (fig. VIII.32) resembles the Beth She’an monastery screen (Avi-Yonah 1981a: Pl. 16:4-5; see also p. 189-190).

c) Further proof which demonstrates that a specific artist or workshop was employed simultaneously by various communities is revealed when a comparison is made between the mosaic pavements of the Beth She'an small synagogue B, the House of Leontis (both in the same building) (figs. IX.37, 42; Pls. 68-70, 85), and room L of the Christian monastery of the Lady Mary at Beth She'an (Pl. 107) (Fitzgerald 1939: 9, Pls. XVI-XVII). I should like to propose that all three mosaic pavements are executed by the same artist (or workshop); this proposition is based on stylistic similarities, and a comparison of the following constituents of composition of the mosaics of the synagogue, House of Leontis and room L of the monastery:

i) The amphorae of the synagogue and room L are identical.

ii) The vine branches, grape clusters and leaves of the designs are identical in the synagogue and room L.

iii) The areas between the medallions of the mosaics of room L, and the synagogue and the middle panel in the House of Leontis are all filled with birds and beasts.

iv) Details of decoration are also similar: the bird in the left-hand corner of room L and the birds in the wide ornate border of the synagogue pavement are similar; the execution of the animals is similar: there is a resemblance between the ram and buffalo in the synagogue, the giraffe and buffalo in room L, and the cow in the House of Leontis. Rendition of eyes in all the beasts, in the room L, synagogue and House of Leontis mosaics, is similar. The guinea-fowl flanking a vase and inscription in the synagogue (Pl. 107) may be compared with a similarly constructed bird in the House of Leontis (Pl. 69): the same free, curved line may be seen in the body and in the legs of the birds.

v) Human figures bear a resemblance to each other in both the House of Leontis and room L: Odysseus is similar, particularly in his hair, to the hunter in the upper left medallion in room L. In his posture he resembles the man with the flute in room L.

d) The inhabited scrolls pavements (figs. IX.41-43; Pls. 85-87), including those of both synagogues and churches, are considered by Avi-Yonah (1981d) to have been executed by the "School of Gaza" mosaicists, who worked in the southwestern part of the Land of Israel. He bases this claim upon composition, patterns, and on a recurring motif (also Dauphin 1976: 130). The present writer cannot accept this theory, however, because of chronological, stylistic and other reasons (see Hachlili 1986): the "common denominator" of all the pavements is the repetition of patterns and motifs, due simply to the use of a pattern book, and not to the unifying element of a "school" (see also pp. 310-316).

From the inscriptions, the style of carving and the mosaic executions, it can be concluded that artists were producing works of art which satisfied the demands of the local clientele. Moreover, it is possible to infer that the same artists or workshops manufactured sometimes for Jews, Christians and pagans. Some artists may have been non-Jews working for a mixed clientele, using pattern books favoured by each of the different arts and religions. Similar designs would be used in all cases, but specific symbols for each client would be added to the synagogue or church mosaic pavement or chancel screen.

B. Pattern Books

The consistent and frequent use of identical compositions, motifs and patterns, and the wide range of themes found in mosaic art, sculpture and funerary art suggest the existence and use in antiquity of pattern books or sketch books (Avi-Yonah 1981b: 375; 1960a: 21; Kitzinger 1965b: 7; Dauphin 1978). Furthermore, the designs, which were often depicted in a stereotyped manner, have been found at various sites widely separated in distance and time. The zodiac is an example of this phenomenon. In addition, the widespread use of zoological and botanical subjects which could hardly have been known at first hand from nature, also proves that many themes and motifs were codified into pattern books which were passed on from generation to generation.

From an analysis of the existing material it is possible to surmise that the pattern books were arranged as discussed below, according to two criteria: composition and general subjects. It is very probable that these books which included designs, motifs and patterns were inherited by the artists' families. If this is so it might explain the time range of some of the themes.

1) Pattern books for mosaic pavements

a) A client desiring an artist to create and construct a mosaic floor would be shown various pattern books from which he could choose a combination of designs according to his wishes, or the wishes of the community he represented. Each pattern book would contain all the designs for a specific purpose, for example, for a whole room, for a border, for a specific motif, and so on. These pattern books would be divided into the following topics: books which comprise compositions showing the basic layout of an entire pavement, or designs for complete rooms of various sizes (long, square), or compositions for geometric or floral carpets (Naʿaran, Ḥuseifa, Ḥammath Gader, Jericho, figs. XI.4, 5, 12, 13), or inhabited scrolls designs (Maʿon, Gaza, Beth Sheʾan B, figs. IX.41-43).

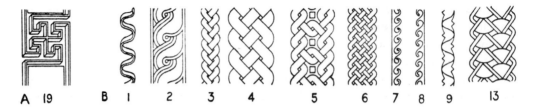

3. Mosaic Border Patterns.

b) Sketch books for pavement borders (Avi-Yonah 1981b: 285). These include geometric designs such as the guilloche (Beth ᵓAlpha, House of Leontis, fig. 3:B2 and Pls. 68-70, 102), the five- or six-strand guilloche (Ḥammath Gader, Ḥammath Tiberias, Beth Sheᵓan A, Naᶜaran, figs. 3:B6, B13; XI.1, 2, 4, 12) and the wave-strands (Torah shrine panel border in Beth Sheᵓan A, Naᶜaran, bottom border of the Gaza David mosaic, figs. 3:B7; XI.4 and Pls. 67, 103). Other interesting recurring border patterns include a fret with square "peopled" panels (fig. 3:A19) at Susiya and Maᶜoz Ḥayim (Pls. 75, 95), and interlacing flowers pointing alternately inwards and outwards in the Maᶜon border (Pl. 87), and in some of the circles of the frontal carpet at Naᶜaran (figs. 3:B9, XI.4; Avi-Yonah, 1960b: 25, note 1, dates this design appearance to the fifth century).

c) Sketch files for various motifs:

i) Birds and beasts. These were actually botanical and zoological catalogues which were influenced by Hellenistic interest in the natural sciences and by the existence of the gardens of the Ptolemies (Avi-Yonah 1960a: 21; Dauphin 1978: 408 (dealing only with mosaic inhabited scrolls pavements)).

ii) Geometric designs, objects, plants, fruits and architectural motifs.

iii) Humans.

These sketch files or pattern books may have been used by craftsmen of sculpture as well as by mosaicists, although pattern books for mosaicists were probably much richer in variety of codified motifs. This is demonstrated by the inhabited scroll pavements in both synagogues and churches (figs. IX.41-43 and the front carpet of Naᶜaran, fig. XI. 11), as well as by some floors which exhibit catalogues of birds, such as the Beth Sheᵓan monastery chapel G (Fitzgerald 1939: Pl. XIV).

d) Pattern files for narrative scenes such as hunting, village and rural life, attested to by the vintage scenes characteristic of Christian floors (see, for instance, room L of the Beth Sheᵓan monastery, Pl. 107). [It is noteworthy that only one vintage scene is found among all the synagogue ornamentation: the Chorazin frieze fragment (Pl.

47).] Few rural scenes are depicted on synagogue pavements: a hen lays an egg at Ma‘on (fig. X.34b), and a hen and chicks, and a figure holding a goose are found in the nave border scroll at Beth ʾAlpha (fig. X.33a, b).

e) Sketch files for other motifs which were either popular or possessed symbolic connotations. These were especially distinguished and may have been contained in a separate sketch book, or may have belonged to an existing file of catalogues for birds and animals. These motifs include: the animal chase (figs. IX.33b, 42; X.15; p. 339), birds pecking grapes (also on lintels at Chorazin, Dikke and Kanef, see p. 337 figs. VIII.52i, j; X.27), the bird cage, the peacock with open tail, the peacock rendered *en-face* with spread feathers (fig. X.29) the bird of prey and the eagle, depicted frontally (figs. X. 22, 23). All these motifs occur on both synagogue and church pavements.

f) Sketch books for heraldic motifs, used constantly by Jews for sculpture and mosaic pavements, but also by Christians and pagans. These files possibly had sketches depicting: a wreath flanked by different objects or figures such as eagles and Nikae (figs. VIII.45, 46; X.1), lions flanking a vase, or bulls' heads (figs. X.4, 6, 7, 16; p. 329); rams or sheep flanking amphorae (Beth Sheʾan synagogue B, fig. IX.42), the Torah shrine and menoroth panel (Susiya, Pl. 104), or a plant (Na‘aran, fig. X.17); these were used also in synagogue architectural ornamentation as well as in funerary art. Many of these heraldic motifs also occur on church mosaic floors. For example, churches in the town of Nebo have mosaics with animals facing each other with either a vase or plants between them (Saller and Bagatti 1949: Pls. 14:1; 20; 21:1; 28:1; 30:1; 34:1; 37:3; 39:2; Saller 1941: Pls. 105: 1-2; 109:1, which is the only example of animals flanking a sanctuary in church mosaics).

g) Copy books for mythological themes used not only by pagans, but also by Jews and Christians. Jewish examples include motifs in synagogue architectural ornamentation (Pls. 45, 46 and fig. X.21) and on the mosaic floor in the House of Leontis at Beth Sheʾan (fig. IX.37). Christian examples include the Haditha mosaic floor (Avi-Yonah 1972), and depictions of Orpheus in many paintings, carvings and mosaics including a Jerusalem church floor (Barash 1980: figs. 4-21). The same theme in synagogues occurs on the Gaza mosaic floor: David depicted as Orpheus, and in the Dura Europos synagogue painting (Pls. 66, 67; fig. IX.36).

2) Jewish Pattern Books

It may be confidently assumed that pattern books existed containing uniquely Jewish subjects; these subjects may be divided into the following topics:

a) Codified files (for mosaic pavements) consisting of complete floor designs divisible into smaller units. This feature is characteristic of many of the synagogue pavements: Ḥammath Tiberias, Beth ʾAlpha, Beth Sheʾan A, Jericho, Susiya, Naʿaran, Ḥuseifa and Ḥammath Gader (figs. XI.1-5, 9-13).

b) Files of mosaic pavement panel compositions which have different motifs, such as the Torah shrine panel including menoroth and ritual objects (Ḥammath Tiberias, Beth ʾAlpha, Susiya, Beth Sheʾan A, Naʿaran, Pls. 101-105), the zodiac panel (fig. IX.39-40; p. 305ff.) and panels of inscriptions flanked by animals (Ḥammath Gader, Ḥammath Tiberias, Beth ʾAlpha, Beth Sheʾan B, (fig. XI.14; p. 361).

c) Special sketch books for Jewish motifs and symbols intended to decorate synagogue floors, architecture and other objects, as well as to ornament funerary articles. These sketch books probably contained the menorah, ritual objects, the Ark, the conch and the zodiac. Sometimes a group of these symbols is added to a synagogue pavement which otherwise depicts a fashionable design such as the inhabited scrolls (see Maʿon and Beth Sheʾan synagogue B, figs. IX.41, 42). It may be assumed that particular animals were also included in these sketch books, due to their symbolic connotations, for example, lions and eagles rendered either singly or in heraldic fashion.

d) Sketch books of Biblical scenes, considered by some scholars to have derived from illustrated manuscripts (see p. 288). They probably contained models of Biblical cycles, condensed and conflated into scenes which could be depicted in confined spaces (also Weitzmann 1957: 89-90).

Mosaic remains testify to the frequent use of these Jewish pattern books which would have been used by the Jewish community when deciding upon synagogue ornamentation. The artists themselves, consequently, need not necessarily have been Jewish.

Dauphin (1978: 408) proposes that these sketch books consisted of one sketch of one particular subject, such as one type of bird or animal, per page. These would be typologically arranged in separate files, and each workshop or artist would possess at least one complete set of files.

The best evidence proving the existence of such sketch books is the zodiac panel design (figs. IX.39, 40) which occurs on at least four synagogue mosaic pavements widely separated in space and time (the Ḥammath Tiberias mosaic is dated to the fourth century whereas the Beth ʾAlpha and Naʿaran mosaics are dated to the sixth century). The scheme as well as the content of these four mosaics is identical and is only found in Jewish art (figs. IX,38, Pls. 71-74). Differences among them of style and execution are to be imputed to the variability of the individual artists' skill and style. Exactly the same explanation may be given about the Torah shrine panel (Pls. 101-105). Thus, this uniformity of form and content can only be a result of models being taken from sketch books.

A further justification for the existence of such sketch books is that size of animals or objects is always uniform without any consideration for actual proportion. The inhabited scrolls pavement at Maᶜon, for instance, shows similar-sized birds and elephants; they all are made to fit the medallions, suggesting that any particular artist did not interpret the drawing but simply copied it (fig. IX.41; Pl. 87). (The eight pavements with the inhabited scroll designs, proposed by Avi-Yonah (1981d) to belong to the "School of Gaza," actually prove the existence of pattern books which included this specific design; these pavements, in fact, differ in many stylistic details (see Hachlili 1987), suggesting that various artists executed the same chosen designs.)

An interesting question concerns the identity of those who actually chose the patterns. Some scholars suggest that the artist chose the details of the composition and motifs after a general order had been given (Dauphin 1978: 408-409). On the other hand, it seems more likely that the patron was free to choose whatever he liked from the pattern books and sketch files. The appearance of Jewish symbols and designs in Jewish synagogal and funerary art attest to the involvement of the donors and the community, and perhaps also of the artists, in choosing the layout, composition and motifs, much assisted by the Jewish pattern books. This must have been also true of local workshops which produced chancel screens with Jewish symbols on them for synagogues and with Christian symbols on them for churches (see p. 190 fig. VIII.32).

Jews must have sometimes chosen patterns from general pattern books that served Christians as well. This would explain the similarity of the inhabited scrolls pattern depicted on synagogue pavements as well as on church floors (figs. IX.41-43; Pl. 86). Whenever the Jews wanted to add specific significance to an ornamented floor, however, they would insert Jewish symbols, for instance, at Maᶜon and Beth Sheʾan B (fig. IX.41-42; Pls. 85, 87). These symbols would clearly indicate the difference between Jewish and Christian floors, and would emphasize the function of the building, that it was a synagogue. One can also infer that Jewish houses were decorated according to the taste of the owners, with patterns or motifs chosen from a general pattern book, and with little desire for expressions of Judaism: for example in the House of Leontis at Beth Sheʾan the floor is mainly decorated with a mythological scene, with only a small five-branched menorah inserted into the inscription (Pl. 69). However, synagogues were treated differently: in them, Jewish symbols were of necessity displayed prominently.

CHAPTER SIXTEEN

DATING OF THE SYNAGOGUES

Dating of synagogues is based on material remains and excavation data such as inscriptions, coins, pottery, architecture, and art, as well as on historical considerations. The most reliable evidence for dating of synagogues consists of inscriptions, which supply accurate dates for the construction or restoration of synagogue buildings. However, only three inscriptions have been found in synagogue buildings which provide absolute dates:

1) The Hebrew inscription on the Nabratein lintel (Pl. 108). The synagogue was built 494 years after the destruction of the Temple, that is, in 564 CE (Avigad 1960a; Naveh 1978: 4-6).

2) A Greek dedicatory inscription within a medallion in the pavement of the southernmost aisle of the Gaza synagogue (Pl. 86a) mentions the year 569 of the era of Gaza, that is, 508/9 CE (Avi-Yonah 1966).

3) The reign of the emperor Justinian I (518-527 CE) is mentioned in the Aramaic inscription of the Beth ʾAlpha mosaic floor (fig. XI.14c) (Naveh 1978: 72-73). The same artists executed a room in Beth Sheʾan A synagogue, which is thus dated to the same period (p. 385).

Several other inscriptions have been found which furnish dates by inference: the Beth Sheʾan B small synagogue should be dated to about the mid-sixth century, as its mosaic pavement was probably executed by the same mosaicist who worked in room L of the Beth Sheʾan monastery (see p. 390 Pls. 85, 107), which is dated by inscription to 567-569 CE (Fitzgerald 1939: 1, 9, 16). A Greek inscription from ʾAscalon dating to 604 CE (Lifshitz 1967: no. 70) is known but no synagogue has yet been found. At Dabbura in the Golan, a lintel is carved with an inscription (fig. VIII.46b) mentioning R. Eliezar ha-Qappar, head of a school, a famous Tannaitic sage who lived at the end of the second-early third centuries.

An interesting votive inscription was found at Kasyon (Galilee) during the nineteenth century and was never seen again until June 1984, when it was rediscovered by the author and Z. Maoz (Pl. 109). This inscription, carved on a lintel face whose left part is missing, commemorates a dedication by the Jews of a building in honour of Septimius Severus, thus dated to 197 CE. Kohl and Watzinger (1916: 209) discuss the Kasyon inscription but conclude that Kasyon was a pagan temple. It is difficult to determine the plan of this building, which seems to be atypical of synagogal architecture. (But see Foerster 1972: 103-105). Further excavation is required, however, to determine if the Kasyon building is in fact a synagogue, as well as to discover the missing left part of the newly rediscovered lintel as it probably mentions what type of building the Jews dedicated to Severus (whether synagogue or temple).

Dates given by inscriptions, found in the excavated synagogue buildings therefore, all pertain to the sixth century as it is not yet clear whether the Kasyon inscription belongs to a synagogue, and no synagogue has yet been found at Dabbura.

Coins found in many excavations offer another means of providing dates for the construction, reconstruction and restoration of many synagogues. The Golan synagogues of ʿEn Neshut, Kanef, and Kazrin are dated by coins to the fifth-sixth centuries (Maoz 1980: 24). ʿEn Gedi (Barag *et al.* 1981: 119) and Rimmon synagogues (Kloner 1983b: 67-69) have various levels which are dated by coins. In the Galilean synagogues, coins determine the dating of Gush Ḥalav (Meyers *et al.* 1979: 45; 1981: 75, 77) and Nabratein (rebuilding of synagogue III in the sixth century, Meyers *et al.* 1982: 36). At ʿAmmudim coins and pottery date the synagogue to the late third and early fourth centuries (Levine 1981: 80-81). At Chorazin coins of two groups were found (Meshorer 1973): a) those dated 134-340 CE; and b) those dated 390-early fifth century; thus dating Chorazin to the third-fourth century, with a fifty year gap 340-390 CE. Chorazin is mentioned by Eusebius as being in ruins at the beginning of the fourth century (Yeivin 1973: 157) (See table 2 for dating of each synagogue).

The most spirited debate among scholars concerns the date of the Galilean synagogues, and Capernaum in particular. The Galilean synagogues of Meiron, Gush Ḥalav, Nabratein II, Shemʿa and ʿAmmudim were erected in the late third century. Meiron was abandoned in 360 CE, Shemʿa was destroyed by an earthquake in 419 CE, whereas Gush Ḥalav thrived until the mid-sixth century (Meyers 1981b: 77). Several of the Galilean synagogues, it is asserted, were destroyed by the earthquakes of 306, 363, and 419 (Russel 1980) and were subsequently restored.

The latest finds from Capernaum date the construction of the synagogue to the end of the fourth- early fifth centuries (Corbo 1975: 113-169; Loffreda 1973, 1981). This is based on pottery and coins found in the fill under the pavement of the synagogue (see the discussion of the Capernaum dating in Loffreda 1981; cf. Foerster (1981b) and Avi-Yonah (1981f) who contend that due to architectural, stylistic and historical considerations, Capernaum is to be dated to the second-third centuries (also Chen 1980a).

Architectural, artistic and stylistic considerations offer dating data as well. For example, the main feature of synagogal architecture, the Torah shrine, changed its form during the various periods. The aedicula is the earliest form of Torah shrine but even so persisted until the sixth century in several synagogues. The development of the niche took place in the early fourth century. The apse was a completely new innovation, constructed in synagogues erected during the sixth century (see p. 180). Therefore synagogues including apses (with the exception of the Golan and Galilee synagogues, none of which have apses) must be dated to the sixth century. (The synagogues with apses at Ḥammath Gader III and Maʿoz Ḥayim II may possibly have been built by the late fifth century.)

Ornamentation of the synagogues is also taken into consideration for dating purposes: mosaic floors already appear in the late third century (Ḥammath Tiberias B level I, ʿEn-Gedi I, H. ʿAmmudim, pp. 222-223), even though at that time they only display geometric designs, whereas from the fourth century on, mosaic pavements also portray figurative art (Ḥammath Tiberias B level IIa zodiac, Pl. 71, Marous, fig. VIII.57, pl. 48). Representational art appears in the fourth century in architectural decoration also, thus providing dates for Capernaum, Chorazin and other synagogal figurative sculpture (such as the Nabratein aedicula lintel, and ʿAmmudim synagogue facade lintel, figs. VIII.12, 18). The Biblical scenes depicted on mosaic floors are dated to the fifth century (Gerasa) and the sixth century (Beth ʾAlpha and Naʿaran).

The destruction of the images in the Naaran synagogue is probably to be dated to the late sixth century, due to iconoclasm contemporary with a thematic change to inscriptions, and floral and geometric designs which replaced figurative art in mosaic pavements. The destruction of figurative sculpture at Capernaum is usually explained as being due to Jewish iconoclasts (cf. KW 1916: 202). However, in the Chorazin and other Golan synagogues, the sculpture has survived in complete form. This phenomenon therefore might be explained by the brittleness of limestone sculpture, which is more easily destroyed than the hard basalt reliefs.

Architectural ornamentation of carved lintels, friezes, and architraves is a common feature of the northern part of the Land of Israel, as well as of Syria. The art is local with Oriental elements dominant; even the classical forms are interpreted in a local accent, which makes it difficult to date stylistically: local tradition would have been strong enough to retain a style for several generations of craftsmen and masons. This is proved by the Galilean and Golan synagogues, similar in plan, architectural features and ornamentation style, although dated to periods from the late third until the seventh centuries.

An example of this chronological difficulty is to be found in lintel type I, characteristic of several of the Galilean synagogues such as ʾArbel, Barʿam, Meiron, Gush Ḥalav and Nabratein, figs. VIII.43, 44; p. 206). The similarity of their mouldings, decoration and size should indicate a corresponding date in the late third century for the construction of all these synagogues' facades. However, these lintels continue to decorate the synagogue facades throughout the life of the synagogues—until the fourth century at Meiron and at least until the sixth century at Gush Ḥalav. Thus, the dating of the Nabratein lintel to phase II is arbitrary. The sixth century inscription was added to the lintel in phase III (as suggested by Avigad 1960). Moreover, by the time Nabratein III was rebuilt, as indicated by the inscription, that is in 564 CE, Gush Ḥalav had already been destroyed (551 CE). (The Dikke synagogue side entrance lintel fragment also belongs to type I. This may indicate a fourth century date for the construction of this synagogue, or even later, if an earlier model from the Galilee synagogues was employed in the moulding.)

After considering the data presented and the excavation reports published during the last decade, we may sum up the following (see table 2):

The only synagogue dated by excavation to the late second century is Nabratein I. Synagogues constructed in the late third century include: ꜥAmmudim, Gush Ḥalav, Meiron, Nabratein II, Shemꜥa, Ḥammath Tiberias IIB, Caesarea, ꜥEn-Gedi and Rimmon I (it is possible to include ꜣArbel and Barꜥam here). Some of these synagogues were paved with mosaics.

Synagogues erected in the fourth century include: Capernaum, Chorazin, Marous, Maꜥoz Ḥayim, Reḥov, ꜣEshtemoꜥa and Susiya. Most of these synagogues possessed mosaic floors. Several synagogues were rebuilt and restored: Gush Ḥalav II, Ḥammath Tiberias II A with its mosaic floor and Rimmon II.

Synagogues erected in the fifth century include: probably most of the Golan synagogues (table 2), Beth Sheꜣan A and Gerasa. Restored and reconstructed synagogues include Maꜥoz Ḥayim II, Reḥov II , Caesarea and probably Ḥammath Gader III.

Synagogues constructed during the sixth century include: Beth ꜣAlpha, Beth Sheꜣan B, Maꜥon, Gaza, Jericho and Naꜥaran. These all have elaborately decorated mosaic pavements, and each contains an apse. Contemporarily restored synagogues include Nabratein III, Gush Ḥalav II continues in use, Ḥammath Tiberias III, Maꜥoz Ḥayim III, Reḥov III, Susiya II, Rimmon III and ꜥEn-Gedi III. Most of these synagogues continued into the early seventh century, and most were probably destroyed during the Persian occupation or during the Arab Conquest.

In conclusion, synagogues in the Land of Israel were constructed continuously during the Roman-Byzantine periods. Synagogue construction seems to be most prolific during two periods: during the mid or late third and early fourth centuries when most of the Galilean synagogues were erected; and during the sixth century, when many of the characteristic Byzantine synagogues were built. Each synagogue consequently should be examined separately to determine its date, by analysis of the data revealed by its excavation, and by its artistic style and historical context.

CHAPTER SEVENTEEN

CONCLUSIONS

Jewish art and architecture (as defined in this book) flourished in two distinctive periods: the first is that of the Second Temple, and the second is the period of Late Antiquity. Differences between these two periods are significant, and are primarily political and social. During the Second Temple period the Land of Israel was a Jewish state having a central Temple in Jerusalem. The ruling classes although Hellenized, retained parts of their faith and laws. The art of the period, shows connections with the neighbouring Graeco-Roman culture. At the same time Jewish art withstood foreign influences by evolving strictly aniconic features; it is characterized together with the other arts of the period by highly skilled indigenous stonework, by the predominant Oriental elements of endless patterns, by the element of *horror vacui*, by plasticity of carving and by symmetrical stylization.

Jewish art of the Second Temple period concentrates on extensive architectural projects consisting of large complexes and structures, not only in Jerusalem where the Temple itself was rebuilt, but also throughout the country in major winter and summer palace complexes, in a magnificent harbour and other architectural installations. This art also includes the ornamentation and embellishment of such structures, as well as of funerary structures such as tombs, sarcophagi and ossuaries. The strictly aniconic and non-symbolic art characterizing the Second Temple period is the outcome of Judaism's struggle against paganism and idolatry. By the rigid observance of the prohibition against animate images, the Jews retained their own identity and distinctiveness.

The aniconic and non-symbolic quality of the art of the Second Temple period completely disappears during the period of Late Antiquity. In Late Antiquity, art and architecture are influenced by political and social changes in the Land of Israel, most particularly by the destruction of the Temple and the removal of the centre of Jewish life to the Galilee. The prevailing architectural structure is now the synagogue, which replaces the Temple as the centre of Jewish religious, national and social life. In addition, the decline of paganism and the rise and expansion of Christianity causes a change in the Jewish attitude towards its art; it now expresses its ornamentation and decorative architecture by figurative and symbolic means. With the destruction of the Temple, a need for a concrete visual image becomes strongly felt. Thus, only during this period do the Temple implements take on a symbolic significance in synagogal and funerary art. The art of the period of Late Antiquity is an expression of Jewish communal and local life, in contrast to the national spirit of the Second Temple period art.

A continuation and connection may be traced between the arts of the two different periods, the Second Temple period and that of Late Antiquity:

1) The traditon of relief and sculptured architecture continues in Late Antiquity and in a limited manner follows the decorative style of Second Temple period art.

2) There is a continuation of the tradition of floral and geometric motifs which characterize Second Temple period art, especially the rosette which is its most prominent motif. This may have been due to traditional pattern books which were kept and handed down from generation to generation.

3) Stylistic tendencies such as symmetrical stylization, tripartite division of architectural ornamentation, and Oriental elements are basic features of the art of both periods.

4) Vestiges of the Temple, its architecture, ritual and ceremony can be detected in Jewish art of Late Antiquity: symbolic art uses the menorah and the ritual utensils as reminders of the Temple vessels and ceremonies; as well as the priestly course lists on stone slabs found in several synagogues.

5) Distinguishing features of Jewish art such as the unidentical symmetry and unfinished funerary art can be seen already in the art of the Second Temple period but are more prevalent in the Jewish art of Late Antiquity.

Thus spiritual and religious tendencies expressed in stylistic features and motifs in the art of the Second Temple period continue into the art of the Jews in Late Antiquity.

An important innovation of Jewish art in Late Antiquity consists of the construction of the synagogue and its art and architecture. The synagogue plan was determined by the prominent place of the Torah shrine on the Jerusalem-oriented wall which in turn established the arrangement of the interior of the synagogue and its orientation. Synagogue ornamentation was determined by the local community but surrounding cultural influences did have a strong attraction: for instance, the facade decoration of Galilean and Golan synagogues is influenced by the style and execution of the neighbouring Syrian-Hauran architecture. By comparison, the mosaic pavement of the synagogue is an expression of an established art tradition which depicts its nave ornamentation in a programmed style, using certain iconographical themes for the panels. These characteristic features of synagogue architecture and decoration are distinctive in Jewish art of Late Antiquity and helped Judaism in maintaining its identity in a world of Christian expansion and the decline of paganism.

Jewish art contains a symbolic vocabulary consisting of the menorah, the ritual objects (the shofar, incense shovel, ethrog and lulav), the Ark of the Scrolls and the conch. Acquiring their symbolic significance and prominence in the arts only after the destruction of the Temple, they thus preserve its memory by expressing a remembrance of the Temple and its ceremonies. Other images were borrowed from Jewish religious life and tradition, such as Biblical scenes, and the zodiac which interpreted the yearly calendar by a depiction of the four seasons, the twelve months, day and night, thus turning it into an elaborate, visual and expressive scheme. The ornamentation of synagogue floors is expressed in a scheme of panels firmly related to the iconography portrayed in them. It is an original, organized scheme, which determined each panel's allotted place and iconographical theme: for example, the Torah shrine and menoroth motif is depicted on the panel closest to the actual Torah shrine; while carpets of vine trellis medallions had the addition of Jewish symbols.

Jewish society from the third century on allowed representational art which portrayed figurative and symbolic themes. Moreover, even the Hand of God was considered a fit subject to be figuratively represented; it was placed within the Sacrifice of Isaac pavement, at Beth ʾAlpha, which was continually being trodden upon. This liberal attitude lasted only until the second half of the sixth century. With increased anti-Jewish legislation, aniconic art was resumed, and iconoclastic deeds are encountered on the Naᶜaran mosaic pavement, where the images are eradicated. The later synagogues of Jericho and ᶜEn-Gedi portray non-figurative, purely decorative designs. This is in accordance with the contrasting attitudes to art displayed throughout Late Antiquity by the Jews and Christians in the Land of Israel. Whenever churches would display aniconic art, the Jews would depict iconography on their synagogue pavements. Subsequently, in the later sixth century, when churches began to display images on their floors, the Jews returned to the prohibition against human and animal images in their art.

Stylistically the tendencies displayed by Jewish art can be seen to be part of an Oriental art of the period and the area, similar to a certain extent to other neighbouring arts, such as Nabatean and Palmyrene art. Reliefs and sculpture did not constitute an art by themselves and their primary function was solely as architectural decoration, within which they formed a whole together with other architectural elements. Figurative representation appears in compositions of scenes where the figures bear no relation to each other and where they are sometimes represented side by side (see for instance Beth ʾAlpha, the Sacrifice of Isaac). Static groups are rendered lacking any dramatic tension. The mythological representations are not

depicted in a narrative story, but rather in a series of separate renditions showing
no connection between them (see the House of Leontis at Beth She'an). The style
of figurative rendition is usually in an hierarchic and impersonal manner. This impression is frequently emphasized by the unusually large size of the figures' eyes.
Representations of humans lack any personal features; the posture is static and two-
dimensional, and the whole figure is schematically rendered.

Jewish art is an example of an art lacking figurative tradition, a weakly-developed
visual sense, and an environment with strong external cultural influences. It is based
on the ability and skill with which the artists related to the needs and requirements
of their clientele whose prerequisites were based mainly on decorative demands.

Themes and designs in ancient art are often derived from copy books of patterns,
some of which probably served both synagogues and churches, and some of which
presumably were traditional pattern books passed on from generation to generation.
There were, very possibly, special pattern books for the Jewish clientele, including
unique designs and symbols. These designs most probably included among them the
unidentical symmetric pattern.

The assumption is postulated here that the selection of symbols and subjects for
synagogue ornamentation was deliberately limited. They were chosen by the Jewish
community and by its donors, who made their choice from available pattern books.
Certain original aspects of ancient Jewish art which continually occur could be explained as being the result of the specific needs of the Jewish community, of its traditions, and of artists' innovations.

Jewish art was essentially a decorative art with both ornamental and iconographic
functions. It was an art which consisted of an indigenous local tradition, with at the
same time appropriations from the surrounding Graeco-Roman and Christian
cultures; it possessed an Oriental style, and was characterized by the use of specific
symbols, motifs and iconography. Despite those elements borrowed from
neighbouring cultures, however, Jewish art retained within it the fundamental
beliefs, customs and traditions of the Jewish people.

BIBLIOGRAPHY

Alföldi-Rosenbaum, E.
1975   A Nilotic Scene on Justianic Floor Mosaics in Cyrenaican churches. *La Mosaïque Greco-Romaine* II: 149-153. Paris.

Avigad, N.
1950-51   The Rock-carved Facades of the Jerusalem Necropolis. *IEJ* 1:96-109.
1954a   Remains of Ancient Jewish Art in the Galilee. *EI* 7: 18-23 (Hebrew).
1954b   *Ancient Monuments in the Kidron Valley*. Jerusalem (Hebrew).
1956   The Necropolis. *Sepher Yerushalayim* (ed. M. Avi-Yonah): 320-335, (Hebrew).
1960a   A Dated Lintel-inscription from the Ancient Synagogue of Nabratein. *Bulletin Rabinowitz* III: 49-56. Jerusalem.
1960b   An Aramaic Inscription from the Synagogue at Umm el-ʿAmed in Galilee. *Bulletin Rabinowitz* III: 62-64. Jerusalem.
1962   The mosaic pavement of the Beth ʾAlpha synagogue and its place in the history of Jewish Art. *Beth Sheʾan Valley*: 63-70 (the 17th Archaeology Convention). (Hebrew).
1967   On the Form of Ancient Synagogues in Galilee. *All the Land of Naphtali*: 91-100. Jerusalem (Hebrew).
1975   The Architecture of Jerusalem in the Second Temple Period. *Jerusalem Revealed.* (ed. Y. Yadin):14-20.
1976   *Beth Sheʿarim III*: Catacombs 12-23. Jerusalem.
1981   The Galilean Synagogue and its predecessors. *ASR*: 42-44.
1983   *Discovering Jerusalem*. Jerusalem.

Avigad, N. *et al.*
1961   The Expedition to the Judean Desert, 1960. *IEJ* 11: 3-72.
1962   The Expedition to the Judean Desert, 1961. *IEJ* 12: 167-262.

Avi-Yonah, M.
1934   A Sixth-Century Synagogue at Isfiya. *QDAP* 3: 118-131.
1956   The Second Temple. *The Book of Jerusalem* I: 392-418. Jerusalem (Hebrew).
1957   Places of Worship in the Roman and Byzantine Periods. *Antiquity and Survival* 3: 262-272. The Hague.
1960a   *Israeli Mosaics*: 15-24. Unesco.
1960b   The Mosaic Pavement of Maʿon (Nirim). *Bulletin Rabinowitz* III: 25-35.
1961a   Synagogue Architecture in the Classical Period. *Jewish Art*: 155-190. (ed. C. Roth).
1961b   *Oriental Art in Roman Palestine*. Rome.
1964   The Caesarea Inscription of the Twenty-Four Priestly Courses. *The Teacher's Yoke: Studies in Memory of Henry Trantham*: 46-57. Texas.
1966   An Ancient Synagogue at Gaza. *BIES* 30: 221-223 (Hebrew).
1968   The Facade of Herod's Temple, An Attempted Reconstruction. *Religions in Antiquity, Essays in Memory of E.R. Goodenough*: 327-334. (ed. J. Neusner). Leiden.
1972   The Haditha Mosaic Pavement. *IEJ* 22: 118-122.
1973   Goodenough's Evaluation of the Dura Paintings: A Critique. *The Dura-Europos Synagogue: A Re-evaluation (1932-1972)*: 117-135. (ed. J. Gutmann). Montana.
1975   *Ancient Mosaics*. London.
1981a   Oriental Elements in the Art of Palestine in the Roman and Byzantine Periods. *Art in Ancient Palestine*. Selected Studies: 1-117. Jerusalem.

1981b   Mosaic Pavements in Palestine. *Art in Ancient Palestine*. Selected Studies: 283-382.
             Jerusalem.
1981c   La Mosaïque Juive dans ses relations avec la mosaïque classique. *Art in Ancient
             Palestine*. Selected Studies: 383-388. Jerusalem.
1981d   Une Ecole de mosaique a Gaza au sixieme siecle. *Art in Ancient Palestine*. Selected
             Studies: 389-395. Jerusalem.
1981e   Le Symbolisme du Zodiaque dans l'art Jude-Byzantine. *Art in Ancient Palestine*.
             Selected Studies: 396-397. Jerusalem.
1981f   Notes on Recent Excavations at Capernaum. *ASR*:60-62.
1981g   The Mosaics of Mopsuestia - Church or Synagogue? *ASR*:186-190.
1981h   Ancient Synagogues. *Art in Ancient Palestine*: 271-281.

Avi-Yonah, M., Avigad, N., Aharoni, Y., Dunayevski, I. and Gutman, S.
1957   Masada, Survey and Excavations, 1955-1956. *IEJ* 7.

Baccache, E. and Tchalenko. G.
1979-1980   *Eglises de Village de La Syrie du Nord*. Text and Plates.

Bahat, D.
1973   A Synagogue Chancel-Screen from Tel Rehob. *IEJ* 23: 181-183.
1981a   A Synagogue at Beth-She'an. *ASR*: 82-85.
1981b   David's Tower and its name in Second Temple Times. *EI* 15: 396-400 (Hebrew).

Bahat, D., and Broshi, M.
1975   Excavations in the Armenian Garden. *Jerusalem Revealed*: 55-56. (ed. Y. Yadin).
             Jerusalem.

Balty, J.
1981   La Mosaïque antique au Proche-Orient. *Aufsteig und Niedergang der Romischen Welt* II:
             12.2: 347-429. Berlin. New-York.

Bar-Adon, P.
1977   Another Settlement of the Judean Desert Sect at ʿEn el-Ghuweir on the Dead Sea.
             BASOR 227: 1-25.

Barag, D.
1977   Maʿon. *Encyclopedia of Archaeological Excavations in the Holy Land*, vol. III: 333-334.
             Jerusalem.

Barag, D., Porat, Y., and Netzer, E.
1981   The Synagogue at ʿEn-Gedi. *ASR*: 116-119.

Baramki, D.C. and Avi-Yonah, M.
1936   An Early Byzantine Synagogue near Tell es Sultan. *QDAP* 6: 73-77.

Barash, M.
1980   The David Mosaic of Gaza. *Assaph, Studies in Art History I : 1-42*. Tel Aviv University.

Ben-Dov, M.
1982   *The Dig at the Temple Mount*. Jerusalem (Hebrew).
1983   *Jerusalem's Fortifications*. Jerusalem (Hebrew).

Bennet, C.
1965   Tombs of the Roman Period, in Kenyon K. *Excavation at Jericho* II. London.

Benoit, P.
1975   The Archaeological Reconstruction of the Antonia Fortress. *Jerusalem Revealed*: 87-89.
             (ed. Y. Yadin). Jerusalem.

Benoit , P. *et al*
1961   *Les Grottes de Murabbʿat*. Discoveries in the Judaean Desert 2. Oxford.

Braslavi, J.
1967   Symbols and Mythological Figures in the Early Synagogues in Galilee. *All the Land
             of Naphtali*: 106-129. Jerusalem (Hebrew).

Bratschkova, M.
    1938   Die Muschel in der antiken Kunst. *Bulletin de l'Institut Archaeologique Bulgare* 11: 1-131.
Broshi, M.
    1975   Excavation in the House of Caiaphas, Mount Zion. *Jerusalem Revealed*: 57-70 (ed. Y.
                    Yadin). Jerusalem.
    1981   The Cities of Eretz-Israel in the Herodian Period. *Qadmoniot* 14: 70-79 (Hebrew).
Brown, D.F.
    1942   The Arcuated Lintel and Its Symbolic Interpretation. *AJA* 44: 391-398.
Budde, L.
    1969   *Antike Mosaiken in Kilikien* I. Recklinghausen.
Bull, R.J.
    1982   Caesarea Maritima — The Search for Herod's City. *BAR* 8: 24-40.
Butler, H.C.
    1903   *Architecture and Other Arts*. New York.
    1915-1919   *Ancient Architecture in Syria* V, VI, VII. Leiden.
    1923   Nabatean Temple Plans and Plans of Syrian Churches. *Studien Zur Kunst Des Ostens*:
                    9-18. Vienna.
    1929   *Early Churches in Syria*. Princeton.
Chiat, M.J.
    1979   *A Corpus of Synagogue Art and Architecture in Roman and Byzantine Palestine* I-IV. Thesis.
                    University Microfilm International.
    1981   First-century Synagogue Architecture: Methodological Problems. *Ancient Synagogues,
                    the State of Research*. ed. J. Gutmann. Ann Arbor.
Chen, D.
    1978   The Design of the Ancient Synagogues in Galilee I. *Liber Annuus* 28: 193-202.
    1980a   The Design of the Ancient Synagogues in Galilee II. *Liber Annuus* 30: 255-258.
    1980b   The Design of the Ancient Synagogues in Judea: Masada and Herodium. *BASOR*
                    239: 37-40.
Cohen, R.
    1980   The Marvelous Mosaics of Kissufim. *BAR* 6: 16-23.
Corbo. V.
    1963   L'Herodion Di Gebal Fureidis. *Liber Annuus* 13: 219-277.
    1975   *Cafarnao* I. Jerusalem.
    1976   La Citta romana di Magdala. *Studia Hierosolymitana* 1: 365-368.
    1979   Macheronte, La Reggia Fortezza Erodiana. *Liber Annuus* 29:315-326.
    1982   Resti della Sinagoga del Primo Secolo a Cafarnao. *Studia Hierosolymitana* 3: 313-357.
Cross, F.M.
    1961   *The Ancient Library of Qumran*. New York.
Crowfoot, J.A., Kenyon, K.M. and Sukenik, E.L.
    1942   *The Buildings at Samaria*. London.
Damati, E.
    1982   The Palace of Ḥilkiya. *Qadmoniot* 15: 117-121 (Hebrew).
Dar, S.
    1984   Excavations in the Synagogue of Kh. Summaqa. *Qadmoniot* 17: 72-75 (Hebrew).
Dauphin, C.M.
    1974   *"Inhabited Scrolls" from the 4 - 7 Centuries A.D. in Asia Minor and the Eastern Provinces of
                    the Byzantine Empire*. Thesis. University of Edinburgh (unpublished).
    1976a   A New Method of Studying Early Byzantine Mosaic Pavement, with Special
                    Reference to the Levant. *Levant* 8: 113-149.
    1976b   Note on the Method of Laying Early Byzantine Mosaics. *Levant* 8: 155-158.
    1978   Byzantine Pattern Books and "Inhabited Scroll" Mosaics. *Art History* 4: 401-423.

Davies, P.R.
    1982   *Qumran*. Guildford, Surrey.
Demsky, A.
    1985   The Trumpeter's Inscription from the Temple Mount. *EI* 18 (Avigad Volume): 40-42
                (Hebrew).
De Vaux, R.
    1973   *Archaeology and the Dead Sea Scrolls*. London.
Dimant, D.
    1984   Qumran Sectarian Literature in *Jewish Writing of the Second Temple Period*, vol II (ed.
                M. E. Stone). Assen.
Dothan, M.
    1981   The Synagogue at Ḥammath-Tiberias. *ASR*: 63-69.
    1983   *Ḥammath-Tiberias*. Jerusalem.
Dunayevski, I.
    1960   Reconstruction (II) Maʿon. *Bulletin Rabinowitz* III: 22-23.
Ehrenstein, T.
    1923   *Das Alte Testament im Bilde*. Vienna.
Figueras, P.
    1983   *Decorated Jewish Ossuaries*. Leiden.
Finney, P.C.
    1977-78   Orpheus-David: A connection in Iconography between Greco-Roman Judaism and
                Early Christianity? *Journal of Jewish Art* 3-5: 6-15.
Fischer, M.
    1984   The Corinthian Capitals of the Capernaum Synagogue - A Late Roman Architectural
                Feature in Eretz-Israel. *EI* 17: 305-311 (Hebrew).
Fitzgerald, G.M.
    1939   *A Sixth Century Monastery at Beth-Shan*. Philadelphia.
Fitzmyer, J.A.
    1975   *The Dead Sea Scrolls. Major Publications and Tools for Study*. Missoula.
Foerster, G.
    1972   *Galilean Synagogues and their Relation to Hellenistic and Roman Art and Architecture*. Thesis.
                Hebrew University, Jerusalem (Hebrew, unpublished).
    1981a   The Synagogue at Masada and Herodium. *ASR*: 24-29.
    1981b   Notes on Recent Excavations at Capernaum. *ASR*: 57-59.
    1983a   H. Shura Synagogue. *Hadashot Archaeologiot*: 7-9 (Hebrew).
    1983b   Ḥammath Gader Synagogue. *Hadashot Archaeologiot*: 11-12 (Hebrew).
Foss, C.
    1976   *Byzantine and Turkish Sardis*. Cambridge.
Frey, J.B.
    1952   *Corpus Inscriptionum Judaicarum* II. Rome.
Frova, A. *et al.*
    1965   *Scavi di Caesarea Maritima*. Milan.
Gafni, Y.
    1981   Reinterment in the Land of Israel: Notes on the Origin and Development of the
                Custom. *The Jerusalem Cathedra* 1: 96-104.
Galling, K.
    1956   Erwagungen zur antiken Synagogue. *ZDPV* 72: 163-178.
Geva, H.
    1983   Excavations in the Jerusalem Citadel, 1979-1982. *IEJ* 33: 58-61.
Gichon, M.
    1978   Roman Bath-Houses in Eretz-Israel. *Qadmoniot* 11: 37-53 (Hebrew).

Glueck, N.
    1965   *Deities and Dolphins.* New York.
Golb, N.
    1980   The Problem of Origin and Identification of the Dead Sea Scrolls. *Proceedings of the American Philosophical Society* 124: 1-24.
Goldman, B.
    1966   *The Sacred Portal*: A Primary Symbol in Ancient Judaic Art. Detroit.
Goodenough, E.
    1953-1968 *Jewish Symbols in the Greco-Roman Period* I-XIII, New-York.
Grabar, A.
    1960   Recherches sur les sources juives de l'art Paleo-chretien. *Cahiers Archeologiques* XI: 41-71.
    1962   *Ibid* XII: 115-152.
    1964   *Ibid* XIV: 49-57.
    1966   Un Theme de l'iconographie chretienne: l'oiseau dans la cage. *Cahiers Archeologiques* XVI: 9-16.
    1967   *The Beginning of Christian Art.* New-York.
    1968   *Christian Iconography*, *A Study of its Origins.* New York.
Gutman, S.
    1981   The Synagogue at Gamla. ASR: 30-34.
Gutman, S, *et al.*
    1981   Excavation in the Synagogue at Ḥorvat Susiya. *ASR*: 123-128.
Gutmann, J.
    1971a   The History of the Ark. *ZAW* 83: 22-30.
    1971b,   ed. *No Graven Images*: *Studies in Art and the Hebrew Bible.* New York.
    1973,   ed. *The Dura-Europos Synagogue*: *A Re-evaluation* (1932-1942). Montana.
    1975,   ed. *The Synagogue*: *Studies in Origins, Archaeology and Architecture.* New York.
    1981,   ed. *Ancient Synagogues*: *The State of Research.* Ann Arbor.
    1984   The Sacrifice of Isaac: Variations on a Theme in Early Jewish and Christian Art. *Festschrift für Josef Fink.* (Köln-Vien): 115-122.
Hachlili, R.
    1971   *Sacred Architecture and Decoration in the Hellenistic-Roman East.* Thesis. Hebrew University, Jerusalem (Hebrew, unpublished).
    1976   The Niche and the Ark in Ancient Synagogues. *BASOR* 223: 43-53.
    1977   The Zodiac in Ancient Jewish Art: Representation and Significance. *BASOR* 228: 61-77.
    1978   A Jerusalem Family in Jericho. *BASOR* 230: 45-56.
    1979   The Goliath Family in Jericho, Funerary Inscriptions from a First Century Monumental Tomb. *BASOR* 235: 31-66.
    1980a   A Second Temple Period Necropolis in Jericho. *BA* 43: 235-240.
    1980b   The Conch Motif in Ancient Jewish Art. *Assaph. studies in Art History* I : 57-65 .Tel Aviv University.
    1981   The *Nefesh*: The Jericho Column Pyramid. *PEQ* 113: 33-38.
    1984a   Was the Abecedarium ''magical'' already in the First century C.E.? *Cathedra* 31 : 27-30 (Hebrew).
    1984b   Names and Nicknames of Jews in Second Temple Times. *EI* 17 (Brawer volume): 188-211. (Hebrew).
    1985   A Jewish Funerary Wall Painting of the First Century C.E. *PEQ* 117: 112-127.
    1987   On the Gaza School of Mosaicists. *EI* 19 (Avi-Yonah volume) (Hebrew;to be published).

Hachlili, R., and Killebrew, A.
    1983a   Jewish Funerary Customs during the Second Temple Period in Light of the Excava-
                tions at the Jericho Necropolis. *PEQ* 115: 109-139.
    1983b   Was the Coin-on-Eye custom a Jewish Burial Practice in the Second Temple Period?
                BA 46: 147-153.
Hachlili, R., and Merhav, R.
    1985   The Menorah in the First and Second Temple Times in the Light of the Sources and
                Archaeology. *EI* 18 (Avigad Volume): 256-267. (Hebrew).
Hachlili, R., and Smith, P.
    1979   The Geneology of the Goliath Family. *BASOR* 235: 67-73.
Haran, M.
    1959   The Ark and the Cherubim; Their Symbolic Significance in Biblical Ritual. *IEJ* 9:
                30-38, 89-94.
    1963   The Disappearance of the Ark. *IEJ* 13: 46-58.
Hestrin, R.
    1960   A New Aramaic Inscription from Alma. *Bulletin Rabinowitz* III: 65-67.
Hiram A.
    1962   Die Entwicklung der Antiken Synagogen und Altchrislichen Kirchenbauten im
                Heiligen Lande. *Weiner Jahrbuch für Kunstgeschichte* XIX : 7-63.
Hohlfelder, R.L.
    1982   Caesarea Beneath the Sea. *BAR* 8: 42-47.
Huttenmeister, F.
    1982   The Holy Ark and the Development of Ancient Synagogues. *Proceedings of the Eighth
                World Congress of Jewish Studies*: 1-7 (Hebrew).
Huttenmeister, F. and Reeg, G.
    1977   *Die Antiken Synagogen in Israel.* Wiesbaden.
Ilan, Z.
    1980   Jewish Menorot from the Golan. *Qadmoniot* 51-52; 117-119. (Hebrew)
Ilan, Z. and Damati, E.
    1984-5   Marous - An Ancient Jewish Fortified Village in Upper Galilee. *Israel Land and Nature*
                10: 61-69.
    1985   The Mosaic from the Synagogue at Ancient Meroth. *The Israel Museum Journal* IV :
                51-56.
Jeremias, J.
    1969   *Jerusalem in the Time of Jesus.* London.
Kelso, J.L. and Baramki, D.C.
    1955   The Excavation of New Testament Jericho. *AASOR* 29-30: 1-49.
Kitzinger, E.
    1951   Studies on Late Antique and Early Byzantine Floor Mosaics. *Dumbarton Oaks* 6: 81ff.
    1965a   Stylistic Developments in Pavements. Mosaics in the Greek East from Constantine
                to Justinian. *La Mosaïque Greco-Romaine* I: 341-351. Paris.
    1965b   *Israeli Mosaics of the Byzantine Period.* New York.
    1976   *The Art of Byzantion and the Medieval West.* London.
    1977   *Byzantine Art in the Making.* London.
Kloner, A.
    1974   A Lintel with a Menorah fron Judean Shephela. *IEJ* 24: 197-200.
    1980a   *The Necropolis of Jerusalem in the Second Temple Period.* Thesis. Hebrew University (un-
                published, Hebrew).
    1980b   Hurvat Rimmon, 1979. *IEJ* 30: 226-228.

1980c   A Burial Cave of the Second Temple Period at Givat HaMivtar, Jerusalem. *Jerusalem in the Second Temple Period* (A. Shalit memorial volume): 191-224. (eds. A. Oppenheimer, U. Rappaport, M. Stern). (Hebrew).

1981   Ancient Synagogues in Israel: An Archaeological Survey. *ASR*: 11-18.

1983a   The Subterranean Hideaways of the Judean Foothills and the Bar Kokhba Revolt. *The Jerusalem Cathedra* 3: 114-135.

1983b   The Synagogue of Horvat Rimon. *Qadmoniot* 16: 65-71. (Hebrew).

Kochavi, M.

1981   The History and Archaeology of ʾAphek-ʾAntipatris. *BA* 44: 75-86.

Kohl, H., and Watzinger, C.

1916   *Antike Synagogen in Galilaea*: 107-111. Leipzig.

Kon, M.

1947   *The Tombs of the Kings.* Tel Aviv (Hebrew).

Kraeling, C.H., ed.

1938   *Gerasa, City of the Decapolis.* New Haven. Conn.

1979   *The Excavation at Dura-Europos: The Synagogue*, VIII, Ktav Publishing House. N.Y.

Krauss, S.

1922   *Synagogale Altertümer.* Berlin - Vien.

Lavin, I.

1963   The Hunting Mosaics of Antioch and their Sources. *Dumbarton Oaks* 17: 179-287.

Leon, H.J.

1949   Symbolic Representations in the Jewish Catacombs of Rome. *JAOS* 69: 87-90.

1960   *The Jews of Ancient Rome.* Rome.

Leveen, J.

1944   *The Hebrew Bible in Art.* London.

Levi, D.

1947   *Antioch Mosaic Pavements* I, II. London. New York.

Levi, S.

1960   The Ancient Synagogue at Maꜥon (Nirim). *Bulletin Rabinowitz III*: 6-13.

Levine, L.I.

1975a   *Caesarea under Roman Rule.* Leiden.

1975b   *Roman Caesarea. (Qedem* 2) Jerusalem.

1981a   Excavations at Hurvat ha-ꜥAmmudim. *ASR*: 78-81.

1981b   The Inscription in the ꜥEn-Gedi Synagogue. *ASR*: 140-145.

1982   Excavations at the Synagogue of Horvat ꜥAmmudim. *IEJ* 32: 1-12.

Levine, L.I., ed.

1981   *Ancient Synagogues Revealed.* Jerusalem.

Levine, L.I. and Netzer, E.

1978   New Light on Caesarea. *Qadmoniot* 11: 70-75. (Hebrew).

Lifshitz, B.

1967   *Donateurs et fondateurs dans les Synagogues Juives (Cahiers de la Revue Biblique* 7). Paris.

Loffreda, S.

1973   The Late Chronology of the Synagogue of Capernaum. *IEJ* 23: 37-42.

1981   The Late Chronology of the Syngogue of Capernaum. *ASR*: 52-56.

Luria, B.

1973   The Town of the Priests in the Second Temple Period. *HUCA* 44: 1-18 (Hebrew).

Lyttelton, M.

1974   *Baroque Architecture in Classical Antiquity.* London.

Maoz, Z.

1972   *Torah Shrine in Ancient Synagogues: Art and Reality.* (unpublished manuscript, Hebrew).

1980   *The Jewish Settlements and Synagogues in the Golan.* The Society for the Protection of Nature, Kazrin (Hebrew).

1981a   The Synagogue of Gamla and the Typology of the Second Temple Synagogue. *ASR*: 35-41.

1981b   The Art and Architecture of the Synagogue of the Golan. *ASR*: 98-115.

Maoz, Z., Killebrew, A., and Hachlili, R.

1987   *Excavation at Kazrin Synagogue* (to be published).

Mazar, A.

1975   The Aqueducts of Jerusalem. *Jerusalem Revealed*: 79-84. (ed. Y. Yadin). Jerusalem.

Mazar, B.

1973   *Beth She'arim* I. Jerusalem.

1975a   The Archaeological Excavations near the Temple Mount. *Jerusalem Revealed*: 25-40. (ed. Y. Yadin). Jerusalem.

1975b   *The Mountain of the Lord - Excavating in Jerusalem.* New York.

1978   Herodian Jerusalem in the Light of the Excavation South and South-West of the Temple Mount. *IEJ* 28: 230-237.

Mayer, L.A., and Reifenberg, A.

1936   The Jewish Buildings of Nawe. *BJPES* 4: 1-8 (Hebrew).

Meshorer, Y.

1973   Coins from the Excavations at Khorazin. *EI* 11: 158-162. (Hebrew)

1982   *Ancient Jewish Coinage*, I, II. New York.

Meyers, C.L.

1976   *The Tabernacle Menorah: a Synthetic Study of a Symbol from the Biblical Cult.* AASOR Dissertation Series 2.

Meyers, E.M.

1971   *Jewish Ossuaries: Reburial and Rebirth.* Rome.

1980   Ancient Synagogues in Galilee: Their Religious and Cultural Setting. *BA* 43: 97-108.

1981a   The Synagogue at Horvat Shema. *ASR*: 71-74.

1981b   Excavations at Gush Halav in the Upper Galilee. *ASR*: 75-77.

Meyers, E.M., Kraabel, T.A., and Strange, J.

1976   *Ancient Synagogue Excavations at Khirbet Shema', Upper Galilee, Israel, 1970-1972.* Durham.

Meyers, E.M., Meyers, C.L., and Strange, J.

1978   Meiron 1974-1975. Excavations at Meiron in Upper Galilee 1974, 1975. *AASOR* Preliminary Reports. (ed. D.N. Freedman).

Meyers, E.M., Meyers, C.L., Strange, J.F., and Hanson, R.S.

1979   Preliminary Report on the 1977-8 Seasons at Gush Halav (el-Jish). *BASOR* 233: 33-58.

Meyers, E.M., and Meyers, C.L.

1981   Finders of a Real Lost Ark. *BAR*: 24-39.

1982   The Ark in Art: A Ceramic Rendering of the Torah Shrine from Nabratein. *EI* 16: 176*-185*.

Meyers, E.M., Meyers, C.L., and Strange, J.F.

1981a   The Ark of Nabratein - A First Glance. *BA* 44: 237-243.

1981b   Preliminary Report on the 1980 Excavations at en-Nabratein, Israel. *BASOR* 244: 1-25.

1981c   *Excavations at Ancient Meiron, Upper Galilee, Israel.* 1971-72, 1974-1975. Cambridge MA. AASOR.

1982   Second Preliminary Report on the 1981 Excavations at en-Nabratein, Israel. *BASOR* 246: 35-54.

Narkiss, M

1935   The Snuff-Shovel as a Jewish Symbol. *JPOS* 15: 14-28.

Naveh, J.
1973   An Aramaic Tomb Inscription Written in Paleo-Hebrew Script. *IEJ* 23: 82-91.
1978   *On Stone and Mosaic: The Aramaic and Hebrew Inscriptions from Ancient Synagogues.* Jerusalem (Hebrew).

Negev, A.
1967   The Chronology of the Seven-Branched Menorah. *EI* 8: 193-210 (Hebrew).
1975   Caesarea. *EAE* I: 279-285.

Netzer, E.
1975a   The Hasmonean and Herodian Winter Palaces at Jericho. IEJ 25: 89-100.
1975b   Cypros. *Qadmoniot* 8: 54-61 (Hebrew).
1977   The Winter Palaces of the Judean Kings at Jericho at the End of the Second Temple Period. *BASOR* 228: 1-13.
1980a   The Triclinia of Herod as the Prototype of the Galilean Synagogue Plan. *Jerusalem in the Second Temple Period*: 108-118. (eds. A. Oppenheimer, A. Rappaport, and M. Stern) (Hebrew).
1980b   The Hippodrome that Herod Built at Jericho. *Qadmoniot* 13: 104-107 (Hebrew).
1981a   *Greater Herodium, Qedem* 13. Jerusalem.
1981b   Herod's Building Projects: State Necessity or Personal Need? A Symposium. *The Jerusalem Cathedra* 1: 48-80. Jerusalem.
1981c   The Herodian Triclinia - A Prototype for the "Galilean-Type" Synagogue. *ASR*: 49-51.
1982a   Ancient Ritual Baths (*Miqvaot*) in Jericho. *The Jerusalem Cathedra* 1: 106-111.
1982b   Recent Discoveries in the Winter Palaces of the Second Temple Period at Jericho. *Qadmoniot* 15: 22-29 (Hebrew).
1983   The winter Palaces and the King's estate in Jericho. *Jericho (Kardom Series)*: 95-112 (Hebrew).

Netzer, E. and Ben-Arieh, S.
1983   Remains of an Opus Reticulatum Building in Jerusalem. *IEJ* 33: 163-175.

Neusner, J.
1975a   Notes on Goodenough's Jewish symbols I - VII. *Early Rabbinic Judaism* (Leiden): 152-173.
1975b   Jewish Use of Pagan Symbols after 70 in *Early Rabbinic Judaism* (Leiden): 174-187.
1981   The Symbolism of Ancient Judaism: The Evidence of the Synagogues. *Ancient Synagogues. The State of Research.* (ed. J. Gutmann).

Nock, A. D.
1955   Goodenough, E. R., Jewish Symbols in the Greco-Roman Period, Vols. 1-8. *Gnomon* 27: 558-572.
1957   *Ibid.* 29: 524-533.
1960   *Ibid.* 32: 728-736.

Orfali, G.
1922   *Capernaum et ses Ruins.* Paris.

Ovadia, A.
1969   Excavations in the Area of the Ancient Synagogue at Gaza. (Preliminary Report). *IEJ* 19: 193-198.
1981   The Synagogue at Gaza. *ASR*: 129-131.

Pinkerfeld, J.
1980   David's Tomb. *Bulletin Rabinowitz* III: 41-43.

Pritchard, J.B., (ed.)
1950   *Ancient Near Eastern Texts relating to the Old Testament.* Princeton.

Raban, A., and Hohlfelder,
1981   The Ancient Harbors of Caesarea Maritima. *Archaeology* 34: 56-60.

Rahmani, L.Y.
   1959   Transformation of an Ornament. *Atiqot* 2 (English series): 188-189.
   1960   The Maꞌon Synagogue - The Small Finds. *Bulletin Rabinowitz III*: 14-18.
   1961   Jewish Rock-Cut Tombs in Jerusalem. *Atiqot* 3: 93-120.
   1967   Jason's Tomb. *IEJ* 17: 61-100.
   1968   Jerusalem Tomb Monuments on Jewish Ossuaries. *IEJ* 18: 220-225.
   1974   A Table-Top of the Late Second Temple Period. *Atiqot* 7: 65-68 (Hebrew).
   1977   *The Decoration of Jewish ossuaries as Representation of Jerusalem Tombs.* Thesis, Hebrew University Jerusalem. (unpublished, Hebrew).
   1980   Depictions of Menoroth on Ossuaries. *Qadmoniot* 51-52: 114-117 (Hebrew).
   1981-1982   Ancient Jerusalem's Funerary Customs and Tombs. *BA* 44: 171-177 (summer); 229-235 (fall); 43-53 (winter); *BA* 45: 109-119 (spring).
Roth, C.
   1953   Jewish Antecedents of Christian Art. *Journal of the Warburg and Courtland Institute* 16: 24-44.
Roussin, L.
   1981   The Beit Leontis Mosaic: An Eschatological Interpretation. *Journal of Jewish Art* 8: 6-19.
Russel, K. W.
   1980   The Earthquake of May 19 A.D. 363. *BASOR* 238: 47-64.
Safrai, S.
   1963   Was there a Women's Gallery in the Synagogues of Antiquity? *Tarbiz* 22: 329-338 (Hebrew).
   1965   *Pilgrimage at the Time of the Second Temple.* Tel Aviv. (Hebrew)
   1976   The Temple; The Synagogue; Home and Family; *The Jewish People in the First Century*, II: 865-944. (eds. S. Safrai, and M. Stern). Assen.
Saller, S. J.
   1941   *The Memorial of Moses on Mount Nebo.* Jerusalem.
Saller, S.Y., and Bagatti, B.
   1949   *The Town of Nebo.* Jerusalem.
Schürer, E., Vermes, C., and Millar, A.
   1973   *The History of the Jewish people in the Age of Jesus Christ* (175 B.C. - A.D. 135), vol. I.
   1979   vol. II (1979). Edinburgh.
Schapiro, M.
   1960   *Israel Ancient Mosaics.* Unesco.
Schwabe M. and Lifshitz B.
   1974   *Beth Sheꞌarim II.* Jerusalem.
Seager, A.R.
   1972   The Building History of the Sardis Synagogue. *AJA* 76: 425-435.
   1975   The Architecture of the Dura and Sardis Synagogues. *The Synagogue.* (ed. J. Gutmann). New York.
   1981   Ancient synagogue Architecture: An Overview. *Ancient Synagogues. the State of Research*: 39-47. (ed. J. Gutmann).
Seager, A. R. and Kraabel, A. T.
   1983   The Synagogue and the Jewish Community. *Sardis from Prehistoric to Roman Times*: 168-190. (ed. G. Hanfmann). Cambridge and London.
Slousch, N.
   1921   Hammath by Tiberias. *Journal of the Jewish Palestine Exploration Society* I: 5-37. (Hebrew)
Smith, A.M.
   1922   The Iconography of the Sacrifice of Isaac in Early Christian Art. *AJA* 26: 159-173.

Smith, M.
    1958   The Image of God. *John Rylands Library* 40: 473-512.
    1967   Goodenough's "Jewish Symbols" in Retrospect. *Journal of Biblical Literature* 86: 53-68.
Strange J. F. and Shanks H.
    1983   Synagogue where Jesus Preached Found at Capernaum. *BAR* IX, 6: 25-31.
Sukenik, E.L.
    1931   Designs of the Torah Shrine in Ancient Synagogues in Palestine. *PEQ* : 22-25.
    1932   *The Ancient synagogue of Beth ꞌAlpha.* Jerusalem.
    1933   Designs of the Lectern in Ancient Synagogues in Palestine. *JPOS* 13: 221-225.
    1934   *Ancient Synagogues in Palestine and Greece.* London.
    1935   *The Ancient Synagogue of El-Hammeh.* Jerusalem.
    1949   The Present State of Ancient Synagogues Studies. *Bulletin Rabinowitz* I: 8-23.
    1951a   The Ancient Synagogue at Yafa, near Nazareth. *Bulletin Rabinowitz* II: 6-24.
    1951b   A New Discovery at Beth ꞌAlpha. *Bulletin Rabinowitz* II: 26.
Sussmann, J.
    1981   The Inscription in the Synagogue at Rehob. *ASR*: 146-151.
Sussman, V.
    1982   *Ornamented Jewish Oil-Lamps*, Jerusalem.
Testini, P.
    1958   Aquileia e Grado. *Rivista di Archeologia Cristiana* 34: 169-181.
Thompson, M.L.
    1973   Hypothetical Models of the Dura Paintings. *The Dura Europos Synagogue: A Re-Evaluation* (1932-1972): 31-52. (ed. J. Gutmann). Montana.
Tsafrir, Y.
    1981   On the Architectural Origins of the Ancient Galilean Synagogues - A Reconsideration. *Cathedra* 20: 29-46 (Hebrew).
    1982   The Desert Fortresses of Judea in the Second Temple Period. *The Jerusalem Cathedra* 2: 120-145.
Tsafrir, Y. and Magen, Y.
    1984   Two Seasons of Excavations at the Sartaba/Alexandrium Fortress. *Qadmoniot* 17: 26-32 (Hebrew).
Tzaferis, V.
    1982   The Ancient Synagogue at Ma'oz Hayyim. *IEJ* 32: 215-244.
Urbach, E.E.
    1959   The Rabbinical Laws of Idolatry in the Second and Third Centuries in the Light of Archaeological and Historical Facts. *IEJ* 9: 149-165; 229-245.
Vitto, F.
    1974   The Ancient Synagogue at Reḥov. *Atiqot* 7: 111-113 (Hebrew).
    1980   The Synagogue at Reḥov, 1980. *IEJ* 30: 214-217.
    1981a   The Synagogue at Reḥob. *ASR*: 90-94.
    1981b   A Byzantine Synagogue in the Beth Shean Valley. *Temples and High Places in Biblical Times*: 164-167.
    1983   Le decor mural des anciennes synagogues a la lumiere de nouvelles decouvertes. *Internationaler Byzantinsten Kongress*. Vien. 4-9 October 1981.
Vincent, R.P.L.H.
    1919   Le Sanctuaire Juif d'Ain Doug. *RB* 16: 532-563.
    1921   Le Sanctuaire Juif d'Ain Doug. *RB* 30: 442-443.
    1961   Un Sanctuaire dans La Region de Jericho, La Synagogue de Naᶜaran. *RB* 68: 163-177.
Vermes, G.
    1978   *The Dead Sea Scrolls, Qumran in Perspective*, Ohio.

Watzinger, C.
    1905   *Griechische Holzsarkophage aus der Zeit Alexanders des Grossen.* Leipzig.
Weitzmann, K.
    1957   Narration in Early Christendom. *AJA* 61: 83-91.
    1971a   The Illustration of the Septuagint. *No Graven Image*: 201-231. (ed. J. Gutmann). New York.
    1971b   The Question of the Influence of Jewish Pictorial Sources on Old Testament Illustrations. *No Graven Image*: 309-328. (ed. J. Gutmann). New York.
Wendel, C.
    1950   *Der Thoraschrein im Altertum.* Halle.
Wiegand, Th.
    1921   *Baalbek.* Berlin.
Wright, G. R. H.
    1961   The Archaeological Ramains at el Mird in the Wilderness of Judaea. *Biblica* 42: 1-21.
Yadin, Y.
    1963   *The finds from the Bar Kokhba Period in the Cave of the Letters.* Jerusalem.
    1965   The Excavation of Masada - 1963/64. *IEJ* 15: 1-120.
    1966   *Masada,* New York.
    1971   *Bar Kokhba.* New York.
    1981   The Synagogue at Masada. *ASR*: 19-23.
    1983   *The Temple Scroll.* vols. I-III. Jerusalem.
Yarden, L.
    1971   *The Tree of Light*: A Study of the Menorah - the Seven-Branched Lampstand. London.
Yeivin, S.
    1942   Notes to the Excavation at Beth She'arim. *BJPES* 9: 69-76 (Hebrew).
    1946   The Painting of the Sacrifice of Isaac in the Beth Alpha Synagogue. *BJPES* 2: 20-24 (Hebrew).
Yeivin, Z.
    1973   Excavations at Khorazin. *EI* 11: 144-157 (Hebrew).
    1974   Inscribed Marble Fragments from the Khirbet Susia Synagogue. *IEJ* 24: 201-209.
    1981   The Synagogue of Eshtemoa. *ASR*: 120-122.
    1985   Reconstruction of The Southern Interior Wall of the Khorazin Synagogue. *EI* 18 (Avigad Volume): 268-276. (Hebrew)
Zevulun, U., and Olenik, Y.
    1978   *Function and Design in the Talmudic Period.* Tel Aviv, Museum Haaretz catalogue.
Zlotnick, D.
    1966   *The Tractate 'Mourning' (Semahot).* New Haven, Conn.
Zori, N.
    1966   The house of Kyrios Leontis at Beth She'an. *IEJ* 16: 123-134.
    1967   The Ancient Synagogue at Beth Sh'an. *EI* 8: 149-167 (Hebrew).

GLOSSARY

Aedicula	Stone structure housing the Ark.
Ark of the Covenant	A chest which stood in Solomon's Temple and contained the Tablets of the Law.
Ark of the Scrolls	A chest which housed the Torah.
Apse	A semi-circular recess in a synagogue or church building.
Aniconic art	The absence of representations of humans and animals in art.
Bema	A raised platform in front of the niche or apse of a synagogue, probably employed in the reading of the Torah.
Ethrog	A citron.
Genizah	A hiding place in the synagogue for its treasure and for discarded scrolls.
Halakha (pl. = *Halakhot*)	Accepted decisions in rabbinic law.
Incense Shovel	Rectangular fire pan with handle.
Lulav	Palm branch.
Menorah (pl. = Menoroth)	Seven-branched candelabrum.
Miqveh (pl. = *Miqvaoth*)	A ritual bath.
Mishna (*M*)	Codification of Jewish oral law, compiled ca. 200 C.E.
Nefesh	A memorial above a tomb.
Ossilegium	Secondary burial of bones in ossuaries.
Passover (*Pesach*)	The feast of the first month (Nisan), "the feast of the unleavened bread" (Ex.12:14).
Pentecost (*Shavuoth*)	"The feast of the harvest" or "the day of the first fruit" (Ex.23:16).
Parochet	A veil covering the Torah shrine.
"Seat of Moses" (*Cathedra d'Moshe*)	A chair, especially for the head of the community.
Shofar (pl. = Shofaroth)	A ram's horn, a ritual object.
"Syrian gable"	A triangular gable with a base cut by an arch.
Tabernacles (*Sukkoth*)	The feast of the seventh month; the feast of ingathering (Ex. 23:16).
Table of Shewbread	One of the three ritual objects in the Temple sanctuary.
Tannaitic	Rabbinic tradition (pre-200 CE) of the Mishna period.
Torah shrine	An architectural structure either an aedicula, niche or apse, containing the Ark of the Scrolls.
Talmud	A corpus of Jewish ceremonial and civil law, compiled in two corpora: first, the Jerusalem Talmud (*J.*), ca. 400 CE, and second, the Babylonian Talmud (*B.*), ca. 650 CE.
Tosefta (*T.*)	Collected corpus of traditions and teachings connected with the Mishna.
Zealots	A Jewish group active in Jerusalem during the Jewish War against Rome (66-70 CE), which fought at Masada (the last stronghold of the war) until 73 CE.

CHRONOLOGY OF THE HASMONAEAN AND HERODIAN DYNASTIES IN THE SECOND TEMPLE PERIOD

The Hasmoneans

Jonathan	152-142 BCE
Simeon	142-134 BCE
John Hyrcanus I	134-104 BCE
Aristobulus I	104-103 BCE
Alexander Jannaeus	103-76 BCE
Salome Alexandra (Shlomzion)	76-67 BCE
Aristobulus II	67-63 BCE
John Hyrcanus II	63-40 BCE
Matthias Antigonus	40-37 BCE

The Herodians

Herod the Great	37-4 BCE
Herod Archelaus	4 BCE-6CE
Herod Antipas	4 BCE-39 CE
Philip	4 BCE-34 CE
Herod Agrippa I	37-44 CE
Agrippa II	53-100 CE

The Jewish War (against Rome) 66-70 CE
Destruction of Jerusalem and Temple - 70 CE
Fall of Masada - 73 CE
The Bar Kokhba War - 132-135 CE

"Tomb of the Kings" 80, 104-105, 107, 380
Torah 18-19, 88, 138-139, 166-167, 182-183, 199, 267, 272, 275, 278-279, 285, 328
Torah Shrine 87-88, 135, 141, 143, 156, 166-187, 189-192, 195-200, 213, 222, 227-228, 230-233, 270-273, 275-280, 284-285, 294, 321-323, 328, 330, 332-333, 336-337, 352, 361-362, 374, 377, 379, 388, 392-395, 397-398, 402-403
Triclinium 15, 33, 36, 87, 227
Triple portal 143, 156-160
Twelve Tribes 295-297

Unidentical Symmetry 330, 376-378, 402, 404

Vase 330, 339, 365, 377, 390, 393
Veil 187, 191-192, 275

Victories 206-207, 340
Vine 66, 80, 116, 212, 216, 220, 224, 310, 312, 315, 318, 338-340, 353, 365, 367, 371, 390, 403

Wall Painting 55, 65, 67-71, 115-119
Willow 131, 256, 267
Workshop 43, 78-79, 113-115, 120, 122, 189, 313, 316, 333, 382-391, 394
Wreath 206-207, 212-213, 216-217, 219, 224, 227, 280, 318, 327, 329-332, 340, 354, 365, 376, 387, 389, 393

Zealots 84, 86, 88
Zodiac, Zodiac Signs 225-226, 236, 287, 294, 297, 301-309, 327-328, 330, 341-343, 352-353, 361, 370-371, 377, 379, 391, 394, 398, 403

INDEX OF NAMES AND PLACES

PLATES

1. Reconstruction of the Second Temple by Avi-Yonah (Holy Land Hotel, Jerusalem).

2. General View of Temple Mount Excavations, Jerusalem.

3. Monumental Stairway near Double Gates, Jerusalem.

4. General View, Masada.

5. General View Herodium.

a

b

c

6a-c. Mosaic Floors in Houses, Upper City, Jerusalem.

a

b

7a,b. Masada Mosaics.

8. The Nazarite Sarcophagus, Jerusalem.

a

b

c

9a-c. Stone Fragments of Ornamented Domes, Huldah Gates, Jerusalem.

10a. Masada Synagogue.

10b. Herodium synagogue.

11. Gamla Synagogue.

12. Jericho Cemetery.

13. Ossuary with Bones from Jericho.

14. Inscribed Ossuary from Jericho: "Yehoezer son of Yehoezer Goliath" in Greek, upper line, and in Aramaic, lower line.

15. Inscribed bowl from Jericho.

16. Tomb of Zechariah, Jerusalem.

a

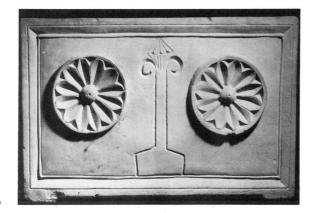

b

c

17a-c. Decorated Ossuaries, Jerusalem.

18. Ornamented Ossuary, Jerusalem (on exhibit, Israel Museum, Jerusalem).

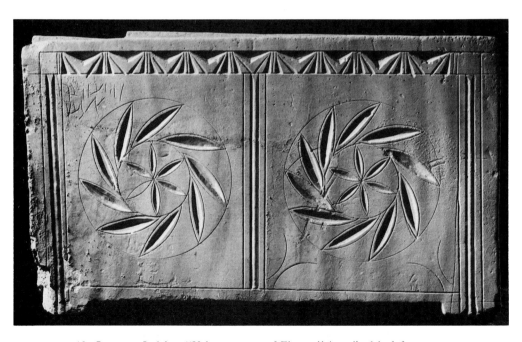

19. Ossuary, Jericho: "Yehoezer, son of Eleazar" inscribed in left corner.

20. General View of Qumran.

21. Bar'am Synagogue, facade.

22. Meiron Synagogue, facade.

23. Aedicula Capital, Umm el-Kanatir.

24. Aedicula Lintel, Nabratein.

25. Aedicula *in situ*, Marous.

26. ʿEn Samsam Relief.

28. An Aedicula Relief, Chorazin.

27. Dura Europos Niche.

29a. ʿAssalieh Lintel.

29b. Tybe Lintel.

30. "Shell" Sarcophagus, Beth Sheʿarim.

32. Torah Shrine Relief, Pekiin.

31. Torah Shrine Relief, Beth Shecarim.

33. Tomb Door, Kefar Yasif.

34. Stone Plaque (on exhibit, Israel Museum, Jerusalem).

35. An Aedicula Relief Fragment, Zumimra.

36. Ḥammath Tiberias Screen (on exhibit, Hecht Museum, Haifa University).

38. Consols, Capernaum.

37a,b. Screen, ʾAscalon (on exhibit, Israel Museum, Jerusalem).

39a. Synagogue Facade, Chorazin.

39b. Synagogue Facade, Kazrin.

40a. Main Portal, Barᶜam Synagogue.　　　40b. Side Portal, Barᶜam Synagogue.

41a. Kazrin synagogue.

41b. ʾEshtemoʿa synagogue.

41c. Susiya synagogue.

42a-f. Capitals: a) Capernaum; b) Caesarea;
c) and d) ʿEn Neshut; e) Kazrin; f) Peḥora,
pedestal (ʿEn Neshut).

43. Frieze Fragment, Capernaum.

44. Frieze Fragment, Capernaum.

45. Frieze Fragment, Chorazin.

46. Frieze Fragment with Mask, Chorazin.

a

b

47a,b. Frieze Fragments with Vintage Scene.

48. Marous Mosaic.

49. Mosaic Panel with Inscription, Ḥammath
Tiberias.

51. Mosaic Inscriptions, ʿEn-Gedi.

50. Mosaic Emblem, Jericho.

52. Mosaic Inscriptions, Reḥev.

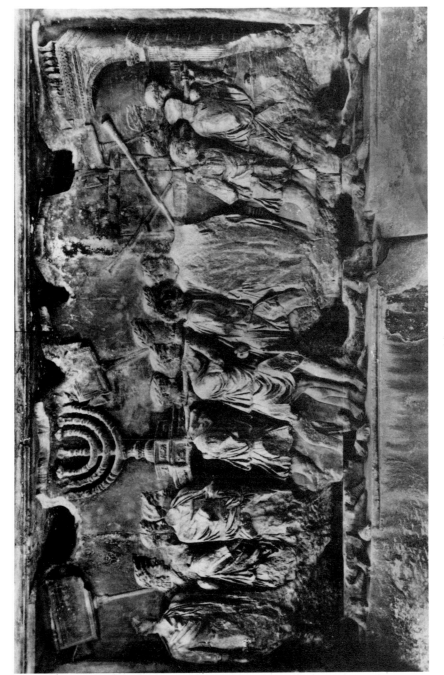

53. Arch of Titus, Rome.

a

b

54a,b. Stone Menorah, Ḥammath Tiberias (on exhibit, Israel Museum, Jerusalem).

55. Tirath Zvi, Mosaic.

a

b

56a,b. Menoroth on Mosaic Floor, Ḥuseifa.

57. Bronze Menorah, ʿEn-Gedi.

58. Ivory Plaque from Beth She'an.

a   b

59a,b. Menorah and Table on Coins of Mattathias Antigonus.

60. Ḥulda Mosaic.

61. Tiberias Mosaic.

63. Ark on Mosaic, Jericho.

62. Lamps with Menoroth and Ritual objects (on exhibit, Israel Museum, Jerusalem).

64. Sacrifice of Isaac, Beth ᵓAlpha.

65. Noah's Ark, Gerasa.

67. David of Gaza (after 1968 Excavations).

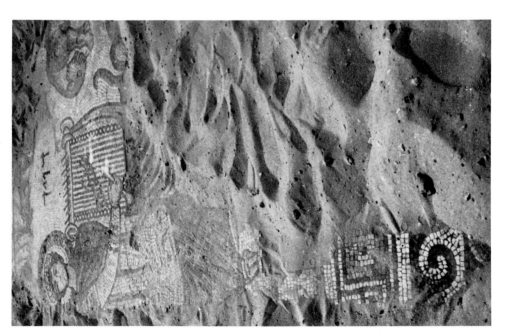

66. David of Gaza (at the beginning of excavations).

68. Upper Panel, House of Leontis, Beth
She'an.

69. Central Panel, House of Leontis, Beth
She'an.

70. Lower Panel, House of Leontis, Beth She'an.

72. Zodiac, Ḥuseifa.

71. Zodiac, Hammath Tiberias.

73. Zodiac, Beth ʾAlpha.

74. Zodiac, Naʿaran.

75. Remains of Zodiac Circle, Left Corner, Susiya.

76. Sun God, Mosaic, Beth ʾAlpha.

77. Sun God, Mosaic, Naʿaran.

78. Sun God, Mosaic, Hammath Tiberias.

BETH ALPHA

HAMMATH TIBERIAS

a

BETH ALPHA

HAMMATH TIBERIAS

b

BETH ALPHA

HAMMATH TIBERIAS

c

79a-c. Zodiac Signs: a) Aries, b) Taurus, c)Gemini.

BETH ALPHA

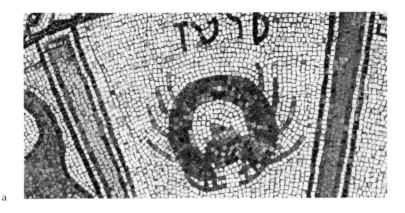

a

BETH ALPHA | **HAMMATH TIBERIAS** | **NAᶜARAN**

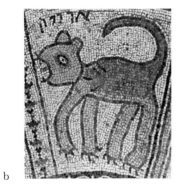  

b

BETH ALPHA | **HAMMATH TIBERIAS**

c

80a-c. Zodiac Signs: a) Cancer, b) Leo, c) Virgo.

BETH ALPHA   HAMMATH TIBERIAS   NAʿARAN

a

BETH ALPHA   HAMMATH TIBERIAS

b

BETH ALPHA

c

81a-c. Zodiac Signs: a) Libra, b) Scorpio, c) Sagittarius.

BETH ALPHA   HAMMATH TIBERIAS

BETH ALPHA   HAMMATH TIBERIAS

BETH ALPHA   HAMMATH TIBERIAS

82a-c. Zodiac Signs: a) Capricorn, b) Aquarius, c) Pisces.

BETH ALPHA

HAMMATH TIBERIAS

SPRING

a

BETH ALPHA

HAMMATH TIBERIAS

SUMMER

b

83a,b. Seasons: a) *Nisan* (Spring) and b) *Tammuz* (Summer).

NA'ARAN

HUSEIFA

AUTUMN

a

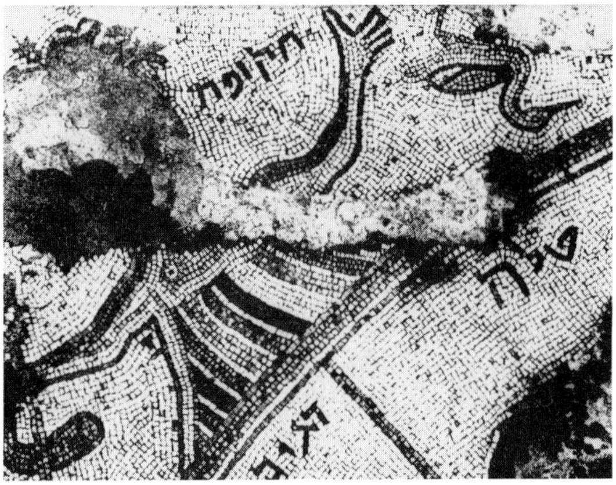

BETH ALPHA

HAMMATH TIBERIAS

AUTUMN

a

BETH ALPHA

HAMMATH TIBERIAS

WINTER

b

84a-b. Seasons: a) *Tishri* (Autumn) and b) *Tebeth* (Winter)

85. Mosaic Floor, Beth She'an B.

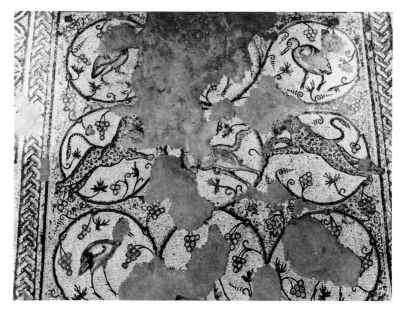

a

b

c

86a-c. "Inhabited Scroll" Mosaic, Gaza.

87. Upper Part of Mosaic, Maʿon.

88. ʿEn Samsam Relief, Detail.

a

b

89a,b. Two Stone Plaques.

90. ʿEn Neshut Lioness.

91. Carved Lintel from Wadi el-Hammam, Tiberias.

92. Basalt Lion from Mishrafawi.

93. Chorazin Gable.

94. Fragment with Eagle, Dikke.

95. Maʿoz Ḥayim Mosaic.

b

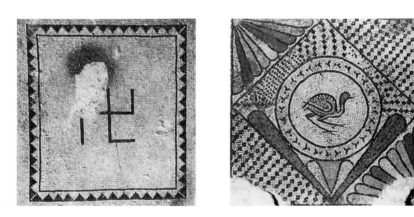

a

c

96a-c. Mosaic Pavements, ʿEn-Gedi.

97a. Lower Part of Mosaic Pavement, Maᶜon.

98. Relief, Dabbura.

b

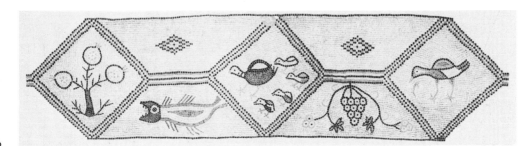

c

97b,c. Parts of the Mosaic Frame, Beth ᵓAlpha.

a

b

99a,b. Gaza screens.

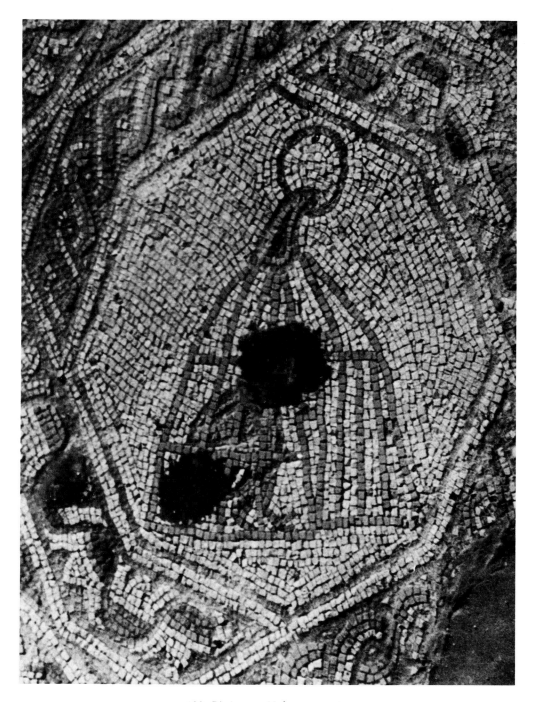

100. Bird cage, Na'aran mosaic.

101. Panel of Jewish Symbols, Ḥammath Tiberias.

102. Panel of Jewish Symbols, Beth ʾAlpha.

103. Panel of Jewish Symbols, Beth Sheʾan A.

104. Panel of Jewish Symbols, Susiya.

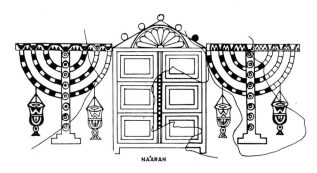

105. Panel of Jewish Symbols, Naʿaran.

106. Inscription, Beth She'an B.

107. Room L, Monastery, Beth She'an.

108. Lintel with Inscription, Nabratein.

109. Lintel with Inscription, Kasyon.